ENGLISH POEMS

ENGLISH POEMS

SELECTED AND EDITED, WITH ILLUSTRATIVE AND
EXPLANATORY NOTES AND BIBLIOGRAPHIES

By

WALTER C. BRONSON

OLD ENGLISH AND MIDDLE ENGLISH PERIODS
450–1550

Granger Index Reprint Series

BOOKS FOR LIBRARIES PRESS

FREEPORT, NEW YORK

First Published 1910
Reprinted 1970

STANDARD BOOK NUMBER:

8369-6119-6

LIBRARY OF CONGRESS CATALOG CARD NUMBER:

70-109135

MANUFACTURED
BY
HALLMARK LITHOGRAPHERS, INC.
IN THE U.S.A.

PREFACE

This volume is the first in order, although the last to appear, in a series of four volumes of English Poems, intended especially for use with college classes. The aim and method of the series as a whole have been set forth in the prefaces to the other volumes and need not be repeated here, the less because the present volume differs considerably from the rest. It cannot well be used separately, as the later volumes can, but derives its chief value from its connection with the series: for the thorough study of Old English and Middle English poetry it is quite inadequate, but in an introductory survey course in English literature it may serve a useful end. To increase the value of the book for this purpose, some specimens of the early drama are given, although plays are elsewhere excluded from the series and some of those here included exceed the strict chronological limits of the period.

In a book of this character it was necessary to turn the Old English poems into modern English. In the present translation, made by Elsie Straffin Bronson, A.M., the aim has been to reproduce the effect as well as the sense of the original, and something of smoothness and ease has therefore been sacrificed, when necessary, in the effort to keep to an Anglo-Saxon vocabulary and preserve the directness and rugged strength of the Old English; an incidental result is the retention of much of the alliteration which is so marked a feature of the verse and which is usually lost when words of foreign origin replace native words. In the case of Middle English, translation was not absolutely necessary; and it has seemed best to abstain also from modernizing the text except by substituting "th" for "þ" and by following present usage in regard to "u" and "v," capitalization, and punctuation. By the aid of glossary and notes even the untrained student can get the meaning of Middle English without great difficulty, and by working thus through a few pages of the original he will come into closer touch with the spirit of the literature than by reading many pages in translation.

The sources of the texts are indicated in the notes. In preparation of the notes and glossary I have used freely the material in the standard editions of the authors and works represented, and acknowledge especially my indebtedness to the publications of the Early English Text Society, the Chaucer Society, and the Scottish Text Society, to Skeat's editions of Langland and Chaucer, to Gollancz's and Osgood's editions of "The Pearl," and to Wells's edition of "The Owl and the Nightingale." I am also glad to express my obligations to the authorities of the Bodleian Library, Oxford, particularly for access to a rare edition of "The Foure PP"; and to my colleague, Professor A. K. Potter, for the privilege of using his rotographs of the first edition of Hawes and for aid in interpreting the text. To my wife I am indebted for preparing the copy, the table of contents, and the indices, for aid in writing notes and making the glossary, and most of all for translating the Old English poems.

W. C. B.

BROWN UNIVERSITY
May 9, 1910

CONTENTS

		PAGE
PREFACE		v

OLD ENGLISH POEMS, DONE INTO MODERN ENGLISH PROSE

From Beowulf

The Cleansing of Heorot 1
The Fight with the Dragon 19
Charms 30
The Frisian Wife 31
Riddle

The Moon and the Sun 31
The Wanderer 31
The Banished Wife's Lament 33
Cædmon's Hymn 34
From the Phœnix

The Happy Land 34
From Genesis

Satan's Speech 36
Judith 38
The Battle of Maldon 44

EARLY MIDDLE ENGLISH POEMS

From Poema Morale 49
From The Brut 51
From A Bestiary

Natura Leonis 56
From The Owl and the Nightingale 57
From Cursor Mundi 61
From The Pearl 66
From The Proverbs of Hendyng 74
Cuckoo Song 75
Alysoun 76
Springtime 77
Ubi Sunt Qui ante Nos Fuerunt 78
The Virgin's Song to Her Baby Christ 79

MIDDLE ENGLISH METRICAL ROMANCES

From The Lay of Havelok the Dane 79

From Syr Gawayn and the Grene Knyght
    The Stranger at King Arthur's Court   83
    Sir Gawayn at the Green Chapel   91

JOHN GOWER

From Confessio Amantis   100

WILLIAM LANGLAND

From The Vision of William concerning Piers the Plowman
    The Prologue   102

GEOFFREY CHAUCER

From The Book of the Duchesse   108
From The Hous of Fame   112
The Legend of Good Women
    From The Prologue   122
From The Canterbury Tales
    The Prologue   127
    The Nonne Preestes Tale   148
Truth   163
The Complaynt of Chaucer to His Purse .   .   .   164

THOMAS HOCCLEVE

Mi Maister Chaucer   165

JOHN LYDGATE

London Lyckpeny   166

JAMES I OF SCOTLAND

From The Kingis Quair   170

ROBERT HENRYSON

From The Testament of Cresseid   177

WILLIAM DUNBAR

Sanct Salvatour, Send Silver Sorrow   184
From The Goldyn Targe   185
The Dance of the Sevin Deidly Synnis   189

GAWIN DOUGLAS

From The Proloug of the XII Buk of Eneados .   .   193

SIR DAVID LYNDSAY

From The Dreme
    The Prolog   194

STEPHEN HAWES

    From The Pastime of Pleasure
        How Graunde Amoure Was Receyved of La Belle Pucell .   197
        Howe Remembraunce Made His Epytaphy on His Grave .   200

JOHN SKELTON

    From Why Come Ye Nat to Court   201

BALLADS

    St. Stephen and Herod   203
    From A Gest of Robyn Hode
        The VII. Fytte   204
        The VIII. Fytte   211
    The Hunting of the Cheviot   216
    Johnie Cock   224
    Jock o the Side   226
    Sir Patrick Spens   231
    Sir Hugh, or The Jew's Daughter   232
    The Three Ravens   234
    Edward   235
    The Twa Sisters   237
    The Cruel Brother   239
    Babylon, or The Bonnie Banks o Fordie   .   .   .   240
    Sweet William's Ghost   242
    Lord Thomas and Fair Annet   243
    Kemp Owyne   247
    Thomas Rymer   249
    The Wee Wee Man   251
    Mary Hamilton   252
    Bonnie George Campbell   254

MIRACLE PLAYS

    The Deluge   254
    Abraham's Sacrifice   265

MORALITY PLAYS

    Everyman   272
    From The Mariage of Witt and Wisdome
        The First Scene   296
        The Second Scene   300
        The Fifte Scene   306
        The Eighth Scene   308
        The Tenth Scene   ,   ,   ,   ,   ,   310

JOHN HEYWOOD

    The Foure PP 312

NOTES 343

GLOSSARY 365

BIBLIOGRAPHY 409

INDEX OF AUTHORS 421

INDEX OF TITLES 421

INDEX TO FIRST LINES 422

OLD ENGLISH POEMS

DONE INTO MODERN ENGLISH PROSE

FROM

BEOWULF

THE CLEANSING OF HEOROT

So then Healfdene's son seethed always over his time of care, nor might the wise warrior turn away his woe: the strife was too strong, loathsome and long-lasting, that came upon the people —dire wrack spitefully grim, greatest bale by night. This, Grendel's deeds, the thane of Hygelac found out from home, a good man among the Geats; he was in might the strongest of mankind in the day of this life, high-born. and powerful. He bade gear him a good wave-crosser; he said he would seek this warking over the swan-road, this great prince, since he had need of men. Wise men blamed him little for the journey, though he was dear to them: they whetted his strong courage and saw lucky signs.

The good man had chosen champions of the Geat people, the keenest he could find; with fourteen others he sought the sea-wood. A man, sea-crafty, pointed out landmarks. Time went forward: the float was on the waves, the boat beneath the hill. Ready heroes mounted on the stem; streams whirled the sea against the sand; warriors bore to the lap of the bark bright trappings, war-armor gayly garnished; men on a willing journey shoved out the wooden ship. Then over the wavy sea, sped by the wind, went the float, foamy-necked, most like to a bird, until the bark with twisted stem had waded up to about the same hour of the next day, when the sailors saw land, sea-cliffs gleaming, steep hills, wide headlands; then the sound at the end of the sea was crossed. Then quickly the Weder-folk went up on the plain and fastened the sea-wood; shirts of mail, war-weeds, rattled; they thanked God because the wave-paths were made easy for them.

Then from the wall the guard of the Scyldings, he who must hold the sea-cliffs, saw them bearing over the gangway bright

shields, ready armor; a fiery longing fretted him in his mind-
thoughts, to know what those men were.   Then the thane of
Hrothgar went riding on his steed to the shore, and with force
he shook the spear, the mighty-wood, in his hands, and asked
in well-weighed words: "What armor-bearers are ye, clad with
burnies, who thus have come leading a high keel over the sea-street,
a ring-stemmed ship hither over the deep seas? I was end-guard,
held sea-watch, so that no one hateful might work harm on the
land of Danes with a ship-army. Not once have men bearing
linden shields more openly begun to come hither; nor knew ye
at all leave-word of war-makers, consent of kinsmen. Never did
I see upon earth greater earl than is one of you, a warrior in
armor; that is no hall-man honored with weapons, unless his
glance belies him, his peerless look. Now I must know your kin,
ere ye fare farther from here on Danes' land as false spies. Now
ye dwellers-afar, sea-crossers, hearken to my onefold thought:
haste is best in making known whence your comings are."

To him the eldest made answer, the wise one of the band
unlocked his word-hoard: "We are Geat-people in kin, and
Hygelac's hearth-sharers. My father was known to the peoples,
a high-born chief called Ecgtheow; he bided many a winter ere
he turned away, an old man, from earthly courts: well nigh
every wise man far and wide throughout the world keeps him well
in mind. We have come with friendly heart to seek thy lord, the
son of Healfdene, stronghold of the people; be thou good to us
in guidance. We have a great errand to the mighty lord of the
Danes: there shall be nothing hidden, as I ween. Thou knowest
whether it is so, as we truly heard say, that among the Scyldings
I know not which of scathers, hidden one of hateful deeds, in
dark nights shows through terror unknown spite, shame and
slaughter. I may teach Hrothgar counsel thereof, through great-
ness of heart, how he, wise and good, may overmaster the fiend,
if ever this baleful business is to turn back from him, help come
again, and these care-waves grow cooler; or else he will ever
afterwards endure hard times, dire need, so long as there stands
in a high place the best of houses."

The warder spoke where he sat on his steed, liegeman unafraid:
"Between these two, words and works, must a sharp shield-
warrior who thinketh well know the difference. I hear that this
is a band friendly to the lord of the Scyldings. Go bring forth
your weapons and war-weeds; I will lead you; likewise I will bid

my kinsman-thanes to hold your float with honor against any foe, your new-tarred bark on the sand, until the wood with curved neck bears the dear man back over the sea-streams to Weder-mark. To such a framer of good it is given that he shall come whole out of the battle-rush." Then they went; the float stayed still, the broad-bosomed ship rested on its rope fast at anchor. Boar-likenesses shone over the cheek-guards, covered with gold, stained and fire-hardened: a boar held watch. In war-mood they hurried, men hastened, together they marched down, until they could get sight of the timbered hall, stately and golden-hued. Among earth-dwellers that was the greatest before all of houses under heavens, in which that mighty one abode: its gleam was bright over many lands. To them then the man bold in battle showed the court of the brave shining, that they might go to it straight. One of the war-heroes, he turned his steed and spoke a word after: "It is time for me to go. May the all-wielding Father in mercy keep you safe in your ways. I will to the sea, to keep ward against foeman bands."

The street was of colored stones; the path led the men all together. The war-burny shone, hard, hand-locked, the bright ring-iron sang in the armor, when first they came going to the hall in their griesly garnishings. Sea-weary they set down wide shields, mightily hard, against the wall of the hall, and then bent them to the bench. Burnies rang, men's war-mail; spears, sea-men's armor, stood all together, ash-wood gray above; the iron-armed band was worthy in weapons. Then a proud hero there asked the warriors about their high birth: "Whence bring ye plated shields, gray shirts of mail and mask-helmets, heap of army-shafts? I am Hrothgar's herald and liegeman. I have not seen so many men of stranger-folk more brave-like. I ween that ye have sought Hrothgar for pride, by no means under ban, but for strength of heart."

Then answered him the one strong in courage,—the proud chief of the Weders spoke a word after, hardy under his helmet: "We are Hygelac's board-sharers; Beowulf is my name. I will say out my errand to the son of Healfdene, mighty chief, thy lord, if he will grant us that we may greet him, so good."

Wulfgar spoke, that was chief of the Wendlas,—his brave heart was known to many, his war-might and wisdom: "Of that I will ask the friend of the Danes, lord of the Scyldings, dealer of rings, as thou dost beg: the mighty chief I will ask about thy undertaking, and will make known to thee quickly the answer that the good man thinks well to give me back." He turned then hastily to where Hrothgar sat, old and very hoar, with his band of earls; he went with courage strong till he stood before the shoulders of the Danes' lord—he knew the custom of the doughty. Wulfgar spoke to his friend-lord: "Hither have fared, come from afar over the stretch of ocean, Geat-folk; the eldest the warriors call Beowulf. They beg, my lord, that they may pass words with thee. Do not thou give them a denial of thy replies, gracious Hrothgar. They seem in war-gear worthy of earls' high honor: at least the chief is doughty, who led the warrior-wights hither."

Hrothgar spoke, helm of the Scyldings: "I knew him when he was a boy. His old father was called Ecgtheow, to whom at home Hrethel of the Geats gave his only daughter; his hardy child has now come hither and sought his faithful friend. Sea-crossers who bore the gift-money for the Geats thither for favor said then that he, the battle-strong, had the might of thirty men in his hand-grip. Him holy God has in mercy sent to us, to the West-Danes, as I have hope, against Grendel's griesly deeds; I shall give the good man treasures for his daring. Be thou in haste: bid the kindred-band go in all together to see me. Say to them also in words that they are welcome to the Dane-folk."

Then Wulfgar went to the door of the hall and gave out word within: "My victory-lord, chief of the East-Danes, bade say to you that he knows your high birth, and ye are welcome to him here, over the sea-waves, hardy-hearted. Now ye may go in your war-gear, under army-masks, to see Hrothgar; let your battle-boards and wooden death-shafts here bide the outcome of your words."

Then the mighty one arose, about him many a wight, a picked band of thanes; some waited there, and kept the battle-dress, as the hardy one bade them. They hastened together, as the man led, under Heorot's roof; strong of heart he went, hardy under his helmet, till he stood on the daïs. Beowulf spoke—on him the burny shone, the armor-net linked by the skill of the smith: "Hail to thee, Hrothgar! I am Hygelac's kinsman and kinsman-thane. I have undertaken many mighty deeds in my youth. The matter of Grendel became known to me openly on my home turf; sea-farers say that this hall, this best house, stands idle and unused of any wight after evening-light becomes hidden under heaven's brightness. Then my people, the best, wise men, taught me counsel, lord Hrothgar, that I should seek thee, because they knew the strength of my might: they looked upon it themselves, when I came out of battle stained from foes, where I bound five, destroyed the kin of eotens, and on the waves slew nickers by night, endured dire straits, drove out the scourge of the Weders (they suffered woe), ground down the fierce ones. And now with Grendel, with the monster, the giant, must I try out the thing alone. Now then I will beg of thee, prince of the Bright-Danes, bulwark of the Scyldings, one boon, that thou deny me not, stronghold of warriors, noble friend of the folk, now I am come thus from afar, that I alone, and the band of my earls, this hardy troop, may cleanse Heorot. I have also learned that the monster recks not of weapons in his rashness. I then forego—so may Hygelac, my lord, be blithe of mood toward me—the bearing of sword or wide shield, yellow buckler, to battle; but I with my grip shall grapple with the fiend and struggle for life, foe with foe. There must he whom death takes believe in the doom of the Lord. I ween that he, if he must come out master, will eat the Geat-folk in the war-hall unafraid, as he often did the strength of the Hrethmen. Thou needst not hide my head, but he will have me, stained with blood, if death takes me: he will bear away my bloody corpse, will think to taste it; he that goes alone will eat it unmournfully, will mark with my blood the moor-haunts. Neither needst thou care longer for the feeding of my body. Send off to Hygelac, if battle take me, the best of war-shrouds, that covers my breast, finest of armor; that was left me by Hrethel, the work of Weland. Fate goeth ever as she must."

Hrothgar spoke, helm of the Scyldings: "To fight off our foe and give kindly help hast thou sought us, my friend Beowulf. Thy father fought out the greatest feud—he was hand-slayer of Heatholaf among the Wylfings. Then the Weder-kin might not keep him for fear of war. Thence he sought the South-Dane folk over the rolling waves, the Honor-Scyldings: then was I first ruling the Dane-folk, and in my youth holding the gem-rich hoard-burg of heroes. Then was Heorogar dead, lifeless was my elder brother, child of Healfdene; he was better than I. Afterwards I settled the feud with a fee: I sent to the Wylfings, over the water's ridge, old treasures; he swore me oaths. Sorrow is it for me in my soul to .tell any one of men what shame Grendel has wrought me in Heorot with his hate-thoughts, what sudden spites: my hall-band, my war-troop, has waned; fate swept them off in Grendel's grim grasp. God may easily cut off the rash scather from his deeds. Full oft warriors drunken with beer boasted over the ale-can that they in the beer-hall would bide Grendel's onset with griesly sword-edges. Then was the mead-hall, lordly abode, at morningtide blood-stained, when daylight gleamed, all the bench-boards steeped in blood, the hall drenched in sword-blood; I had the less of faithful men, bold and doughty ones, since death had taken them off. Sit now to the feast and unseal thy thoughts, thy victory-pride to the men, as thy soul whets thee."

Then was room made at the bench in the beer-hall for the Geat-men all together; there the stout-hearted ones went to sit, proud in might. The thane minded his task who bore in his hand the garnished ale-can, poured out bright mead. At whiles a bard sang clear-voiced in Heorot; there was mirth of men, no little doughtiness of Danes and Weders.

. . . .

Then Hrothgar, bulwark of the Scyldings, went out of the hall with his band of men; the war-chief would seek Wealhtheow, his queen, for bed-fellow. The glory of kings had set a hall-guard against Grendel, as men heard,—he minded a special task about the Danes' chief, gave watch for the monster. Truly the Geats' chief eagerly trusted his proud might and the Maker's favor. Then he doffed his iron burny and the helmet from his head, gave up his jeweled sword, the pick of irons, to his waiting-thane, and bade him hold the war-gear. Then the good man spoke some boastful words, Beowulf of the Geats, ere he mounted his bed: "'I count not myself meaner in army-might of war-works than Grendel himself; therefore I will not kill him with the sword and so take his life, although I may. He knows not of these good helps, that he may strike at me and hew my shield, though he be strong in spite-works; but we two in the night must do without the sword, if he dares seek war without weapons; and afterwards may wise God, the holy Lord, award glory on which-soever hand may seem to Him meet." Then the bold in battle laid him down—the cheek-bolster received the earl's face; and about him many a keen seaman bent to hall-rest. None of them thought that he should ever thereafter seek home-love, folk or free burg where he was brought up: but they had learned that, ere this, slaughter-death had taken off far too many Dane-folk in the wine-hall. But the Lord gave them webs of war-speed gave to the Weder-folk comfort and help, so that they all over-came their foe through the strength of one man, by his own might; the truth is made known that mighty God has ruled over mankind forever. In the dark night came stalking the goer-in-shadow. The shooters slept who were to hold the horned house, all but one. It was known to men that the unresting scather might not cast them under the shades when the Maker willed not; but he, waking in anger at the wroth foe, waited, in raging mood, for the outcome of the strife.

Then from the moor under the misty hills came Grendel walking: God's ire he bore. The wicked scather was minded to ensnare some one of mankind in that high hall. Beneath the clouds he went, to where he best knew a wine-house, gold-hall of men, bright with platings of gold; nor was that the first time that he had sought Hrothgar's home. Never found he in his life-days, before or after, hardier heroes for hall-thanes. The wight with no part in joys came then journeying to the house. The door soon sprang open, fast with fire-bands, after he laid hold of it with his hands: the baleful-minded burst open the mouth of the house, being swollen with rage. Quickly after that the fiend trod on the shining floor; he went in ireful mood; from his eyes came a light not fair, most like to flame. He saw in the house many men, a kindred-band sleeping all together, a crowd of kinsman-warriors. Then his heart laughed aloud; he meant, dire monster, ere day came to part the life of each one from his body, since hope of his fill of food was fallen to him. It was not fate, any longer, that he should seize more of mankind after that night. Hygelac's kinsman, mightily strong, beheld how the wicked scather was going to fare with his fear-grips. The monster meant not to tarry, but he quickly, the first time, seized a sleeping man, slit him unawares, bit his bone-locker, drank the blood from his veins, swallowed huge bits. Soon he had devoured all the life-less body, feet and hands. Forth he stepped, nearer, and then seized with his hand the great-hearted warrior at rest. With his hand the fiend reached out; quickly the hero laid hold, with hostile thoughts, and leaned against his arm. Soon the herder of crimes found out that he had met in no other man in the world, in the corners of earth, a greater hand-grip. He grew fearful in mind, in heart: none the sooner could he get away. His heart was eager to be gone—he wanted to flee into darkness, to seek the haunt of devils: there was no work for him there, such as he had found before in his life-days. Then Hygelac's good kinsman bethought him of his evening-speech, stood upright and grappled with him fast; his fingers burst; the monster was moving outward; the earl stepped further. The great one was minded wheresoever he might to turn loose and flee away thence to the fen-hollows: he knew his fingers' power was in the grips of a fierce foe. That was a dire journey that the harm-scather took to Heorot. The lordly hall was full of din; panic came upon all the Danes, the castle-dwellers, upon each of the bold ones and upon the earls. Ireful were both the fierce and mighty champions. The house was in uproar. Then was it great wonder that the wine-hall withstood the two bold in battle, that it fell not to the ground, that fair earth-building; but it was made so fast by smith's work with cunning thoughts, by iron bands within and without. There from its base started many a mead-bench, as I have heard, garnished with gold, where the fierce ones fought; of that the wise men of the Scyldings never thought before, that any man with power might ever break it in pieces, splendid and bone-decked as it was, or force it apart with cunning, unless flame's embrace swallowed it in smoke. Noise went up, new enough; dire fear stood upon the North-Danes, upon each one of those who heard weeping from the wall, heard the striver against God singing a griesly lay, a song of defeat—hell's thrall bewailing his sore. He held him fast, he who was strongest of men in might in the day of this life.

The stronghold of earls would not for anything let the death-dealing comer go alive, nor deemed he his life-days of use to any folk. There many an earl of Beowulf's brandished an old heir-loom-sword, wanted to guard the life of their lord and chief, mighty leader, wheresoever they might. They knew not when they went through the strife, hardy-hearted battle-men, and thought to hew him upon each side and seek his soul, that not even the pick of irons upon earth, no war-bill, could touch that unresting scather, but he had foresworn victory-weapons, every edge. His life-parting was to be wretched in the day of this life, and his ghost, gone elsewhere, must journey afar to the rule of fiends. Then he found out, he who before had wrought many a crime against mankind in mirthful mood, he, foe to God, that his body would not last him, but Hygelac's brave kinsman had him by the hand: each was hateful to the other, living. The dire monster endured a body-sore: a clear wound not to be eased was on his shoulder; his sinews sprang apart, his bone-lockers burst. To Beowulf war-glory was given: Grendel was to flee thence life-sick under the fen-slopes, to seek his joyless dwelling; he knew the more surely that his life's end was gone, the number of his days. All Danes had their wish fulfilled after that slaughter-rush. Then he who erewhile came from afar, wise and stout-hearted, had cleansed Hrothgar's hall, had saved from spite; he rejoiced in his night-work, his mighty feats. The chief of the Geat-men had carried out his boast to the East-Danes, as all the sufferings were made good, the sorrows sent by the foe, which they before went through and for dire need had to endure, no little bitterness. That was clear token, when the bold in battle laid down the hand, arm and shoulder—there was all of Grendel's claw together—under the roomy roof.

Then in the morning, as I have heard, there was many a warrior about the gift-hall; from far and near folk-leaders fared throughout the wide-ways to view the wonder, the traces of the foe. His life-parting seemed not sorry to any of the men who viewed the track of the gloryless one, how he, in weary mood, bore away thence his life-steps to the mere of the nickers, over-come in strife, doomed and routed. There was the sea welling with blood—the dire swing of waves welled up all mingled with hot gore, sword-blood; the·death-doomed dyed it, when, with no part in joys, he laid down his life, his heathen soul, in the fen-shelter; there hell took him.

· · · · · · · ·

There was the pick of feasts; men drank wine; they knew not fate, grim shaper-aforetime, as it was fallen to many an earl. When evening came, and Hrothgar went him to his lodge, the mighty one to his rest, uncounted earls guarded the house, as they had oft done before. They bared the bench-boards; it was overspread with beds and bolsters. One of the stewards, ready and doomed, bowed to his floor-rest. They set at their heads battle-shields, bright board-woods; there on the bench over an atheling was easy to see his helmet high-towering in battle, his ringed burny, his mighty onset-spear. It was their way, that they were often ready for war both at home and in the field, and either of them even at such times as need befell their lord: that was a good folk.

Then they sank to sleep. One sorely paid for his evening-rest, as full often befell them when Grendel guarded the gold-hall and did wrong, until the end came, death after sins. It became plain, widely known to men, that an avenger still lived after the loathed one, a long time after the war-care: Grendel's mother, woman, monster-wife, was mindful of her woe, she whose it was to dwell in the dreadful water, the cold streams, after Cain became sword-slayer of his only brother, his father's son—then went the guilty one, marked with murder, fleeing man's mirth, and dwelt in the waste. Thence woke many a fate-sent ghost. Of these was Grendel one, hateful sword-wolf, who found at Heorot a waking man awaiting war. There the monster was grasping at him; yet was he mindful of the strength of his might, his large and lasting gift which God had granted him, and he believed in the Almighty's grace for him, comfort and help; thereby he overcame the fiend, felled hell's ghost. Then he departed downcast, with no part in mirth, to see his dwelling of death—the foe of mankind. And his mother, still greedy and sad of mood, would go a sorrowful way to wreak her son's death; she came then to Heorot, where the Ring-Danes slept throughout that hall. Then a change came there soon to the earls, after Grendel's mother made her way in. The griesly dread was even so much less as is the might of maids, the war-terror of a woman, beside a weaponed man, when the bound blade forged with the hammer, the sword stained with blood, strong in its edges, face to face shears down the boar's image over the helmet. Then in the hall was the hard-edged sword tugged over settles, and many a broad shield heaved fast to the hand: a man minded not the helmet or the broad burny when the dread got hold on him. She was in haste, and would go out from there to save her life, when she was found; quickly she had seized fast upon one atheling; then she went to the fen. He whom she killed at his rest was a man in comradeship most dear to Hrothgar between the seas, a mighty shield-warrior, a hero of stedfast fame. Beowulf was not there, but another dwelling had before been assigned to the mighty Geat, after the treasure-giving. Noise grew high in Heorot; she had seized the well-known hand in its gore; care was renewed, was risen again in the dwellings. That was not a good exchange when they must buy on both sides with the lives of friends.

Then was the old king, hoar battle-man, in sad mood, when he knew his chief thane was lifeless, his dearest man dead. Quickly was Beowulf fetched to the bower, victory-blessed warrior; just at daybreak he went with the earls, the high-born champion himself with his comrades, where the wise one waited whether the Almighty should ever will to work a change for him after this woe-spell. Then went along the floor the war-worthy man with his hand-troop—the hall-wood dinned—until he greeted with words the wise lord of the Ingwines, and asked him if he had a pleasant night, after the pressing summons.

Hrothgar spoke, helm of the Scyldings: "Ask not after pleasant things; sorrow is renewed for the Dane-folk. Æschere is dead, Yrmenlaf's elder brother, my man wise in runes and my counsel-bearer, shoulder-comrade when we guarded our heads in battle, when troops clashed, boars crashed. Such should an earl be, an atheling good before others, as Æschere was. There came to him in Heorot a wandering slaughter-guest for hand-slayer; I know not whither the dire carrion-proud monster has taken her back-journeys, made famous by her feast. She avenged that feud in which thou didst kill Grendel yesternight in fierce wise with hard grips, for that he had too long cut down and made few my people. He fell in battle, having forfeited his life, and now came another mighty scather; she would avenge her son, and has carried the feud far, as may appear heavy heart-bale to many a thane who weeps in soul for the treasure-giver. Now that hand lies low that was strong for you in well-nigh all wishes.

"I have heard the land-dwellers, my people, hall-rulers, say that they saw two such great march-steppers holding the moors, stranger-ghosts: one of them was, as they might most surely know, a likeness of a woman; the other, wretched-shapen, in man's form trod the paths of the banned, only he was greater than any other man—him in days of yore earth-dwellers named Grendel; they know not his father, whether any lurking ghost was begotten before him. They guard the hidden land, wolf-slopes, windy headlands, dread fen-paths, where the mountain-stream goes downwards under the mists of the headlands, the flood under ground. It is not far hence by mile-mark where that mere stands, over which hang rimy groves—a wood fast to its roots overhangs the water. Each night may be seen there a dread wonder, fire on the flood. There lives not one of the children of men so wise that he knows the bottom. Though the heath-stepper pressed by the hounds, the hart with strong horns, seeks the holt-wood, having fled from afar, he will give up his life on the bank ere he will hide his head within. That is no canny place: from it a blending of waves rises up wan to the clouds, when the wind stirs the hateful storms, till the air grows dark and the heavens weep. Now is the counsel again with thee alone. Thou knowest not yet the land, the dread place, where thou mayest find the one of many sins; seek if thou dare. I shall pay thee for the feud with a fee, with old treasures, as I did before, with twisted gold, if thou comest away."

Beowulf spoke, son of Ecgtheow: "Do not sorrow, wise man; it is better for every man that he avenge his friend than that he mourn much. Each of us must abide the end of this world's life; let him who may win glory before death: that is afterwards best for a noble man done with life. Arise, guard of the realm: let us go quickly to see the track of Grendel's kinsman. I vow it to thee: he shall not get off to cover, either in earth's bosom or in the mountain-wood or in ocean's depth, go where he will. This day do thou have patience with each of thy woes, as I hope thou wilt."

Then the aged man leaped up, and thanked God, the mighty Lord, for what this man said. Then was a horse bridled for Hrothgar, a steed with twisted hair; the wise prince went in state; a troop of shield-bearers marched on foot. Traces were plain far and wide along the wood-paths, a track over the ground; straight she went over the murky moor, and bore lifeless the best of the kinsman-thanes who watched over the home with Hrothgar. Then the child of athelings went over steep stone-slopes, narrow trails, strait single-paths, an unknown way, deep headlands, many nicker-houses; he, with a few wise men, went before to see the plain, until he suddenly found the mountain-trees leaning over the hoary stone, the joyless wood; the water stood beneath, bloody and troubled. For all the Danes, friends of the Scyldings, it was grievous in heart to endure, a suffering for many a thane and each of the earls, when they came upon Æschere's head on the sea-cliff. The flood welled with blood (folk looked upon it), with hot gore. From time to time the horn sang the ready war-song. All the troop sat down. Then they saw along the water many of the worm-kind, strange sea-dragons, trying the channel, likewise nickers lying on headland-slopes, that often at morning time make a sorrowful raid on the sail-road— worms and wild beasts. They fell away, bitter and swollen with rage: they sensed the sound, the war-horn singing. The chief of the Geats with an arrow-bow parted one from life in his wave-struggle, so that the hard war-dart stood in his vitals; he was the slower at swimming in the sea, because death carried him off. Quickly was he hard pressed on the waves with boar-spears sword-hooked, set upon by force and tugged to the headland, a wondrous wave-bearer; the men looked upon the griesly guest.

Beowulf geared himself with earl-weeds, was in no wise careful for his life. The war-burny, woven with hands, wide and cunningly stained, must try the channel, that which could cover his body so that battle-grasp might not scathe his breast or ireful foeman's clutch his life; but the white helmet guarded his head, and must mingle with the mere-depths, seek the turmoil of the sea, though decked with treasure, held with lordly chains, as the weapon-smith wrought it in days of old, made it wondrously, set it with swine-shapes, so that afterwards no brand or battle-swords might bite it. That was not then the smallest of mighty helps that Hrothgar's spokesman lent him in need—Hrunting was the hilted sword's name: it was one among the first of the old treasures; the edge was iron, smeared with poison-twigs, hardened with battle-blood; never in battle did it fail any man who clasped his hands about it, who durst go griesly journeys, to battle-fields of foes. That was not the first time that it had to do a work of strength. Indeed Ecglaf's son, strong in might, was not mindful of what he said before, drunken with wine, when he lent that weapon to a better sword-warrior: he himself durst not risk life under the wave-struggle, do a warrior's deed; there he lost glory, fame for strength. It was not so with that other, after he had geared him for the fight.

Beowulf spoke, son of Ecgtheow: "Think now, mighty son of Healfdene, wise prince, gold-friend of men, now I am ready for the venture, of what we two have said before: if I at thy need should lose my life, that thou wouldst ever be in a father's place to me when I am gone hence. Be thou a protector for my kinsman-thanes, my hand-comrades, if battle takes me; likewise send to Hygelac the treasures that thou gavest me, dear Hrothgar. Then may the lord of the Geats know by the gold, the son of Hrethel see, when he gazes upon that treasure, that I found a dealer of rings good in manly parts and had joy of him while I might. And do thou let Hunferth, a wide-known man, have my old heirloom, jeweled wave-sword, hard-edged; I will work me glory with Hrunting or death shall take me."

After these words the chief of the Weder-Geats hastened with stout heart, would in no wise bide an answer; the welling surge received the battle-man. Then was there a day's while ere he might get sight of the bottom-plain. Soon she who had held the compass of the floods for a hundred half-years, sword-eager, grim and greedy, found that some one of men from above was searching there the abode of stranger-wights. Then she grasped at him, seized the warrior in her fearful grips; none the sooner did she put hurt into the hale body: outside the ring-mail covered him about, so that she might not clutch through the army-coat, the locked limb-shirt, with her hateful fingers. Then the she-wolf of the mere, when she came to the bottom, bore to her house the prince of rings in such wise that he might not (though he was brave) wield weapons at all; but by reason of it many monsters troubled him in the deep, many a sea-beast with its battle-tusks broke his army-shirt, worried the warrior. Then the earl was aware that he was in he knew not what war-hall, where no water hurt him a whit, nor could the fear-grip of the flood touch him, because of the roofed hall; he saw firelight, a glittering gleam shining bright. Then the good man got sight of the she-wolf of the sea-bottom, the mighty mere-wife; he gave a mighty rush with the battle-bill, his hand withheld not the swing, so that the ring-sword sang its greedy war-song on her head. Then the stranger found out that the battle-flasher would not bite, or harm her life, but the edge failed the chief at need; ere this it went through many hand-meetings, often sheared a helmet, a doomed man's army-dress; then was the first time for the dear treasure that its glory failed. Still was he resolute, nowise slow of strength, mindful of mighty deeds—the kinsman of Hygelac. The ireful warrior threw away then the chased sword bound with jewels, so that it lay on the earth, stiff and steel-edged; he trusted to his strength, his mighty hand-grip. So must a man do when he thinks to gain lasting praise in war, and cares not at all about his life. Then the chief of the War-Geats seized Grendel's mother by the shoulder—he mourned not at all for the strife; the hardy in battle, as he was swollen with rage, hurled his life-foe so that she bent to the floor. Quickly she paid him back hand-meed with grim grasps, and clutched at him; then, weary of mood, the strongest of warriors, fighter on foot, stumbled so that he fell. Then she sat upon the hall-guest, and drew her dagger, broad, brown-edged, and would avenge her child, her only son. On his shoulder lay the braided breast-net; that saved his life, withstood the inthrust of point and edge. Then had the son of Ecgtheow, champion of the Geats, perished under the wide sea-bottom but that the battle-burny gave him help, the hard army-net, and holy God, the wise Lord, brought about war-victory—the Ruler of the heavens easily judged it aright. Afterwards he stood up again.

Then he saw among the armor a bill rich in victories, an old sword of eotens, with doughty edges, the worship of warriors; that was the pick of weapons, but that it was greater than any other man might bear to battle-play, good and well garnished, a work of giants. He seized then the belted hilt, the wolf of the Scyldings, fierce and sword-grim, drew the ring-sword, hopeless of life struck irefully, so that the hard blade griped at her neck, broke the bone-rings; the bill went all through the doomed flesh-covering; she fell to the floor. The sword was bloody; the man was glad of his· work. The gleam flashed up: light stood within, even as the candle of the sky shines clearly from heaven. He looked along the house, then turned beside the wall; the thane of Hygelac, ireful and resolute, lifted up the hard weapon by the hilt. The edge was not worthless to the warrior, but he wanted to pay Grendel quickly for many war-rushes which he made upon the West-Danes much oftener than a single time, when he slew Hroth-gar's hearth-sharers in their sleep, ate fifteen men of the Dane-folk while they slept, and bore off as many others, a loathly prey. For that he gave him his pay, the fierce champion, insomuch that he saw Grendel lying war-weary in his resting-place, lifeless, so had the battle at Heorot scathed him before. The corpse gaped wide when it felt his stroke after death, the hard sword-swing; and then he cut off the head.

Soon the wise men who looked on the mere, with Hrothgar, saw that the welling of waves was all mingled, the sea stained with blood. The gray-haired old men spoke together about the good hero, said that they did not look for the atheling again, that he should come, glorious in victory, to seek their mighty prince; since, from that, it seemed to many that the sea-wolf of the mere had broken him to pieces. Then came the noon of the day: the bold Scyldings gave up the headland; the gold-friend of men went him home thence. The strangers sat there sick at heart, and stared at the mere; they wished and yet had no hope that they might see their friend-lord himself.

Then the sword, the war-bill, on account of the blood began to dwindle away in battle-icicles; that was a wonder, that it all melted most like to ice, when the Father loosens the bond of frost, unwinds the fetters of the pool—He Who has the wielding of times and seasons: that is the true Maker. He took no more of the treasure-goods in the dwelling, the chief of the Weder-Geats, though he saw many there, but only the head, together with the hilt decked with jewels: the sword had melted before, the adorned blade had burned up, so hot was that blood, so poisonous that stranger-ghost that met death in there. Soon he was swimming, he who erewhile in fight abode the war-fall of wroth ones; up through the water he dived; the blending waves were all cleansed, the broad abodes, when the stranger-ghost left her life-days and this fleeting earthly shape. The stout-hearted helm of seamen came then swimming to land; he joyed in his sea-booty, the mighty burden that he had with him. The picked troop of thanes went then to him, thanked God, joyed in their chief, for that they might see him sound. Then were the helmet and burny quickly loosed from the stirring hero. The lake became still, the water under the clouds, stained with slaughter-blood. Forth thence, glad at heart, they fared by foot-tracks, measured the earth-way, the well-known street, those kingly-bold men. From the sea-cliff they bore the head, with hardship for each one of them, though very brave; four men had to work hard to bear Grendel's head on the slaughter-pole to the gold-hall, till they came forthwith to the hall, bold and warlike, the fourteen Geats marching; amid them the lord of men, proud in the troop, trod the mead-plains. Then the chief of the thanes went in, the man keen in deeds, worthy in glory, battle-bold warrior, to greet Hrothgar. Then was Grendel's head borne by the hair on to the floor where men drank, a fearful thing before the earls and the lady with them; a wondrous sight men looked upon.

· · · · · · · · · · · · · ·

Then again, as before, for the strength-brave hall-sitters was a feast fairly set anew. The night-helm loured dark over the lordly men. The doughty all arose; the old Scylding with gray-streaked hair wanted to seek his bed. With boundless longing the Geat, strong shield-warrior, listed to rest; soon the hall-thane, he who for courtesy looked out for all the thane's needs, such as in that day sea-goers should have, led him forth, weary of his way, come from afar. Then the great-hearted rested him; the house towered roomy and gold-hued; the guest slept within till the black raven, blithe-hearted, heralded heaven's joy; then came the bright sun speeding over the ground. The warriors hastened, the athelings were eager to fare back to their folk; the bold-minded comer wanted to get to his keel far thence. The hardy one then bade Ecglaf's son bear Hrunting, bade him take his sword, his dear iron; he spoke him thanks for the loan, said he reckoned it a good war-friend, mighty in battle; by no means in his words did he blame the sword's edge. That was a man of mind! And when the warriors were about to set off, ready in their gear, the atheling dear to the Danes went to the high seat where the other was; the battle-brave hero greeted Hrothgar.

Beowulf spoke, son of Ecgtheow: "Now we sea-goers, come from afar, wish to say that we are going to seek Hygelac. Here we have been well waited on after our wishes; thou hast treated us well. If, then, on earth I may gain any whit more of thy heart-love than I have yet done, lord of men, I shall soon be ready for war-works. If over the stretch of the floods I learn that thy neighbors bind thee down with dreads, as those that hate thee at times have done, I will bring thee thousands of thanes, heroes to help thee. I know of Hygelac, lord of the Geats, though he be young, shepherd of the folk, that he will further me by words and works so that I may honor thee well and bear to thy help the spear-holt, an army's aid, where thou hast need of men. If then Hrethric, the king's son, take service at the courts of the Geats, he may find there many friends; far countries are better sought by him who is strong in himself."

Hrothgar spoke to him in answer: "Those word-sayings the wise Lord sent into thy soul: never heard I man in so young life speak more wisely; thou art strong of might and old in mind, wise in word-sayings. I count it a likelihood, if it happens that the spear, the sword-grim battle, illness or iron, take Hrethel's son, thy chief, shepherd of the folk, and thou hast thy life, that the Sea-Geats will have none better than thee to choose for king, hoard-warden of heroes, if thou wilt hold the realm of thy kins-men. Thy mind's mood likes me well, the longer the better, dear Beowulf. Thou hast brought it to pass that there shall be friend-ship between the folk, Geat-people and Spear-Danes, and strife shall rest, foemen-hatreds that they erewhile went through. While I wield the wide realm there shall be treasures between us: with goods shall many a one greet another over the diver's bath; over the sea the ring-bark shall bring gifts and love-tokens. I know the people are fast welded, towards foe and towards friend, alto-gether blameless in the old way."

Then, besides, the stronghold of earls, the son of Healfdene gave him within the hall twelve treasures, and bade him seek his own dear folk with the gifts, in sound health, and come again quickly. Then the king good in lineage, prince of the Scyldings, kissed that best thane, and clasped him round the neck; tears fell from him, the gray-haired man. Of both those things he had hope, old and very wise as he was, and stronger hope of the second, that they might see each other again, brave in council. The man was so dear to him that he could not keep back the heaving of his breast, but in his heart, fast in the bonds of his mind, a hidden longing for the dear man burned in his blood. From him, there, Beowulf, gold-proud warrior, trod the grassy earth exulting in treasure. The sea-goer that was riding at anchor awaited her owner-lord. Then was Hrothgar's gift often talked of as they went: that was a king every way blameless, until old age, that has often scathed many, took from him the joys of his might.

There came then to the flood many brave liegemen; ring-mail they bore, locked limb-shirts. The land-guard found out the earls' journey back, as he did before; he did not greet the guests with harm from the cliff's nose, but rode towards them, and said that as men welcome to the Weder-folk the bright-mailed warriors went to ship. Then on the sand was the sea-wide bark laded with war-weeds, the ring-stemmed ship with horses and costly things; the mast towered over Hrothgar's hoard-treasures. To the boat-ward he gave a sword bound with gold, so that thereafter he was deemed the more worthy on the mead-bench because of the treasure, the heirloom. He went on to the bark to stir the deep water, left the Danes' land. Then by the mast was a sort of sea-robe, a sail made fast by a rope; the sea-wood groaned; there the wind over the waves did not part the wave-floater from her way; the sea-goer went on, floated foamy-necked forth over the waves, the bound stem over the sea-streams, till they might get sight of the Geats' cliffs, the well-known headlands; the keel bounded up, urged by the wind, and stood on land. Quickly was the haven-guard ready at the sea, he who a long time before had looked far at the flood, eager for the dear men; he bound the broad-bosomed ship with anchor-bands fast to the sand, lest the force of the waves might drive away from them their winsome wood.

THE FIGHT WITH THE DRAGON

That came to pass afterwards by battle-crashes in later days, when Hygelac lay dead and battle-swords under the shield-cover brought bane to Heardred, when among his victory-people the hardy war-wolves, Battle-Scylfings, sought him, beset with spite the nephew of Hereric—after that the broad realm went to Beowulf's hand. He ruled well for fifty winters (he was a wise king then, an old guardian of the fatherland), until on dark nights a dragon began to make raids, that on a high mound watched over a hoard, a steep stone-barrow; a path lay under, unknown to men. Some one of men went in there, ... seized from the heathen hoard [a cup] . . . . bright with gold; nor [did] he [give] it [back] afterwards, though by thief's craft [the keeper was tricked] while he slept. The people [found out], ... the warrior-folk, that he was angered.

By no means of his own accord or with his own will did he seek the mass of worm-hoards, he who sorely scathed him; but because of dire stress this slave of some one of the children of men fled from hate-blows, in need of a house, and made his way therein, a man sin-haunted. Soon it came about that . . . . griesly terror stood upon the guest; . . . . as the fear seized him, he saw the treasure-vessel.

There were many such old treasures in that earth-house, as in days of yore some one of men had thoughtfully hidden them there, a great legacy of noble kin, dear jewels. All those men death had taken in earlier times, and the one from the doughty of that people who still roamed there longest became a mourner bereft of friends, yet looked forward to old age, that he might for a little time enjoy the long-kept treasures. A barrow all ready stood on the plain near the water-waves, all new by the head-land, made fast by close craft; into that the keeper of rings bore the heavy deal of earls' treasures, of plated gold, and spoke a few words: "Hold thou now, Earth, now that men might not, the ownings of earls. Lo, good men got it first in thee; war-death, dread life-bale, has taken off each man of my people, who has given up this life; they have seen hall-joy. I have no one who may bear the sword, or polish the plated flagon, dear drink-vessel; the doughty have gone elsewhere. The hard helmet, decked with gold, shall lose its platings; the burnishers sleep whose task it was to make ready the battle-mask; and likewise the army-coat, which in battle endured, over the crash of shields, the bite of iron swords, shall crumble after the hero; the ringed burny may not fare far after the war-chief, by the side of warriors. There is no joy of the harp, no mirth of the glee-wood, nor does the good hawk swing through the hall, nor the swift horse paw the castle-yard. Baleful death has sent forth many of living kind." So in mournful mood one man bemoaned his sorrow for all, wept in woe day and night, till the flood of death laid hold of his heart.

The old twilight-scather found the joy-hoard standing open,— the burning one that seeks barrows, naked spite-dragon, and flies at night enfolded in fire; him earth-dwellers dread greatly. He must seek a hoard in the earth, where, old in winters, he guards heathen gold; yet is it no whit the better for him. So for three hundred winters the people-scather held in the earth a hoard-house mightily strong, till one man put him in angry mood; he bore a plated flagon to a prince of men, and begged his lord for a peace-treaty. Then was the hoard found, the hoard of rings plundered; the wretched man's boon was granted. The lord saw the ancient work of men for the first time. Then the worm awoke, strife was renewed; he sniffed of the stone, stout-hearted found the foe's foot-track—in his hidden craft he had stepped too far forth, near the dragon's head. So may the undoomed easily get off from woe and banishment, whom the Wielder's favor keeps. The hoard-warden sought eagerly along the ground, would find the man who had done him harm in his sleep; hot and fierce of mood he went oft round the mound, all the outside of it; no man was there in the waste. Yet he was glad of the war, the battle-work; at times he turned back to the barrow, sought the costly vessel; he soon found that some one of men had sought out the gold, the high treasures. The hoard-warden could hardly wait till evening came; then was the keeper of the barrow angry,—the loathsome foe would pay back with flame for the dear drink-vessel. Then was day gone, according to the worm's will; no longer would he bide on the wall, but went forth with burning, made ready with fire. Terrible was the beginning for the folk in the land, even as it was quickly ended in their treasure-giver's sore.

Then the guest began to spew gledes, to burn bright dwellings; the burning ray stood forth for mischief to men; naught living would the loathsome air-flyer leave there. The worm's war was widely seen, near and far the spite of the pressing foe, how the war-scather hated and humbled the Geat-people. Back he shot to the hoard, the hidden warrior-hall, ere day-time; he had enfolded the land-folk with flame, with burning and brand; he trusted the barrow, his warfare and his wall; his hope belied him. Then was the terror made known to Beowulf, quickly forsooth, that his own home, best of buildings, the Geats' gift-stool, was melting in surges of fire. That was a grief to the good man in his breast, greatest of heart-sorrows: the wise one weened that he had bitterly angered the Wielder, the eternal Lord, against the old laws; his breast within welled with dark thoughts, as was not his wont. The fire-dragon had burned down with his gledes the people's fastness, the water-land without, the earth-holding; therefore the war-king, prince of the Weders, learned vengeance upon him. Then the stronghold of warriors, lord of earls, bade make him a well-adorned war-board all of iron; well he knew that holt-wood might not help him, a linden shield against fire. The atheling good before all was to meet the end of his loan-days, this world's life, and the worm with him, though he had long held the hoard-wealth. The prince of rings scorned to seek the wide-flyer with a band, a large army; not at all did he dread the fight: he counted the worm's warfare for naught, its hardiness and its strength, for that he himself ere this, risking close straits, had got through many struggles, battle-crashes, since he, victory-blessed man, had cleansed Hrothgar's hall and gripped to death in battle Grendel's kinsman of loathsome kind. Not the least was the hand-to-hand meeting where Hygelac was slain, when the Geats' king in the war-rushes, the lord-friend of the folk, Hrethel's son, in Friesland died of sword-drinks, beaten by the bill; thence Beowulf came off by his own might, did swimming-work: he alone had on his arm thirty suits of war-gear when he went down to the sea. By no means did the Hetware need to be exultant over their foot-war, they who bore their linden shields forward against him; few came again from that battle-wolf to return home. Then the son of Ecgtheow swam over the stretch of still waters, wretched and alone, back to his people, where Hygd offered him the hoard and realm, rings and prince's stool: she did not trust her child, that he could hold the seats of the fatherland against alien folk, now Hygelac was dead. None the sooner might the wretched people by any means prevail upon the atheling to be Heardred's lord or to choose the kingdom; yet he upheld him among the folk with friendly lore, with kindness and honor, till he became older and ruled the Weder-Geats. Him banished men sought over sea, the sons of Ohthere; they had rebelled against the helm of the Scylfings, the best of sea-kings, who dealt out treasure in the Swede-realm, a famous prince. That came to be his life's bound: there, without food, the son of Hygelac was allotted a life-wound through swings of the sword. And the child of Ongentheow went him back to return home, when Heardred lay dead, let Beowulf hold the prince's stool, rule the Geats. That was a good king. In later days he took thought of requital for the prince's fall: he became a friend to needy Eadgils, furthered with folk the son of Ohthere over the wide sea, with warriors and weapons; he had vengeance afterwards for his cold care-journeys—took the king's life.

So had he got through every struggle, every savage slaying and work of strength, this son of Ecgtheow, till that one day when he was to wage war with the worm. One of twelve men, the lord of the Geats went, then, swollen with anger, to see the dragon. He had learned whence the feud arose, the baleful spite against heroes; to his lap had come the marvelous treasure-vessel, through the finder's hand. He was a thirteenth man in the band, the one who set afoot the beginning of the battle; a captive, sad at heart and despised, he had to lead the way thence to the plain. He went against his will to where he knew was an earth-hall, a mound under the earth near the sea-surge, the wave-strife, which was full within of jewels and wire-work. A warden uncanny, a ready war-wolf, old under the earth, held the gold-treasures; it was no easy bargain for any man to go there. Then the king hardy in war sat down on the headland while he bade farewell to his hearth-sharers, the gold-friend of the Geats. His heart was sad within him, wavering and looking to death; fate was very near at hand, that must greet the old man, seek out the hoard of his soul, part in sunder his life and body: not long then was the atheling's life wound about with flesh.

Beowulf spoke, son of Ecgtheow: "In youth I got through many war-rushes, many battle-times; I remember it all. I was seven winters old when the prince of treasures, lord-friend of the folk, took me from my father: King Hrethel held me and had me, gave me treasures and feasts, and remembered our kinship; I was no whit more hateful to him in his life, as a warrior in his burgs, than any one of his own children, Herebeald and Hæthcyn or my Hygelac. For the eldest a murder-bed was strewn, unnaturally, by a kinsman's deeds, when Hæthcyn struck him, his lord-friend, with an arrow from his horn-bow, missed his mark and shot down his kinsman, one brother another, with a bloody shaft. That was a fight not to be paid with a fee, a sin criminally done, wearying to the heart; yet the atheling had to lose his life unwreaked, nevertheless. So is it sad for an old man to abide that his boy shall ride young on the gallows; then he utters a dirge, a sorry song, when his son hangs for a comfort to the raven and he cannot help him—old and infirm, can do nothing. Always is he reminded, each morning, of his child's passing away; he cares not to await another heir in his burgs, when the one has proved his deeds through the pangs of death. Full of sorrow and care he sees in his son's bower a wine-hall at waste, a resting place for winds, of revel bereft: the riders sleep, the heroes, in the grave; no sound of the harp is there, no games in the yards, as there were before.

"He goes then to his sleeping-place and sings his sorrow-lay, a lone man for an only one lost; all has seemed to him too roomy, meadows and dwelling-place. So the helm of the Weders bore a heart welling with sorrow for Herebeald; no whit might he make good the feud on the life-slayer, nor any sooner vent his hate on the warrior by hateful deeds, though he was not dear to him. Then with that sorrow which his sore brought upon him, he gave up the joy of men, chose God's light. When he went from life he left to his sons, as a rich man does, the land and the folk-burg. Then was there hatred and strife between Swedes and Geats, a struggle together over the wide water, hard army-hate, after Hrethel died; and the sons of Ongentheow were bold and warlike, would not hold friendship over sea, but often made a dire inroad about Hreosnabeorh. That my kinsman-friends wreaked on them, the feud and the crime, as was well known, though another paid for it with his life, a hard bargain: the war was fatal for Hæthcyn, lord of the Geats. Then in the morning I heard that one kinsman took vengeance on another's slayer with the sword's edge, where Ongentheow sought out Eofor: the war-helmet fell apart; the old Scylfing fell, sword-pale; the hand remembered enough of the feud, did not withhold the life-blow. In the war, as was granted me, I paid him [Hygelac] with my bright sword for the treasures that he gave me; he gave me land, an abode, home-joy. He had no need to seek a worse war-wolf among the Gifths or the Spear-Danes or in Swede-realm, and buy him for a price: I would always be foremost in his troop, alone in front; and so through life shall I do battle while this sword holds out, that has often lasted me early and late, since I, for doughty deeds, was hand-slayer of Dæghrefn, champion of the Hugs. By no means might he bring the fretwork, the breast-riches, to the Frisian king, but in battle the banner-keeper fell, the atheling in his strength; the edge was not his slayer, but the battle-grip broke his heart's wellings, his bone-house. Now shall the bill's edge, the hand and the hard sword, war for the hoard."

Beowulf spoke, uttered boasting words, for the last time: "I got through many wars in my youth; yet will I, old warden of the folk, seek the feud and do famously, if the wicked scather will come out of his earth-hall and seek me." Then he greeted each of the men for the last time, the keen helmet-bearer his dear comrades: "I would not bear a sword, a weapon against the worm, if I knew how else I might carry out my boast in griping with the monster, as I did once with Grendel: but there I look for hot battle-fire, breath and venom; therefore I have upon me shield and burny. I will not flee from the barrow's warden a foot's space, but it shall befall us two at the wall as fate fixes for us, the Creator of every man. I am keen of mood, so that I keep back my boast against the war-flyer. Do ye await on the barrow, covered with your burnies, warriors in gear, which of us two may the better live through his wound after the slaughter-rush. It is not your undertaking, nor is it meet for a man, save me alone, that he deal his might against the monster, win earl-ship. With my strength I shall gain gold, or battle, dread life-bale, will take your lord."

The strong warrior then arose by his shield, hardy under his helmet, bore his sword-shirt under the stone-cliffs, trusted to one man's strength: not such is the coward's way. Then he who, good in manly parts, had lived through a great number of wars, battle-crashes, when troops clashed, saw by the wall a stone-arch standing, and a stream breaking out thence from the barrow; the welling of the stream there was hot with battle-fires. He might not without burning endure for any while the deep near the hoard, because of the dragon's flame. Then the chief of the Weder-Geats let a word go out from his breast, since he was angry—the stout-hearted stormed: his voice came roaring in, battle-bright, under the hoary stone. Hate was stirred up; the hoard-warden knew the man's speech; there was no more time to seek for friendship. Forth came the monster's breath, first, out of the stone, hot battle-sweat; the earth dinned. The hero under

the barrow, lord of the Geats, swung up his board-shield against
the griesly guest; then was the ring-coiler ready in heart to seek
strife. Ere this the good war-king had drawn his sword, the old
heirloom, not slow of edge—to each of the bale-plotters came
terror from the other. Stout-hearted stood the lord of friends
against his tall shield, while the worm bent quickly together: he
waited in his gear. Then the burning one, bent up, went gliding
on, hastening to his fate. The shield covered the great prince
well, life and body, for a shorter while than his wish sought, if he
was to prevail at that time, on the first day: since fate did not
allot to him victory in the battle. The lord of the Geats lifted up
his hand, struck the griesly foe with his weighty heirloom so that
its edge weakened, brown on the bone, bit less strongly than its
folk-king had need of, beset with troubles. Then was the barrow's
warden in fierce mood after the battle-stroke: he threw out
slaughter-fire; wide sprang the battle-flames. The gold-friend of
the Geats did not boast triumphant victory: his war-bill failed,
naked in the struggle, as it by no means should, an iron good
before all. It was no easy course for the famous son of Ecgtheow
to give up the ground-plain; against his will he must take up
his dwelling elsewhere, as every man shall leave his loan-days.
It was not long, then, before the monster-warriors met each other
again. The hoard-warden heartened him—his breast swelled with
breath anew; he who formerly ruled the folk was pressed in close
straits, enfolded in fire. By no means did his hand-comrades,
children of athelings, stand about him in a band, with battle-
virtue; but they bent to the wood, looked after their lives. In one
of them his soul welled with sorrow: naught may ever set aside
kinship, to the man who thinks rightly.

Wiglaf was his name, son of Weohstan, a dear shield-warrior
prince of the Scylfings, kinsman of Ælfhere. He saw his lord
suffering heat under his army-mask; then he remembered the
favors that he had formerly given him, the wealthy homestead of
the Wægmundings, and every folk-right, the same as his father
had. He could not keep back—his hand clutched his shield, the
yellow linden, and tugged at his old sword. That was an heir-
loom among men from Eanmund, son of Ohthere, whom, a friend-
less wanderer, Weohstan slew in strife by the sword's edge, and
bore to his kinsmen the brown-stained helmet, the ringed burny,
and the old sword of eotens that Onela gave him, his kinsman's
war-weeds, ready army-gear; he did not speak about the feud,

though he had overthrown his brother's child. He held the fretted armor many a half-year, bill and burny, till his boy might win earlship like his father before him; then he gave him, among the Geats, a countless number of war-weeds of each kind, when he went from life, old, on his way forth.

Then was the first time for the young fighter that he was to make a war-rush with his noble lord. His heart did not melt nor his kinsman's heirloom weaken in the war: that the worm found out when they had come together. Wiglaf spoke many right words, said to his comrades (his heart was sad): "I remember the time that we were taking mead, when we, in the beer-hall, vowed to our lord, who gave us these rings, that we would repay him for the war-gear, helmets and hard swords, if need like this befell him. Of his own will he chose us in the army for this undertaking, reminded us of great deeds, and gave me these treasures, because he reckoned us good spear-warriors, bold helmet-bearers; though our lord thought to do this strength-work alone, shepherd of the folk, since he among men has done the most great things, daring deeds. Now is the day come when our lord has need of the might of good warriors: let us go to him, help our battle-chief, while the heat lasts, the grim glede-terror. God knows of me that I had much liefer that the fire enfold my body with my gold-giver. Methinks it is not fitting that we bear shields back home unless we may first fell the foe, guard the life of the Weders' prince. I know well that these were not his deserts from of old, that he alone from the doughty of the Geats should suffer sorrow, sink in the strife. For us two shall sword and helmet, burny and shield-covering, be in common." Then he went through the slaughter-reek, bore his war-helmet to his lord's help, spoke a few words: "Dear Beowulf, do all well, as thou in thy youth-days of yore didst say that thou wouldst not let glory fail with thee living. Now must thou, strong in deeds, resolute atheling, guard thy life with all thy might; I will help thee."

After these words the worm came on in ire, dire foeman-guest, for a second time, flashing with wellings of fire, to beset his foes, hateful men. With waves of flame the shield burned up to the rim; the burny could give no help to the young spear-warrior; but the young man bravely went under his kinsman's shield when his own was burned away by the gledes. Then again the war king minded him of great deeds, struck with main strength with his battle-bill, so that it stood in the [dragon's] head, driven by hate. Nægling broke: Beowulf's sword failed in the fight, ancient and gray-marked. It was not given him that edges of irons might help him in battle; that hand was too strong, which in its swing overtaxed every sword, as I have heard, when he bore to the fight a weapon wondrously hard: no whit was it the better for him. Then was the people-scather, the fierce fire-dragon, for a third time mindful of the feud—rushed upon the brave one where room offered him, hot and battle-grim, and encircled all his neck with biting bones. He was made bloody with life-blood; the blood welled in waves.

Then I heard that at the folk-king's need the earl showed endless courage, craft and keenness, as was natural to him. He heeded not the [dragon's] head (but the brave man's hand was burned where he helped his kinsman), so that he smote the spite-guest a little downwards, the man in armor, in such wise that the sword dived in, bright and plated, and the fire began to wane afterwards. Then the king himself again had use of his wits, drew his slaughter-knife, biting and battle-sharp, that he wore on his burny: the helm of the Weders cut the worm in two in the middle. They felled the foe, strength drove out life, and they had both killed him, the kinsman-athelings; such a man should a warrior be, a thane at need.

For the prince that was the last victory-while, through his own deeds, of his work in the world. The wound which the earth-dragon had given him erewhile began to burn and swell; he soon found that baleful venom was welling in his breast, poison within him. Then the atheling went to sit on a seat by the wall, wise-thinking, and looked upon the work of giants, how the stone-arches, firm on their columns, hold up the everlasting earth-house within. With his hand the thane boundlessly good laved him with water, sword-gory as he was, the famous prince, his friend-lord, battle-sated; and he loosened his helmet. Beowulf made speech—he spoke in spite of his hurt, the wound deathly pitiful; he knew well that he had spent his days' while of earth's joy; then was all the number of his days departed, death nearer than could be told: "Now I would give my war-weeds to my son, if it were so given me that any heir belonging to my body came after me. Fifty winters have I held this people; there was not one folk-king of the neighbors who durst greet me with swords, beset me with dread. I bided in my home for the times that were set, held well what was mine; neither sought wily spites nor swore me many oaths in unrighteousness. Sick with life-wounds I may have joy of all that: therefore the Ruler of men need not blame me for murder of kinsmen when my life goes from my body. Now do thou go quickly and see the hoard under the hoary stone, dear Wiglaf, now that the worm lies still, sleeps sorely wounded, bereft of its riches. Be now in haste, that I may get sight of the ancient wealth, the gold-treasure, may see well the bright cunning gems, so that I may the softer, after the wealth of treasures, let go my life and my people, that I have long held."

Then I heard that the son of Weohstan after these word-sayings quickly obeyed his wounded lord, battle-sick: bore his ring-mail, his braided battle-sark, under the barrow's roof. He that exulted in victory, the brave kinsman-thane, saw when he went by the seat many treasure-jewels, gold glittering as it lay on the ground, a wonder on the wall, and the den of the worm, the old twilight-flyer. Flagons stood there, vessels of former men, wanting the burnisher, bereft of adornments. There was many a helmet, old and rusty, many an arm-ring cunningly twisted. A treasure, gold on the ground, may easily befool any one of mankind, hide it he who will. Likewise he saw resting there a banner all golden, high over the hoard, greatest wonder of handiwork, woven by hand-craft; from it came a gleam, so that he could see the ground-plain, look over the jewels. There was not a sign of the worm, but the sword's edge had taken him. Then I heard that a single man plundered the hoard in the mound, the old work of giants—at his own will loaded into his lap cups and dishes; he also took the banner, brightest of beacons. The old lord's bill—its edge was iron—had erewhile scathed him who was a long while care-taker of these treasures, and waged the flame-terror hot before the hoard, fierce-welling at midnight, till he died the bloody death. The messenger was in haste, yearning to go back, the jewels with him; a longing fretted him to know whether, in his high spirits, he should find the prince of the Weders, sick and strengthless, alive in the meadow-place where he had left him before.

With the treasures he found the great prince, his lord, all bloody, at the end of life; he began again to sprinkle him with water, till a word's point broke through his breast-hoard. Beowulf spoke—the old man in his sorrow looked upon the gold: "For these jewels which I here gaze upon I utter thanks, in words, to the Lord of all, the King of Glory, everlasting Lord, that I might get such things for my people ere my death-day. Now that I have sold for the hoard of treasures the laying-down of my old life, do still the people's need; I may not be here longer. Bid the great in battle make a mound, bright after the funeral fire, at the sea-cape; it shall be lifted high on Whale's Ness as a reminder to my people, so that seafarers who drive high ships from afar over the mists of the floods shall call it henceforth Beowulf's Barrow." The bold-minded prince took from his neck the golden ring-mail: he gave to the thane, the young spear-warrior, his gold-hued helmet, his ring and his burny, and bade him use them well. "Thou art the last left of our kin, the Wægmundings; fate has swept off all my kinsmen to the fixed doom, the earls in their strength; I must after them." That was the last word from the old man's breast-thoughts ere he met the fire, the hot flame-wellings: his soul went from his breast to seek the reward of the steadfast in truth.

. . . .

Now the wise son of Weohstan called from the crowd seven of the king's thanes together, the best, and went, one of eight, under the foe's roof; one warrior bore in his hand a fire-gleam, and went in front. Then was no taking of lots who should plunder that hoard, when the men saw any part staying in the hall without a warden, lying likely to be lost; little did any mourn that they bore out the dear treasures hastily. They shoved the dragon also, the worm, over the cliff-wall—let the wave take, the flood enfold, the keeper of the jewels. There was twisted gold loaded on a wain, altogether uncounted. The atheling, the hoary warrior, was borne to Whale's Ness.

Then the Geat people made ready for him a funeral pile firm on the earth, hung with helmets, battle-boards, and bright burnies as he had begged; there in the midst the heroes lamenting laid the great prince, their dear lord. Then the warriors began to kindle on the barrow the greatest of funeral fires; the wood-smoke arose swart above the glow, the flame roared, mingled with weeping (the tumult of winds was laid), till it had broken the bone-house, hot on the breast. Sad in their souls and with heart-care they bemoaned their lord's death; likewise his wife, in care and sorrow, with hair bound up, [sang for Beowulf] a sad lay, said over and over that she [dreaded] for herself hard [harm-days], many slaughter-falls, [a warrior's] terror, shame and [a slave's need]. Heaven swallowed the smoke. Then the Weder-people made a mound on the cliff, that was high and broad, widely seen by wavefarers, and built in ten days the beacon of him that was strong in battle; what was left of the brands they enclosed with a wall, as very wise men might most worthily devise it. They put in the barrow rings and jewels, all such adornments as men of warlike mind had taken erewhile from the hoard; they let the earth hold the treasure of earls, gold in the grit, where it now lives still, as useless to men as it was before. Then about the mound rode battle-bold children of athelings, twelve in all: they would bemoan their cares, lament for the king, utter the word-lay and speak about the man; they praised his earlship and doughtily judged of his strength-work, as it is meet that a man honor his friend-lord in words and love him in heart when he must go forth from the fleeting body. So the Geat people, his hearth-sharers, bemoaned the fall of their lord. They said that he was a world-king, of men the mildest and kindest to men, gentlest to the people and most eager for praise.

CHARMS

I

Against a swarm of bees. Take earth, throw it over with thy right hand under thy right foot, and say: "I take under foot; I have found it. Lo, earth avails against every creature, and against mischief and against forgetfulness, and against the great tongue of man." Throw gravel over when they swarm, and say: "Sit ye, victory-women, sink to earth! never shall ye fly wild to wood! be ye as mindful of my good as is every man of food and land!"

II

Against a sudden stitch. Feverfew, and the red nettle that grows in through the house, and dock; boil in butter.

Loud were they, lo, loud, when over the hill they rode, were of one mind when over the land they rode! Do thou shield thee now, that thou mayest escape this spite. Out, little spear, if herein it be! I stood under linden, under a light shield, where the mighty women made ready their might, and they sent yelling spears; I will send them another again, a flying arrow against them in front: out, little spear, if herein it be! There sat a smith and forged a little knife, wounded with iron strongly: out, little spear, if herein it be! Six smiths sat, slaughter-spears wrought: out, spear—not in, spear! if herein be a piece of iron, witches' work, it shall melt! If thou wert shot in skin, or wert shot in flesh, or wert shot in blood, or wert shot in limb, never be thy life worn out! If it were shot of gods, or were shot of elves, or were shot of witches, now I will help thee: this to thee for cure of gods' shot, this to thee for cure of elves' shot, this to thee for cure of witches' shot: I will help thee. Flee to the mountain-head! Be thou whole! Lord help thee!

Take then the knife, put it in the liquid.

THE FRISIAN WIFE

Dear to the Frisian wife is the welcome one, when the ship stands still: his keel is come, and her man is come home, her own provider; and she calls him in, washes his clothing stained with sea-weed, and gives him new garments. Sweet is it on land for him whom his love constrains.

RIDDLE

THE MOON AND THE SUN

I saw a wight wondrously bearing booty between horns, a bright air-vessel cunningly geared bearing booty home from the war-journey: he would build him a bower in the burg, fashion it skilfully if so he might. Then came over the wall's roof a wondrous wight who is known to all earth-dwellers: he took away then the booty, and drove the wretch home against his will; went himself thence to go west with his wars, sped him forth. Dust rose to heaven, dew fell on earth, night came forth: no man knew after of that wight's journey.

THE WANDERER

Oft a lonely man looks for favor, for the Maker's mercy, though with heart of care over the water-ways he must lcng stir with his hands the rime-cold sea, follow the paths of the banished: fate is full relentless!

So quoth a wanderer, mindful of his hardships, of cruel slaughters and the fall of friendly kinsmen: "Often alone at each dawn must I talk of my care: there is now none living to whom I dare speak my heart clearly. In sooth I know that for an earl it is a noble custom that he bind fast his heart-locker, hold his hoard-chamber, think as he will. The weary mind may not withstand fate, nor the sad heart frame help: wherefore yearners for glory oft bind the dreary heart fast in their breast-chambers. So must

I, often wretched and full of care, parted from my country, far from free kinsmen, seal my heart with fetters, since in bygone years the darkness of earth enwrapped my gold-friend, and I, downcast, went thence in wintry care over the mingling of waves, all dreary sought the hall of a dealer of treasure, where, far or near, I might find him who knew mercy in the mead-hall or would comfort me, friendless, entertain me with joy.

"He can tell who knows, how cruel is sorrow for a comrade to him who has few dear protectors: the exile-path attends him, not twisted gold, a chill heart-locker, not the fruit of the earth; he remembers hallmen and receiving of treasure, how in his youth his gold-friend entertained him at the feast—joy has all failed! Wherefore he knows who must long do without the counsels of his dear friend-lord, when sorrow and sleep together often bind the wretched wanderer—it seems to him in his mind that he embraces and kisses his lord, and lays on his knee hands and head, as he at times before enjoyed the gift-stool, in days of yore. Then the friendless man awakes again, sees before him fallow waves, sea-birds bathing, spreading their feathers, rime and snow falling, mingled with hail. Then are his heart's wounds the heavier, sore after the loved one—sorrow is renewed. Then the mind recalls the memory of kinsmen, greets it joyfully, surveys it eagerly. The comrades of warriors swim again away—the spirit of the floating ones brings not there many well-known speech-words; care is renewed for him who must very often send his weary heart over the mingling of waves.

"Therefore I may not understand in this world why my heart turns not black, when I think over all the life of earls, how they suddenly give up the hall-floor, brave kinsman-thanes. So this world every day perishes and falls; therefore a man may not become wise ere he has a deal of winters in the world-realm. The wise man must be patient, must be neither too hot-hearted nor too hasty in words, nor too weak a warrior nor too heedless, nor too fearful nor too fain nor too greedy, nor ever too eager in boast before he knows well. A man must wait, when he speaks a boast, till, proud-spirited, he knows well whither hearts' thought will turn. The wise hero must perceive how ghastly it is when all this world's wealth stands waste, as now throughout this earth various walls stand blown upon by the wind, covered with hoar-frost, the dwellings storm-beaten. The wine-halls are crumbling, rulers lie bereft of joy; all the doughty have fallen, proud by the wall: some war took off, carried on the way forth; one a bird bore away over the high sea; one the hoary wolf dealt to death; one a sad-faced earl hid in an earth-cave. So the Creator of men laid waste this earth, till, reft of burghers' revels, the old works of giants stood idle. He then who has wisely thought of this wall-place, and deeply thinks this dark life through, wise in spirit often remembers far back a great number of slaughters, and says this word: 'Where has the horse gone? where has the kinsman gone? where has gone the giver of treasures? where have gone the seats at feasts? where are the hall-joys? Alas, the bright cup! alas, the burny-warrior! alas, the king's strength! How is time gone, grown dark under the night-helm, as if it were not! Now on the track of the dear host stands a wall wondrous high, adorned with worm-shapes: the might of ashen spears has taken off the earls, weapons greedy for slaughter—fate, the well-known. And storms beat the stone-cliffs; the snow-storm falling binds the earth, winter's terror when it comes wan; the shadow of night darkens, sends on from the north a cruel hail-storm for harm to men. All is full of hardship in earth's realm; the decree of fate changes the world under the heavens: here is wealth fleeting, here is friend fleeting, here is man fleeting, here is kinsman fleeting; all this earth's foundation becomes idle!' "

So quoth the wise man in his mind, sat apart in counsel with himself. Good is he who keeps his troth; never shall the hero reveal his anger too hastily from his breast, unless he first knows the remedy; an earl must act boldly. Well is it for him who seeks favor, comfort from the Father in Heaven, where stands all our safety.

THE BANISHED WIFE'S LAMENT

By myself, full sad, I utter this song of my own lot. I may say that what miseries I have endured since I grew up, new or old, were never greater than now: ever I suffer the torment of my exile!

First my lord went hence from his people over the waves' tossing; in early morning I had care where, in what land, my chieftain was. Then I went, a friendless exile, for my sore need, to go and seek him I served. The man's kinsmen began, through secret thought, to plan that they should part us, that we two should live in this world-realm most wide apart and most hatefully, and I should be filled with longing.

My lord bade me take up my dwelling here: I had few dear ones in this landstead, few faithful friends. Therefore is my heart sad, since I have found the man who is full well matched with me one of hard fortunes, gloomy-hearted, concealing his thought, thinking evil, with blithe bearing. Full oft we two vowed that naught else should part us save death alone: that is also changed —our friendship is now as if it never were! Far and near must I endure the enmity of my much-beloved! I am bidden to dwell among groves of wood, under an oak-tree in the earth-cavern; old is this earth-hall—I am all filled with longing; dim are the dells, high the downs, bitter the burg-towns, overgrown with briers, a joyless dwelling. Full oft my lord's departure has filled me here with wrath. Friends are on earth living beloved, keeping the marriage-bed, when I alone in early morning go under the oak-tree in the earth-cavern! There I must sit the summer-long day; there I may weep my banishment, many hardships, wherefore I may never rest from my mind-care or all that longing that in this life has laid hold upon me.

Ever shall the young man be sad in mind, hard the thought of his heart; so also shall he have a blithe bearing, even with breast-care, a band of constant sorrows; within himself be all his world's joy—be it full widely exiled in a far folk-land, so that my friend shall sit under a stone-slope, hoar-frosted by storm, weary in heart, overflowed with water in a dreary hall! My friend will endure much mind-care; he will remember too often a more joyful dwelling. Woe is his who must await his love with useless longing!

CÆDMON'S HYMN

Now should we praise the Keeper of heaven's kingdom, the Maker's might and His mind-thought, the Father-of-Glory's work, as He, the eternal King, each wonder's beginning established. He first shaped for earth's children the heaven as roof—the holy Creator; and then Mankind's Keeper, eternal King, the Lord Almighty, after prepared the world, the land for men.

FROM

THE PHŒNIX

THE HAPPY LAND

I have heard that far hence in eastern parts is the noblest of lands, famous among men. That part of the earth is not accessible to many earth-owners over the world, but is removed through the Maker's might from evil-doers. Beautiful is all the plain, made blissful with joys, with the fairest odors of earth: peerless is that island, noble the Maker, of high mind and rich in might, Who established that land. There the door of the heavenly kingdom is often open before the blessed, the joy of its melodies is revealed. That is a winsome plain, green forésts, roomy under the skies. No rain nor snow there, nor frost's breath nor fire's blast, nor fall of hail or hoar-frost, nor sun's heat nor lasting cold, nor warm weather nor winter shower, may anywise destroy, but the plain stands blessed and sound; that noble land is blowing with blossoms.

There stand neither hills nor steep mountains, nor do stone-cliffs tower high, as here with us, nor valleys nor dales, nor hill-caves, mounds nor slopes, nor does aught that is rough slope there; but the noble field flourishes under the clouds blowing with joys. That bright land is twelve fathoms higher (so wise men through wisdom make known to us by hearsay in their writings) than any of the hills that here with us tower bright and high under the stars of heaven. Mild is that victory-plain; a sunny grove shines there, a joyful wood: the bright fruits that grow do not fall, but the trees forever stand green, as God commanded them; winter and summer alike the wood is hung with fruits; the leaves never fade under the air, nor will flame scathe them for ever and ever till change comes to the world. As when of yore the strength of waters covered all the world, a sea-flood the circuit of the earth, then the noble plain stood altogether sound, kept against the oncoming of the fierce waves, blessed and pure through God's grace: so it shall abide in bloom till the coming of the last fire, the Lord's doom, when the halls of death, men's chambers of darkness, shall be opened.

There is no foe in the land, nor weeping nor wretchedness, no token of woe, nor old age nor misery, nor cruel death nor loss of life, nor coming of wrong, nor sin nor strife nor sore revenge, nor trouble of poverty nor want of wealth, nor sorrow nor sleep nor grievous sickness, nor winter storm nor rough change of weather under the heavens, nor does the hard frost beat any one with cold icicles. There neither hail nor hoar-frost falls to the earth, nor windy cloud, nor does water fall there, troubled by the air; but there water-streams, wondrous wells, spring forth, with fair flood-wellings water the earth—winsome water from the midst of the wood, which every month breaks forth cold as the sea from the earth's turf, goes through all the grove gloriously at times: it is the King's command that twelve times the joy of water-floods shall play over that glorious land. The groves are hung with fruits fair-grown: there the holy adornments of the wood do not fade under the heavens; there the blossoms, beauty of forest-trees, fall not fallow on the earth, but the branches on the trees are always splendidly laden, fruits renewed in all time. On the grass-plain the brightest of groves stand green, joyfully adorned by the Holy One's might. The holt is not broken in hue, where the holy fragrance dwells throughout the joy-land; it shall not be changed for ever and ever, till the Wise One Who shaped it in the beginning shall end His former work.

FROM

GENESIS

SATAN'S SPEECH

Then spoke the proud king, who was erewhile fairest of angels, whitest in heaven and beloved of his Lord, dear to God, till they became too foolhardy, so that God Himself, the mighty, became ireful in mood against him for his pride, cast him into that torture, down upon that bed of death, and shaped him a name thereafter —the Highest said that he should be called Satan thenceforth, and bade him care for the ground of that swart hell, by no means fight against God. Satan made speech, spoke sorrowing, he who should henceforth hold hell and care for its ground—who was before God's angel, white in heaven, till his heart and his pride, strongest of all, led him astray, that he would not worship the word of the Lord of Hosts. His proud mind welled within him about his heart, and wrathful torment was hot without him; then he spoke these words: "This narrow place is very unlike the other that we knew before, high in heaven's kingdom, that my Lord lent me, though because of the All-Ruler we may not have it, may not possess our realm. Yet He has not done right, that He has felled us by fire to the bottom, to this hot hell, taken from us heaven's kingdom, and has marked it out to settle with mankind. That is the greatest of sorrows to me, that Adam, who was wrought of earth, shall hold my strong seat, be in bliss, and we suffer this torment, harm in this hell. Oh woe! had I power of my hands, and might I for one time get out, be out one winter-hour, then with this troop I—but iron bands lie about me, a chain of fetters rides me. I am powerless: such hard bonds of hell have seized me fast. Here is a great fire above and below; I never saw a more loathly landscape; the flames die not down, hot over hell. A bond of rings, chain cruelly hard, has hindered me from motion, taken from me my power to move—my feet are bound, my hands held fast; the ways of these hell-gates are blocked up, so I may nowise get from these limb-bonds. Round about me lie great bars of hard iron forged hot: thus has God fastened me by the neck. So I know He knew my thought, and the Lord of Hosts knew also that evil should come to us two, Adam and me, about that heavenly kingdom, if I had power of my hands. But we suffer now throes in hell, that are darkness and heat, grim, fathomless; God Himself has swept us down to these swart mists. Although He may not impute any sin to us, that we have worked hatred against Him in the land, He has yet robbed us of the light, cast us into the greatest of all torments: nor may we do vengeance for that, requite Him with any hatred, that He has robbed us of the light. He has now marked out a middle-yard, where He has made man after His likeness, with whom He will again settle the kingdom of heaven with pure souls.

"We must therefore think eagerly, that we may pay back our wrong on Adam, if ever we may, and on his children likewise, and balk Him there of His will, if we may any way devise it. I now trust no further the light which He thinks long to enjoy, the riches with His angels' strength; we may never win that, to soften the mood of mighty God. Let us turn it now from the children of men, that heavenly kingdom, now we may not have it: bring it about that they lose His favor, that they transgress what He commanded with His word; then will He be wrathful in mood against them, turn them from His favor; then shall they seek this hell, and these grim grounds—then may we have them for our followers, children of men in these fast bonds. Begin now to think about the expedition. If I have given any thane princely treasures in days of yore, while we sat blessed in the good realm and had power of our thrones, then he might never at a dearer time pay me returns for my gift,—if any of my thanes would now be a consenter to it, that he might come out, up hence through this prison, and had craft in him so that he could fly with a feather-coat, go on a cloud, where Adam and Eve stand wrought on the earth-realm, surrounded with wealth, and we are cast down hither into this deep dale. Now they are much worthier in the sight of the Lord, and may have the wealth which we should have in the heavenly kingdom, our realm by right: this good is decreed to mankind. That is such a sorrow to me in my mind, grieves me in my heart, that they possess the heavenly kingdom forever. If any of you may anywise compass it that they forsake God's word, His teaching, soon will they be the more hateful to Him; if they break His commandment then He will be angry with them; thereafter will the wealth be turned from them and torment will be prepared for them, some hard harm-share. Do ye all think of it, how ye may betray them. Then may I rest me softly in these fetters, if that kingdom is lost to them. He who achieves that, for him is reward ready for ever after of what we may still win of benefits herein in this fire: with myself will I let him sit, whoever comes to say, in this hot hell, that they unworthily in words and deeds the teaching of the King of heaven [have forsaken]."

JUDITH

She doubted not the Glorious Creator's gifts in this wide earth. There found she ready protection with the great Prince, when she had most need of favor from the highest Judge, that He, Ruler of creation, would protect her against the highest danger: this the glorious Father in Heaven granted her who had ever firm faith in the Almighty. Then I heard Holofernes willingly wrought a bidding to wine, and made ready a feast splendid with all wonders. To it the king of men bade all the chief thanes; with great haste the shield-warriors performed it, came journeying to the mighty prince, leader of the folk. That was the fourth day after Judith, wise in thought, woman fair as an elf, first sought him.

Then they went to sit down to the feast, in pride went to the wine-drinking, all his comrades in evil, bold warriors in the burny. There were deep bowls borne often along the benches, likewise also cups and flagons borne full to the sitters-in-hall: they took it, the strong shield-warriors, doomed to death, though the mighty one, terrible lord of earls, had no thought of it. Then Holofernes, gold-friend of men, became joyful in the pouring of wine; he laughed and was loud, made a noise and a din, so that the children of men might hear from afar how the man of fierce mood stormed and yelled—proud and made wanton by mead, often admonished the bench-sitters to bear themselves well. So through all the day the wicked one drenched his retainers with wine, the stout-hearted dealer of treasure, till they lay in a swoon—overdrenched all his doughty men as if they were smitten by death, drained of every good thing.

So the king of men bade serve the sitters-in-hall till the dark night drew near to the children of men. Then, filled with wickedness, he bade fetch the blessed maid in haste to his bed-rest, loaded with armlets and adorned with rings. The serving-men quickly did as their prince, chief of burny-warriors, bade them: in a twinkling they stepped to the guest-house, where they found Judith, wise in thought, and then quickly the shield-warriors began to lead the bright maid to the high tent wherein the mighty one always rested him at night, Holofernes hateful to the Savior. There was a fair fly-net all of gold hung about the folk-leader's bed, so that the baleful one, king of warriors, might look through on any one of heroes' children that came in there, and no one of mankind on him, unless the proud prince bade some one of the men strong in war come nearer him for counsel. Quickly they brought the wise woman to the resting-place; the men, gloomy of mind, went then to make known to their lord that the holy woman was brought to his bower-tent. Then the famous prince of cities became blithe in mood, thought to defile the bright maiden with spot and with stain; the Judge of glory, Shepherd of strength, would not let that be, but He kept him from that thing, the Lord, Ruler of hosts. Then went the devilish one, wanton with a troop of men, baleful, to seek his bed, where he was to lose his life forthwith in a single night: he had awaited his end, an end on earth ungentle, such a one as he had worked after erewhile, the harsh-hearted prince of men, while he dwelt in this world under the clouds' roof. The mighty one fell on the midst of his bed so drunken with wine as if he knew no counsel in his witplace. The warriors stepped out of the house in great haste, the wine-sated men who had led to bed for the last time the traitor, the hateful oppressor.

Then was the Savior's glorious servant strongly mindful how she might most easily take the terrible one's life ere the impure, full of defilement, awoke. She with the twisted locks, the Maker's maid, took then a sharp sword, hardened by scourings, and drew it from the sheath with her right hand. She then began to name by name the Guardian of the sky, Savior of all world-dwellers, and spoke this word: "Thee, God of creation, and Spirit of comfort, and Son of the All-Ruler, I will pray for Thy mercy to me in my need, Trinity's Glory. Strongly is my heart now heated, and my mind is sad, greatly troubled with sorrows. Give me, King of the sky, victory and true faith, that I with this sword may hew down this dealer of murder. Grant me my salvation, strong-hearted Prince of men; never had I greater need of Thy mercy: avenge now, mighty Lord, bright Dealer of glory, that I am thus angry in mind, hot in my breast."

Then the highest Judge inspired her with courage forthwith, as He doth every one of dwellers here who seek Him for their help with understanding and with righteous faith. She became then free in mind—hope was renewed for the holy one. She took the heathen man fast by his hair, tugged him toward her with her hands, shamefully, and skillfully laid down the baleful one, the hateful man, so she might most easily wield the wretched one well. Then she with the twisted locks smote with the bright sword the scather-foe whose thoughts were of hate, and cut through half his neck, so that he lay in a swoon, drunken and wounded. He was not dead yet, altogether lifeless. Earnestly a second time the woman strong of courage smote the heathen hound, so that his head rolled forth on the floor: the foul body lay lifeless behind, and the spirit turned elsewhere under the deep earth and there was thrown down, fettered by torture ever after, surrounded by worms, bound by torments, harshly enchained in hell-fire after the journey hence. Nor need he hope at all, enveloped in darkness, that he may away from that worm-hall; but there shall he dwell for ever and ever forth without end in that dark home, without joy of hope.

So had Judith gained very great glory in war, as God granted her, King of the sky, Who lent her victory. Then the wise maid quickly brought the warrior's head, so bloody, in the vessel in which her attendant, a fair-cheeked virgin of noble virtues, carried thither food for them both; and Judith gave it then, so gory, into her hand, to her maid, the thoughtful-minded, to bear home. Then they went forth thence, both the women bold of courage, till they came proud-hearted, maidens exultant, out from the army, so that they might clearly see shining the walls of that beautiful city Bethulia. They, then, adorned with rings, hastened their steps forwards till they had come, glad-hearted, to the wall-gate. There sat warriors, men watching kept guard in the fortress, as Judith, maid cunning in thought, had bidden that sad-hearted folk before, when she went away on her undertaking, the woman strong in courage. Now was she come again, dear to the people, and forthwith the woman wise of thought, bade one man come to meet her from the wide city, let her in with haste through the wall's gate; and she spoke this word to the victor-folk: "I may tell you a thought-worthy thing, that ye need no longer mourn in your heart: the Maker, Glory of kings, is kindly towards you; it has become known widely through the world that to you is granted glorious gain, a bright future and fame for the hateful things that ye have long endured." Then the city-dwellers became blithe when they had heard how the holy woman spoke over the high wall. The host was in joy; the folk hastened towards the fortress-gate, men and women together, in troops and multitudes; in bands and crowds they thronged and ran by thousands towards the Prince's maid, old and young: the heart of each man in that mead-city was gladdened when they perceived that Judith was come back to her home, and then in haste they let her in, with reverence.

The wise woman decked with gold then bade her servant, the thoughtful-minded, to uncover the warrior's head and show it, bloody, to the city-people as a proof how she had succeeded in the war. The noble one spoke then to all the folk: "Here, victory-strong heroes, leaders of the people, ye may clearly gaze upon the head of that most hateful heathen warrior, Holofernes, dead: who of all men wrought for us most murders, sore sorrows, and would add more yet, but God did not grant him longer life that he might afflict us with hateful wrongs; I thrust out life from him, through God's help. Now I will ask every man of these city-people, shield-warriors, that ye hasten at once to the fight; when the God of creation, the good King, sends from the east a gleam of light, bear forth your linden shields, boards before your breasts and burny-covers, bright helmets into the troop of the foe, with bright swords to slay the folk-leaders, fated chieftains. Your enemies are doomed to death, and ye shall have glory, honor in battle, as the mighty Lord hath given you token through my hand."

Then the band of the bold got ready quickly, keen for the fight; nobly strong marched men and comrades; they bore banners of victory, fared forth straight on to the fight, heroes under helmets from the holy city in that same red dawn; shields dinned, resounded loudly. For this the lank wolf in the forest rejoiced, and the dark raven, bird greedy for slaughter: both knew that the men of the people thought to provide them their fill on fated ones; and on their track flew the eagle yearning for flesh—dewy-feathered, dark-coated, horny-beaked, he sang a battle-song. The warriors marched, heroes to battle, covered with their boards, their hollow linden shields—those who a while before had endured the foreigners' reproach, the heathen's insult. That was fiercely paid back to them, to all the Assyrians, in the spear-play, when the Hebrews had come to the camp under war-banners. Quickly then they let fly forth from their horn-bows showers of arrows, war-adders, shafts strong and hard; loud stormed the raging warriors, sent spears into the throng of the hardy ones. The heroes, dwellers in the land, were angry against the hateful tribe; stern of mood they marched; not softly did the stout-hearted awaken their old foe, mead-weary. With their hands the men drew from their sheaths bright-decked swords with tried edges, and earnestly slew the hate-thinking warriors of the Assyrians; not one did they spare of that army-folk, neither low nor high, of living men that they might overcome.

So the kinsman-thanes in the morningtide pursued the foreign tribe all the time, till the chief guards of the army-folk, who were angry, perceived that the Hebrew men were showing them strong sword-swings. They went to make it known in words to the chiefest of the chief thanes, awakened the banner-warriors and with fear told them sudden tidings, morning-terror to the mead-weary, dire sword-play. Then I heard that the heroes doomed to slaughter cast off sleep forthwith, and men sad at heart thronged in crowds to the bower-tent of the baleful one, Holofernes: they meant only to assure their lord of their help before the terror sat upon him, the might of the Hebrews. All thought that the prince of men and the bright maid were together in the fair tent, Judith the noble, and the man wanton-minded, terrible and fierce; yet there was not one of the earls that durst awaken the fighter, or find out how the banner-warrior had fared with the holy woman, the Maker's maid. The force drew near, the Hebrew folk, fought mightily with hard blades, fiercely repaid with shining swords their former quarrels, old grudges; the glory of the Assyrians was weakened in that day's work, their pride brought low. Warriors stood about their chief's tent mightily resolute, gloomy of mind. They began to make a noise all together, to cry aloud and gnash the teeth, without God, enduring anger with their teeth; then was their glory at an end, their wealth and their deeds of strength. The earls thought to awaken their friend-lord; no whit did they succeed. After a time one of the battle-men became bold enough to venture, hardy in war, in to the bower-tent, as need drove him. He found his gold-giver lying pale on the bed, without breath, robbed of life. He fell forthwith cold to the ground, in sad mood began to tear his hair and his robe together, and spoke this word to the warriors that were outside there in sadness: "Here is shown our own fate, our future is betokened, that at this time has pressed near with wars—when we shall be lost together, perish in the strife: here, hewn with the sword, lies our guardian beheaded."

In sad mood then they threw down their weapons, went weary-hearted to hasten in flight. Men fought on their track, folk strong in might, till the most part of the army lay on the victory-plain, bought low in battle, hewn with swords, for a joy to wolves and a comfort also to birds greedy for slaughter. Those of the hateful shield-warriors that lived, fled. On their track went the troop of Hebrews honored with victory, exalted with glory; the Lord God, almighty King, helped them well. Quickly, with bright swords, the strong-hearted heroes made a war-path through the throng of their foes, hewed the linden, cut the shield-fortress; the shooters, Hebrew men, were enraged in the war; the thanes at that time strongly desired spear-fighting. There on the dust fell the highest part of the chief number of the flower of Assyrian earls, the hateful tribe; only a little came alive to their native land. Nobly bold they turned, the warriors in retreat, into the slaughter, among the reeking corpses: there was room for the land-dwellers to take from those most hateful ones, their old foes now lifeless, bloody armor, bright trappings, shields and broad swords, brown helmets, dear treasures. Gloriously on the battle-ground had the country's guards overcome their foes, with swords put to sleep old enemies; they rested behind who were in life of living kind most hateful to them. Then all the tribe, greatest of nations, for the space of one month, proud, with twisted locks, carried and brought to the bright city of Bethulia helmets and hip-swords, hoary burnies, men's war-trappings fretted with gold, more of noble treasure than any man of cunning thought may tell: all that the men of the people gained by their courage, keen under their banners in battle, through the wise teaching of Judith, brave maid. From that same journey the spear-strong earls brought her for a meed the sword and bloody helmet of Holofernes, likewise his wide burny decked with red gold; and all that the stout-hearted king of warriors owned of treasure or private wealth, rings and bright jewels, they gave to that bright woman of ready thought. For all that Judith said praise to the Lord of Hosts, Who gave her honor, glory in the realm of earth, likewise a meed in heaven, reward of victory in the splendor of the sky, because she had true faith ever in the Almighty; truly at the end she did not doubt the reward that she had long yearned for. So glory be to the dear Lord for evermore, Who made wind and air, skies and roomy plains, likewise rushing streams and joys of heaven through His own mercy.

THE BATTLE OF MALDON

Then he bade each of the youths let go his horse, drive it far away, and go forth, think to his hands and give his mind to brave thoughts. Offa's kinsman then first found that the earl would brook no cowardice: he let his dear hawk fly from his hands to the wood, and stepped to the battle; by that one might know that the youth would not weaken in the war when he took to weapons. Eadric would also stand by him, by his chief, his lord in the fight; he began then to bear forth his spear to the war; he had brave thoughts while he might hold with his hands the shield and broad sword; he carried out his boast when he had to fight before his lord. There Byrhtnoth began to hearten his men, rode and gave counsel, taught the warriors how they should stand and hold their place, and bade that they should hold their shields rightly, fast with their hands, and not be at all afraid. When he had arrayed the folk fairly he alighted among the people where he liked best, where he knew his hearth-troop was most faithful.

Then the herald of the Vikings stood on the shore, called stoutly, spoke with words, and with boasting announced the seafarers' errand to the earl, where he stood on the bank: "Bold seamen have sent me to thee and bidden me say to thee that thou must quickly send rings for defense; and it is better for you that ye buy off this spear-rush with tribute, than that we deal so hard a battle. We need not spill each other if ye are rich enough for this; we will bind peace for the gold. If thou wilt agree, thou that art most powerful here, that thou wilt redeem thy people, give the seamen at their own choice goods for peace, and take peace at our hands, we will go to ship with the payment, fare away over sea, and keep peace with you."

Byrhtnoth spoke, held up his shield, brandished his slender ashen spear, spoke with words, wrathful and resolute, gave him back answer: "Hearest thou, sea-farer, what this folk saith? They will give you spears for tribute, poisoned point and old sword, the weapons that are of no worth to you in battle. Messenger of the seamen, take back word again, tell thy people a much more hateful story, that here stands a noble earl with his band, who will defend this land, the country of Æthelred my king, folk and field; the heathen shall fall in battle. Methinks it is too base that ye go to ship with our money unfought, now ye have come hither thus far in upon our land. Not so softly shall ye gain treasure: point and edge shall reconcile us first, grim warplay, ere we give tribute."

Then he bade his men bear the shield, go on till they all stood on the river-bank. There the band might not get to the other for the water: there a flood came flowing after the ebb, water-streams interlocked. It seemed to them too long to when they should bear spears together. They stood there in pomp by Panta stream, the flower of the East-Saxons, and the spearmen; no one of them might injure another, except who took his fall through an arrow's flight. The flood went out; the sailors stood ready, many Vikings, eager for war. Then the stronghold of heroes bade a war-hardy warrior hold the bridge, one who was named Wulfstan, bold among his kin (that was Ceola's son), who shot with his spear the first man who stepped there most boldly upon the bridge. There stood with Wulfstan warriors unafraid, Ælfere and Maccus, two brave men: they would not make flight at the ford, but firmly defended themselves against the foe while they might wield weapons. When they perceived that, and surely saw that they found bitter bridge-guards there, the hateful guests began to play a trick: they begged that they might have the passage, fare over the ford and lead their troops. Then the earl, because of his pride, began to leave too much land to the hateful tribe. Byrhthelm's son began to call then over the cold water (the heroes listened): "Now room is made for you, come at once to us, men to the war; God only knows who may prevail over the slaughter-field."

Then the slaughter-wolves advanced, cared not for the water: the band of Vikings carried shields over the bright water, west over Panta—the shipmen bore linden shields to land. There facing the fierce foe stood Byrhtnoth ready with his men: he bade them make the war-hedge with their shields and hold the ranks firm against the foe. Then was the fight near, glory in battle; the time was come that fated men should fall there. There was clamor raised, ravens flew, the eagle greedy for carrion: there was a cry upon earth. Then from their hands they let fly spears file-hard, ground darts; bows were busy; the shield took the point; bitter was the battle-rush; heroes fell on either hand—youths lay dead. Wulfmær was wounded, chose slaughter-rest: Byrhtnoth's kinsman, his sister's son, was sorely hewed with swords. Then was requital given to the Vikings: I heard that Edward smote one strongly with his sword, withheld not the swing, so that the fated fighter fell at his feet; for that his chief gave thanks to him, to the chamberlain, when he had a chance. So the stern-minded youths stood firm in the battle, thought eagerly who there might first with his point get the life in a doomed man, warriors with weapons; the slain fell on the earth. They stood stedfast, and Byrhtnoth spurred them on, bade that each youth who would win glory in fight from the Danes should give his thoughts to war.

Then one hardy in war went forward, raised up his weapon, his shield for cover, and stepped towards the hero; so went the resolute earl to the man: each of them thought evil to the other. Then the sea-warrior sent a spear from the south so that the lord of warriors was wounded. He shoved then with the shield so that the shaft came asunder and the spear broke and sprang back. The warrior was enraged: with his spear he pierced the proud Viking who gave him the wound. Wise was the war-man: he let his dart go through the youth's neck; his hand guided it so that he reached the life in the sudden-scather. Then with haste he shot another so that his burny burst: he was wounded in the breast through the ring-mail; the poisoned point stood in his heart. The earl was the blither; the brave man laughed, uttered thanks to the Maker for the day's work which the Lord had granted him. Then one of the youth let a javelin fly from his hand so that it 'went forth through Æthelred's noble thane. By his side stood a youth ungrown, a boy in the fight, Wulfstan's son, young Wulfmær, who full boldly drew from the hero the bloody spear; he let it go back again, very sharp; the point went in, so that he lay on the earth who had hit his prince so hard just before. Then an armed man went to the earl—he wanted to fetch the hero's bracelets, his armor and rings and chased sword. Then Byrhtnoth drew his sword from the sheath, broad and brown-edged, and smote upon his burny; too quickly a shipman hindered him, when he maimed the earl's arm; the fallow-hilted sword fell then to the ground; no longer might he hold the hard blade, wield a weapon. Yet the hoary warrior spoke the word, heartened the youth, bade his good comrades go forth; he might not then stand longer firm on his feet, but he looked to heaven: "I thank Thee, Ruler of nations, for all the joys that I have had in the world; now, merciful Maker, I have the greatest need that Thou grant my spirit the blessing that my soul may journey to Thee, into Thy power, Prince of Angels, may go with peace; I entreat Thee that the hell-scathers may not bring me low." Then the heathen knaves hewed him to pieces and both the heroes that stood by him: Ælfnoth and Wulmær both lay dead, who gave their lives along with their lord.

Then those bent from the battle who would not be there. There were Odda's sons first in flight: Godric went from the war, and left the good man who had often given him many a horse; he leaped on the horse that his lord owned, on the trappings that he had no right to; and his brothers with him both galloped away, Godrinc and Godwig, cared not for the war, but turned from the fight and sought the wood, fled to the fastness and covered their lives; and more men than was anywise fitting if they had remembered all the worthy things that he had done for their help—as Offa said to him before, one day, in the meeting-place when he had an assembly, that many spoke bravely there who again at need would not hold out.

Then was the prince of the folk fallen, Æthelred's earl; all the hearth-sharers saw that their lord lay dead. Then proud thanes went forth there, men that were no cowards hastened eagerly: they all wanted one of two things, to let go life or avenge the dear one. So Ælfric's son urged them forth, a warrior young in winters—Ælfwine uttered words, said then (he spoke with strength): "Remember the times that we often spoke at mead, when we raised the boast on the bench, heroes in hall, about hard battle. Now may we try who is bold. I will make known to all my noble line, that I was of great kindred among the Mercians—my grandfather was named Ealhelm, a wise alderman, worldly blessed. Thanes in that nation shall not twit me with being willing to go from this campaign and seek my home, now that my prince lies hewn down in battle. That is the greatest of griefs to me: he was both my kinsman and my lord." Then he went forth, remembered the feud, and with his spear-point reached one sailor among the folk so that he lay on the ground, brought down with his weapon. Then he began to exhort his comrades, his friends and companions, that they should go forth.

Offa spoke, shook his ashen spear-shaft: "Lo thou, Ælfwine,

hast exhorted all, the thanes at need. Now our chief lies low, our earl on the earth, there is need for us all that each of us hearten the other warrior to war, while he may have and hold a weapon, hard blade, spear and good sword. Godric, cowardly son of Odda, has betrayed us all: too many men thought, when he rode on the horse, on that proud steed, that it was our lord. Therefore the folk here on the field were separated, the shield-fortress was broken: may his beginning fail, that he put so many men here to flight." Leofsunu spoke, and raised his linden shield, his board for a cover; he said to the hero: "I promise that I will not flee hence one footstep, but I will go further, avenge my friend-lord in fight. Stedfast warriors about Stourmere need not twit me with words, now my friend has fallen, that I make my way home lordless, turn from the war; but a weapon shall take me, spear-point and iron." He went full ireful, fought firmly—he scorned flight. Then Dunnere spoke, shook his javelin; an old man, he called out over all, bade that every hero avenge Byrhtnoth: "Never may he waver nor care for life who thinks to avenge his lord among the folk."

Then they went forth; they recked not of life. The retainers began to fight hard, raging spear-bearers, and prayed God that they might take vengeance for their friend-lord, and work slaughter upon their foes. The hostage began eagerly to help them; he was of hardy kin among the Northumbrians, Ecglaf's son—his name was Æscferth: he never wavered at the war-play, but sent forth an arrow often; sometimes he shot on a shield, sometimes wounded a man; ever from time to time he gave some one a wound, while he might wield weapons. Then still in front stood Edward the long, ready and eager; he spoke boasting words, that he would not flee a foot-measure of land, give back while his better lay dead: he broke the shield-wall and fought against the men till he had worthily avenged his treasure-giver upon the sea-men, ere he lay dead on the field. So did Ætheric, a noble comrade, ready and eager to go on; earnestly he fought, Sibyrht's brother and very many others clove the hollow shield, made bold defense; the shield's border burst, and the burny sang a griesly song. Then in the war Offa smote a sea-farer so that he fell on the earth, and there Gad's kinsman sought the ground: quickly was Offa hewn down in the battle. Yet he had fulfilled what he promised his lord, as he boasted before to his ring-giver, that they should both ride into the burg, whole to their home, or fall in the army, die of wounds on the slaughter-field: he lay, thane-like, close by his chief. Then was a breaking of shields; seamen came on, enraged by war; often a spear went through a doomed man's life-house. Forth then went Wistan, Thurstan's son, fought against the men; he was, in the throng, slayer of three of them ere he, Wigelin's child, lay dead on the field. There was stern meeting: warriors stood fast in the fight, and warring fell, weary with wounds; the slain fell upon the earth. Oswold and Ealdwold all the while, both the brothers, heartened the men, in words bade their friends and kinsmen that they should endure there at need, use their weapons stoutly. Byrhtwold spoke, held up his shield (he was an old comrade), shook his ash, and full boldly gave the men counsel: "The mind shall be the harder, heart the bolder, courage the greater, as our might lessens. Here lies our prince all forhewn, a good man on the ground; forever may he mourn who thinks now to turn from this war-play. I am old in life: I will not go from here, but I mean to lie beside my lord, by a man so dear." Likewise Æthelgar's son Godric strengthened them all to the war: often he let fly a dart, a slaughter-spear upon the Vikings, as he went foremost among the folk, hewed and laid low, till he fell in battle; that was not the Godric that turned from the war.

EARLY MIDDLE ENGLISH POEMS

FROM

POEMA MORALE

Ich am eldre than ich wes, a winter and ek on lore;
Ich welde more than ich dude, my wyt auhte beo more.
Wel longe ich habbe child ibeo, a werke and eke on dede;
Thah ich beo of wynter old, to yong ich am on rede.
Unneth lif ich habbe ilad, and yet me thinkth ich lede;   5
Hwenne ich me bithenche, ful sore ich me adrede.
Mest al that ich habbe idon is idelnesse and chilce;
Wel late ich habbe me bi-thouht, bute God do me mylce.
Veole idel word ich habbe ispeke seoththe ich speke cuthe;
And feole yonge deden ido, that me of-thincheth nuthe.   10
Al to lome ich habbe agult, on werke and on worde;
Al to muchel ich habbe i-spend, to lutel i-leyd an horde.
Best al that me likede er nu hit me mys-lyketh;

The muchel foleweth his wil, him seolve he bi-swiketh.
Mon, let thi fol lust over-go, and eft hit the liketh.   15
Ich myhte habbe bet i-do, hevede ich eny selhthe;
Nu ich wolde, and i ne may for elde ne for unhelhthe..
Eld is me bi-stolen on er than ich hit wiste;
Ne may ich bi-seo me bi-fore, for smoke ne for myste.
Erewe we beoth to donne god, uvel al to thriste;   20
More eye stondeth mon of mon than him to Cryste.
The wel ne doth hwile he may, hit schal him sore reowe,
Hwenne alle men repen schule that heo ear seowe.
Doth to Gode that ye muwen the hwile ye beoth alyve;
Ne lipne no mon to muchel to childe ne to wyve.   25
The him seolve for-yet for wive other for childe,
He schal cumen on uvele stude bute God him beo milde.

.   .   .   .

    We the breketh Godes has, and gulteth swo ilome,
Hwat sulle we seggen other don ate muchele dome?
We the luveden unriht and evel lif ladden,   30
Hwat sulle we seggen other don thar ængles beth ofdradde?
Hwat sulle we beren us bi-foren, mid hwan sulle we iqueme,
We the nafre god ne duden, than hevenliche Deme?
Ther schule beon deovlen so veole, that wulleth us forwreyen;
Nabbeth heo nowiht for-yete of al that heo iseyen.   35
Al that we mysduden here heo hit wulleth cuthe there,
Bute we habben hit ibet the hwile we her were.
Al heo habbeth in heore wryte that we mysduden here;
Thah we hit nusten, heo weren ure i-fere.

.   .   .   .

    Understondeth nu to me, edye men and arme: 40
Ich wille ou telle of helle pyne, and warny of harme.
Thar is hunger and thurst, uvele tweye ivere;
Theos pyne tholieth ther that were mete-nythinges here.
Thar is wonyng and wop after ulche strete:
Ho vareth from hete to chele, from chele to thar hete;   45
Hwenne heo cumeth in hete, the chele heom thincheth blysse;
Thenne heo cumeth eft to chele, of hete heo habbeth
          mysse. . . . .
Thar is fur an hundred-folde hatture thane be ure;
Ne may hit quenche no salt water, ne Avene streme ne Sture.
That is thet fur that ever barnth, ne may hit nomon quenche. 50
Thar-inne beoth theo that her wes leof povre men to swenche;

Theo that were swikelemen and ful of uvele wrenche;
And theo that ne myhte uvele do, and was hit leof to thenche:
Theo that luved reving and stale and hordom and drunken,
And on deoveles werke blutheliche swunken.   55

.   .   .   .

   Ne may no pyne ne no wone beon in heovene riche,
Thah ther beon wonynges feole and other unyliche:
Summe habbeth lasse murehthe, and summe habbeth more,
Uych after that he dude her and after that heo swunken sore.
Ne wrth ther bred ne wyn ne nones kunnes este: 60
God one schal beon eche lif and blisse [and] eche reste.
Ther nys nouther fou ne grey ne konyng ne hermyne,
Ne oter ne acquerne, bever ne sablyne,
Ne ther ne wurth ful iwis worldes wele none:
Al the murehthe that me us bihat, al hit is God one.   65
Nis ther no murehht so muchel so is Godes syhte:
He is soth sunne and briht and day bute nyhte;
He is uyche godes ful, nys Him nowiht with-ute;
Nis heom nones godes wone that wuneth Hym abute.
Ther is weole bute wone, and reste bute swynke: 70
Hwo may thider cume and nule, hit schal hym sore of-
    thinche.
Ther is blysse bute teone, and lif with-ute dethe:
Theo that schulle wunye ther blithe muwen heo beon ethe.
Ther is yonghede buten ealde, and hele buten unhelthe;
Ther nys seorewe ne no sor, never non unselthe.   75
Seoththe me Dryhten iseo so He is myd-iwisse,
He one may beon and schal englene and monne blisse.

   About 1170.

FROM

THE BRUT

(BY LAYAMON)

Under than com tydinge
To Vortiger, than kinge,
That over see weren icome
Swithe selliche gomes.
Threo sipes gode   5
I-come were mid than flode;
Thar-on threo hundred cnihtes

Alse hit were kempes.
Thes weren the faireste men
That evere come here,   10
Ac hii weren hethene:
That was harm the more.
Theos comen to than kinge,
And faire hine grette,
And seide that hii wolde   15
Him sarvi in his londe,
"Yif us thou wolle
Mid rihte at-holde."
Tho answerede Vortiger
That of eche uvele he was war: 20
"In al mine lifve
That ich ileved habbe,
Bi dai no bi nihte
Ne seh ich soche cnihtes.
For you ich ham blithe,   25
And mid me ye solle bi-lefve.
Ac forst ich wolle wite,
For youre mochele worsipe,
Wat cnihtes beo yeo
And wanene yeo i-comen beo."   30
Tho answerede the other,
That was the elder brother:
"Ich hatte Hengest;
Hors hatte min brother.
We beoth of Alemaine,   35
Of one riche londe,
Of than ilke hende
That Englis his ihote.
Beoth in ure londe
Wonder thenges gonde.   40
Bi eche fiftene yer
That folk his i-somned,
And werpeth thare hire lotes
For to londes seche:
Up wan that lot falleth   45
He mot neod wende;
Ne beo he noht so riche
He mot lond seche.

Forthe wifves goth thare mid childe
Alse the deor wilde,   50
Bi evereche yere
Hii goth mid childe there.
That lot on us ful
That we faren solde,
Ne moste we bi-lefve   55
For life ne for deathe.
Thus hit fareth there;
Thar-fore we beoth nou here.
Nou thou havest ihord, loverd King,
Soth of us and no lesing."   60
Tho saide Vortiger,
That was wis and swithe war,
"And woche beoth youre bi-leve
That yeo an bi-lefeth?"
"We habbeth godes gode   65
That we lovieth in mode:
The on hatte Phebus,
The other Saturnus;
The thride hatte Woden,
That was a mihti thing;   70
The feorthe hatte Jubiter,
Of alle thinges he his war;
The fifthe hatte Merchurius,
That his the hehest over us;
The sixte hatte Appolin,   75
That his a god of gret win;
The sovethe hatte Tervagant,
An heh god in ure lond.
Yet we habbeth an leafdi,
That heh his and mihti;   80
Heo his i-hote Frea;
Heredmen hire lovieth.
To alle theos godes
We worsipe wercheth,
And for hire love   85
Theos dayes we heom gefve:
Mone we gefve Moneday,
Tydea we gefve Tisdei,
Woden we gefve Wendesdei,

Thane Thonre we gefve Thorisdai,   90
Frea thane Friday,
Saturnus than Sateresdai."
Thus saide Hengest,
Cniht alre hendest.
Tho answerede Vortiger;   95
Of alle harme he was war:
"Cnihtes, yeo beoth me leofve,
Ac youre bilefves me beoth lothe.
Ac ich wolle ou at-holde
In min anwolde;   100
For north beoth the Peutes,
Swithe ohte cnihtes,
That ofte doth me same,
And thar-vore ich habbe grame.
And yef ye wolleth me wreke   105
Of [hire] withere dedes,
Ich you wolle geve
Geftes swithe deore."
Tho saide Hengest,
"Al hit sal iworthe thus."   110
Hengest nam lefve,
And to sipe gan wende;
And al hire godes
Hii beore to londe.
Forth hii wende alle   115
To Vortiger his halle.
Bet weren i-scrud
And bet weren ived
Hengestes sweines
Thane Vortiger his cnihtes: 120
Bruttes weren sori
For than ilke sihte.
    Nas noht longe
That ne come tydinge
That tho forth-rihtes   125
Icomen were the Peutes:
"Overal thin lond hii erneth,
And sleath thin folk and bearneth;
And alle thane north ende
Hii falleth to than grunde.   130

Her-of thou most reade,
Other alle we beoth deade!"
The king sende his sonde
To theos cnihtes hinne,
That hii swithe sone   135
To him seolve come.
Thar com Hengest and his brother
And manian other,
That the king Vortiger
Blithe was tho ther.   140
The Peutes dude hire wone;
A this half Umbre hii were icome;
And the king Vortiger
Of hire come was war.
To-gadere hii comen,   145
And manie thar of-sloghen.
The Peutes weren ofte iwoned
Vortiger to overcome,
And tho ithohten al so:
Ac hit bi-ful otherweies tho,   150
For hii hadde mochel care,
For Hengest was thare;
For swithe manie Peutes
Hii sloghen in than fihte.
Tho that non was icome,   155
Tho were Peutes over-come;
And swithe hii awey floghe
On evereche side.
And Vortiger the king
Wende agen to his hin,   160
And to Hengest and his cnihtes
He gef riche geftes.
Ne dorste nevere Peutes
Come in thisse londe,
That hii nere sone of-slaghe   165
And idon of lifdaye.
And Hengest swithe hendeliche
Cwemde than kinge;
Tho hit bi-ful in on time
That the king was swithe blithe.   170

About 1200.

FROM

A BESTIARY

NATURA LEONIS

*i*a

The leun stant on hille:
And he man hunten here,
Other thurg his nese smel
Smake that he negge,
Bi wilc weie so he wile   5
To dele nither wenden,
Alle hise fet-steppes
After him he filleth,
Drageth dust with his stert
Ther he [dun] steppeth,   10
Other dust other deu,
That he ne cunne is finden;
Driveth dun to his den
Thar he him bergen wille.

*ii*a

An other kinde he haveth: 15
Wanne he is ikindled,
Stille lith the leun,
Ne stireth he nout of slepe,
Til the sunne haveth sinen
Thries him abuten;   20
Thanne reiseth his fader him
Mit te rem that he maketh.

*iii*a

The thridde lage haveth the leun:
Thanne he lieth to slepen,
Sal he nevre luken   25
The lides of hise egen.
   Significacio prime nature
Welle heg is tat hil,
That is heven-riche:
Ure Loverd is te leun,
The liveth ther abuven.   30
Wu tho Him likede
To ligten her on erthe,

Migte nevre divel witen,
Thog he be derne hunte,
Hu He dun come,　　　　　　　　　　35
Ne wu He dennede Him
In that defte meiden,
Marie bi name,
The Him bar to manne frame.

*ii*ᵃ *et iii*ᵃ

Tho ure Drigten ded was　　　　　　40
And dolven, also His wille was
In a ston stille He lai
Til it kam the thridde dai;
His fader Him filstnede swo
That He ros fro dede tho,　　　　　　45
Us to lif holden.
Waketh so His wille is,
So hirde for His folde:
He is hirde, we ben sep;
Silden He us wille,　　　　　　　　　50
If we heren to His word,
That we ne gon nowor wille.

Before 1250.

FROM

THE OWL AND THE NIGHTINGALE

(BY NICHOLAS DE GUILDFORD?)

Ich was in one sumere dale,
In one swithe digele hale;
I-herde ich holde grete tale
An ule and one nihtingale.
That plait was stif and starc and strong,　　5
Sum wile softe, and lud among;
And aither agen other swal,
And let that vule mod ut al.
And either seide of otheres custe
That alre-worste that hi wuste;　　　　　10
And hure and hure of otheres songe
Hi heolde plaiding swithe stronge.
　The nihtingale bi-gon the speche,

In one hurne of one beche,
And sat up one vaire bohe,   15
Thar were abute blosme i-nohe,
In ore waste thicke hegge,
I-meind mid spire and grene segge.
Heo was the gladur vor the rise,
And song a vele cunne wise: 20
Bet thuhte the drem that he were
Of harpe and pipe than he nere;
Bet thuhte that he were i-shote
Of harpe and pipe than of throte.

   Tho stod on old stoc thar bi-side,   25
Thar tho ule song hire tide,
And was mid ivi al bi-growe;
Hit was thare ule earding-stowe.

   The nihtingale hi i-seh,
And hi bi-heold and over-seh,   30
And thuhte wel vule of thare ule,
For me hi halt lothlich and fule.
"Unwiht," heo sede, "awei thu fleo!
Me is the wers that ich the seo:
I-wis for thine vule lete   35
Wel oft ich mine song for-lete;
Min heorte at-flith, and falt mi tunge,
Wonne thu art to me i-thrunge;
Me luste bet speten thane singe,
Of thine fule gogelinge."   40

   Theos ule abod fort hit was eve;
Heo ne mihte no leng bileve,
Vor hire heorte was so gret.
That wel neh hire fnast at-schet;
And warp a word thar-after longe: 45
"Hu thincthe nu bi mine songe?
Wenst thu that ich ne cunne singe,
Theh ich ne cunne of writelinge?
I-lome thu dest me grame,
And seist me bothe teone and schame.   50
Gif ich the heolde on mine vote
(So hit bi-tide that ich mote!),
And thu were ut of thine rise,
Thu scholdest singe an other wise!"

The nihtingale gaf answare: 55
"Gif ich me loki wit the bare,
And me schilde with the blete,
Ne recche ich noht of thine threte;
Gif ich me holde in mine hegge,
Ne recche ich never what thu segge.   60
Ich wot that thu art un-milde
With heom that ne muhe from the schilde,
And thu tukest wrothe and uvele
Whar thu might over smale fugele;
Vor-thi thu art loth al fugel-kunne,   65
And alle heo the driveth heonne,
And the bi-schricheth and bi-gredet,
And wel narewe the bi-ledet;
And ek for-the the sulve mose
Hire thonkes wolde the to-tose.   70
Thu art lodlich to bi-holde,
And thu art loth in monie volde:
Thi bodi is short, thi sweore is smal,
Grettere is thin heved than thu al;
Thin eyen beoth col-blake and brode,   75
Riht swo heo weren i-peint mid wode;
Thu starest so thu wille abiten
Al that thu miht mid clivre smiten;
Thi bile is stif and scharp and hoked,
Riht so an owel that is croked;   80
Thar-mid thu clackest oft and longe,
And that is on of thine songe.
Ac thu thretest to mine fleshe,
Mid thine clivres woldest me meshe;
The were i-cundur to one frogge,   85
That sit at mulne under cogge:
Snailes, mus, and fule wihte
Beoth thine cunde and thine rihte.
Thu sittest adai, and flihst aniht;
Thu cuthest that thu art on un-wiht.   90
Thu art lodlich and un-clene:
Bi thine neste ich hit mene,
And ek bi thine fule brode—
Thu fedest on heom a wel ful fode."

.   .   .   .

Theos hule luste swithe longe,   95
And was of-teoned swithe stronge.
Heo quath: "Thu hattest nihtingale:
Thu mihtest bet hoten galegale,
Vor thu havest to monie tale.
Lat thine tunge habbe spale!   100
Thu wenest that thes dai beo thin oge:
Lat me nu habbe mine throge;
Beo nu stille, and lat me speke;
Ich wille beon of the a-wreke,
And lust hu ich con me bi-telle   105
Mid rihte sothe with-ute spelle. . . . .
Thu wenist that ech song beo grislich
That thine pipinge nis i-lich:
Mi stefne is bold and noht un-orne;
Heo is i-lich one grete horne,   110
And thin is i-lich one pipe
Of one smale weode un-ripe.
Ich singe bet than thu dest:
Thu chaterest so doth on Irish prest;
Ich singe an eve, a rihte time,   115
And seoththe won hit is bed-time,
The thridde sithe at middelnihte,
And so ich mine song adihte
Wone ich i-seo arise veorre
Other dai-rim other dai-sterre.   120
Ich do god mid mine throte,
And warni men to heore note;
Ac thu singest alle longe niht,
From eve fort hit is dai-liht,
And evre lesteth thin o song   125
So longe so the niht is long,
And evre croweth thi wrecche crei,
That he ne swiketh niht ne dai.
Mid thine pipinge thu adunest
Thas monnes earen thar thu wunest,   130
And makest thine song so un-wiht
That me ne telth of the nowiht.
Evrich murhthe mai so longe i-leste
That heo shal liki wel un-wreste;
Vor harpe and pipe and fugeles songe   135

Misliketh gif hit is to longe.
Ne beo the song never so murie
That he ne shal thinche wel un-murie
Gef he i-lesteth over un-wille.
So thu miht thine song aspille;   140
Vor hit is soth, Alvred hit seide,
And me hit mai in boke rede,
'Evrich thing mai leosen his godhede
Mid unmethe and mid over-dede.'"

About 1250.

FROM
CURSOR MUNDI

Adam past nyne hundride yere;
No wondur thei he wex unfere.
Al for wroughte with his spade,
Of his lif he wex al made.
Upon his spade his brest he leide;   5
To Seth his son thus he seide:
"Son," he seide, "thou most go
To paradis that I coom fro,
To cherubyn that ys gateward,
That kepeth tho gates swithe hard."   10
Seth seide to his fadir there,
"How stondeth hit, fadir, and where?"
"I shal the telle," he seide, "to say
How thou shal take the right way.
Towarde the eest ende of the yondur vale   15
A grene weye fynde thou shale;
In that weye shal thou fynde and se
The steppes of thi modir and me,
For welewed in that gres grene,
That ever siththen hath ben sene.   20
There we coom, goynge as unwise,
Whenne we were out fro paradise
Into this ilke wrecched slade
There my self first was made;
For the greetnes of oure synne   25
Might siththen no gras growe therynne.
That same wol the lede thi gate

Fro hennes to paradis gate."
He seide, "Fadir, say me thi wille
What shal I say the aungel tille?"   30
"Thou shal him saye I am unwelde;
For longe lyved am I in elde,
And so in strif and sorwe stad
That forwery I wex al mad.
Thou him preye sum word me sende   35
Whenne I shal fro this world wende.
Another eronde shal there be,
That he me sende worde bi the
Wher I shal have hit ought in hye
That me was het, the oyl of mercye,   40
Whenne I was dryven fro paradis
And lost hit bi my foly nys;
Ageyn the wille of God I wrought:
Somdel I have hit bought;
Mi sorwe hath ever sithen be newe;   45
Now were hit tyme on me to rewe."
    Seth went forth withouten nay
To paradis the same day.
He fonde the steppes him to wise,
Til he coom to paradise.   50
Whenne he therof had a sight,
He was aferde of that light;
So greet light he say there,
A brennynge fire he wende hit were.
He blessed him as his fadir bad,   55
And went forth and was not drad.
The aungel at the gate he fond;
He asked him of his erond.
Seeth set tale on ende,
And tolde whi he was sende: 60
He tolde him of his fadir care,
And of his elde, and of his fare.
"But sende him worde whenne he shal deye
(Lenger to lyve may he not dreye),
And whenne God had him dight   65
The oyle of mercy that was hight."
Whenne cherubin his eroonde herde,
Mekely he him unswerde,

"To yonder gate thou go and loute,
Thi heed withinne, thi bodi withoute,   70
And tente to thinges with al thi myght
That shul be shewed to thi sight."
Whenne Seth a while had loked in,
He say so mychel wele and wyn
In erthe is no tong may telle: 75
Of floures fruyt and swete smelle,
Of joye and blis so mony a thing.
Amydde the lond he say a spryng
Of a welle of honoure:
Fro hir ronne stremes foure—   80
Fison, Gison, Tigre, and Eufrate;
Al erthe these weten erly and late.
Over that welle thenne loked he,
And say there stonde a mychel tre,
With braunches fele, no barke that bere;   85
Was there no lyf in hem there.
Seth bigon to thenke whye
That this tre bicoom so drye:
And on the steppes thoughte he thon
That dryghed were for synne of mon;   90
That ilke skil dud him to mynne
The tre was dryghe for Adam synne.
He coom tho to that aungel shene,
And tolde him that he had sene.
Whenne he had thus him tolde,   95
He bad him efte go and biholde.
He loked in efte and stode theroute,
And say thingis that made him doute:
This tre that I bifore of seide,
A nedder hit had aboute bi leide.   100
Cherubin, the aungel bright,
Bad him go se the thridde sight.
Him thoughte thenne that he seghe
This for seide tre raughte ful heghe;
Unto the skye raughte the top;   105
A new born childe lay in the crop,
Bounden with his swatheling bonde;
There thoughte him hit lay squelonde.
He was a ferde whenne he hit seghe,

And to the rote he cast his eghe: 110
Him thoughte hit raughte fro erthe to helle;
There he say his brother Abelle;
In his soule he say that sight,
That Kaym sloughe forwaryed wight.
He went ageyn for to shawe 115
To cherubyn al that he sawe.
Cherubyn with chere mylde
Bigan to telle him of that childe:
"That childe," he seide, "withouten wene
Is Goddes Son, that thou hast sene. 120
Thi fadir synne now wepeth he;
He shal hit clense the tyme shal be,
Whenne the plente shal com of tyme.
This is the oyle was highte to hyme,
To him and to his progeny; 125
With pite he shal hem shewe mercy."
Whenne Seth had undirstonden wel
The aungels sayinge ever a del,
His leve he toke of cherubyn.
And thre curnels he gaf to hym, 130
Whiche of that tre he nam
That his fadir eet of, Adam.
"Thi fadir," he seide, "thou shalt say
That he shal deye the thridde day
Aftir thou be comen him to; 135
Loke that thou saye to him so.
But thou shal take the pepyns thre
That I toke of the appel tre,
And put undir his tunge rote.
To mony men thei shul be bote: 140
Thei ben cidre, cipres, and palme fine;
To mony thei shul be medicine.
Thi fadir bi cidre shal thou take;
Hit shal be tre withouten make.
Of cipres, bi that swete savour, 145
Bitokeneth oure swete Saveour;
The mychel swetenes is the Sone.
The palme, to fruyt hit is wone
Mony curnels of o tre, most
Gode giftis of the Holy Goost." 150

Seth was of his eronde feyn,
And soone coom to his fadir ageyn.
"Son," he seide, "hastou sped ought;
Hastou any mercy brought?"
"Sir cherubin, that aungel 155
That porter is, the greteth wel,
And seith the world shal neghe han ende
Ar he the oile may to the sende,
Thourghe birthe of a blessed childe
That shal the world fro shame shilde. 160
For thi deth, he bad me say
Hit shal be this day thridde day."
Adam her of was glad ful blyve,
So glad was he never er his lyve;
Whenne he herde to lyve no more, 165
Tho he lowghe but never ore.
And thus to God gan he crye:
"Lord, inoughe now lyved have I;
Thou take my soule out of my flesshe,
And do hit where Thi wille es!" 170
For of this world he was ful mad,
That never o day therinne was glad:
Nyne hundride yeer and more yare
He lyved here in sorwe and care;
Lever him were to ben in helle 175
Then lenger in this world to dwelle.
    Adam, as him was tolde biforn,
Deyed on the thridde morn.
Graven he was bi Seth thon
In the vale of Ebron. 180
The curnels were put undir his tonge:
Of hem roos thre yerdes yonge,
And sone an ellen hyghe thei wore;
Thenne stode thei stille and wex no more;
Mony a yeer I liche grene, 185
Holynes in hem was sene.
Stille stode tho yerdes thre
Fro Adames tyme to Noe,
Fro Noe tym and fro the flode
To Abraham holy and gode; 190
Fro Abraham yit stille stode thai

Til Moyses that gaf the lay;
Ever stode thei stille in oone,
Withouten waxinge othere woone.
No more of tho yerdes now,   195
But of a story I shal telle yow.

About 1300.

FROM

THE PEARL

Perle plesaunte to prynces paye,
To clanly clos in golde so clere,
Oute of Oryent, I hardyly saye,
Ne proved I never her precios pere:
So rounde, so reken in uche araye,   5
So smal, so smothe her sydez were,
Queresoever I jugged gemmez gaye,
I sette hyr sengeley in synglure.
Allas! I leste hyr in on erbere;
Thurgh gresse to grounde hit fro me yot: 10
I dewyne, for-dolked of luf daungere
Of that pryvy perle with-outen spot.

Sythen in that spote hit fro me sprange,
Ofte haf I wayted wyschande that wele,
That wont watz whyle devoyde my wrange,   15
And heven my happe and al my hele;
That dotz bot thrych my herte thrange,
My breste in bale bot bolne and bele.
Yet thoght me never so swete a sange
As stylle stounde let to me stele;   20
Forsothe ther fleten to me fele,—
To thenke hir color so clad in clot!
O moul, thou marrez a myry mele,—
My privy perle with-outen spot.

That spot of spysez myght nedez sprede,   25
Ther such rychez to rot is runnen;
Blomez blayke and blwe and rede,
Ther schynez ful schyr agayn the sunne.
Flor and fryte may not be fede,
Ther hit doun drof in moldez dunne,   30

For uch gresse mot grow of graynez dede,
No whete were ellez to wonez wonne;
Of goud uche goude is ay by-gonne.
So semly a sede moght fayly not,
That spryngande spycez up ne sponne,   35
Of that precios perle wyth-outen spotte.

To that spot that I in speche expoun
I entred in that erber grene,
In Auguste in a hygh seysoun,
Quen corne is corven wyth crokez kene.   40
On huyle ther perle hit trendeled doun,
Schadowed this wortez ful schyre and schene
Gilofre, gyngure, and gromylyoun,
And pyonys powdered ay by-twene.
Gif hit watz semly on to sene,   45
A fayr reflayr yet fro hit flot,
Ther wonys that worthyly, I wot and wene,
My precious perle wyth-outen spot.

Bifore that spot my honde I spenned
For care ful colde that to me caght;   50
A denely dele in my herte denned,
Thagh resoun sette my selven saght.
I playned my perle that ther watz spenned,
Wyth fyrte skyllez that faste faght;
Thagh kynde of Kryst me comfort kenned,   55
My wreched wylle in wo ay wraghte.
I felle upon that floury flaghte;
Suche odour to my hernez schot,
I slode upon a slepyng-slaghte,
On that precios perle with-outen spot.   60

Fro spot my spyryt ther sprang in space,
My body on balke ther bod in sweven;
My goste is gon in Godez grace,
In aventure ther mervaylez meven.
I ne wyste in this worlde quere that hit wace,   65
Bot I knew me keste ther klyfez cleven;
Towarde a foreste I bere the face,
Where rych rokkez wer to dyscreven;

The lyght of hem myght no mon leven,
The glemande glory that of hem glent,   70
For wern never webbez that wyghez weven
Of half so dere adubmente.

Dubbed wern alle tho downez sydez
With crystal klyffez so cler of kynde;
Holte-wodez bryght aboute hem bydez,   75
Of bollez as blwe as ble of ynde;
As bornyst sylver the lef onslydez,
That thike con trylle on uch a tynde;
Quen glem of glodez agaynz hem glydez,
Wyth schymeryng schene ful schrylle thay schynde. 80
The gravayl that on grounde con grynde
Wern precious perlez of Oryente;
The sunne bemez bot blo and blynde,
In respecte of that adubbement.

The adubbemente of tho downez dere   85
Garten my goste al greffe for-gete;
So frech flavorez of frytez were,
As fode hit con me fayre refete.
Fowlez ther flowen in fryth in fere,
Of flaumbande hwez, bothe smale and grete;   90
Bot sytole stryng and gyternere
Her reken myrthe moght not retrete,
For quen those bryddez her wyngez bete
Thay songen wyth a swete asent:
So gracios gle couthe no mon gete   95
As here and se her adubbement.

So al watz dubbet on dere asyse;
That fryth ther fortwne forth me ferez,
The derthe ther-of for to devyse
Nis no wygh worthe that tonge berez.   100
I welke ay forth in wely wyse;
No bonk so byg that did me derez:
The fyrre in the fryth the feirer con ryse,
The playn, the plonttez, the spyse, the perez,
And rawez and randez and rych reverez,   105
As fyldor fyn her bonkes brent.

I wan to a water by schore that scherez:
Lorde! dere watz hit adubbement!

The dubbemente of tho derworth depe
Wern bonkez bene of beryl bryght; 110
Swangeande swete the water con swepe
Wyth a rownande rourde raykande aryght;
In the founce ther stonden stonez stepe,
As glente thurgh glas that glowed and glyght,
As stremande sternez, quen strothe men slepe, 115
Staren in welkyn in wynter nyght,
For uche a pobbel in pole ther pyght
Watz emerad, saffer, other gemme gente,
That alle the loghe lemed of lyght,
So dere watz hit adubbement. 120

More mervayle con my dom adaunt.
I segh by-yonde that myry mere
A crystal clyffe ful relusaunt;
Mony ryal ray con fro hit rere.
At the fote thereof ther sete a faunt, 125
A mayden of menske, ful debonere;
Blysnande whyt watz hyr bleaunt;
(I knew hyr wel, I hade sen hyr ere;)
As glysnande golde that man con schere,
So schon that schene anunder schore. 130
On lenghe I loked to hyr there;
The lenger, I knew hyr more and more.

The more I frayste hyr fayre face,
Her figure fyn quen I had fonte,
Suche gladande glory con to me glace 135
As lyttel byfore therto watz wonte.
To calle hyr lyste con me enchace,
Bot baysment gef myn hert a brunt;
I segh hyr in so strange a place,
Such a burre myght make myn herte blunt. 140
Thenne verez ho up her fayre frount,
Hyr vysayge whyt as playn yvore,
That stonge myn hert ful stray atount,
And ever the lenger, the more and more.

More then me lyste my drede aros: 145
I stod ful stylle and dorste not calle;
Wyth yghen open and mouth ful clos,
I stod as hende as hawk in halle.
I hope that gostly watz that porpose;
I dred on ende quat schulde byfalle,   150
Lest ho me eschaped that I ther chos,
Er I at steven hir moght stalle.
That gracios gay with-outen galle,
So smothe, so smal, so seme slyght,
Rysez up in hir araye ryalle,   155
A precios pyece in perlez pyght.

Perlez pyghte of ryal prys
There moght mon by grace haf sene,
Quen that frech as flor-de-lys
Doun the bonke con boghe by-dene.   160
Al blysnande whyt watz hir beau mys,
Upon at sydez and bounden bene
Wyth the myryeste margarys, at my devyse,
That ever I segh yet with myn yghen;
Wyth lappez large, I wot and I wene,   165
Dubbed with double perle and dyghte,
Her cortel of self sute schene,
With precios perlez al umbe-pyghte.

A pyght coroune yet wer that gyrle,
Of marjorys and non other ston,   170
Highe pynakled of cler quyt perle,
Wyth flurted flowrez perfect upon:
To hed hade ho non other werle;
Her here heke al hyr umbe-gon.
Her semblaunt sade, for doc other erle;   175
Her ble more blaght then whallez bon;
As schorne golde schyr her fax thenne schon,
On schylderez that leghe unlapped lyghte;
Her depe colour yet wonted non,
Of precios perle in porfyl pyghte,   180

Pyght watz poyned and uche a hemme,
At honde, at sydez. at overture.

Wyth whyte perle and non other gemme,
And bornyste quyte watz hyr vesture.
Bot a wonder perle with-outen wemme   185
In myddez hyr breste watz sette so sure,
A mannez dom moght dryghly demme
Er mynde moght malte in hit mesure;
I hope no tong moght endure
No saverly saghe say of that syght,   190
So watz hit clene and cler and pure,
That precios perle ther hit watz pyght,

Pyght in perle, that precios pyece.
On wyther half water com doun the schore;
No gladder gome hethen into Grece   195
Then I quen ho on brymme wore:
Ho watz me nerre then aunte or nece;
My joy for-thy watz much the more.
Ho profered me speche, that special spece,
Enclynande lowe in wommon lore;   200
Caghte of her coroun of grete tresore,
And haylsed me wyth a lote lyghte.
Wel watz me that ever I watz bore,
To sware that swete in perlez pyghte!

"O perle," quod I, "in perlez pyght,   205
Art thou my perle that I haf playned,
Regretted by myn one, on nyghte?
Much longeyng haf I for the layned,
Sythen into gresse thou me aglyghte;
Pensyf, payred, I am for-payned,   210
And thou in a lyf of lykyng lyghte
In paradys erde, of stryf unstrayned.
What wyrde hatz hyder my juel vayned,
And don me in thys del and gret daunger?
Fro we in twynne wern towen and twayned,   215
I haf ben a joylez juelere."

That juel thenne, in gemmez gente,
Vered up her vyse with yghen graye.
Set on hyr coroun of perle orient,
And soberly after thenne con ho say: 220

"Syr, ye haf your tale myse-tente,
To say your perle is al awaye,
That is in cofer, so comly clente,
As in this gardyn gracios gaye,
Here-inne to lenge forever and play,   225
Ther mys nee mornyng com never ner.
Her were a forser for the, in faye,
If thou were a gentyl jueler.

"Bot, jueler gente, if thou schal lose
Thy joy for a gemme that the watz lef,   230
Me thynk the put in a mad porpose,
And busyez the aboute a raysoun bref:
For that thou lestez watz bot a rose,
That flowred and fayled as kynde hit gef;
Now, thurgh kynde of the kyste that hyt con close, 235
To a perle of prys hit is put in pref.
And thou hatz called thy wyrde a thef,
That oght of noght hatz mad the cler;
Thou blamez the bote of thy meschef;
Thou art no kynde jueler."   240

"I halde that jueler lyttel to prayse,
That lovez wel that he segh wyth yghe;
And much to blame and un-cortoyse,
That levez oure Lorde wolde make a lyghe,
That lelly hyghte your lyf to rayse,   245
Thagh fortune dyd your flesch to dyghe.
Ye setten Hys wordez ful westernays,
That lovez no thynk bot ye hit syghe;
And that is a poynt o sorquydryghe,
That uche god mon may evel byseme,   250
To leve no tale be true to tryghe
Bot that hys one skyl may deme.

Deme now thy-self, if thou con, dayly,
As man to God wordez schulde heve.
Thou saytz thou schal won in this bayly: 255
Me thynk the burde fyrst aske leve,
And yet of graunt thou myghtez fayle.
Thou wylnez over thys water to weve;

Er moste thou cever to other counsayl:
Thy corse in clot mot calder keve;   260
For hit watz for-garte; at paradys greve
Oure yore fader hit con mysseyeme;
Thurgh drwry deth bogh uch ma dreve,
Er over thys dam hym dryghtyn deme."

"Demez thou me," quod I, "my swete   265
To dol agayn, thenne I dowyne.
Now haf I fonte that I for-lete,
Schal I efte for-go hit er ever I fyne?
Why schal I hit bothe mysse and mete?
My precios perle dotz me gret pyne: 270
What servez tresor bot garez men grete
When he hit schal efte with tenez tyne?
Now rech I never for to declyne,
Ne how fer of folde that man me fleme,
When I am partlez of perlez myne.   275
Bot durande doel what may men deme?"

"Thow demez noght bot doel dystresse,"
Thenne sayde that wyght; "why dotz thou so?
For dyne of doel, of lurez lesse,
Ofte mony mon for-gos the mo.   280
The oghte better thy selven blesse,
And love ay God and wele and wo,
For anger gaynez the not a cresse.
Who nedez schal thole be not so thro;
For thogh thou daunce as any do,   285
Braundysch and bray thy brathez breme,
When thou no fyrre may to ne fro,
Thou moste abyde that He schal deme.

Deme Dryghtyn, ever Hym adyte,
Of the way a fote ne wyl He wrythe;   290
Thy mendez mountez not a myte,
Thagh thou for sorghe be never blythe.
Stynst of thy strot, and fyne to flyte,
And sech Hys blythe ful swefte and swythe:
Thy prayer may Hys pyte byte,   295
That mercy schal hyr craftez kythe;

Hys comforte may thy langour lythe,
And thy lurez of lyghtly leme;
For marred other madde, morne and mythe,
Al lys in Hym to dyght and deme."   300

.   .   .   .

Delyt me drof in yghe and ere;
My manez mynde to maddyng malte.
Quen I segh my frely, I wolde be there,
By-yonde the water thagh ho were walte.
I thoght that no thyng myght me dere,   305
To fech me bur and take me halte;
And to start in the strem schulde non me stere,
To swymme the remnaunt, thagh I ther swalte.
Bot of that munt I watz bi-talt:
When I schulde start in the strem astraye,   310
Out of that caste I watz by-calt;
Hit watz not at my Pryncez paye.

Hit payed Hym not that I so flonc
Over mervelous merez, so mad arayed;
Of raas thagh I were rasch and ronk,   315
Yet rapely ther-inne I watz restayed:
For ryght as I sparred un-to the bonc,
That brathe out of my drem me brayde;
Then wakned I in that erber wlonk,
My hede upon that hylle watz layde   320
Ther as my perle to grounde strayd.
I raxled and fel in gret affray,
And sykyng to my self I sayd,
"Now al be to that Pryncez paye!"

About 1370.

FROM

THE PROVERBS OF HENDYNG

Wis mon halt is wordes ynne;
For he nul no gle bygynne,
   Er he have tempred is pype.
Sot is sot, and that is sene;

For he wol speke wordes grene,   5
  Er ther hue buen rype.
"Sottes bolt is sone shote,"
             Quoth Hendyng.

Tel thou never thy fomon
Shome ne teone that the is on,   10
  Thi care ne thy wo;
For he wol fonde, yef he may,
Bothe by nyhtes and by day,
  Of on to make two.
"Tel thou never thy fo that thy fot aketh,"   15
             Quoth Hendyng.

Yef thou havest bred and ale,
Ne put thou nout al in thy male;
  Thou del hit sum aboute.
Be thou fre of thy meeles,   20
Wher-so me eny mete deles
  Gest thou nout with-oute.
"Betere is appel ygeve then y-ete,"
             Quoth Hendyng.

Alle whyle ich wes on erthe,   25
Never lykede me my werthe,
  For none wynes fylle;
Bote myn and myn owen won,
Wyn and water, stoke and ston,
  Al goth to my wille.   30
"Este bueth oune brondes,"
             Quoth Hendyng.

About 1300.

CUCKOO SONG

Sumer is icumen in:
  Lhude sing cuccu!
Groweth sed, and bloweth med,
  And springth the wude nu.
    Sing cuccu!   5

Awe bleteth after lomb;
  Lhouth after calve cu;
Bulluc sterteth, bucke verteth.
  Murie sing cucu!

Cuccu, cuccu, well singes thu, cuccu: 10
  Ne swike thu naver nu.
Sing cuccu, nu, sing cuccu!
  Sing cuccu, sing cuccu, nu!

About 1300.

ALYSOUN

Bytuene Mershe ant Averil,
  When spray biginneth to springe,
The lutel foul hath hire wyl
  On hyre lud to synge.
  Ich libbe in love-longinge   5
  For semlokest of alle thynge:
  He may me blisse bringe;
Icham in hire baundoun.
  An hendy hap ichabbe y-hent;
  Ichot from hevene it is me sent: 10
  From alle wymmen mi love is lent,
Ant lyht on Alysoun.

On heu hire her is fayr y-noh;
  Hire browe broune; hire eye blake—
With lossum chere he on me loh!—   15
  With middel smal, ant wel y-make.
  Bote he me wolle to hire take,
  Forte buen hire owen make,
  Longe to lyven ichulle forsake,
Ant feye fallen a-doun.   20
  An hendy hap, etc.

Nihtes-when y wende ant wake;
  For-thi myn wonges waxeth won:
Levedi, al for thine sake
  Longinge is y-lent me on.   25
  In world nis non so wyter mon

That al hire bounte telle con:
Hire swyre is whittore then the swon,
Ant feyrest may in toune.
    An hendy, etc.   30

Icham for wowyng al for-wake,
  Wery so water in wore,
Lest eny reve me my make;
  Ychabbe y-yirned yore:
  Betere is tholien whyle sore   35
  Then mournen evermore.
  Geynest under gore,
Herkne to my roun.
    An hendi, etc.

About 1300.

SPRINGTIME

Lenten ys come with love to toune,
With blosmen ant with briddes roune,
  That al this blisse bryngeth:
Dayes-eyes in this dales;
Notes suete of nyhtegales;   5
  Uch foul song singeth.
The threstel-coc him threteth oo;
A-way is huere wynter wo,
  When woderove springeth.
This foules singeth ferly fele,   10
Ant wlyteth on huere wynter wele,
  That al the wode ryngeth.

The rose rayleth hire rode;
The leves on the lyhte wode
  Waxen al with wille;   15
The mone mandeth hire bleo;
The lilie is lossom to seo,
  The fenyl ant the fille;
Wowes this wilde drakes;
Miles murgeth huere makes;   20
  Ase strem that striketh stille,

Mody meneth, so doth mo,
Ichot ycham on of tho,
    For love that likes ille.

The mone mandeth hire lyht;   25
So doth the semly sonne bryht,
    When briddes singeth breme;
Deowes donketh the dounes;
Deores with huere derne rounes,
    Domes forte deme;   30
Wormes woweth under cloude;
Wymmen waxeth wounder proude,
    So wel hit wol hem seme
Yef me shal wonte wille of on:
This wunne weole y wole for-gon,   35
    Ant wyht in wode be fleme.

About 1300.

UBI SUNT QUI ANTE NOS FUERUNT

Were beth they that biforen us weren,
Houndes ladden and havekes beren,
    And hadden feld and wode?
        The riche levedies in here bour,
          That wereden gold in here tressour,   5
    With here brighte rode;

Eten and drounken, and maden hem glad;
Here lif was al with gamen y-lad;
    Men kneleden hem biforen;
        They beren hem wel swithe heye: 10
        And in a twincling of an eye
    Here soules weren forloren.

Were is that lawhing and that song,
That trayling and that proude gong,
    Tho havekes and tho houndes?   15
        Al that joye is went away,
        That wele is comen to weylaway,
    To manye harde stoundes.

Here paradis they nomen here,
And nou they lyen in helle y-fere; 20
The fyr hit brennes evere:
Long is ay, and long is o,
Long is wy, and long is wo;
Thennes ne cometh they nevere.

About 1350.

THE VIRGIN'S SONG TO HER BABY CHRIST

Jesu, swete sone dere!
On porful bed list thou here,
And that me greveth sore;
For thi cradel is ase a bere
Oxe and asse beth thi fere; 5
Weope ich mai thar-fore.

Jesu, swete, beo noth wroth,
Thou ich nabbe clout ne cloth
The on for to folde,
The on to folde ne to wrappe, 10
For ich nabbe clout ne lappe;
Bote ley thou thi fet to my pappe,
And wite the from the colde.

About 1350?

MIDDLE ENGLISH METRICAL ROMANCES

FROM

THE LAY OF HAVELOK THE DANE

Grim tok the child, and bond him faste,
Hwil the bondes micte laste,
That weren of ful stronge line:
Tho was Havelok in ful strong pine;
Wiste he nevere er wat was wo. 5
Jhesu Crist, That makede to go
The halte, and the doumbe speken,

Havelok The of Godard wreken!
Hwan Grim him havede faste bounden,
And sithen in an eld cloth wounden, 10
A kevel of clutes, ful un-wraste,
That he [ne] moucte speke ne fnaste
Hwere he wolde him bere or lede;
Hwan he havede don that dede,
Than the swike him gan bede 15
That he shulde him forth [lede]
And him drinchen in the se—
That forwarde makeden he.
In a poke, ful and blac,
Sone he caste him on his bac, 20
Ant bar him hom to hise cleve,
And bitaucte him Dame Leve,
And seyde: "Wite thou this knave,
Also thou wilt my lif have.
I shal dreinchen him in the se; 25
For him shole we ben maked fre,
Gold haven ynou, and other fe:
That havet mi loverd bihoten me."
Hwan Dame [Leve] herde that,
Up she stirte and nouct ne sat, 30
And caste the knave adoun so harde
That hise croune he ther crakede
Ageyn a gret ston, ther it lay:
Tho Havelok micte sei, "Weilawei!
That evere was I kinges bern!" 35
That him ne havede grip or ern,
Leoun or wulf, wulvine or bere,
Or other best that wolde him dere.
  So lay that child to middel nict,
That Grim bad Leve bringen lict, 40
For to don on [him] his clothes:
"Ne thenkeste nowt of mine othes
That ich have mi loverd sworen?
Ne wile I nouth be forloren.
I shal beren him to the se 45
(Thou wost that bi-hoves me),
And I shal drenchen him ther-inne.

Ris up swithe, an go thu binne,
And blou the fir, and lict a kandel."
Als she shulde his clothes handel   50
On for to don, and blawe the fir,
She saw ther-inne a lict ful shir,
Also brict so it were day,
Aboute the knave ther he lay.
Of hise mouth it stod a stem,   55
Als it were a sunne-bem;
Also lict was it ther-inne
So ther brenden cerges thrinne.
"Jhesu Crist!" wat Dame Leve,
"Hwat is that lict in ure cleve?   60
Ris up, Grim, and loke wat it menes,
Hwat is the lict as thou wenes?"
He stirten bothe up to the knave
(For [him] man shal god wille have),
Unkeveleden him, and swithe unbounden,   65
And sone anon [upon] him funden,
Als he tirneden of his serk,
On his rict shuldre a kyne merk,
A swithe brict, a swithe fair.
"Goddot!" quath Grim, "this [is] ure eir,   70
That shal [ben] loverd of Denemark!
He shal ben king strong and stark;
He shal haven in his hand
Al Denemark and Engeland.
He shal do Godard ful wo: 75
He shal him hangen or quik flo,
Or he shal him al quic grave;
Of him shal he no merci have."
Thus seide Grim, and sore gret,
And sone fel him to the fet,   80
And seide, "Loverd, have merci
Of me, and Leve that is me bi!
Loverd, we aren bothe thine,
Thine cherles, thine hine.
Lowerd, we sholen the wel fede,   85
Til that thu cone riden on stede,
Til that thu cone ful wel bere

Helm on heved, sheld and spere.
He ne shal nevere wite, sikerlike,
Godard, that fule swike.   90
Thoru other man, loverd, than thoru the,
Sal I nevere freman be.
Thou shalt me, loverd, fre maken,
For I shal yemen the and waken;
Thoru the wile I fredom have."   95
    Tho was Haveloc a blithe knave.
He sat him up, and cravede bred,
And seide, "Ich am [wel] ney ded,
Hwat for hunger, wat for bondes,
That thu leidest on min hondes,   100
And for [the] kevel at the laste,
That in mi mouth was thriste faste;
Y was ther-with so harde prangled.
That I was ther-with ney strangled."
"Wel is me that thu mayct ete,   105
Goddoth!" quath Leve; "Y shal the fete
Bred and chese, butere and milk,
Pastees and flaunes, al with suilk
Shole we sone the wel fede,
Loverd, in this mikel nede.   110
Soth it is, that men seyt and suereth:
'Ther God wile hilpen, nouct ne dereth.'"
Thanne sho havede brouct the mete,
Haveloc anon bigan to ete
Grundlike, and was [tho] ful blithe;   115
Couthe he nouct his hunger mithe.
A lof he et, Y wot, and more,
For him hungrede swithe sore:
Thre dayes ther-biforn, I wene,
Et he no mete, that was wel sene.   120
Hwan he havede eten, and was fed,
Grim dede maken a ful fayr bed,
Unclothede him, and dede him ther-inne,
And seyde, "Slep sone, with muchel winne;
Slep wel faste, and dred the nouct: 125
Fro sorwe to joye art thu brouct."

About 1300.

FROM

SYR GAWAYN AND THE GRENE KNYGHT

THE STRANGER AT KING ARTHUR'S COURT

Now wyl I of hor servise say yow no more,
For uch wyghe may wel wit no wont that ther were.
An other noyse ful newe neghed bilive,
That the lude myght haf leve lif-lode to cach;
For unethe watz tl.e noyce not a whyle sesed,   5
And the fyrst cource in the court kyndely served,
Ther hales in at the halle dor an aghlich mayster,
On the most on the molde on mesure hyghe:
Fro the swyre to the swange so sware and so thik,
And his lyndes and his lymes so longe and so grete,   10
Half etayn in erde I hope that he were.
Bot mon most I algate mynn hym to bene,
And that the myriest in his muckel that myght ride;
For of bak and of brest al were his bodi sturne,
Bot his wombe and his wast were worthily smale,   15
And alle his fetures folgande, in forme that he hade,
            Ful clene;
        For wonder of his hwe men hade,
        Set in his semblaunt sene;
        He ferde as freke were fade,   20
        And over-al enker grene.

Ande al graythed in grene this gome and his wedes:
A strayt cote ful streght, that stek on his sides;
A mere mantile abof, mensked with-inne,
With pelure pured apert the pane ful clene,   25
With blythe blaunner ful bryght, and his hod bothe,
That watz laght fro his lokkez and layde on his schulderes;
Heme wel haled, hose of that same grene,
That spenet on his sparlyr, and clene spures under,
Of bryght golde, upon silk bordes, barred ful ryche,   30
And scholes under schankes, there the schalk rides.
And alle his vesture verayly watz clene verdure,
Bothe the barres of his belt and other blythe stones,
That were richely rayled in his aray clene,
Aboutte hym-self and his sadel, upon silk werkez,   35
That were to tor for to telle of tryfles the halve,

That were enbrauded abof, wyth bryddes and flyghes,
With gay gaudi of grene, the golde ay in myddes;
The pendauntes of his payttrure, the proude cropure,
His molaynes, and all the metail anamayld was thenne;   40
The steropes that he stod on, stayned of the same,
And his arsounz al after, and his athel sturtes,
That ever glemered and glent al of grene stones.
The fole that he ferkkes on, fyn of that ilke,
Sertayn;   45
A grene hors gret and thikke,
A stede ful stif to strayne,
In brawden brydel quik,
To the gome he watz ful gayn.

Wel gay watz this gome gered in grene,   50
And the here of his hed of his hors swete.
Fayre fannand fax umbe-foldes his schulderes;
A much berd as a busk over his brest henges,
That wyth his highlich here, that of his hed reches,
Watz enesed al umbe-torne, a-bof his elbowes,   55
That half his armes ther under were halched in the wyse
Of a kyngez capados, that closes his swyre.
The mane of that mayn hors much to hit lyke,
Wel cresped and cemmed wyth knottes ful mony,
Folden in wyth fildore aboute the fayre grene,   60
Ay a herle of the here, an other of golde;
The tayl and his toppyng twynnen of a sute,
And bounden bothe wyth a bande of a bryght grene,
Dubbed wyth ful dere stonez, as the dok lasted,
Sythen thrawen wyth a thwong a thwarle knot alofte,   65
Ther mony bellez ful bryght of brende golde rungen.
Such a fole upon folde, ne freke that hym rydes,
Watz never sene in that sale wyth syght er that tyme,
With yghe:
He loked as layt so lyght,   70
So sayd al that hym syghe,
Hit semed as no mon myght
Under his dynttez dryghe.

Whether hade he no helme ne hawbergh nauther,
Ne no pysan, ne no plate that pented to armes,   75

Ne no schafte, ne no schelde, to schwne ne to smyte;
Bot in his on honde he hade a holyn bobbe,
That is grattest in grene, when grevez ar bare,
And an ax in his other, a hoge and un-mete,
A spetos sparthe to expoun in spelle quo-so myght;   80
The hede of an elnyerde the large lenkthe hade,
The grayn al of grene stele and of golde hewen,
The bit burnyst bryght, with a brod egge,
As wel schapen to schere as scharp rasores;
The stele of a stif staf, the sturne hit bi-grypte,   85
That watz wounden wyth yrn to the wandez ende,
And al bigraven with grene, in gracios werkes;
A lace lapped aboute, that louked at the hede,
And so after the halme halched ful ofte,
Wyth tryed tasselez therto tacched in-noghe,   90
On botounz of the bryght grene brayden ful ryche.
This hathel heldez hym in, and the halle entres;
Drivande to the heghe dece, dut he no wothe,
Haylsed he never one, bot heghe he over loked.
The fyrst word that he warp, "Wher is," he sayd,   95
"The governour of this gyng? gladly I wolde
Se that segg in syght, and with hym self speke
            Raysoun."
      To knyghtez he kest his yghe,
      And reled hym up and doun;   100
      He stemmed, and con studie
      Quo walt ther most renoun.

Ther watz lokyng on lenthe, the lude to beholde;
For uch mon had mervayle quat hit mene myght,
That a hathel and a horse myght such a hwe lach,   105
As growe grene as the gres, and grener, hit semed,
Then grene aumayl on golde lowande bryghter.
Al studied that ther stod, and stalked hym nerre,
Wyth al the wonder of the worlde what he worch schulde;
For fele sellyez had thay sen, bot such never are,   110
For-thi for fantoum and fayryye the folk there hit demed.
Ther-fore to answare watz arghe mony athel freke,
And al stouned at his steven, and ston-stil seten,
In a swoghe sylence thurgh the sale riche;
As al were slypped upon slepe, so slaked hor lotez   115

> In hyghe.
> I deme hit not al for doute,
> Bot sum for cortaysye
> Let hym that al schulde loute
> Cast unto that wyghe.   120

Thenn Arthour bifore the high dece that aventure byholdez,
And rekenly hym reverenced, for rad was he never,
And sayde, "Wyghe, welcum iwys to this place;
The hede of this ostel Arthour I hat.
Light luflych adoun, and lenge, I the praye;   125
And quat-so thy wylle is, we schal wyt after."
"Nay, as help me," quod the hathel, "He That on hyghe
            syttes,
To wone any quyle in this won, hit watz not myn ernde:
Bot for the los of the lede is lyft up so hyghe,
And thy burgh and thy burnes best ar holden,   130
Stifest under stel-gere on stedes to ryde,
The wyghtest and the worthyest of the worldes kynde,
Preve for to play wyth in other pure laykez;
And here is kydde cortaysye, as I haf herd carp;
And that hatz wayned me hider, iwys, at this tyme.   135
Ye may be seker bi this braunch that I bere here,
That I passe as in pes, and no plyght seche;
For had I founded in fere, in feghtyng wyse,
I have a hauberghe at home and a helme bothe,
A schelde, and a scharp spere, schinande bryght,   140
Ande other weppenes to welde, I wene wel als;
Bot for I wolde no were, my wedez ar softer.
Bot if thou be so bold as alle burnez tellen,
Thou wyl grant me godly the gomen that I ask,
                Bi ryght."   145
        Arthour con onsware
        And sayd, "Syr cortays knyght,
        If thou crave batayl bare,
        Here faylez thou not to fyght."

"Nay, frayst I no fyght, in fayth I the telle;   150
Hit arn aboute on this bench bot berdlez chylder!
If I were hasped in armes on a heghe stede,
Here is no mon me to mach for myghtez so wayke.

For-thy I crave in this court a Crystemas gomen,
For hit is Yol and Nwe Yer, and here are yep mony: 155
If any so hardy in this hous holdez hym-selven,
Be so bolde in his blod, brayn in hys hede,
That dar stifly strike a strok for an other,
I schal gif hym of my gyft thys giserne ryche—
This ax, that is heve innogh—to hondele as hym lykes;   160
And I schal bide the fyrst bur, as bare as I sitte.
If any freke be so felle to fonde that I telle,
Lepe lyghtly me to, and lach this weppen—
I quit-clayme hit for ever,—kepe hit as his awen;
And I schal stonde hym a strok, stif on this flet,   165
Ellez thou wyl dight me the dom to dele hym an other,
        Barlay,
      And yet gif hym respite,
      A twelmonyth and a day.
      Now hyghe, and let se tite   170
      Dar any her-inne oght say."

If he hem stowned upon fyrst, stiller were thanne
Alle the hered-men in halle, the hygh and the lowe:
The renk on his rounce hym ruched in his sadel,
And runischly his rede yghen he reled aboute,   175
Bende his bresed browez, blycande grene,
Wayved his berde, for to wayte quo-so wolde ryse.
When non wolde kepe hym with carp he coghed ful hyghe,
Ande rimed hym ful richely, and ryght hym to speke:
"What, is this Arthures hous," quod the hathel thenne,   180
"That al the rous rennes of thurgh ryalmes so mony?
Where is now your sourquydrye and your conquestes,
Your gryndel-layk, and your greme, and your grete wordes?
Now is the revel and the renoun of the Rounde Table
Over-walt wyth a worde of on wyghes speche;   185
For al dares for drede, with-oute dynt schewed!"
Wyth this he laghes so loude that the lorde greved;
The blod schot for scham in-to his schyre face
        And lere.
      He wex as wroth as wynde;   190
      So did alle that ther were.
      The kyng, as kene bi kynde,
      Then stod that stif mon nere,

Ande sayde, "Hathel, by heven thyn askyng is nys;
And as thou foly hatz frayst, fynde the be-hoves.   195
I know no gome that is gast of thy grete wordes.
Gif me now thy geserne, upon Godez halve,
And I schal baythen thy bone, that thou boden habbes."
Lyghtly lepez he hym to, and laght at his honde;
Then feersly that other freke upon fote lyghtis.   200
Now hatz Arthure his axe, and the halme grypez,
And sturnely sturez hit aboute, that stryke wyth hit thoght.
The stif mon hym bifore stod upon hyght,
Herre then ani in the hous by the hede and more;
Wyth sturne chere ther he stod, he stroked his berde,   205
And wyth a countenaunce dryghe he drogh doun his cote,
No more mate ne dismayd for hys mayn dintez
Then any burne upon bench hade broght hym to drynk
                    Of wyne.
          Gawan, that sate bi the quene,   210
          To the kyng he can enclyne:
          "I be-seche now with sawez sene,
          This melly mot be myne.

"Wolde ye, worthilych lorde," quod Gawan to the kyng,
"Bid me boghe fro this benche, and stonde by yow there, 215
That I wyth-oute vylanye myght voyde this table,
And that my legge lady lyked not ille,
I wolde com to your counseyl, bifore your cort ryche;
For me think hit not semly, as hit is soth knawen,
Ther such an askyng is hevened so hyghe in your sale,   220
Thagh ye your-self be talenttyf to take hit to your-selven,
Whil mony so bolde yow aboute upon bench sytten,
That under heven, I hope, non hagher er of wylle,
Ne better bodyes on bent, ther baret is rered.
I am the wakkest, I wot, and of wyt feblest,   225
And lest lur of my lyf, quo laytes the sothe;
Bot, for as much as ye ar myn em, I am only to prayse—
No bounte bot your blod I in my bode knowe,—
And sythen this note is so nys that noght hit yow falles,
And I have frayned hit at yow fyrst, foldez hit to me!   230
And if I carp not comlyly, let alle this cort rych
                    Bout blame."
          Ryche to-geder con roun,

And sythen thay redden alle same,
To ryd the kyng wyth croun,   23
And gif Gawan the game.

Then comaunded the kyng the knyght for to ryse;
And he ful radly up ros, and ruchched hym fayre,
Kneled doun bifore the kyng, and cachez that weppen.
And he luflyly hit hym laft, and lyfte up his honde,   240
And gef hym Goddez blessyng, and gladly hym biddes
That his hert and his honde schulde hardi be bothe:
"Kepe the, cosyn," quod the kyng, "that thou on kyrf
        sette;
And if thou redez hym ryght, redly I trowe
That thou schal byden the bur that he schal bede after."   245
Gawan gotz to the gome, with giserne in honde,
And he baldly hym bydez, he bayst never the helder.
Then carppez to Syr Gawan the knyght in the grene,
"Refourme we oure forwardes, er we fyrre passe.
Fyrst I ethe the, hathel, how that thou hattes,   250
That thou me telle truly, as I tryst may."
"In god fayth," quod the goode knyght, "Gawan I hatte,
That bede the this buffet, quat-so bi-fallez after;
And at this tyme twelmonyth take at the another,
Wyth what weppen so thou wylt, and wyth no wygh
        ellez   255
                On lyve."
        That other onswarez agayn,
        "Sir Gawan, so mot I thryve,
        As I am ferly fayn,
        This dint that thou schal dryve.   260

"Bi Gog," quod the grene knyght, "Sir Gawan, me lykes,
That I schal fange at thy fust that I haf frayst here;
And thou hatz redily rehersed, bi resoun ful trwe,
Clanly al the covenaunt that I the kynge asked,
Saf that thou schal siker me, segge, bi thi trawthe,   265
That thou schal seche me thi-self, where-so thou hopes
I may be funde upon folde, and foch the such wages
As thou deles me to day, bifore th:s douthe ryche."
"Where schulde I wale the?" quod Gavan; "Where is
        thy place?

I wot never where thou wonyes, bi Hym That me
      wroght;   270
Ne I know not the, knyght, thy cort, ne thi name.
Bot teche me truly ther-to, and telle me howe thou hattes,
And I schal ware alle my wyt to wynne me theder;
And that I swere the for sothe, and by my seker traweth."
"That is innogh in Nwe Yer, hit nedes no more,"   275
Quod the gome in the grene to Gawan the hende:
"Gif I the telle trwly, quen I the tape have,
And thou me smothely hatz smyten, smartly I the teche
Of my hous and my home and myn owen nome,
Then may thou frayst my fare, and forwardez holde;   280
And if I spende no speche, thenne spedez thou the better,
For thou may leng in thy londe, and layt no fyrre,
            Bot slokes.
      Ta now thy grymme tole to the,
      And let se how thou cnokez."   285
        "Gladly, sir, for sothe,"
      Quod Gawan; his ax he strokes.

The grene knyght upon grounde graythely hym dresses:
A littel lut with the hede, the lere he discoverez;
His longe lovelych lokkez he layd over his croun,   290
Let the naked nec to the note schewe.
Gavan gripped to his ax, and gederes hit on hyght;
The kay fot on the folde he be-fore sette,
Let hit doun lyghtly lyght on the naked,
That the scharp of the schalk schyndered the bones,   295
And schrank thurgh the schyire grece, and scade hit in
      twynne,
That the bit of the broun stel bot on the grounde.
The fayre hede fro the halce hit [felle] to the erthe,
That fele hit foyned wyth her fete there hit forth roled;
The blod brayd fro the body, that blykked on the gren.   300
And nawther faltered ne fel the freke never-the-helder,
Bot stythly he start forth upon styf schonkes,
And runyschly he raght out there-as renkkez stoden,
Laght to his lufly hed and lyft hit up sone;
And sythen boghez to his blonk, the brydel he cachchez, 305
Steppez in to stel-bawe and strydez alofte,
And his hede by the here in his honde haldez;

And as sadly the segge hym in his sadel sette
As non unhap had hym ayled, thagh hedlez he were,
    In stedde.   310
   He brayde his blunk aboute,
   That ugly bodi that bledde;
   Moni on of hym had doute,
   Bi that his resounz were redde:

For the hede in his honde he haldez up even,   315
To-ward the derrest on the dece he dressez the face,
And hit lyfte up the yghe-lyddez, and loked ful brode,
And meled thus much with his muthe, as ye may now here.
"Loke, Gawan, thou be graythe to go as thou hettez,
And layte as lelly til thou me, lude, fynde,   320
As thou hatz hette in this halle, herande thise knyghtes.
To the grene chapel thou chose, I charge the, to fotte;
Such a dunt as thou hatz dalt disserved thou habbez,
To be yederly yolden on Nw Yeres morn.
The Knyght of the Grene Chapel, men knowen me
    mony;   325
For-thi me for to fynde, if thou fraystez, faylez thou never;
Ther-fore com, other recreaunt be calde the be-hoves."
With a runisch rout the raynez he tornez,
Halled out at the hal-dor, his hed in his hande,
That the fyr of the flynt flawe from fole hoves.   330
To quat kyth he be-com, knewe non there,
Never more then thay wyste fram quethen he watz wonnen.
    What thenne?
   The kyng and Gawen thare,
   At that Grene thay laghe and grenne;   335
   Yet breved watz hit ful bare,
   A mervayl among tho menne.

SIR GAWAYN AT THE GREEN CHAPEL

Thenne gyrdez he to Gryngolet, and gederez the rake,
Schowvez in bi a schore, at a schaghe syde,
Ridez thurgh the roghe bonk, ryght to the dale;
And thenne he wayted hym aboute, and wylde hit hym
   thoght,
And seghe no syngne of resette, bisydez nowhere,   5

Bot hyghe bonkkez and brent, upon bothe halve,
And rughe knokled knarrez, with knorned stonez;
The skwez of the scowtes skayved hym thoght.
Thenne he hoved, and wyth-hylde his hors at that tyde,
And ofte chaunged his cher, the chapel to seche.   10
He segh non suche in no syde, and selly hym thoght;
Sone a lyttel on a launde, a lawe as hit were:
A balgh bergh, bi a bonke, the brymme by-syde,
Bi a forgh of a flode, that ferked thare;
The borne blubred ther-inne, as hit boyled hade.   15
The knyght kachez his caple, and com to the lawe,
Lightez doun luflyly, and at a lynde tachez
The rayne, and his riche with a roghe braunche;
Thenne he boghez to the berghe, aboute hit he walkez,
Debatande with hym-self quat hit be myght.   20
Hit hade a hole on the ende and on ayther syde,
And over-growen with gresse in glodes ay where;
And al watz holgh in-with, nobot an olde cave,
Or a crevisse of an olde cragge, he couthe hit noght deme
                    With spelle.   25
        "We, lorde," quod the gentyle knyght,
        "Whether this be the grene chapelle,
          He myght aboute myd-nyght
          The Dele his matynnes telle!"

"Now i-wysse," quod Wowayn, "wysty is here;   30
This oritore is ugly, with erbez over-growen;
Wal bisemez the wyghe wruxled in grene
Dele here his devocioun, on the develez wyse.
Now I fele hit is the fende, in my fyve wyttez,
That hatz stoken me this steven, to strye me here;   35
This is a chapel of meschaunce, that chekke hit by-tyde;
Hit is the corsedest kyrk that ever I com inne!"
With heghe helme on his hede, his launce in his honde,
He romez up to the rokke of tho rogh wonez;
Thene herde he of that hyghe hil, in a harde roche,   40
Biyonde the broke, in a bonk, a wonder breme noyse:
Quat! hit clatered in the clyff, as hit cleve schulde,
As one upon a gryndelston hade grounden a sythe;
What! hit wharred, and whette, as water at a mulne;
What! hit rusched and ronge, rawthe to here.   45

Thenne "Bi Godde," quod Gawayn, "that geré, as I trowe,
Is ryched at the reverence, me renk to mete,
        Bi rote.
    Let God worche we loo,
    Hit helppez me not a mote;   50
    My lif thagh I for-goo,
    Drede dotz me no lote."

Thenne the knyght con calle ful hyghe:
"Who stightlez in this sted, me steven to holde?
For now is gode Gawayn goande ryght here,   55
If any wyghe oght wyl wynne hider fast,
Other now other never his nedez to spede."
"Abyde," quod on on the bonke, aboven over his hede,
"And thou schal haf al in hast that I the hyght ones."
Yet he rusched on that rurde, rapely a throwe,   60
And wyth quettyng a-wharf, er he wolde lyght;
And sythen he keverez bi a cragge, and comez of a hole,
Whyrlande out of a wro, wyth a felle weppen,
A Denez ax nwe dyght, the dynt with to yelde
With a borelych bytte, bende by the halme,   65
Fyled in a fylor, fowre fote large—
Hit watz no lasse, bi that lace that lemed ful bryght.
And the gome in the grene, gered as fyrst,
Bothe the lyre and the leggez, lokkez, and berde,
Save that fayre on his fote he foundez on the erthe,   70
Sette the stele to the stone, and stalked bysyde.
When he wan to the watter, ther he wade nolde,
He hypped over on hys ax, and orpedly strydez,
Bremly brothe on a bent, that brode watz a-boute,
        On snawe.   75
    Sir Gawayn the knyght con mete;
    He ne lutte hym no thyng lowe.
    That other sayde, "Now, sir swete,
    Of steven mon may the trowe."

"Gawayn," quod that grene gome, "God the mot loke! 80
I-wysse thou art welcom, wyghe, to my place,
And thou hatz tymed thi travayl as true mon schulde;
And thou knowez the covenauntez kest uus by-twene:
At this tyme twelmonyth thou toke that the falled,

And I schulde at this Nwe Yere yeply the quyte.　　85
And we ar in this valay, verayly oure one;
Here ar no renkes us to rydde, rele as uus likez.
Haf thy helme of thy hede, and haf here thy pay;
Busk no more debate then I the bede thenne,
When thou wypped of my hede at a wap one."　　90
"Nay, bi God," quod Gawayn, "That me gost lante,
I schal gruch the no grwe, for grem that fallez;
Bot styghtel the upon on strok, and I schal stonde stylle,
And warp the no wernyng to worch as the lykez,
　　　　　No whare."　　95
　　　　He lened with the nek, and lutte,
　　　　And schewed that schyre al bare,
　　　　And lette as he noght dutte;
　　　　For drede he wolde not dare.

Then the gome in the grene graythed hym swythe,　　100
Gederez up hys grymme tole, Gawayn to smyte;
With alle the bur in his body he ber hit on lofte,
Munt as maghtyly, as marre hym he wolde;
Hade hit dryven adoun as dregh as he atled,
Ther hade ben ded of his dynt that doghty watz ever.　　105
Bot Gawayn on that giserne glyfte hym bysyde,
As hit com glydande adoun, on glode hym to schende,
And schranke a lytel with the schulderes, for the scharp
　　　　yrne.
That other schalk wyth a schunt the schene wyth-haldez,
And thenne repreved he the prynce with mony prowde
　　　　wordez:　　110
"Thou art not Gawayn," quod the gome, "that is so goud
　　　　halden,
That never arghed for no here, by hylle ne be vale;
And now thou fles for ferde, or thou fele harmez.
Such cowardise of that knyght cowthe I never here.
Nawther fyked I, ne flaghe, freke, quen thou myntest,　　115
Ne kest no kavelacion, in kyngez hous Arthor;
My hede flagh to my fote, and yet flagh I never.
And thou, er any harme hent, arghez in hert;
Wherfore the better burne me burde be called
　　　　Ther-fore."　　120
　　　　Quod Gawayn, "I schunt onez,

          And so wyl I no more;
          Bot thagh my hede falle on the stonez,
          I con not hit restore.

"Bot busk, burne, bi thi fayth, and bryng me to the
            poynt,   125
 Dele to me my destine, and do hit out of honde,
 For I schal stonde the a strok, and start no more,
 Til thyn ax have me hitte; haf here my trawthe."
"Haf at the, thenne," quod that other, and hevez hit alofte,
 And waytez as wrothely as he wode were;   130
 He myntez at hym maghtyly, bot not the mon ryvez,
 With-helde heterly his honde er hit hurt myght.
 Gawayn graythely hit bydez, and glent with no membre,
 Bot stode stylle as the ston other a stubbe auther,
 That ratheled is in roche grounde, with rotez a hundreth. 135
 Then muryly efte con he mele, the mon in the grene:
"So now thou hatz thi hert holle, hitte me bihoves;
 Halde the now the hyghe hode, that Arthur the raght,
 And kepe thy kanel at this kest, yif hit kever may."
 Gawayn ful gryndelly with greme thenne sayde,   140
"Wy, thresch on, thou thro mon; thou thretez to longe;
 I hope that thi hert arghe wyth thyn awen selven."
"For sothe," quod that other freke, "so felly thou spekez,
 I wyl no lenger on lyte lette thin ernde,
                  Right nowe."   145
          Thenne tas he hym strythe to stryke,
          And frounses bothe lyppe and browe;
          No mervayle thagh hym myslyke,
          That hoped of no rescowe.

He lyftes lyghtly his lome, and let hit doun fayre,   150
With the barbe of the bitte bi the bare nek;
Thagh he homered heterly, hurt hym no more,
Bot snyrt hym on that on syde, that severed the hyde;
The scharp schrank to the flesche thurgh the schyre grece,
That the schene blod over his schulderes schot to the
            erthe.   155
And quen the burne segh the blode blenk on the snawe,
He sprit forth spenne fote more then a spere lenthe,
Hent heterly his helme, and on his hed cast,
Schot with his schulderez his fayre schelde under,

Braydez out a bryght sworde, and bremely he spekez;   160
Never syn that he watz burne borne of his moder,
Watz he never in this worlde wyghe half so blythe:
"Blynne, burne, of thy bur! bede me no mo!
I haf a stroke in this sted with-oute stryf hent;
And if thow rechez me any mo, I redyly schal quyte,   165
And yelde yederly agayn, and ther to ye tryst,
        And foo.
     Bot on stroke here me fallez;
     The covenaunt schop ryght so,
     [Sikered] in Arthurez hallez,   170
     And ther-fore, hende, now hoo!"

The hathel heldet hym fro, and on his ax rested,
Sette the schaft upon schore, and to the scharp lened,
And loked to the leude, that on the launde yede,
How that doghty dredles dervely ther stondez,   175
Armed ful aghlegh; in hert hit hym lykez.
Thenn he melez muryly, wyth a much steven,
And wyth a raykande rurde he to the renk sayde:
"Bolde burne, on this bent be not so gryndel;
No mon here un-manerly the mys-boden habbe,   180
Ne kyd, bot as covenaunde at kyngez kort schaped;
I hyght the a strok, and thou hit hatz; halde the wel payed;
I relece the of the remnaunt, of ryghtes alle other.
Gif I deliver had bene, a boffet, paraunter,
I couthe wrotheloker haf waret, [and] to the haf wroght
     anger.   185
Fyrst I mansed the muryly, with a mynt one,
And rove the wyth no rof, sore with ryght I the profered,
For the forwarde that we fest in the fyrst nyght:
And thou trystyly the trawthe and trwly me haldez;
Al the gayne thow me gef, as god mon schulde.   190
That other munt for the morne, mon, I the profered,
Thou kyssedes my clere wyf, the cossez me raghtez;
For bothe two here I the bede bot two bare myntes,
        Boute scathe.
     Trwe mon trwe restore,   195
     Thenne thar mon drede no wathe;
     At the thrid thou fayled thore,
     And ther-for that tappe ta the.

For hit is my wede that thou werez, that ilke woven
    girdel;
Myn owen wyf hit the weved, I wot wel forsothe.   200
Now know I wel thy cosses, and thy costes als;
And the wowyng of my wyf, I wroght hit myselven;
I sende hir to asay the, and, sothly me thynkkez,
On the fautlest freke that ever on fote yede:
As perle bi the quite pese is of prys more,   205
So is Gawayn, in god fayth, bi other gay knyghtez.
Bot here yow lakked a lyttel, sir, and lewte yow wonted;
Bot that watz for no wylyde werke, ne wowyng nauther,
Bot for ye lufed your lyf; the lasse I yow blame."
That other stif mon in study stod a gret whyle;   210
So agreved for greme he gryed with-inne,
Alle the blode of his brest blende in his face,
That al he schrank for schome, that the schalk talked.
The forme worde upon folde, that the freke meled:
"Corsed worth cowarddyse and covetyse bothe!   215
In yow is vylany and vyse, that vertue disstryez."
Thenne he kaght to the knot, and the kest lawsez,
Brayde brothely the belt to the burne selven:
"Lo! ther the falssyng, foule mot hit falle!
For care of thy knokke cowardyse me taght   220
To a-corde me with covetyse, my kynde to for-sake,
That is larges and lewte, that longez to knyghtez.
Now am I fawty and falce, and ferde haf ben ever;
Of trecherye and un-trawthe bothe bityde sorghe
                And care!   225
      I bi-knowe yow, knyght, here stylle,
      Al fawty is my fare;
      Letez me over-take your wylle,
      And efte I schal be ware."

Thenn loghe that other leude, and luflyly sayde: 230
"I halde hit hardily hole, the harme that I hade.
Thou art confessed so clene, be-knowen of thy mysses,
And hatz the penaunce apert, of the poynt of myn egge,
I halde the polysed of that plyght, and pured as clene
As thou hadez never forfeted sythen thou watz fyrst
    borne.   235

And I gif the, sir, the gurdel that is golde hemmed;
For hit is grene as my goune, Sir Gawayn, ye maye
Thenk upon this ilke threpe, ther thou forth thryngez
Among prynces of prys, and this a pure token
Of the chaunce of the grene chapel, at chevalrous
   knyghtez.   240
And ye schal in this Nwe Yer agayn to my wonez,
And we schyn revel the remnaunt of this ryche fest,
     Ful bene."
    Ther lathed hym fast the lorde,
    And sayde, "With my wyf, I wene,   245
    We schal yow wel acorde,
    That watz your enmy kene."

"Nay, for sothe," quod the segge, and sesed hys helme,
And hatz hit of hendely, and the hathel thonkkez:
"I haf sojorned sadly; sele yow bytyde,   250
And He yelde hit yow yare, That yarkkez al menskes!
And comaundez me to that cortays, your comlych fere,
Bothe that on and that other, myn honoured ladyez,
That thus hor knyght wyth hor kest han koyntly bigyled.
Bot hit is no ferly thagh a fole madde,   255
And thurgh wyles of wymmen be wonen to sorghe:
For so watz Adam in erde with one bygyled,
And Salamon with fele sere, and Samson eft sonez—
Dalyda dalt hym hys wyrde; and Davyth ther-after
Watz blended with Barsabe, that much bale tholed.   260
Now these were wrathed wyth her wyles: hit were a
   wynne huge,
To luf hom wel, and leve hem not; a leude that couthe,
For thes wer forne the freest that folged alle the sele,
Exellently of alle thyse other, under heven-ryche,
     That mused.   265
    And alle thay were bi-wyled,
    With wymmen that thay used:
    Thagh I be now bigyled,
    Me think me burde be excused.

"Bot your gordel," quod Gawayn, "God yow for-yelde! 270
That wyl I welde wyth good wylle, not for the wynne golde
Ne the saynt, ne the sylk, ne the syde pendaundes,

For wele, ne for worchyp, ne for the wlonk werkkez,
Bot in syngne of my surfet I schal se hit ofte:
When I ride in renoun, remorde to myselven   275
The faut and the fayntyse of the flesche crabbed,
How tender hit is to entyse teches of fylthe;
And thus, quen pryde schal me pryk for prowes of armes,
The loke to this luf lace schal lethe my hert.
Bot on I wolde yow pray, displeses yow never: 280
Syn ye be lorde of the yonder londe, ther I haf lent inne,
Wyth yow wyth worschyp—the Wyghe hit yow yelde
That up-haldez the heven and on hygh sittez,—
How norne ye yowre ryght nome, and thenne no more?"
"That schal I telle the trwly," quod that other thenne;   285
"Bernlak de Hautdesert I hat in this londe,
Thurgh myght of Morgne la Faye, that in my hous lenges.
In koyntyse of clergye, bi craftes wel lerned,
The maystres of Merlyn, mony ho [hatz] taken;
For ho hatz dalt drwry ful dere sum tyme,   290
With that conable klerk, that knowes alle your knyghtez
         At hame.
         Morgne the goddes,
         Ther-fore hit is hir name;
         Weldez non so hyghe hawtesse   295
         That ho ne con make ful tame.

"Ho wayned me upon this wyse to your wynne halle,
For to assay the surquidre, yif hit soth were,
That rennes of the grete renoun of the Rounde Table;
Ho wayned me this wonder, your wyttez to reve,   300
For to haf greved Gaynour, and gart hir to dyghe,
With glopnyng of that ilke gomen, that gostlych speked,
With his hede in his honde, bifore the hyghe table.
That is ho that is at home, the auncian lady;
Ho is even thyn aunt, Arthurez half suster,   305
The duches doghter of Tyntagelle, that dere Uter after
Hade Arthur upon, that athel is nowthe.
Therfore I ethe the, hathel, to com to thy naunt,
Make myry in my hous: my meny the lovies;
And I wol the as wel, wyghe, bi my faythe,   310
As any gome under God, for thy grete trauthe."
And he nikked hym naye, he nolde bi no wayes.

Thay acolen and kyssen, [bikennen] ayther other
To the Prynce of Paradise, and parten ryght there,
            On coolde.   315
        Gawayn on blonk ful bene
        To the kyngez burgh buskez bolde;
        And the knyght in the enker grene
        Whider-warde so ever he wolde.

About 1360.

JOHN GOWER

FROM

CONFESSIO AMANTIS

Of Jupiter this finde I write:
How whilom that he wolde wite
Upon the pleigntes whiche he herde,
Among the men how that it ferde,
As of here wrong condicion   5
To do justificacion;
And for that cause doun he sente
An angel, which aboute wente
That he the sothe knowe mai.
So it befell upon a dai   10
This angel, which him scholde enforme,
Was clothed in a mannes forme,
And overtok, I understonde,
Tuo men that wenten over londe;
Thurgh whiche he thoghte to aspie   15
His cause, and goth in compaignie.
This angel with hise wordes wise
Opposeth hem in sondri wise,
Now lowde wordes and now softe,
That mad hem to desputen ofte,   20
And ech of hem his reson hadde.
And thus with tales he hem ladde,
With good examinacioun,
Til he knew the condicioun
What men thei were, bothe tuo;   25
And sih wel ate laste, tho,

That on of hem was coveitous,
And his fela was envious.
And thus, whan he hath knowlechinge,
Anon he feigneth departinge,   30
And seide he mot algate wende.
Bot herkne now what fell at ende:
For thanne he made hem understonde
That he was there of Goddes sonde;
And seide hem, for the kindeschipe   35
That thei have don him felaschipe,
He wole him do som grace ayein;
And bad that on of hem schal sein
What thing him is lievest to crave,
And he it schal of yifte have;   40
And over that ek, forth withal,
He seith that other have schal
The double of that his felaw axeth.
And thus to hem his grace he taxeth.
The coveitous was wonder glad,   45
And to that other man he bad
And seith that he ferst axe scholde:
For he supposeth that he wolde
Make his axinge of worldes good,
For thanne he knew wel how it stod,   50
That he himself be double weyhte
Schal after take; and thus be sleyhte,
Be-cause that he wolde winné,
He bad his fela ferst beginne.
This envious, thogh it be late,   55
Whan that he syh he mot algate
Make his axinge ferst, he thoghte
If he worschipe or profit soghte,
It schal be doubled to his fiere:
That wolde he chese in no manere.   60
Bot thanne he scheweth what he was
Toward envie, and in this cas
Unto this angel thus he seide,
And for his yifte this he preide,
To make him blind of his on yhe,   65
So that his fela nothing syhe.
This word was noght so sone spoke,

That his on yhe anon was loke,
And his felawh forthwith also
Was blind of bothe his yhen tuo.   70
Tho was that other glad ynowh:
That on wept, and that other lowh;
He sette his on yhe at no cost,
Wherof that other two hath lost.
Of thilke ensample, which fell tho,   75
Men tellen now full ofte so.
The worlde empeireth comunly,
And yit wot non the cause why:
For it acordeth noght to kinde
Min oghne harme to seche and finde   80
Of that I schal my brother grieve;
It myhte nevere wel achieve.

About 1383.

WILLIAM LANGLAND

FROM

THE VISION OF WILLIAM CONCERNING

PIERS THE PLOWMAN

THE PROLOGUE

In a somer seson,   whan soft was the sonne,
I shope me in shroudes   as I a shepe were;
In habite as an heremite   unholy of werkes,
Went wyde in this world   wondres to here.
Ac on a May mornynge,   on Malverne hulles,   5
Me byfel a ferly,   of fairy me thoughte.
I was wery, forwandred,   and wente me to reste
Under a brode banke,   bi a bornes side;
And as I lay and lened,   and loked in the wateres,
I slombred in a slepyng,   it sweyved so merye.   10
Thanne gan I to meten   a merveilouse swevene
That I was in a wildernesse,   wist I never where.
As I behelde in-to the est,   an hiegh to the sonne,
I seigh a toure on a toft,   trieliche ymaked;
A depe dale binethe,   a dongeon there-inne,   15

With depe dyches and derke   and dredful of sight.
A faire felde ful of folke   fonde I there bytwene,
Of alle maner of men,   the mene and the˙riche,
Worchyng and wandryng   as the worlde asketh.
   Some putten hem to the plow,   pleyed ful selde,   20
In settyng and in sowyng   swonken ful harde,
And wonnen that wastours   with glotonye distruyeth.
And some putten hem to pruyde,   apparailed hem there-
    after,
In contenaunce of clothyng   comen disgisid.
In prayers and in penance   putten hem manye,   25
Al for love of owre Lorde   lyveden ful streyte,
In hope for to have   hevene-riche blisse;
As ancres and heremites,   that holden hem in here selles,
Coveite nought in contre   to cairen aboute,
For no likerous liflode   her lycam to plese.   30
And somme chosen chaffare,   to cheven the bettere,
As it semeth to owre syght   that suche men thryveth;
And somme murthes to make   as mynstrales conneth,
And geten gold with here glee,   synneles, I leve.
Ac japers and jangelers,   Judas chylderen,   35
Feynen hem fantasies   and foles hem maketh,
And han here witte at wille   to worche yif thei sholde;
That Poule precheth of hem   I nel nought preve it here—
Qui turpiloquium loquitur   is Luciferes hyne.
Bidders and beggeres   fast aboute yede,   40
With her bely and her bagges   of bred ful ycrammed;
Fayteden hem for here fode,   foughten atte ale;
In glotonye, God it wot,   gon hii to bedde,
And rysen up with ribaudye   tho roberdes knaves:
Slepe and sori sleuthe   seweth hem ever.   45
Pilgrymes and palmers   plighted hem togidere
For to seke Seynt James   and seyntes in Rome;
Thei went forth in here way   with many wise tales,
And hadden leve to lye   al here lyf after.
I seigh somme that seiden   thei had ysought seyntes;   50
To eche a tale that thei tolde   here tonge was tempred to lye,
More than to sey soth,   it semed bi here speche.
Heremites on an heep,   with hoked staves,
Wenten to Walsyngham,   and here wenches after.
Grete lobyes and longe,   that loth were to swynke,   55

Clotheden hem in copis   to ben knowen fram othere,
And shopen hem heremites   here ese to have.
I fond there freris,   alle the foure ordres,
Preched the peple   for profit of hem-selven,
Glosed the gospel   as hem good lyked,   60
For coveitise of copes   construed it as thei wolde.
Manye of this maistres freris   mowe clothen hem at lykyng,
For here money and marchandise   marchen togideres.
For sith charite hath be chapman,   and chief to shryve
        lordes,
Many ferlis han fallen   in a fewe yeris.   65
But holychirche and hii   holde better togideres,
The moste myschief on molde   is mountyng wel faste.
    Ther preched a pardoner   as he a prest were,
Broughte forth a bulle   with bishopes seles,
And seide that hym-self myght   assoilen hem alle   70
Of falshed of fastyng,   of vowes ybroken.
Lewed men leved hym wel   and lyked his wordes,
Comen up knelyng   to kissen his bulles;
He bonched hem with his brevet   and blered here eyes,
And raughte with his ragman   rynges and broches.   75
Thus they given here golde   glotones to kepe,
And leveth such loseles,   that lecherye haunten.
Were the bischop yblissed   and worth bothe his eres,
His seel shulde nought be sent   to deceyve the peple.
Ac it is naught by the bischop   that the boy precheth, 80
For the parisch prest and the pardonere   parten the silver
That the poraille of the parisch   scholde have yif thei nere.
Persones and parisch prestes   pleyned hem to the bischop
That here parisshes were pore   sith the pestilence tyme,
To have a lycence and leve   at London to dwelle,   85
And syngen there for symonye,   for silver is swete.
    Bischopes and bachelers,   bothe maistres and doctours,
That han cure under Criste   and crounyng in tokne
And signe that thei sholden   shryven here paroschienes,
Prechen and prey for hem,   and the pore fede,   90
Liggen in London   in Lenten, an elles.
Somme serven the Kyng   and his silver tellen,
In Cheker and in Chancerye   chalengen his dettes
Of wardes and wardmotes,   weyves and streyves.
And some serven as servantz   lordes and ladyes,   95

And in stede of stuwardes sytten and demen,
Here messe and here matynes, and many of here oures
Arn don undevoutlych; drede is at the laste
Lest Crist in consistorie acorse ful manye.
I parceyved of the power that Peter had to kepe,   100
To bynde and to unbynde, as the Boke telleth,
How he it left with love, as owre Lorde hight,
Amonges foure vertues the best of all vertues,
That cardinales ben called and closyng gatis,
There Crist is in kyngdome, to close and to shutte,   105
And to opne it to hem and hevene blisse shewe.
Ac of the cardinales atte courte that caught of that name,
And power presumed in hem a pope to make,
To han that power that Peter hadde, inpugnen I nelle,
For in love and letterure the eleccioun bilongeth;   110
For-thi I can and can naughte of courte speke more.
    Thanne come there a kyng: Knyghthod hym ladde,
Might of the comunes made hym to regne;
And thanne cam Kynde Wytte, and clerkes he made,
For to conseille the kyng and the comune save.   115
The kyng and Knyghthode and Clergye bothe
Casten that the comune shulde hem-self fynde.
The comune contreved of Kynde Witte craftes,
And for profit of alle the poeple plowmen ordeygned,
To tilie and travaile as trewe lyf asketh.   120
The kynge and the comune and Kynde Witte the thridde
Shope lawe and lewte, eche man to knowe his owne.
Thanne loked up a lunatik, a lene thing with-alle,
And knelyng to the kyng clergealy he seyde:
"Crist kepe the, Sire Kyng, and thi kyngriche,   125
And leve the lede thi londe so leute the lovye,
And for thi rightful rewlyng be rewarded in hevene!"
And sithen in the eyre an hiegh an angel of hevene
Lowed to speke in Latyn— for lewed men ne coude
Jangle ne jugge that justifie hem shulde,   130
But suffren and serven; for-thi seyde the angel:
"'Sum rex, sum princeps;' neutrum fortasse deinceps.
O qui jura regis Christi specialia regis,
Hos quod agas melius justus es, esto pius!
Nudum jus a te vestiri vult pietate.   135
Qualia vis metere talia grana sere:

Si jus nudatur,　nudo de jure metatur;
Si seritur pietas,　de pietate metas!"
Thanne greved hym a Goliardeys,　a glotoun of wordes,
And to the angel an heigh answered after,　　　　140
"Dum rex a regere　dicatur nomen habere,
Nomen habet sine re　nisi studet jura tenere."
And thanne gan alle the comune　crye in vers of Latin,
To the kynges conseille　construe ho-so wolde,
"Precepta regis　sunt nobis vincula legis."　　　　145
　　With that ran there a route　of ratones at ones,
And smale mys with hem　mo then a thousande,
And comen to a conseille　for here comune profit;
For a cat of a courte　cam whan hym lyked,
And overlepe hem lyghtlich　and laughte hem at his
　　　　wille,　　　　150
And pleyde with hem perilouslych　and possed hem aboute.
"For doute of dyverse dredes　we dar noughte wel loke;
And yif we grucche of his gamen　he wil greve us alle,
Cracche us, or clawe us　and in his cloches holde,
That us lotheth the lyf　or he lete us passe.　　　　155
Myghte we with any witte　his wille withstonde,
We myghte be lordes aloft　and lyven at owre ese."
A raton of renon,　most renable of tonge,
Seide for a sovereygne　help to hym-selve:
"I have ysein segges," quod he,　"in the cite of London,　160
Beren bighes ful brighte　abouten here nekkes,
And some colers of crafty werk;　uncoupled thei wenden,
Both in wareine and in waste,　where hem leve lyketh;
And otherwhile thei aren elles-where,　as I here telle.
Were there a belle on here beighe,　bi Jhesu, as me
　　　　thynketh,　　　　165
Men myghte wite where thei went,　and awei renne!
And right so," quod his raton,　"reson me sheweth
To bugge a belle of brasse　or of brighte sylver,
And knitten on a colere,　for owre comune profit,
And hangen it upon the cattes hals;　thanne here we
　　　　mowen　　　　170
Where he ritt or rest　or renneth to playe.
And yif him list for to laike,　thenne loke we mowen,
And peren in his presence　ther-while hym plaie liketh;
And yif him wrattheth, be ywar　and his weye shonye."

Alle this route of ratones   to this reson thei assented.   175
Ac tho the belle was ybought   and on the beighe hanged,
Ther ne was ratoun in alle the route,   for alle the rewme
    of Fraunce,
That dorst have ybounden the belle   aboute the cattis nekke,
Ne hangen it aboute the cattes hals,   al Engelonde to
    wynne;
And helden hem unhardy   and here conseille feble,   180
And leten here laboure lost   and alle here longe studye.
A mous that moche good   couthe, as me thoughte,
Stroke forth sternly   and stode biforn hem alle,
And to the route of ratones   reherced these wordes:
"Though we culled the catte,   yut sholde ther come an-
    other   185
To cracchy us and al owre kynde,   though we croupe
    under benches.
For-thi I conseille alle the comune   to lat the catte worthe,
And be we never so bolde   the belle hym to shewe;
For I herde my sire seyn   (is sevene yere ypassed),
There the catte is a kitoun   the courte is fu! elyng;   190
That witnisseth Holi-Write,   who-so wil it rede,
    'Ve terre ubi puer rex est,' etc.
For may no renke there rest have,   for ratones bi nyghte.
The while he caccheth conynges   he coveiteth nought owre
    caroyne,
But fet hym al with venesoun;   defame we hym nevere,
For better is a litel losse   than a longe sorwe,   195
The mase amonge us alle   though we mysse a shrewe.
For many mannes malt   we mys wolde destruye,
And also ye route of ratones   rende mennes clothes,
Nere that cat of that courte   that can yow overlepe;
For had ye rattes yowre wille,   ye couthe nought reule
    yowre-selve.   200
I sey for me," quod the mous,   "I se so mykel after,
Shal never the cat ne the kitoun   bi my conseille be greved,
Ne carpyng of this coler   that costed me nevre.
And though it had coste me catel,   biknowen it I nolde,
But suffre as hym-self wolde   to do as hym liketh,   205
Coupled and uncoupled   to cacche what thei mowe.
For-thi uche a wise wighte I warne   wite wel his owne."—
    What this meteles bemeneth,   ye men that be merye,

Devine ye, for I ne dar,   bi dere God in hevene!
   Yit hoved there an hondreth   in houves of selke,   210
Serjauntz, it semed,   that serveden atte barre;
Plededen for penyes   and poundes the lawe,
And nought for love of owre Lord   unlose here lippes onis:
Thou myghtest better mete the myste   on Malverne hulles
Then gete a momme of here mouthe   but money were
     shewed.   215
Barones and burgeis   and bonde-men als
I seigh in this assemble,   as ye schul here after;
Baxsteres and brewesteres   and bocheres manye,
Wolle-websteres   and weveres of lynnen,
Taillours and tynkeres   and tolleres in marketes,   220
Masons and mynours   and many other craftes,
Of alkin libbyng laboreres   lopen forth somme,
As dykers and delveres,   that doth here dedes ille,
And dryven forth the longe day   with "Dieu vous save,
     dame Emme!"
Cookes and here knaves   crieden "Hote pies, hote!   225
Gode gris and gees!   Go we dyne, go we!"
Taverners un-til hem   tolde the same:
White wyn of Oseye   and red wyn of Gascoigne,
Of the Ryne and of the Rochel,   the roste to defye.
Al this I seigh slepyng,   and sevene sythes more.   230

   1376–77.

GEOFFREY CHAUCER

FROM

THE BOOK OF THE DUCHESSE

Me thoghte thus: that hyt was May,
And in the dawnynge ther I lay
(Me mette thus) in my bed al naked,
And loked forth, for I was waked
With smale foules a grete hepe,   5
That had affrayed me out of my slepe,
Thorgh noyse and swetenesse of her songe;
And, as me mette, they sate amonge,
Upon my chambre-roofe withoute,

Upon the tyles, over al a-boute,   10
And songe, everich in hys wyse,
The moste solempne servise,
By note, that ever man, I trowe,
Had herde, for som of hem song lowe,
Som high, and al of oon acorde.   15
To telle shortly, at oo worde,
Was never harde so swete a steven
But hyt had be a thynge of heven;
So mery a soune, so swete entunes,
That certes, for the toune of Tewnes,   20
I nolde but I had herde hem synge,
For al my chambre gan to rynge
Thorgh syngynge of her armonye:
For instrument nor melodye
Was nowhere herde yet halfe so swete,   25
Nor of acorde halfe so mete;
For ther was noon of hem that feyned
To synge, for ech of hem hym peyned
To fynde out mery crafty notes;
They ne spared not her throtes.   30
And, soothe to seyn, my chambre was
Ful wel depeynted, and with glas
Were al the wyndowes wel y-glased,
Ful clere, and nat an hole y-crased;
That to beholde hit was grete joye: 35
For hoolly al the story of Troye
Was in the glasynge y-wroght thus—
Of Ector and Kynge Priamus,
Of Achilles and Kynge Lamedon,
And eke of Medea and of Jason,   40
Of Paris, Eleyne, and of Lavyne.
And alle the walles with colours fyne
Were peynted, bothe text and glose,
Of al the "Romaunce of the Rose."
My wyndowes weren shette echon,   45
And throgh the glas the sonne shon
Upon my bed with bryghte bemes,
With many glade gilde stremes;
And eke the welken was so faire;
Blew, bryght, clere was the ayre,   50

And ful attempre, for sothe, hyt was,
For nother to colde nor hoote yt was,
Ne in al the welkene was a cloude.
    And as I lay thus, wonder loude
Me thoght I herde an hunte blowe   55
Tassay hys horne and for to knowe
Whether hyt were clere or hors of soune.
And I herde goynge, bothe up and doune,
Men, hors, houndes, and other thynge,
And al men speke of huntynge—   60
How they wolde slee the hert with strengthe,
And how the hert had, upon lengthe,
So moche embosed, I not now what.
Anoon-ryght, whan I herde that,
How that they wolde on huntynge goon,   65
I was ryght glad, and up anoon;
Tooke my hors, and forthe I went
Out of my chambre: I never stent
Til I come to the feld withoute.
Ther overtoke I a gret route   70
Of huntes and eek of foresteres,
With many relayes and lymeres;
And hyed hem to the forest faste,
And I with hem. So at the laste
I asked oon, ladde a lymere,   75
"Say, felowe, who shal hunte here?"
Quod I; and he answered ageyn,
"Syr, themperour Octovyen,"
Quod he, "and ys here faste by."
"A Goddes halfe, in goode tyme," quod I;   80
"Go we faste!" and gan to ryde.
Whan we came to the forest-syde,
Every man didde, ryght anoon,
As to huntynge fel to doon.
The mayster-hunte anoon, fote-hoot,   85
With a grete horne blew thre moot
At the uncoupylynge of hys houndes.
Withynne a whyle the herte founde ys,
Y-halowed, and rechased faste
Long tyme; and so, at the laste,   90
This hert rused and stale away

Fro alle the houndes a prevy way.
The houndes had overshette hem alle,
And were on a defaute y-falle;
Therwyth the hunte wonder faste   95
Blewe a forloyn at the laste.
    I was go walked fro my tree;
And as I wente, ther came by mee
A whelpe, that fauned me as I stoode,
That hadde y-folowed, and coude no good.   100
Hyt came and crepte to me as lowe,
Ryght as hyt hadde me y-knowe;
Held doun hys hede and joyned hys erys,
And leyde al smothe doun hys herys.
I wolde han caught hyt, and anoon   105
Hyt fledde, and was fro me goon;
And I him folwed. And hyt forthe went
Doune by a floury grene went
Ful thikke of gras, ful softe and swete,
With floures fele, faire under fete,   110
And litel used, hyt semed thus:
For bothe Flora and Zephirus,
They two that make floures growe,
Had made her dwellynge ther, I trowe;
For hit was, on to beholde,   115
As thogh the erthe envye wolde
To be gayer than the heven,
To have mo floures, swiche seven
As in the welkyn sterris bee.
Hyt had forgete the povertee   120
That wynter, thorgh hys colde morwes,
Had mad hyt suffre, and his sorwes:
All was forgeten, and that was sene,
For al the woode was waxen grene;
Swetnesse of dewe had mad hyt waxe.   125
Hyt ys no need eke for to axe
Where there were many grene greves,
Or thikke of trees, so ful of leves;
And every tree stood by himselve
Fro other wel ten fete or twelve.   130
So grete trees, so huge of strengthe,
Of fourty or fifty fedme lengthe,

Clene withoute bough or stikke,
With croppes brode, and eke as thikke—
They were nat an ynche a-sonder—   135
That hit was shadwe over-al under,
And many an herte and many an hynde,
Was both before me and behynde.
Of founes, sowres, bukkes, does
Was ful the woode, and many roes,   140
And many squirelles, that sete
Ful high upon the trees, and ete,
And in hir maner made festys.
Shortly, hyt was so ful of bestys
That thogh Argus, the noble countour,   145
Sete to rekene in his countour,
And reken with his figurs ten—
For by tho figurs mowe al ken,
Yf they be crafty, rekene and noumbre,
And tel of every thinge the noumbre,—   150
Yet shulde he fayle to rekene evene
The wondres, me mette in my swevene.

1369.

FROM

THE HOUS OF FAME

This egle, of whiche I have yow tolde,
That shone with fethres as of golde,
Which that so hyghe gan to sore,
I gan beholde more and more,
To se her beaute and the wonder.   5
But never was ther dynt of thonder,
Ne that thyng that men calle foudre—
That smyte somtyme a tour to poudre,
And in his swifte comynge brende,—
That so swithe gan descende   10
As this foule, whan hyt behelde
That I a-roume was in the felde;
And with hys grym pawes stronge,
Withyn hys sharpe nayles longe,
Me, fleynge, at a swappe he hente,   15
And with hys sours agayn up wente,

Me caryinge in his clawes starke
As lyghtly as I were a larke:
How high, I can not telle yow,
For I came up I nyste how;   20
For so astonyed and a-sweved
Was every vertu in my heved,
What with his sours and with my drede,
That al my felynge gan to dede,
For-why hit was to grete affray.   25
    Thus I longe in hys clawes lay,
Til at the laste he to me spake
In mannes vois, and seyde, "Awake!
And be not so a-gast, for shame!"
And called me tho by my name.   30
And, for I shulde the bet abreyde
(Me mette), "Awake!" to me he seyde
Ryght in the same vois and stevene
That useth oon I coude nevene.
And with that vois, soth for to seyne,   35
My mynde came to me ageyne;
For hyt was goodely seyde to me,
So was hyt never wonte to be.
    And herewithal I gan to stere,
And he me in his feet to bere,   40
Til that he felt that I had hete,
And felte eke that my herte bete.
And tho gan he me to disporte,
And with wordes to comforte,
And seyde twyes, "Seynte Mary!   45
Thou arte noyouse for to cary!
And nothynge nedeth hit, pardee:
For al-so wis God helpe me
As thou noon harme shalt have of this;
And this cas, that betydde the is,   50
Is for thy lore and for thy prowe.
Let see! darst thou yet loke nowe?
Be ful assured, boldely,
I am thy frende." And therwith I
Gan for to wondren in my mynde.   55
"O God," thought I, "That madeste kynde,
Shal I noon other weyes dye?

Wher Joves wol me stellefye,
Or what thinge may this sygnifye?
I neyther am Ennok, ne Elye,   60
Ne Romulus, ne Ganymede—
That was y-bore up, as men rede,
To hevene with daun Jupiter,
And made the goddys botiler."
  Lo, this was tho my fantasye!   65
But he that bar me gan espye
That I so thoghte, and seyde this:
"Thou demest of thyselfe amis;
For Joves ys not theraboute—
I dar wel put the out of doute—   70
To make of the as yet a sterre.
But er I bere the moche ferre,
I wol the telle what I am,
And whider thou shalt, and why I cam
To do thys, so that thou take   75
Goode herte and not for fere quake."
"Gladly," quod I. "Now wel," quod he:
"First I, that in my fete have the,
Of which thou haste a fere and wonder,
Am dwellynge with the god of thonder,   80
Whiche that men callen Jupiter,
That doth me flee ful ofte fer
To do al hys comaundement.
And for this cause he hath me sent
To the: now herke, be thy trouthe!   85
Certeyn, he hath of the routhe
That thou so longe trewely
Hys blynde nevew Cupido,
Hast served so ententyfly
And fair Venus [goddesse] also,   90
Withoute guerdoun ever yit;
And never the lesse hast set thy witte—
Although that in thy hede ful lyte is—
To make bookes, songes, dytees,
In ryme, or elles in cadence,   95
As thou best canst, in reverence
Of Love and of hys servantes eke,
That have hys servyse soght, and seke;

And peynest the to preyse hys art,
Althogh thou haddest never parte: 100
Wherfore, al-so God me blesse,
Joves halt hyt grete humblesse
And vertu eke, that thou wolt make,
A-nyghte, ful ofte thyn hede to ake,
In thy studye so thou writest,   105
And ever-mo of love enditest,
In honour of hym and in preysynges,
And in his folkes furtherynges,
And in hir matere al devisest,
And noght hym nor his folk despisest,   110
Although thou maist go in the daunce
Of hem that hym lyst not avaunce.
Wherfore, as I seyde, y-wis,
Jupiter considereth this,
And also, beau sir, other thynges: 115
That is, that thou hast no tydynges
Of Loves folke, yf they be glade,
Ne of noght elles that God made;
And noght only fro fer contree
That ther no tydynge cometh to thee,   120
But of thy verray neygheboris,
That dwellen almost at thy doris,
Thou herest neyther that ne this;
For when thy labour doon al ys,
And hast made al thy rekenynges,   125
In stede of reste and newe thynges,
Thou gost home to thy house anoon,
And, al so dombe as any stoon,
Thou sittest at another booke,
Tyl fully dasewed ys thy looke,   130
And lyvest thus as an heremyte,
Although thyn abstynence ys lyte.
And therfore Joves, thorgh hys grace,
Wol that I bere the to a place,
Whyche that hight the House of Fame,   135
To do the som disport and game.
In som recompensacioun
Of labour and devocioun
That thou hast had, lo! causeles,

To Cupido, the recheles!"   140

.   .   .   .

    And with this word, sothe for to seyne,
He gan alway upper to sore,
And gladded me ay more and more,
So feythfully to me spake he.
Tho gan I to loken under me,   145
And behelde the ayerishe bestes,
Cloudes, mystes, and tempestes,
Snowes, hayles, reynes, wyndes,
And thengendrynge in hir kyndes,
Al the wey thrugh whiche I came.   150
"O God," quod I, "That made Adame,
Moche ys Thy myght and Thy noblesse!"
And tho thought I upon Boesse,
That writ, "A thought may flee so hye,
Wyth fetheres of Philosophye,   155
To passen everyche element;
And whan he hath so fer y-went,
Than may be seen, behynde hys bak,
Cloude and al that I of spak."
Tho gan I wexen in a were,   160
And seyde, "I wote wel I am here,
But wher in body or in gost
I noot, y-wys; but, God, Thou wost!"
For more clere entendement
Nadde He me never yet sent.   165
And than thought I on Marcyan,
And eke on Anteclaudian,
That sooth was her descripsioun
Of alle the hevens regioun,
As fer as that I sey the preve;   170
Therfore I can hem now beleve.
    With that this egle gan to crye:
"Lat be," quod he, "thy fantasye!
Wilt thou lere of sterres aught?"
"Nay, certenly," quod I, "ryght naught;   175
And why? for I am now to olde."
"Elles I wolde thee have tolde,"
Quod he, "the sterres names, lo,
And al the hevens sygnes therto,

And which they ben." "No fors," quod I.　　180
"Yis, parde," quod he; "wostow why?
For when thou redest poetrye,
How goddes gonne stellifye
Bryddis, fishe, beste, or him or hyr,
As the Ravene, or eyther Bere,　　185
Or Arionis harpe fyne,
Castor, Polux, or Delphyne,
Or Athalantes doughtres sevene,
How alle these arn set in hevene;
For though thou have hem ofte on honde,　　190
Yet nostow not wher that they stonde."
"No fors," quod I, "hyt is no nede:
I leve as wel, so God me spede,
Hem that write of this matere
As though I knew her places here;　　195
And eke they shynen here so bright,
Hyt shulde shenden al my syght
To loke on hem." "That may wel be,"
Quod he. And so forthe bare he me
A while; and than he gan to crye,　　200
That never herd I thing so hye,
"Now up the hede; for alle ys well;
Seynt Julyane, lo, bon hostell!
Se here the House of Fame, lo!
Maistow not heren that I do?"　　205
"What?" quod I. "The grete soun,"
Quod he, "that rumbleth up and doun
In Fames House, ful of tydynges,
Bothe of feire speche and chidynges,
And of fals and soth compouned.　　210
Herkne wel; hyt is not rouned.
Herestow not the grete swogh?"
"Yis, parde," quod I, "wel ynogh."
"And what soune is it lyke?" quod hee.
"Peter! lyke betynge of the see,"　　215
Quod I, "ayen the roches holowe,
Whan tempest doth the shippes swalowe—
And lat a man stonde, out of doute,
A myle thens and here hyt route;
Or elles lyke the last humblynge　　220

After a clappe of oo thundrynge,
Whan Joves hath the aire y-bete.
But yt doth me for fere swete."
"Nay, dred the not therof," quod he,
"Hyt is nothinge will beten the;　　　　225
Thow shalt non harme have, trewely."
And with this worde both he and I
As nygh the place arryved were
As men may casten with a spere.
I nyste how, but in a strete　　　　230
He sette me faire on my fete,
And seyde, "Walke forth a pace,
And take thyn aventure or case
That thou shalt fynde in Fames place."

   .   .   .   .   .   .

   Whan I was fro thys egle goon,　　　　235
I gan beholde upon this place.
And certein, or I ferther pace,
I wol yow al the shap devyse
Of hous and citee, and al the wyse
How I gan to this place aproche,　　　　240
That stood upon so hygh a roche
Hier stant ther non in Spayne.
But up I clombe with alle payne:
And though to clymbe yt greved me,
Yit I ententyf was to see,　　　　245
And for to pouren wonder low,
If I coude any weyes know
What maner stoon this roche was;
For hyt was lyke a thynge of glas
But that hyt shoon ful more clere;　　　　250
But of what congeled matere
Hyt was, I nyste redely.
   But at the laste espied I,
And founde that hyt was, every dele,
A roche of yse and not of stele.　　　　255
Thought I, "By Seynt Thomas of Kent,
This were a feble fundament
To bilden on a place hye!
He oughte him lytel glorifye
That her-on bilt, God so me save!"　　　　260

Tho sawgh I the halfe y-grave
With famouse folkes names fele,
That had y-ben in mochel wele,
And her fames wide y-blowe.
But wel unnethes coude I knowe   265
Any lettres for to rede
Her names by; for, out of drede,
They were almost of-thowed so
That of the lettres oon or two
Were molte away of every name,   270
So unfamouse was wox hir fame:
But men seyn, "What may ever last?"
Tho gan I in myn herte cast
That they were molte awey with hete,
And not awey with stormes bete;   275
For on that other syde I sey
Of this hille, that northewarde lay,
How hit was writen ful of names
Of folkes that hadden grete fames
Of olde tymes, and yet they were   280
As fresh as men had writen hem here
The selfe day ryght, or that houre
That I upon hem gan to poure.
But wel I wiste what yt made;
Hyt was conserved with the shade.   285
Alle this writynge that I sigh,
Of a castel stoode on high;
And stoode eke on so colde a place
That hete myght hit not deface.

Tho gan I up the hille to gon,   290
And fonde upon the cop a wone,
That al the men that ben on lyve
Ne han the cunnynge to descrive
The beaute of that ylke place,
Ne coude casten no compace   295
Swich another for to make
That myght of beaute ben hys make,
Ne so wonderlych y-wrought;
That hit astonyeth yit my thought,
And maketh alle my wyt to swynke   300
On this castel to bethynke;

So that the grete beaute,
The cast, the curiosite,
Ne can I not to yow devyse—
My wit ne may me not suffise.   305
But natheles alle the substance
I have yit in my remembrance;
For-whi me thoughte, by Seynt Gyle,
Alle was of stone of beryle,
Both the castel and the toure,   310
And eke the halle, and every boure,
Wythouten peces or joynynges.
But many subtile compassinges,
Babewynnes and pynacles,
Ymageries and tabernacles,   315
I say; and ful eke of wyndowes
As flakes falle in grete snowes.
And eke in ech of the pynacles
Weren sondry habitacles,
In which stoden, alle withoute   320
(Ful the castel, alle aboute),
Of alle maner of mynstrales
And gestiours, that tellen tales,
Both of wepinge and of game,
Of alle that longeth unto Fame.   325

.   .   .   .   .   .

But in this lusty and ryche place,
That Fames Halle called was,
Ful moche prees of folke ther nas,
Ne crowdyng, for to mochil prees.
But al on hye, above a dees,   330
Sit in a see imperiall
That made was of a rubee all,
Which that a carbuncle ys y-called,
I saugh, perpetually y-stalled,
A femynyne creature,   335
That never formed by Nature
Nas swich another thing y-seye:
For altherfirst, soth for to seye,
Me thoughte that she was so lyte
That the lengthe of a cubite   340
Was lengere than she semed be;

But thus sone, in a whyle, she
Hir tho so wonderliche streight
That with hir fete she erthe reight,
And with hir heed she touched hevene,   345
Ther as shynen sterres sevene.
And therto eke, as to my witte,
I saugh a gretter wonder yitte,
Upon her eyen to beholde;
But certeyn I hem never tolde: 350
For as fele yen had she
As fetheres upon foules be,
Or weren on the bestes foure
That Goddis trone gunne honoure,
As John writ in thapocalips.   355
Hir heere, that oundy was and crips,
As burned gold hyt shoon to see;
And, sothe to tellen, also she
Had also fele up-stondyng eres
And tonges, as on bestes heres;   360
And on hir fete wexen, saugh I,
Partriches wynges redely.
But, Lorde! the perrie and the richesse
I saugh sittyng on this goddesse!
And, Lord! the hevenysh melodye   365
Of songes, ful of armonye,
I herde aboute her trone y-songe,
That al the paleys-walles ronge!
So song the myghty Muse, she
That cleped ys Caliope,   370
And hir eighte sustren eke,
That in her face semen meke.
And evermo, eternally,
They songe of Fame, as tho herd I:
"Heryed be thou and thy name,   375
Goddesse of rcnoun or of fame!"
Tho was I war, lo, atte laste,
As I myn eyen gan up caste,
That thys ylke noble quene
On her shuldres gan sustene   380
Bothe the armes and the name
Of tho that hadde large fame:

Alexander, and Hercules
That with a sherte hys lyf lees!
Thus fonde I syttinge this goddesse,   38₅
In nobley, honour, and richesse;
Of which I stynte a whyle nowe,
Other thinge to tellen yowe.

1383?–84?

THE LEGEND OF GOOD WOMEN

FROM

THE PROLOGUE

A thousand tymes have I herd men telle
That ther is joye in heven and peyne in helle,
And I acorde wel that hit is so;
But, natheles, yit wot I wel also
That ther nis noon dwellyng in this contree   5
That eyther hath in hevene or helle y-be,
Ne may of hit noon other weyes witen
But as he hath herd seyd or founde it writen,
For by assay ther may no man it preve.
But God forbede but men shulde leve   10
Wel more thing then men han seen with eye!
Men shal nat wenen every thing a lye
But yf himself yt seeth or elles dooth;
For, God wot, thing is never the lasse sooth
Thogh every wight ne may it nat y-see.   15
Bernarde the monke ne saugh nat all, pardee!
   Than mote we to bokes that we fynde,
Thurgh which that olde thinges ben in mynde,
And to the doctrine of these olde wyse,
Yeve credence, in every skylful wise,   20
That tellen of these olde appreved stories,
Of holynesse, of regnes, of victories,
Of love, of hate, of other sondry thynges,
Of whiche I may not maken rehersynges.
And yf that olde bokes were a-wey,   25
Y-lorne were of remembraunce the key;
Wel oghte us, thanne, honouren and beleve
These bokes, there we han noon other preve.

And as for me, though that I conne but lyte,
On bokes for to rede I me delyte,   30
And to hem yive I feyth and ful credence,
And in myn herte have hem in reverence
So hertely that ther is game noon
That fro my bokes maketh me to goon,
But yt be seldom, on the holyday;   35
Save, certeynly, whan that the month of May
Is comen, and that I here the foules synge,
And that the floures gynnen for to sprynge,
Farewel my boke and my devocioun!

Now have I than suche a condicioun   40
That, of alle the floures in the mede,
Thanne love I most thise floures white and rede,
Suche as men callen daysyes in our toun.
To hem have I so grete affeccioun,
As I seyde erst, whanne comen is the May,   45
That in my bed ther daweth me no day
That I nam up, and walkyng in the mede
To seen this floure aye in the sonne sprede,
Whan hit uprysith erly by the morwe.
That blisful sighte softneth al my sorwe,   50
So glad am I whan that I have presence
Of it, to doon al maner reverence,
As she, that is of alle floures flour,
Fulfilled of al vertue and honour,
And ever y-lyke faire and fresh of hewe;   55
And I love it, and ever y-like newe,
And evere shal, til that myn herte dye:
Al swere I nat, of this I wol nat lye,
Ther loved no wight hotter in his lyve.

And whan that hit is eve, I renne blyve,   60
As sone as evere the sonne gynneth weste,
To seen this flour, how it wol go to reste
For fere of nyght, so hateth she derknesse!
Hir chere is pleynly sprad in the brightnesse
Of the sonne, for ther yt wol unclose.   65
Allas! that I ne had Englysh, ryme or prose,
Suffisant this flour to preyse aryght!
But helpeth, ye that han connyng and myght,
Ye lovers, that can make of sentement:

In this case oghte ye to be diligent　　　　　70
To forthren me somewhat in my labour,
Whethir ye ben with the leef or with the flour;
For wel I wot that ye han here-biforne
Of makynge ropen, and lad awey the corne,
And I come after, glenyng here and there,　　　75
And am ful glad yf I may fynde an ere
Of any goodly word that ye han left.
And thogh it happen me rehercen eft
That ye han in your freshe songes sayede,
For-bereth me, and beth nat evele apayede,　　　80
Syn that ye see I do yt in the honour
Of love, and eke in service of the flour
Whom that I serve as I have witte or myght.
She is the clerenesse and the verray lyght,
That in this derke worlde me wynt and ledyth.　　　85
The hert in-with my sorweful brest yow dredith,
And loveth so sore that ye ben verrayly
The maistresse of my witte, and nothing I.
My worde, my werke, ys knyt so in youre bonde
That, as an harpe obeieth to the honde　　　90
And maketh it soune after his fyngerynge,
Ryght so mowe ye oute of myn herte bringe
Swich vois, ryght as yow lyst, to laughe or pleyne.
Be ye my gide and lady sovereyne!
As to myn erthely god, to yowe I calle,　　　95
Bothe in this werke and in my sorwes alle.

　　But wherfore that I spake, to yive credence
To olde stories and doon hem reverence,
And that men mosten more thyng beleve
Than men may seen at eigh or ellis preve?　　　100
That shal I seyn whanne that I see my tyme;
I may not al atones speke in ryme.

　　My besy gost, that thursteth alwey newe
To seen this flour so yong, so fresh of hewe,
Constreyned me with so gledy desire　　　105
That in myn herte I feele yet the fire
That made me to ryse er yt wer day—
And thys was now the firste morwe of May—
With dredful herte and glad devocioun
For to ben at the resureccioun　　　110

Of this flour, whan that it shuld unclose
Agayne the sonne, that roos as rede as rose
That in the brest was of the beste that day,
That Agenores doghtre ladde away.
And downe on knees anon-right I me sette,   115
And, as I coude, this freshe flour I grette,
Knelyng alwey, til it unclosed was,
Upon the smale softe swote gras,
That was with floures swote enbrouded al,
Of swich swetnesse and swich odour overal   120
That, for to speke of gomme or herbe or tree,
Comparisoun may noon y-maked bee;
For yt surmounteth pleynly alle odoures,
And eke of riche beautee alle floures.

    Forgeten had the Erthe his pore estat   125
Of Wyntir, that hym naked made and mat,
And with his swerd of colde so sore greved:
Now hath thatempre sonne all that releved
That naked was, and clad yt new agayn.
The smale foules, of the seson fayn,   130
That from the panter and the nette ben scaped,
Upon the foweler, that hem made a-whaped
In wynter, and distroyed hadde hire broode,
In his dispite hem thoughte yt did hem goode
To synge of hym, and in hir songe dispise   135
The foule cherle that, for his covetyse,
Had hem betrayed with his sophistrye.
This was hire song: "The foweler we defye,
And al his crafte!" And somme songen clere
Layes of love, that joye it was to here,   140
In worshipynge and preysinge of hir make.
And, for the newe blisful somers sake,
Upon the braunches ful of blosmes softe,
In hire delyt, they turned hem ful ofte,
And songen, "Blessed be Seynt Valentyne!   145
For on his day I chees yow to be myne,
Withouten repentyng, myn herte swete!"
And therwith-alle hire bekes gonnen mete,
Yeldyng honour and humble obeysaunces
To love; and diden hire othere observaunces   150
That longeth unto love and to nature—

Construeth that as yow lyst, I do no cure.
And tho that hadde doon unkyndenesse—
As dooth the tydif, for new-fangelnesse—
Besoghte mercy of hir trespassynge,   155
And humblely songen hire repentynge,
And sworen on the blosmes to be trewe,
So that hire makes wolde upon hem rewe;
And at the laste maden hire acord.
Al founde they Daunger for a tyme a lord,   160
Yet Pitee, thurgh his stronge gentil myght,
Forgaf, and made Mercy passen Ryght,
Thurgh innocence and ruled curtesye.
But I ne clepe nat innocence folye,
Ne fals pitee; for "vertue is the mene,"   165
As Ethik seith, in swich maner I mene.
And thus thise foweles, voide of al malice,
Acordeden to love, and laften vice
Of hate, and songen alle of oon acorde,
"Welcome, Somer, oure governour and lorde!"   170
        And Zepherus and Flora gentilly
Yaf to the floures, softe and tenderly,
Hire swoote breth, and made hem for to sprede,
As god and goddesse of the floury mede;
In whiche me thoght that I myght, day by day,   175
Dwellen alwey, the joly month of May,
Withouten slepe, withouten mete or drynke.
A-doune ful softely I gan to synke;
And, lenynge on myn elbowe and my syde,
The longe day I shoope me for tabide,   180
For nothing ellis (and I shal nat lye)
But for to loke upon the dayesye,
That men by reson wel hit calle may
The "dayesye"—or elles the "ye of day,"—
The emperice and floure of floures alle.   185
I pray to God that faire mote she falle!
And alle that loven floures, for hire sake!
But natheles, ne wene nat that I make
In preysing of the flour agayn the leef,
No more than of the corn agayn the sheef;   190
For, as to me, nys lever noon ne lother:
I nam with-holden yit with never nother.

Ne I not who serveth leef, ne who the flour;
Wel brouken they her service or labour;
For this thing is al of another tonne,   195
Of olde storye, er swiche thinge was begonne.
    Whan that the sonne out of the south gan west,
And that this floure gan close and goon to rest,
For derknesse of the nyght, the which she dred,
Home to myn house ful swiftly I me sped   200
To goon to reste, and erly for to ryse
To seen this flour to sprede, as I devyse.

1385?

FROM

THE CANTERBURY TALES

THE PROLOGUE

Whan that Aprille with his shoures soote
The drought of March hath perced to the roote,
And bathed every veyne in swich licour,
Of which vertu engendred is the flour;
Whan Zephirus eek with his swete breeth   5
Inspired hath in every holt and heeth
The tendre croppes, and the yonge sonne
Hath in the Ram his halfe cours y-ronne,
And smale fowles maken melodye,
That slepen al the nyght with open eye,   10
So priketh hem nature in hir corages:
Than longen folk to goon on pilgrymages,
And palmers for to seken straunge strondes,
To ferne halwes couthe in sondry londes;
And specially, from every shires ende   15
Of Engelond, to Caunterbury they wende,
The holy blisful martir for to seke,
That hem hath holpen whan that they were seeke.
    Bifel that in that sesoun on a day,
In Southwerk at the Tabard as I lay   20
Redy to wenden on my pilgrymage
To Caunterbury with ful devout corage,
At nyght were come into that hostelrye
Wel nyne and twenty in a compaignye,

Of sondry folk, by aventure y-falle   25
In felaweshipe, and pilgrimes were they alle,
That toward Caunterbury wolden ryde.
The chambres and the stables weren wyde,
And wel we weren esed atte beste.
And shortly, whan the sonne was to reste,   30
So hadde I spoken with hem everychon
That I was of hir felaweshipe anon,
And made forward erly for to ryse,
To take our wey ther as I yow devyse.

    But natheles, whil I have tyme and space,   35
Er that I ferther in this tale pace,
Me thynketh it acordaunt to resoun
To telle yow al the condicioun
Of ech of hem, so as it semed me,
And whiche they weren and of what degree,   40
And eek in what array that they were inne:
And at a knyght, than, wol I first bigynne.

    A Knyght ther was, and that a worthy man,
That fro the tyme that he first bigan
To riden out, he loved chivalrye,   45
Trouthe and honour, fredom and curteisye.
Ful worthy was he in his lordes werre,
And thereto hadde he riden, no man ferre,
As wel in cristendom as in hethenesse,
And ever honoured for his worthynesse.   50
At Alisaundre he was, whan it was wonne.
Ful ofte tyme he hadde the bord bigonne
Aboven alle naciouns in Pruce.
In Lettow hadde he reysed and in Ruce;
No Cristen man so ofte of his degree.   55
In Gernade at the seege eek hadde he be
Of Algezir, and riden in Belmarye.
At Lyeys was he, and at Satalye,
Whan they were wonne; and in the Grete See
At many a noble armee hadde he be.   60
At mortal batailles hadde he been fiftene,
And foughten for our feith at Tramyssene
In lystes thries and ay slayn his foo.
This ilke worthy knyght hadde been also
Somtyme with the lord of Palatye,   65

Agayn another hethen in Turkye.
And evermore he hadde a sovereyn prys.
And though that he were worthy, he was **wys,**
And of his port as meek as is a mayde.
He never yet no vileinye ne sayde   70
In al his lyf, unto no maner wight.
He was a verray parfit gentil knyght.
But for to tellen yow of his array,
His hors were goode, but he was nat **gay;**
Of fustian he wered a gipoun   75
Al bismotered with his habergeoun,
For he was late y-come from his viage,
And wente for to doon his pilgrymage.
    With hym ther was his sone, a yong Squyer,
A lovyer and a lusty bacheler,   80
With lokkes crulle as they were leyd in presse.
Of twenty yeer of age he was, I gesse.
Of his stature he was of evene lengthe,
And wonderly deliver, and greet of strengthe.
And he hadde been somtyme in chivachye,   85
In Flaundres, in Artoys, and Picardye,
And born hym wel, as of so litel space,
In hope to stonden in his lady grace.
Embrouded was he, as it were a mede
Al ful of fresshe floures, white and rede.   90
Syngyng he was, or floytyng, al the day.
He was as fresh as is the month of May.
Short was his gowne, with sleves longe and **wyde.**
Wel coude he sitte on hors and faire ryde.
He coude songes make and wel endite,   95
Juste and eek daunce, and wel purtreye and write.
So hote he lovede that by nyghtertale
He slepte no more than doth a nyghtyngale.
Curteys he was, lowly, and servisable,
And carf biforn his fader at the table.   100
    A Yeman hadde he, and servaunts namo
At that tyme, for hym liste ride so.
And he was clad in cote and hood of grene;
A sheef of pecok arwes brighte and kene
Under his belt he bar ful thriftily—   105
Wel coude he dresse his takel yemanly;

His arwes drouped noght with fetheres lowe,—
And in his hand he bar a myghty bowe.
A not-heed hadde he, with a broun visage.
Of wode-craft wel coude he al the usage.   110
Upon his arm he bar a gay bracer,
And by his syde a swerd and a bokeler,
And on that other syde a gay daggere,
Harneised wel, and sharp as poynt of spere;
A Cristofre on his brest of silver shene.   115
An horn he bar; the bawdrik was of grene:
A forster was he, soothly, as I gesse.

    Ther was also a Nonne, a Prioresse,
That of hir smylyng was ful symple and coy;
Hir gretteste ooth was but by Seinte Loy;   120
And she was cleped Madame Eglentyne.
Ful wel she song the service dyvyne,
Entuned in hir nose ful semely;
And Frensh she spak ful faire and fetisly,
After the scole of Stratford-atte-Bowe,   125
For Frensh of Parys was to hir unknowe.
At mete wel y-taught was she withalle:
She leet no morsel from hir lippes falle,
Ne wette hir fyngres in hir sauce depe;
Wel coude she carie a morsel, and wel kepe   130
That no drope ne fel upon hir brest.
In curteisye was set ful moche hir lest.
Hir over-lippe wyped she so clene
That in hir coppe ther was no ferthyng sene
Of grece whan she dronken hadde hir draughte;   135
Ful semely after hir mete she raughte.
And sikerly she was of greet disport,
And ful plesaunt, and amyable of port;
And peyned hir to countrefete chere
Of court, and been estatlich of manere,   140
And to ben holden digne of reverence.
But for to speken of hir conscience,
She was so charitable and so pitous
She wolde wepe if that she sawe a mous
Caught in a trappe, if it were deed or bledde.   145
Of smale houndes hadde she, that she fedde
With rosted flesh, or milk and wastel breed.

But sore wepte she if oon of hem were deed,
Or if men smoot it with a yerde smerte:
And al was conscience and tendre herte. 150
Ful semely hir wimpel pynched was;
Hir nose tretys; hir eyen greye as glas;
Hir mouth ful smal, and therto softe and reed;
But sikerly she hadde a fair forheed—
It was almost a spanne brood, I trowe, 155
For, hardily, she was nat undergrowe.
Ful fetys was hir cloke, as I was war.
Of smal coral aboute hir arm she bar
A peire of bedes, gauded al with grene;
And theron heng a brooch of gold ful shene, 160
On which ther was first write a crowned "A,"
And after, "Amor vincit omnia."
    Another nonne with hir hadde she,
That was hir chapeleyne, and preestes thre.
    A Monk ther was, a fair for the maistrye, 165
An outridere, that lovede venerye;
A manly man, to been an abbot able.
Ful many a deyntee hors hadde he in stable;
And whan he rood, men myghte his brydel here
Gynglen in a whistlyng wynd as clere 170
And eek as loude as doth the chapel belle.
Ther as this lord was keper of the celle,
The reule of Seint Maure or of Seint Beneit,
By cause that it was old and som-del streit,
This ilke monk leet olde thynges pace, 175
And held after the newe world the space.
He yaf nat of that text a pulled hen,
That seith that hunters been nat holy men;
Ne that a monk, whan he is rechelees,
Is likned til a fish that is waterlees 180
(This is to seyn, a monk out of his cloystre)—
But thilke text held he nat worth an oystre.
And I seyde his opinioun was good:
What! sholde he studie, and make hymselven wood,
Upon a book in cloystre alwey to poure, 185
Or swynken with his handes and laboure,
As Austyn bit? How shal the world be served?
Lat Austyn have his swynk to hym reserved.

Therfore he was a pricasour aright;
Grehoundes he hadde, as swift as fowel in flight: 190
Of prikyng and of huntyng for the hare
Was al his lust; for no cost wolde he spare.
I seigh his sleves purfiled at the hond
With grys, and that the fyneste of a lond;
And for to festne his hood under his chyn   195
He hadde of gold wroght a ful curious pyn—
A love-knot in the gretter ende ther was.
His heed was balled, that shoon as any glas,
And eek his face, as he hadde been anoynt.
He was a lord ful fat and in good poynt;   200
His eyen stepe, and rollynge in his heed,
That stemed as a forneys of a leed;
His bootes souple, his hors in greet estat.
Now certeinly he was a fair prelat;
He was nat pale as a forpyned goost.   205
A fat swan loved he best of any roost.
His palfrey was as broun as is a berye.
      A Frere ther was, a wantoun and a merye;
A lymytour, a ful solempne man.
In alle the ordres foure is noon that can   210
So muche of daliaunce and fair langage.
He hadde maad ful many a mariage
Of yonge wommen, at his owne cost.
Unto his ordre he was a noble post.
Ful wel biloved and famulier was he   215
With frankeleyns overal in his contree,
And eek with worthy wommen of the toun;
For he hadde power of confessioun,
As seyde hymself, more than a curat,
For of his ordre he was licentiat.   220
Ful swetely herde he confessioun,
And plesaunt was his absolucioun.
He was an esy man to yeve penaunce
Ther as he wiste to have a good pitaunce:
For unto a povre ordre for to yive   225
Is signe that a man is wel y-shrive;
For if he yaf, he dorste make avaunt
He wiste that a man was repentaunt,
For many a man so hard is of his herte

He may nat wepe althogh hym sore smerte; 230
Therfore, in stede of wepyng and preyeres,
Men moote yeve silver to the povre freres.
His tipet was ay farsed ful of knyves
And pynnes, for to yeven faire wyves.
And certeinly he hadde a merye note; 235
Wel coude he synge and pleyen on a rote.
Of yeddynges he bar outrely the pris:
His nekke whit was as the flour-de-lys;
Therto he strong was as a champioun.
He knew the tavernes wel in every toun, 240
And everich hostiler and tappestere
Bet than a lazar or a beggestere;
For unto swich a worthy man as he
Acorded nat, as by his facultee,
To have with seke lazars aqueyntaunce: 245
It is nat honest, it may nat avaunce,
For to deelen with no swich poraille,
But al with riche and sellers of vitaille.
And overal, ther as profit sholde arise,
Curteis he was and lowly of servyse. 250
Ther nas no man nowher so vertuous.
He was the beste beggere in his hous,
For thogh a wydwe hadde noght a sho,
So plesaunt was his "In principio"
Yet wolde he have a ferthyng er he wente. 255
His purchas was wel bettre than his rente.
And rage he coude as it were right a whelpe.
In love-dayes ther coude he muchel helpe;
For there he was nat lyk a cloysterer,
With a thredbare cope, as is a povre scoler, 260
But he was lyk a maister or a pope.
Of double worsted was his semy-cope,
That rounded as a belle out of the presse.
Somwhat he lipsed, for his wantounesse,
To make his English sweete upon his tonge; 265
And in his harpyng, whan that he hadde songe,
His eyen twynkled in his heed aryght,
As doon the sterres in the frosty nyght.
This worthy lymytour was cleped Huberd.
    A Marchant was ther, with a forked berd, 270

In mottelee; and hye on horse he sat,
Upon his heed a Flaundrissh bever hat;
His bootes clasped faire and fetisly.
His resouns he spak ful solempnely,
Sownynge alway thencrees of his wynnyng.   275
He wolde the see were kept for any thyng
Bitwixe Middelburgh and Orewelle.
Wel coude he in eschaunge sheeldes selle.
This worthy man ful wel his wit bisette:
Ther wiste no wight that he was in dette,   280
So estatly was he of his governaunce,
With his bargaynes and with his chevisaunce.
For sothe he was a worthy man withalle;
But, sooth to seyn, I noot how men him calle.

A Clerk ther was of Oxenford also,   285
That unto logyk hadde long y-go.
As leene was his hors as is a rake;
And he nas nat right fat, I undertake,
But looked holwe and thereto soberly.
Ful thredbar was his overest courtepy,   290
For he hadde geten hym yet no benefice,
Ne was so worldly for to have office;
For hym was levere have at his beddes heed
Twenty bookes, clad in blak or reed,
Of Aristotle and his philosophye,   295
Than robes riche or fithele or gay sautrye.
But al be that he was a philosophre,
Yet hadde he but litel gold in cofre;
But al that he myght of his freendes hente
On bookes and on lernynge he it spente,   300
And bisily gan for the soules preye
Of hem that yaf hym wherwith to scoleye.
Of studie took he most cure and most heede.
Noght o word spak he more than was needе,
And that was seyd in forme and reverence,   305
And short and quyk, and ful of hy sentence.
Sownynge in moral vertu was his speche;
And gladly wolde he lerne and gladly teche.

A Sergeant of the Lawe, war and wys,
That often hadde been at the parvys,   310
Ther was also, ful riche of excellence.

Discreet he was, and of greet reverence;
He semed swich, his wordes weren so wise.
Justice he was ful often in assise,
By patente and by pleyn commissioun: 315
For his science and for his heigh renoun,
Of fees and robes hadde he many oon.
So greet a purchasour was nowher noon;
Al was fee symple to hym in effect;
His purchasyng myghte nat been infect.   320
Nowher so bisy a man as he ther nas,
And yet he semed bisier than he was.
In termes hadde he caas and doomes alle
That from the tyme of Kyng William were falle.
Therto he coude endite, and make a thyng;   325
Ther coude no wight pynche at his writyng;
And every statut coude he pleyn by rote.
He rood but hoomly in a medlee cote
Girt with a ceint of silk, with barres smale;
Of his array telle I no lenger tale.   330
   A Frankeleyn was in his compaignye.
Whyt was his berd as is a dayesye;
Of his complexioun he was sangwyn.
Wel loved he by the morwe a soppe in wyn:
To lyven in delit was ever his wone;   335
For he was Epicurus' owne sone,
That heeld opinioun that pleyn delit
Was verraily felicitee parfit.
An housholdere, and that a greet, was he;
Seint Julian he was in his contree.   340
His breed, his ale, was alweys after oon;
A bettre envyned man was nevere noon.
Withouten bake mete was nevere his hous,
Of fish and flesh, and that so plentevous
It snewed in his hous of mete and drynke,   345
Of alle deyntees that men coude thynke.
After the sondry sesons of the yeer,
So chaunged he his mete and his soper.
Ful many a fat partrich hadde he in mewe,
And many a breem and many a luce in stewe.   350
Wo was his cook but if his sauce were
Poynaunt and sharpe, and redy al his geere.

His table dormant in his halle alway
Stood redy covered al the longe day.
At sessiouns ther was he lord and sire.   355
Ful ofte tyme he was knyght of the shire.
An anlas and a gipser al of silk
Heng at his girdel, whit as morne milk.
A shirreve hadde he been, and a countour.
Was nowher such a worthy vavasour.   360

    An Haberdasshere and a Carpenter,
A Webbe, a Dyere, and a Tapycer;
And they were clothed alle in o lyveree
Of a solempne and greet fraternitee.
Ful fresh and newe hir geere apiked was;   365
Hir knyves were chaped noght with bras,
But al with silver wrought ful clene and weel,
Hir girdles and hir pouches everydeel.
Wel semed ech of hem a fair burgeys,
To sitten in a yeldehalle on a deys.   370
Everich, for the wisdom that he can,
Was shaply for to been an alderman,
For catel hadde they ynogh and rente;
And eek hir wyves wolde it wel assente,
And elles certeyn were they to blame: 375
It is ful fair to been cleped *ma dame,*
And goon to vigilyes al bifore,
And have a mantel roialliche y-bore.

    A Cook they hadde with hem for the nones,
To boille the chiknes with the mary-bones,   380
And poudre-marchant tart and galyngale.
Wel coude he knowe a draughte of London ale.
He coude roste, and seethe, and broille, and frye,
Maken mortreux, and wel bake a pye.
But greet harm was it, as it thoughte me,   385
That on his shyne a mormal hadde he.
For blankmanger, that made he with the beste.

    A Shipman was ther, wonynge fer by weste:
For aught I woot, he was of Dertemouthe.
He rood upon a rouncy, as he couthe,   390
In a gowne of faldyng to the knee.
A daggere hangynge on a laas hadde he
Aboute his nekke, under his arm adoun.

The hote somer hadde maad his hewe al broun;
And certeinly he was a good felawe.   395
Ful many a draughte of wyn had he y-drawe
From Burdeux-ward, whyl that the chapman sleepe.
Of nyce conscience took he no keepe.
If that he faught, and hadde the hyer hond,
By water he sente hem hoom to every lond.   400
But of his craft to rekene wel his tydes,
His stremes and his daungers hym besides,
His herberwe and his moone, his lodemenage,
Ther nas noon swich from Hulle to Cartage.
Hardy he was, and wys to undertake;   405
With many a tempest hadde his berd been shake.
He knew alle the havenes, as they were,
Fro Gootlond to the cape of Fynystere,
And every cryke in Britaigne and in Spayne.
His barge y-cleped was the Maudelayne.   410
    With us ther was a Doctour of Phisik.
In al this world ne was ther noon hym lyk
To speke of phisik and of surgerye,
For he was grounded in astronomye:
He kepte his pacient a ful greet del   415
In houres, by his magyk naturel;
Wel coude he fortunen the ascendent
Of his images for his pacient.
He knew the cause of everich maladye,
Were it of hoot or cold or moyste or drye,   420
And where engendred and of what humour.
He was a verray parfit practisour.
The cause y-knowe, and of his harm the roote,
Anon he yaf the sike man his boote.
Ful redy hadde he his apothecaries,   425
To sende hym drogges, and his letuaries;
For ech of hem made other for to wynne:
Hir frendschipe nas nat newe to bigynne.
Wel knew he the olde Esculapius,
And Deyscorides, and eek Rufus;   430
Olde Ypocras, Haly, and Galyen;
Serapion, Razis, and Avycen;
Averrois, Damascien, and Constantyn;
Bernard, and Gatesden, and Gilbertyn.

Of his diete mesurable was he;   435
For it was of no superfluitee,
But of greet norissyng and digestible.
His studie was but litel on the Bible.
In sangwyn and in pers he clad was al,
Lyned with taffata and with sendal;   440
And yet he was but esy of dispence:
He kepte that he wan in pestilence;
For gold in phisik is a cordial,
Therfore he loved gold in special.

    A good Wyf was ther of biside Bathe;   445
But she was som-del deef, and that was scathe.
Of cloth-makyng she hadde swiche an haunt
She passed hem of Ypres and of Gaunt.
In al the parishe wyf ne was ther noon
That to the offrynge bifore hir sholde goon;   450
And if ther dide, certeyn so wrooth was she
That she was out of alle charitee.
Hir coverchiefs ful fyne were of ground;
I dorste swere they weyeden ten pound,
That on a Sonday were upon hir heed.   455
Hir hosen weren of fyn scarlet reed,
Ful streite y-teyd; and shoes ful moyste and newe.
Bold was hir face, and fair, and red of hewe.
She was a worthy womman al hir lyve:
Housbondes at chirche-dore she hadde fyve,   460
Withouten other compaignye in youthe—
But therof nedeth nat to speke as nouthe;—
And thries hadde she been at Jerusalem;
She hadde passed many a straunge strem;
At Rome she hadde been, and at Boloigne,   465
In Galice at Seint Jame, and at Coloigne:
She coude moche of wandrynge by the weye.
Gat-tothed was she, soothly for to seye.
Upon an amblere esily she sat,
Y-wympled wel, and on hir heed an hat   470
As brood as is a bokeler or a targe;
A foot-mantel aboute hir hipes large,
And on hir feet a paire of spores sharpe.
In felaweshipe wel coude she laughe and carpe.

Of remedies of love she knew perchaunce,   475
For she coude of that art the olde daunce.
   A good man was ther of religioun,
And was a povre Persoun of a toun;
But riche he was of holy thoght and werk.
He was also a lerned man, a clerk,   480
That Cristes gospel trewely wolde preche;
His parishens devoutly wolde he teche.
Benygne he was, and wonder diligent,
And in adversitee ful pacient;
And swich he was y-preved ofte sithes.   485
Ful looth were hym to cursen for his tithes,
But rather wolde he yeven, out of doute,
Unto his povre parishens aboute
Of his offryng and eek of his substaunce:
He coude in litel thyng han suffisaunce.   490
Wyd was his parishe, and houses fer asonder;
But he ne lafte nat, for reyn ne thonder,
In siknesse nor in meschief to visite
The ferreste in his parishe, moche and lite,
Upon his feet, and in his hand a staf.   495
This noble ensample to his sheep he yaf:
That first he wroghte, and afterward he taughte.
Out of the gospel he tho wordes caughte,
And this figure he added eek therto:
That if gold ruste, what shal iren do?   500
For if a preest be foul, on whom we truste,
No wonder is a lewed man to ruste;
And shame it is, if a preest take keepe,
A [filthy] shepherde and a clene sheepe;
Wel oghte a preest ensample for to yive,   505
By his clennesse, how that his sheep sholde live.
He sette nat his benefice to hyre,
And leet his sheep encombred in the myre,
And ran to London, unto Seinte Poules,
To seken hym a chaunterie for soules,   510
Or with a bretherhed to been withholde;
But dwelte at hoom, and kepte wel his folde,
So that the wolf ne made it nat myscarie:
He was a shepherde and not a mercenarie.
And though he holy were, and vertuous,   515

He was to synful man nat despitous,
Ne of his speche daungerous ne digne,
But in his techyng discreet and benygne.
To drawen folk to heven by fairnesse,
By good ensample, this was his bisynesse: 520
But it were any persone obstinat,
What so he were, of heigh or lowe estat,
Hym wolde he snybben sharply for the nonys.
A bettre preest I trowe that nowher non is.
He wayted after no pompe and reverence,   525
Ne maked him a spiced conscience;
But Cristes lore and his apostles twelve
He taughte, but first he folwed it hymselve.
    With hym ther was a Plowman, was his brother,
That hadde y-lad of dong ful many a fother.   530
A trewe swynkere and a good was he,
Lyvynge in pees and parfit charitee.
God loved he best with al his hoole herte
At alle tymes, thogh hym gamed or smerte,
And thanne his neighebour right as hymselve.   535
He wolde thresshe, and therto dyke and delve,
For Cristes sake, for every povre wight,
Withouten hyre, if it lay in his myght.
His tithes payed he ful faire and wel,
Bothe of his propre swynk and his catel.   540
In a tabard he rood upon a mere.
    Ther was also a reve and a millere,
A somnour and a pardoner also,
A maunciple, and myself; ther were namo.
    The Millere was a stout carl, for the nones: 545
Ful byg he was of brawn and eek of bones;
That proved wel, for overal ther he cam
At wrastlynge he wolde have alwey the ram.
He was short-sholdred, brood, a thikke knarre;
Ther nas no dore that he nolde heve of harre,   550
Or breke it, at a rennyng, with his heed.
His berd as any sowe or fox was reed,
And therto brood às though it were a spade.
Upon the cop right of his nose he hade
A werte; and theron stood a tuft of herys   555
Reed as the bristles of a sowes erys.

His nose-thirles blake were and wyde.
A swerd and a bokeler bar he by his syde.
His mouth as greet was as a greet forneys.
He was a janglere and a goliardeys, 560
And that was most of synne and harlotries.
Wel coude he stelen corn, and tollen thries;
And yet he hadde a thombe of gold, pardee.
A whit cote and a blew hood wered he.
A baggepipe wel coude he blowe and sowne, 565
And therwithal he broghte us out of towne.

A gentil Maunciple was ther of a temple,
Of which achatours myghte take exemple
For to be wise in byynge of vitaille;
For wheither that he payde or took by taille, 570
Algate he wayted so in his achate
That he was ay biforn and in good state:
Now is nat that of God a ful fair grace,
That swich a lewed mannes wit shal pace
The wisdom of an heepe of lerned men? 575
Of maistres hadde he mo than thries ten,
That weren of lawe expert and curious;
Of whiche ther weren a dozeyne in that hous,
Worthy to been stywardes of rente and lond
Of any lord that is in Engelond, 580
To make hym lyve by his propre good,
In honour dettelees but he were wood,
Or lyve as scarsly as hym list desire;
And able for to helpen al a shire
In any cas that myghte falle or happe: 585
And yet this manciple sette hir aller cappe.

The Reve was a sclendre colerik man.
His berd was shave as ny as ever he can;
His heer was by his erys round y-shorn;
His top was dokked, lyk a preest, biforn. 590
Ful longe were his legges, and ful lene,
Y-lyk a staf; ther was no calf y-sene.
Wel coude he kepe a gerner and a bynne;
Ther was noon auditour coude on him wynne.
Wel wiste he, by the droghte and by the reyn, 595
The yeldynge of his seed and of his greyn.
His lordes sheepe, his neet, his dayerye,

His swyn, his hors, his stoor, and his pultrye,
Was hoolly in this reves governyng,
And by his covenaunt yaf the rekenyng,　　　600
Syn that his lord was twenty yeer of age:
Ther coude no man brynge hym in arrerage.
Ther nas baillif, ne herde, ne other hyne,
That he ne knew his sleighte and his covyne;
They were adrad of hym as of the deeth.　　　605
His wonyng was ful fair upon an heeth;
With grene trees shadwed was his place.
He coude bettre than his lord purchace.
Ful riche he was astored prively;
His lord wel coude he plesen subtilly,　　　610
To yeve and lene hym of his owne good,
And have a thank, and yet a cote and hood.
In youthe he lerned hadde a good myster:
He was a wel good wrighte, a carpenter.
This reve sat upon a ful good stot,　　　615
That was al pomely grey, and highte Scot.
A long surcote of pers upon he hade,
And by his syde he bar a rusty blade.
Of Northfolk was this reve, of which I telle,
Biside a toun men clepen Baldeswelle.　　　620
Tukked he was, as is a frere, aboute,
And evere he rood the hyndreste of oure route.

　　A Somnour was ther with us in that place,
That hadde a fyr-reed cherubynnes face,
For sawcefleem he was, with eyen narwe.　　　625
As hoot he was, and lecherous, as a sparwe,
With scalled browes blake, and piled berd:
Of his visage children were aferd.
Ther nas quyk-silver, litarge, ne brimstoon,
Boras, ceruce, ne oille of tartre noon,　　　630
Ne oynement that wolde clense and byte,
That hym myghte helpen of the whelkes white,
Ne of the knobbes sittynge on his chekes.
Wel loved he garleek, oynons, and eek lekes,
And for to drynken strong wyn reed as blood:　　　635
Thanne wolde he speke, and crie as he were wood.
And whan that he wel dronken hadde the wyn,
Than wolde he speke no word but Latyn.

A fewe termes hadde he, two or thre,
That he had lerned out of som decree; 640
No wonder is—he herde it al the day,
And eek ye knowen wel how that a jay
Can clepen "Watte" as well as can the Pope.
But whoso coude in other thyng hym grope,
Thanne hadde he spent al his philosophie: 645
Ay "Questio quid juris!" wolde he crie.
He was a gentil harlot and a kynde;
A bettre felawe sholde men noght fynde:
He wolde suffre for a quart of wyn
A good felawe to have his concubyn 650
A twelf-monthe, and excuse hym atte fulle;
And prively a fynch eek coude he pulle.
And if he fond owher a good felawe,
He wolde techen hym to have non awe,
In swich cas, of the erchedeknes curs 655
But if a mannes soule were in his purs,
For in his purs he sholde y-punysshed be:
"Purs is the erchedeknes helle," seyde he.
But wel I woot he lyed right in dede:
Of cursyng oghte ech gilty man hym drede— 660
For curs wol slee right as assoillyng savith,—
And also war hym of a *significavit*.
In daunger hadde he at his owne gise
The yonge girles of the diocise,
And knew hir conseil and was al hir reed. 665
A gerland hadde he set upon his heed,
As greet as it were for an ale-stake;
A bokeler hadde he maad hym of a cake.
 With hym ther rood a gentil Pardoner
Of Rouncivale, his freend and his compeer, 670
That streight was comen fro the court of Rome.
Ful loude he song, "Com hider, love, to me."
This somnour bar to hym a stif burdoun;
Was nevere trompe of half so greet a soun.
This pardoner hadde heer as yelow as wex, 675
But smothe it heng as doth a strike of flex;
By ounces henge his lokkes that he hadde,
And therwith he his shuldres overspradde,
But thynne it lay, by colpons oon and oon:

But hood, for jolitee, wered he noon,   680
For it was trussed up in his walet:
Hym thoughte he rood al of the newe jet;
Dischevele, save his cappe he rood al bare.
Swiche glarynge eyen hadde he as an hare.
A vernycle hadde he sowed upon his cappe.   685
His walet lay biforn hym in his lappe,
Bret-ful of pardoun comen from Rome al hoot.
A voys he hadde as smal as hath a goot.
No berd hadde he, ne nevere sholde have;
As smothe it was as it were late y-shave.   690
But of his craft, fro Berwik into Ware,
Ne was ther swich another pardoner:
For in his male he hadde a pilwe-beer,
Which that, he seyde, was Our Lady veyl;   695
He seyde he hadde a gobet of the seyl
That Seint Peter hadde whan that he wente
Upon the see, til Jhesu Crist hym hente;
He hadde a croys of latoun, ful of stones,
And in a glas he hadde pigges bones.   700
But with thise relikes, whan that he fond
A povre person dwellynge upon lond,
Upon a day he gat hym more moneye
Than that the person gat in monthes tweye;
And thus, with feyned flaterye and japes,   705
He made the person and the peple his apes.
But trewely to tellen, atte laste,
He was in chirche a noble ecclesiaste:
Wel coude he rede a lessoun or a storie,
But alderbest he song an offertorie;   710
For wel he wiste, whan that song was songe
He moste preche, and wel affile his tonge
To wynne silver, as he ful wel coude;
Therefore he song so meriely and loude.

Now have I told you shortly, in a clause,   715
The staat, tharray, the nombre, and eek the cause
Why that assembled was this compaignye
In Southwerk, at this gentil hostelrye,
That highte the Tabard, faste by the Belle.
But now is tyme to yow for to telle   720
How that we baren us that ilke nyght,

Whan we were in that hostelrie alyght.
And after wol I telle of our viage,
And al the remenaunt of our pilgrimage.
    But first I pray yow, of your curteisye, 725
That ye narette it nat my vileynye
Thogh that I pleynly speke in this matere,
To telle you hir wordes and hir chere,
Ne thogh I speke hir wordes proprely.
For this ye knowen al so wel as I: 730
Who-so shal telle a tale after a man,
He moot reherce, as ny as evere he can,
Everich a word, if it be in his charge,
Al speke he never so rudeliche or large;
Or ellis he moot telle his tale untrewe, 735
Or feyne thyng, or fynde wordes newe.
He may nat spare, althogh he were his brother;
He moot as wel seye o word as another.
Crist spak Hymself ful brode in Holy Writ,
And wel ye woot no vileynye is it. 740
Eek Plato seith, whoso can hym rede,
The wordes moote be cosyn to the dede.
Also I prey yow to foryeve it me,
Al have I nat set folk in hir degree
Here in this tale, as that they sholde stonde: 745
My wit is short, ye may wel understonde.
    Greet cheere made our hoste us everichon;
And to the soper sette he us anon,
And served us with vitaille at the beste:
Strong was the wyn, and wel to drynke us leste. 750
A semely man our hoste was, withalle,
For to been a marshal in an halle:
A large man he was with eyen stepe;
A fairer burgeys was ther noon in Chepe;
Boold of his speche and wys, and wel y-taught, 755
And of manhod hym lakkede right naught.
Eek therto he was right a mery man;
And after soper pleyen he bigan,
And spak of myrthe amonges othere thynges,
Whan that we hadde maad our rekenynges; 760
And seyde thus: "Now, lordynges, trewely
Ye been to me right welcome hertely;

For by my trouthe, if that I shal nat lye,
I saugh nat this yeer so mery a compaignye
Atones in this herberwe as is now.   765
Fayn wolde I doon yow myrthe, wiste I how.—
And of a myrthe I am right now bythoght,
To doon yow ese, and it shal coste noght.
Ye goon to Caunterbury: God yow speede!
The blisful martir quite yow youre meede!   770
And wel I woot, as ye goon by the weye,
Ye shapen yow to talen and to pleye;
For trewely, confort me myrthe is noon
To ride by the weye doumb as a stoon:
And therfor wol I maken yow disport,   775
As I seyde erst, and doon yow som confort.
And if yow lyketh alle, by oon assent,
For to stonden at my jugement,
And for to werken as I shal yow seye,
Tomorwe, whan ye riden by the weye,   780
Now, by my fader soule, that is deed,
But ye be merye I wol yeve yow myn heed.
Hold up your hond, withouten more speche!"
    Our counseil was nat longe for to seche:
Us thoughte it was noght worth to make it wys;   785
And graunted hym withouten more avys,
And bad hym seye his verdit as hym leste.
    "Lordynges," quod he, "now herkneth for the beste;
But take it not, I prey yow, in desdeyn.
This is the poynt, to speken short and pleyn,   790
That ech of yow, to shorte with our weye,
In this viage, shal telle tales tweye,
To Caunterbury-ward (I mene it so),
And hom-ward he shal tellen othere two,
Of aventures that whilom han bifalle.   795
And which of yow that bereth hym beste of alle—
That is to seyn, that telleth in this cas
Tales of best sentence and most solas—
Shal have a soper at oure aller cost,
Here in this place, sittynge by this post,   800
Whan that we come agayn fro Caunterbury.
And for to make yow the more mery,
I wol myselven goodly with yow ryde,

Right at myn owne cost, and be youre gyde.
And who-so wole my jugement withseye   805
Shal paye al that we spenden by the weye.
And if ye vouchesauf that it be so,
Tel me anon, withouten wordes mo,
And I wol erly shape me therfore."
    This thyng was graunted, and our othes swore 810
With ful glad herte; and preyden hym also
That he wold vouchesauf for to do so,
And that he wolde been oure governour,
And of our tales juge and reportour,
And sette a soper at a certeyn pris,   815
And we wol reuled been at his devys,
In heigh and lowe: and thus, by oon assent,
We been acorded to his jugement.
And therupon the wyn was fet anon:
We dronken; and to reste wente echon,   820
Withouten any lenger taryynge.
    A-morwe, whan that day gan for to sprynge,
Up roos oure host, and was oure aller cok,
And gadrede us togidre, alle in a flok;
And forth we riden, a litel more than pas,   825
Unto the wateryng of Seint Thomas.
And there oure host bigan his hors areste,
And seyde: "Lordynges, herkneth if yow leste.
Ye woot youre foreward, and I it yow recorde.
If even-song and morwe-song accorde,   830
Lat se now who shal telle the firste tale.
As evere mote I drynke wyn or ale,
Who-so be rebel to my jugement
Shal paye for al that by the weye is spent.
Now draweth cut, er that we ferrer twynne: 845
He which that hath the shorteste shal bigynne.
Sir Knyght," quod he, "my mayster and my lord,
Now draweth cut, for that is myn acord.
Cometh neer," quod he, "my lady Prioresse;
And ye, sir Clerk, lat be your shamefastnesse.   840
Ne studieth noght. Ley hond to, every man!"
    Anon to drawen every wight bigan;
And shortly for to tellen as it was,
Were it by aventure or sort or cas,

The sothe is this, the cut fil to the knyght;   845
Of which ful blithe and glad was every wyght.
And telle he moste his tale, as was resoun,
By foreward and by composicioun,
As ye han herd; what nedeth wordes mo?
And whan this goode man saugh that it was so,   850
As he that wys was and obedient
To kepe his foreward by his free assent,
He seyde: "Syn I shal bigynne the game,
What, welcome be the cut, a Goddes name!
Now lat us ryde, and herkneth what I seye."   855
And with that word we ryden forth oure weye;
And he bigan with right a mery chere
His tale anon, and seyde in this manere.

1386?

THE NONNE PREESTES TALE

A povre wydwe, somdel stope in age,
Was whilom dwellyng in a narwe cotage,
Beside a grove, stondyng in a dale.
This wydwe, of which I telle yow my tale,
Syn thilke day that she was last a wyf,   5
In pacience ladde a ful symple lyf,
For litel was hir catel and hir rente.
By housbondrie of swich as God hir sente,
She foond hirself and eek hir doghtren two.
Thre large sowes hadde she, and namo,   10
Three kyne, and eek a sheep that highte Malle.
Ful sooty was hir bour, and eek hir halle,
In which she eet ful many a sclendre meel:
Of poynaunt sauce hir neded never a deel;
No deyntee morsel passed thurgh hir throte,   15
Hir diete was accordant to hir cote.
Repleccioun ne made hir never sik;
Attempre diete was al hir phisik,
And exercise and hertes suffisaunce.
The goute lette hir nothyng for to daunce,   20
Napoplexie shente nat hir heed.
No wyn ne drank she, neither whit ne reed;

Hir bord was served most with whit and blak,
Milk and broun breed, in which she foond no lak,
Seynd bacoun, and somtyme an ey or tweye,   25
For she was as it were a maner deye.
    A yeerd she hadde, enclosed al aboute
With stikkes, and a drye dych withoute;
In which she hadde a cok, hight Chauntecleer.
In al the land of crowying nas his peer: 30
His voys was merier than the mery orgon
On messe-dayes that in the chirche gon;
Wel sikerer was his crowyng in his logge
Than is a clokke or an abbey orlogge.
By nature knew he ech ascencioun   35
Of equinoxial in thilke toun;
For whan degrees fiftene were ascended,
Thanne crew he, that it myghte nat been amended.
His comb was redder than the fyn coral,
And batailled as it were a castel wal.   40
His byl was blak, and as the jeet it shoon;
Lyk asure were his legges and his toon;
His nayles whiter than the lylye flour;
And lyk the burned gold was his colour.
This gentil cok hadde in his governaunce   45
Sevene hennes, for to doon al his plesaunce,
Whiche were his sustres and his paramours,
And wonder lyk to him as of colours.
Of whiche the faireste hewed on hir throte
Was cleped faire damoysele Pertelote.   50
Curteys she was, discreet, and debonaire,
And compaignable, and bar hyrself so faire,
Syn thilke day that she was seven nyght old,
That trewely she hath the herte in hold
Of Chauntecleer loken in every lith;   55
He loved hir so that wel was hym therwith.
But swich a joye was it to here hem synge,
Whan that the brighte sonne bigan to sprynge,
In sweete accord, "My lief is faren in londe";
For thilke tyme, as I have understonde,   60
Beestes and briddes coude speke and synge.
    And so bifel that in a dawenynge,
As Chauntecleer among his wyves alle

Sat on his perche, that was in the halle,
And next hym sat this faire Pertelote,   65
This Chauntecleer gan gronen in his throte,
As man that in his dreem is drecched sore.
And whan that Pertelote thus herde hym rore,
She was agast and seyde, "O herte deere,
What eyleth yow, to grone in this manere?   70
Ye been a verray sleper; fy for shame!"
And he answerde and seyde thus: "Madame,
I pray yow that ye take it nat agrief:
By God, me thoughte I was in swich meschief,
Right now, that yet myn herte is sore afright.   75
Now God," quod he, "my sweven rede aright,
And keep my body out of foul prisoun!
Me mette how that I romed up and doun
Withinne our yeerde; where as I saugh a beest,
Was lyk an hound, and wolde han maad areest   80
Upon my body, and han had me deed.
His colour was bitwixe yelow and reed;
And tipped was his tayl, and bothe his eeris,
With blak, unlyk the remenant of his heeris;
His snowte smal, with glowynge eyen tweye.   85
Yet of his look for feere almost I deye.
This caused me my gronyng, doutelees."

    "Avoy!" quod she; "fy on yow, hertelees!
Allas!" quod she, "for, by that God above,
Now han ye lost myn herte and al my love;   90
I can nat love a coward, by my feith:
For certes, what so any womman seith,
We alle desiren, if it myghte bee,
To han housbondes hardy, wise, and free,
And secree, and no nygard, ne no fool,   95
Ne hym that is agast of every tool,
Ne noon avauntour, by that God above!
How dorste ye seyn, for shame, unto youre love,
That any thyng myghte make yow aferd?
Have ye no mannes herte, and han a berd?   100
Allas! and conne ye been agast of swevenys?
No thyng, God wot, but vanitee, in swevene is:
Swevenes engendren of replecciouns,
And ofte of fume and of complecciouns,

Whan humours been to habundant in a wight.   105
Certes this dreem, which ye han met to-nyght,
Cometh of the grete superfluitee
Of youre rede *colera,* pardee,
Which causeth folk to dremen in hir dremes
Of arwes, and of fyre with rede lemes,   110
Of grete beestes, that they wol hem byte,
Of contek, and of whelpes grete and lyte;
Right as the humour of malencolie
Causeth ful many a man, in sleepe, to crie,
For feere of blake beres or boles blake,   115
Or elles blake develes wole hym take.
Of othere humours coude I telle also,
That werken many a man in sleepe ful wo;
But I wol passe as lightly as I can.
Lo Caton, which that was so wys a man,   120
Seyde he nat thus, 'Ne do no fors of dremes'?
Now, sire," quod she, "whan we flee fro the bemes,
For Goddes love, as tak som laxatyf.
Up peril of my soule and of my lyf,
I counseille yow the beste—I wol nat lye—   125
That bothe of colere and of malencolye
Ye purge yow. And for ye shal nat tarie,
Though in this toun is noon apothecarie,
I shal myself to herbes techen yow,
That shul ben for youre hele and for youre prow;   130
And in oure yeerd tho herbes shal I fynde,
The whiche han of hire propretee, by kynde,
To purgen yow bynethe and eek above.
Foryet not this, for Goddes owne love!
Ye been ful coleryk of compleccioun.   135
Ware the sonne in his ascencioun
Ne fynde yow nat repleet of humours hote;
And if it do, I dar wel leye a grote
That ye shul have a fevere terciane,
Or an agu, that may be youre bane.   140
A day or two ye shul have digestyves
Of wormes, er ye take your laxatyves
Of lauriol, centaure, and fumetere,
Or elles of ellebor, that groweth there,
Of catapuce, or of gaitrys beryis,   145

Of erbe yve, growyng in oure yeerd, ther mery is:
Pekke hem up right as they growe, and ete hem yn.
Be merye, housbonde, for your fader kyn!
Dredeth no dreem! I can say yow namore."

"Madame," quod he, *"graunt mercy of youre lore!*   150
But natheles, as touchyng daun Catoun,
That hath of wysdom swich a greet renoun,
Though that he bad no dremes for to drede,
By God, men may in olde bookes rede
Of many a man, more of auctoritee   155
Than evere Caton was, so moot I thee,
That al the revers seyn of this sentence,
And han wel founden by experience
That dremes ben significaciouns
As wel of joye as of tribulaciouns   160
That folk enduren in this lif present.
Ther nedeth make of this noon argument;
The verray preve sheweth it in dede.
Oon of the gretteste auctours that men rede
Seith thus: that whilom two felawes wente   165
On pilgrimage, in a ful good entente;
And happed so, they coomen in a toun
Whereas ther was swich congregacioun
Of peple, and eek so streit of herbergage,
That they ne founde as muche as o cotage,   170
In which they bothe myghte logged bee;
Wherfore they mosten, of necessitee,
As for that nyght, departen compaignye;
And ech of hem goth to his hostelrye,
And took his loggyng as it wolde falle.   175
That oon of hem was logged in a stalle,
Fer in a yeerd, with oxen of the plough;
That other man was logged wel y-nough,
As was his aventure or his fortune,
That us governeth alle as in commune.   180
And so bifel that, longe er it were day,
This man mette in his bed, ther as he lay,
How that his felawe gan upon hym calle
And seyde, 'Allas! for in an oxes stalle
This nyght I shal be mordred ther I lye.   185
Now help me, deere brother, or I dye!

In alle haste com to me!' he sayde.
This man out of his sleepe for feere abrayde;
But whan that he was wakened of his sleepe,
He turned hym, and took of it no keepe: 190
Hym thoughte his dreem nas but a vanitee.
Thus twies in his slepyng dremed hee.
And atte thridde tyme yet his felawe
Cam, as hym thoughte, and seide, 'I am now slawe:
Bihold my bloody woundes, depe and wyde! 195
Arys up erly in the morwe-tyde;
And at the west gate of the toun,' quod he,
'A carte ful of donge ther shaltow se,
In which my body is hid ful prively:
Do thilke carte arresten boldely. 200
My gold caused my mordre, sooth to sayn.'
And tolde hym every point how he was slayn,
With a ful pitous face, pale of hewe.
And truste wel, his dreem he foond ful trewe.
For on the morwe, as soone as it was day, 205
To his felawes in he took the way;
And whan that he cam to this oxes stalle,
After his felawe he bigan to calle.
The hostiler answerde hym anon
And seyde, 'Sire, your felawe is agon; 210
As soone as day he wente out of the toun.'
This man gan fallen in suspecioun,
Remembrynge on his dremes that he mette;
And forth he goth, no lenger wolde he lette,
Unto the west gate of the toun, and fond 215
A dong-carte, as it were to donge lond,
That was arrayed in that same wise
As ye han herd the dede man devyse.
And with an hardy herte he gan to crye
Vengeaunce and justice of this felonye: 220
'My felawe mordred is this same nyght,
And in this carte he lith gapyng upright!
I crye out on the ministres,' quod he,
'That sholden kepe and reulen this citee!
Harrow! allas! here lith my felawe slayn!' 225
What sholde I moore unto this tale sayn?
The peple out-sterte, and cast the cart to grounde;

And in the myddel of the dong they founde
The dede man that mordred was al newe.
O blisful God, That art so just and trewe,   230
Lo, how that Thou biwreyest mordre alway!
Mordre wol out; that se we day by day.
Mordre is so wlatsom and abhomynable
To God, That is so just and resonable,
That He ne wol nat suffre it heled be: 235
Though it abyde a yeer, or two, or thre,
Mordre wol out; this my conclusioun.
And right anon, ministres of that toun
Han hent the carter, and so sore hym pyned,
And eek the hostiler so sore engyned,   240
That they biknewe hire wikkednesse anon,
And were anhanged by the nekke-bon.
    "Here may men seen that dremes been to drede.
And certes, in the same book I rede,
Right in the nexte chapitre after this,—   245
I gabbe nat, so have I joye or blis,—
Two men that wolde han passed over see,
For certeyn cause, into a fer contree,
If that the wynd ne hadde been contrarie,
That made hem in a citee for to tarie,   250
That stood ful merye upon an haven-syde.
But on a day, agayn the eventyde,
The wynd gan chaunge, and blew right as hem leste.
Jolif and glad they wente unto hir reste,
And casten hem ful erly for to saille.   255
But herkneth! to that oo man fel a greet mervaille.
That oon of hem, in slepyng as he lay,
Hym mette a wonder dreem, agayn the day.
Hym thoughte a man stood by his beddes syde,
And hym comaunded that he sholde abyde,   260
And seyde hym thus: 'If thou tomorwe wende,
Thow shalt be dreynt; my tale is at an ende.'
He wook, and tolde his felawe what he mette,
And preyde hym his viage for to lette;
As for that day, he preyde hym to abyde.   265
His felawe, that lay by his beddes syde,
Gan for to laughe, and scorned him ful faste.
'No dreem,' quod he, 'may so myn herte agaste

That I wol lette for to do my thynges.
I sette nat a straw by thy dremynges,   270
For swevenes been but vanytees and japes.
Men dreme al day of owles or of apes,
And eek of many a mase therwithal;
Men dreme of thyng that nevere was ne shal.
But sith I see that thou wolt here abyde,   275
And thus forslewthen wilfully thy tyde,
God wot it reweth me; and have good day!'
And thus he took his leve, and wente his way.
But er that he hadde halfe his cours y-seyled,
Noot I nat why, ne what myschaunce it eyled,   280
But casuelly the shippes botme rente,
And shipe and man under the water wente
In sighte of othere shippes it bisyde,
That with hem seyled at the same tyde.
And therfore, faire Pertelote so deere,   285
By swiche ensamples olde maistow leere
That no man sholde been to recchelees
Of dremes; for I sey thee, doutelees,
That many a dreem ful soore is for to drede.
  "Lo, in the lyf of Seint Kenelm, I rede,   290
That was Kenulphus sone, the noble kyng
Of Mercenrike, how Kenelm mette a thyng:
A lite er he was mordred, on a day,
His mordre in his avisioun he say.
His norice hym expouned every del   295
His sweven, and bad hym for to kepe hym wel
For traisoun; but he nas but seven yeer old,
And therfore litel tale hath he told
Of any dreem, so holy was his herte.
By God, I hadde lever than my sherte   300
That ye hadde rad his legende, as have I.
Dame Pertelote, I sey yow trewely,
Macrobeus, that writ the avisioun
In Affrike of the worthy Cipioun,
Affermeth dremes, and seith that they been   305
Warnynge of thynges that men after seen.
And, forthermore, I pray yow looketh wel
In the Olde Testament, of Daniel,
If he held dremes any vanitee.

Reed eek of Joseph, and ther shul ye see   310
Wher dremes ben somtyme—I sey nat alle—
Warnynge of thynges that shul after falle.
Looke of Egipt the kyng, daun Pharao,
His bakere and his butiller also,
Wher they ne felte noon effect in dremes.   315
Who-so wol seken actes of sondry remes
May rede of dremes many a wonder thyng.
Lo Cresus, which that was of Lyde kyng,
Mette he nat that he sat upon a tree,
Which signified he sholde anhanged bee?   320
Lo here Andromacha, Ectores wyf,
That day that Ector sholde lese his lyf,
She dremed, on the same nyght biforn,
How that the lyf of Ector sholde be lorne
If thilke day he wente into bataille.   325
She warned hym, but it myghte nat availle:
He wente for to fighte natheles,
But he was slayn anon of Achilles.
But thilke tale is al to long to telle,
And eek it is ny day; I may nat dwelle.   330
Shortly I seye, as for conclusioun,
That I shal han of this avisioun
Adversitee. And I seye, forthermore,
That I ne telle of laxatyves no store,
For they been venimous, I wot it wel;   335
I hem defye, I love hem never a del.
      "Now let us speke of myrthe, and stynte al this.
Madame Pertelote, so have I blis,
Of o thyng God hath sent me large grace:
Fcr whan I see the beautee of youre face,   340
Ye been so scarlet-reed aboute youre eyen
It maketh al my drede for to dyen;
For, also siker as 'In principio,'
'Mulier est hominis confusio.'
(Madame, the sentence of this Latyn is,   345
'Womman is mannes joye and al his blis.') . . . .
I am so ful of joye and of solas   350
That I defye bothe sweven and dreem."
      And with that word he fley doun fro the beem
(For it was day), and eek his hennes alle;

And with a chuk he gan hem for to calle,
For he hadde founde a corn, lay in the yerd.   355
Royal he was; he was namore aferd. . . . .
He looketh as it were a grym leoun,
And on his toos he rometh up and doun;   360
Hym deigned nat to sette his foot to grounde.
He chukketh whan he hath a corn y-founde,
And to hym rennen thanne his wyves alle.
Thus roial, as a prince is in an halle,
Leve I this Chauntecleer in his pasture;   365
And after wol I telle his aventure.
    Whan that the monthe in which the world bigan,
That highte March, whan God first maked man,
Was compleet, and passed were also
(Syn March bigan) thritty dayes and two,   370
Bifel that Chauntecleer, in al his pryde,
His seven wyves walkynge by his syde,
Caste up his eyen to the brighte sonne,
That in the signe of Taurus hadde y-ronne
Twenty degrees and oon, and somwhat more;   375
And knew by kynde, and by noon other lore,
That it was pryme, and crew with blisful stevene.
"The sonne," he sayde, "is clomben up on hevene
Fourty degrees and oon, and moore, y-wis.
Madame Pertelote, my worldes blis,   380
Herkneth thise blisful briddes, how they synge;
And se the fresshe floures, how they sprynge!
Ful is myn hert of revel and solas."
But sodeynly hym fil a sorweful cas;
For evere the latter ende of joye is wo.   385
Got wot that worldly joye is soone ago;
And if a rethor coude faire endite,
He in a cronycle saufly myghte it write
As for a sovereyn notabilitee.
Now every wys man, lat hym herkne me;   390
This storie is also trewe, I undertake,
As is the book of Launcelot de Lake,
That wommen holde in ful greet reverence.
Now wol I come agayn to my sentence.
    A colfox, ful of sly iniquitee,   395
That in the grove hadde woned yeres three,

By heigh imaginacioun forn-cast,
The same nyght thurghout the hegges brast
Into the yerd, ther Chauntecleer the faire
Was wont, and eek his wyves, to repaire;   400
And in a bed of wortes stille he lay,
Til it was passed undern of the day,
Waitynge his tyme on Chauntecleer to falle,
As gladly doon thise homycides alle,
That in await liggen to mordre men.   405
O false mordrour, lurkynge in thy den!
O newe Scariot, newe Genylon!
False dissimilour, O Greek Synon,
That broghtest Troye al outrely to sorwe!
O Chauntecleer, acursed be that morwe   410
That thou into that yerd flaugh fro the bemes!
Thou were ful wel y-warned, by thy dremes,
That thilke day was perilous to thee.
But what that God forwot moot nedes bee,
After the opinioun of certein clerkis.   415
Witnesse on hym, that any parfit clerk is,
That in scole is greet altercacioun
In this mateere, and greet disputisoun,
And hath ben of an hundred thousand men.
But I ne can not bulte it to the bren,   420
As can the holy doctour Augustyn,
Or Boece, or the bishope Bradwardyn,
Wheither that Goddes worthy forwityng
Streyneth me nedely for to doon a thyng—
Nedely clepe I symple necessitee;   425
Or elles if free choys be graunted me
To do that same thyng or do it noght,
Though God forwot it er that it was wroght;
Or if His wityng streyneth never a del
But by necessitee condicionel.   430
I wil nat han to do of swich mateere;
My tale is of a cok, as ye may heere,
That took his conseil of his wyf, with sorwe,
To walken in the yerd upon that morwe
That he hadde met the dreem that I of tolde.   435
Wommennes conseils been ful ofte colde;
Wommannes conseil broghte us first to wo,

And made Adam fro paradys to go,
Ther as he was ful merye and wel at ese.
But for I noot to whom it myght displese   440
If I conseil of wommen wolde blame,
Passe over, for I seyde it in my game.
Rede auctours, where they trete of swich mateere,
And what they seyn of wommen ye may heere.
Thise been the cokkes wordes, and nat myne;   445
I can noon harm of no womman divyne.
    Faire in the sond, to bathe hire merily,
Lyth Pertelote, and alle hire sustres by,
Agayn the sonne; and Chauntecleer so free
Song merier than the mermayde in the see—   450
For Phisiologus seith, sikerly,
How that they syngen wel and merily.
And so bifel that, as he caste his eye
Among the wortes, on a boterflye,
He was war of this fox that lay ful lowe: 455
Nothyng ne liste hym thanne for to crowe,
But cride anon, 'cok! cok!' and up he sterte,
As man that was affrayed in his herte;
For naturelly a beest desireth flee
Fro his contrarie, if he may it see,   460
Though he never erst hadde seyn it with his eye.
    This Chauntecleer, whan he gan hym espye,
He wolde han fled but that the fox anon
Seyde: "Gentil sire, allas! wher wol ye gon?
Be ye affrayed of me that am your freend?   465
Now certes, I were worse than a feend,
If I to yow wolde harm or vileynye.
I am nat come your conseil for tespye;
But, trewely, the cause of my comynge
Was only for to herkne how that ye synge: 470
For trewely ye have as mery a stevene
As eny aungel hath that is in hevene;
Therwith ye han in musyk more feelynge
Than hadde Boece, or any that can synge.
My lord youre fader—God his soule blesse!—   475
And eek youre moder, of hire gentilesse,
Han in myn hous y-been, to my greet ese;
And certes, sire, ful fayn wolde I yow plese.

But for men speke of syngyng, I wol saye,
So mote I brouke wel myne eyen tweye,   480
Save yow I herde never man so synge
As dide youre fader in the morwenynge:
Certes, it was of herte, al that he song;
And for to make his voys the moore strong,
He wolde so peyne hym that with bothe his eyen   485
He moste wynke, so loude he wolde cryen,
And stonden on his tiptoon therwithal,
And strecche forth his nekke long and smal.
And eek he was of swich discrecioun
That ther nas no man in no regioun   490
That hym in song or wisedom myghte passe.
I have wel rad in daun Burnel the Asse,
Among his vers, how that ther was a cok,
For that a preestes sone yaf hym a knok
Upon his leg whil he was yong and nyce,   495
He made hym for to lese his benefice.
But, certeyn, ther nis no comparisoun
Bitwixe the wisedom and discrecioun
Of youre fader and of his subtiltee.
Now syngeth, sire, for Seinte Charitee: 500
Lat se, conne ye youre fader countrefete?"
    This Chauntecleer his wynges gan to bete,
As man that coude his traysoun nat espie
So was he ravished with his flaterie.
(Allas, ye lordes! many a fals flatour   505
Is in your courtes, and many a losengeour,
That plesen yow wel more, by my feith,
Than he that soothfastnesse unto yow seith.
Redeth Ecclesiaste of flatterye;
Beth war, ye lordes, of hir trecherye.)   510
This Chauntecleer stood hye upon his toos,
Strecchynge his nekke, and held his eyen cloos,
And gan to crowe loude for the nones;
And daun Russel, the fox, sterte up atones,
And by the gargat hente Chauntecleer,   51
And on his bak toward the wode hym beer,
For yet ne was ther no man that hym sewed.
    O destinee, that mayst nat been eschewed!
Allas, that Chauntecleer fleigh fro the bemes!

Allas, his wyf ne roghte nat of dremes!   520
And on a Friday fil al this meschaunce.
O Venus, that art goddesse of plesaunce,
Syn that thy servant was this Chauntecleer,
And in thy service dide al his poweer,
More for delit than world to multiplye,   525
Why woltestow suffre hym on thy day to dye?
O Gaufred, deere maister soverayn,
That, whan thy worthy kyng Richard was slayn
With shot, compleynedest his deth so sore,
Why ne hadde I now thy sentence and thy lore,   530
The Friday for to chide, as diden ye?—
For on a Friday soothly slayn was he.
Thanne wolde I shewe yow how that I coude pleyne
For Chauntecleres drede and for his peyne.

    Certes, swich cry ne lamentacioun   535
Was nevere of ladyes maad, whan Ylioun
Was wonne, and Pirrus with his streite swerd
Whan he hadde hent kyng Priam by the berd
And slayn hym—as saith us *Eneydos*,—
As maden alle the hennes in the clos,   540
Whan they had seyn of Chauntecleer the sighte.
But sovereynly dame Pertelote shrighte
Ful louder than dide Hasdrubales wyf,
Whan that hir housbonde hadde lost his lyf,
And that the Romayns hadde brent Cartage—   545
She was so ful of torment and of rage
That wilfully into the fyr she sterte,
And brende hirselven with a stedefast herte.
O woful hennes, right so criden ye
As, whan that Nero brende the citee   550
Of Rome, cryden senatoures wyves
For that hir housbondes losten alle hir lvyes:
Withouten gilt this Nero hath hem slayn.
Now turne I wole to my tale agayn.

    This sely wydwe and eek hir doghtres two   555
Herden thise hennes crye and maken wo;
And out at dores sterten they anon,
And syen the fox toward the grove gon
And bar upon his bak the cok away;
And cryden, "Out! harrow! and weylaway!   560

Ha, ha, the fox!" And after hym they ran,
And eek with staves many another man;
Ranne Colle our dogge, and Talbot, and Gerland,
And Malkyn with a dystaf in hir hand;
Ran cow and calf, and eek the verray hogges,   565
So were they fered for berkyng of the dogges
And shoutyng of the men and wommen eek.
They ronne so, hem thoughte hir herte breek;
They yelleden as feendes doon in helle.
The dokes cryden as men wolde hem quelle,   570
The gees for feere flowen over the trees,
Out of the hyve cam the swarm of bees,
So hydous was the noyse, a! *benedicite!*
Certes, he Jakke Straw and his meynee
Ne made nevere shoutes half so shrille,   575
Whan that they wolden any Flemyng kille,
As thilke day was maad upon the fox.
Of bras they broghten bemes, and of box,
Of horn, of boon, in whiche they blewe and powped,
And therwithal they shriked and they howped: 580
It semed as that hevene sholde falle.
    Now, goode men, I pray yow herkneth alle!
Lo, how fortune turneth sodeynly
The hope and pryde eek of hir enemy!
This cok, that lay upon the foxes bak,   585
In al his drede, unto the fox he spak
And seyde: "Sire, if that I were as ye,
Yet sholde I seyn—as wys God helpe me,—
'Turneth agayn, ye proude cherles alle!
A verray pestilence upon yow falle!   590
Now am I come unto the wodes side,
Maugree youre heed, the cok shal here abyde;
I wol hym ete in feith, and that anon!'"
The fox answerede, "In feith, it shal be don"—
And as he spak that word, al sodeynly   595
This cok brak from his mouth delyverly,
And heighe upon a tree he fleigh anon.
And whan the fox saugh that he was y-gon,
"Allas!" quod he, "O Chauntecleer, allas!
I have to yow," quod he, "y-doon trespas,   600
In-as-muche as I maked yow aferd

Whan I yow hente and broghte out of the yerd.
But, sire, I dide it in no wikke entente:
Com doun, and I shal telle yow what I mente.
I shal seye sooth to yow, God help me so." 605
"Nay, thanne," quod he, "I shrewe us bothe two,
And first I shrewe myself, bothe blood and bones,
If thou bigyle me ofter than ones.
Thou shalt namore, thurgh thy flaterye,
Do me to synge and wynken with myn eye; 610
For he that wynketh whan he sholde see,
Al wilfully, God lat hym nevere thee!"
"Nay," quod the fox, "but God yeve him meschaunce,
That is so undiscreet of governaunce,
That jangleth whan he sholde holde his pees." 615
  Lo, swich it is for to be recchelees
And necligent, and truste on flaterye.
But ye that holden this tale a folye,
As of a fox, or of a cok and hen,
Taketh the moralitee, goode men; 620
For Seint Paul seith that al that writen is,
To oure doctrine it is y-write, y-wis:
Taketh the fruyt, and lat the chaf be stille.
  Now, goode God, if that it be Thy wille,
As seith my lord, so make us alle goode men, 625
And brynge us to His heighe blisse! Amen.
1387?

TRUTH

Fle fro the prees, and dwelle with sothfastnesse;
Suffice unto thi good, though it be smal:
For hord hath hate, and clymbynge tykelnesse;
Prees hath envye, and wele blent overal.
Savour no more than the byhove shal; 5
Werke wel thiselfe, that other folke canst rede:
And trouthe shal delivere, it is no drede.

Tempest the noght al croked to redresse,
In trust of hyr that turneth as a bal;
Gret reste stant in lytel bisynesse. 10
And eek be war to sporne ageynst an al;

Stryve noght as doth the crokke with the wal.
Daunte thiself, that dauntest otheres dede:
And trouthe shal delivere, it is no drede.

That the is sent, receyve in boxomnesse;   15
The wrastlynge for this worlde axeth a fal.
Here nys non hom, here nys but wyldernesse;
Forth, pilgrim, forth! Forth, beste, out of thi stal!
Knowe thy contree; lok up, thank God of al;
Hold the hye-wey, and lat thi gost the lede: 20
And trouthe shal delivere, it is no drede.

ENVOY

Therfore, thou vache, leve thine old wrechedenesse;
Unto the worlde leve now to be thral;
Crie Him mercy That of Hys hie godnesse
Made the of nought, and in especial   25
Draw unto Hym, and pray in general
For the, and eke for other, hevenelyche mede:
And trouthe schal delyvere, it is no drede.

After 1386?

THE COMPLAYNT OF CHAUCER TO HIS PURSE

To yow, my purse, and to non other wight,
Complayne I, for ye be my lady dere!
I am so sory, now that ye be lyght;
For, certes, but ye make me hevy chere,
Me were as leef be layde upon my bere: 5
For whiche unto your mercy thus I crye:
Beth hevy ageyne, or elles mote I dye!

Now voucheth-sauf this day, or hyt be nyght,
That I of yow the blisful soune may here,
Or see your colour lyke the sonne bryght,   10
That of yelownesse hadde never pere.
Ye be my lyfe, ye be myn hertes stere,
Quene of comfort and of good companye:
Beth hevy ageyne, or elles mote I dye!

Now purse, that ben to me my lyves lyght,⠀⠀⠀⠀⠀15
And saveour, as doun in this worlde here,
Oute of this toune helpe me thurgh your myght,
Syn that ye wole nat bene my tresorere;
For I am shave as nye as any frere.
But yet I pray unto your curtesye:⠀⠀⠀⠀⠀20
Beth hevy ayen, or elles mote I dye!

LENVOY DE CHAUCER

O conquerour of Brutes Albyoun!
Whiche that by lygne and free eleccioun
Been verray kynge, this song to yow I sende;
And ye, that mowen alle myn harme amende,⠀⠀⠀⠀⠀25
Have mynde upon my supplicacioun!

1399?

THOMAS HOCCLEVE

MI MAISTER CHAUCER

O maister deere and fadir reverent,
⠀⠀Mi maister Chaucer, flour of eloquence,
Mirour of fructuous entendement,
⠀⠀O universel fadir in science,
⠀⠀Allas, that thou thyn excellent prudence⠀⠀⠀⠀⠀5
⠀⠀⠀⠀In thi bed mortel mightist naght by-qwethe!
⠀⠀⠀⠀What eiled Deth? allas! whi wold he sle the?

O Deth, thou didest naght harme singuleer
⠀⠀In slaghtere of him, but al this land it smertith.
But nathelees yit hast thou no power⠀⠀⠀⠀⠀10
⠀⠀His name sle: his hy vertu astertith
⠀⠀Unslayn fro the, whiche ay us lyfly hertyth
⠀⠀⠀⠀With bookes of his ornat endytyng,
⠀⠀⠀⠀That is to al this land enlumynyng.

⠀⠀.⠀⠀⠀⠀.⠀⠀⠀⠀.⠀⠀⠀⠀.⠀⠀⠀⠀.⠀⠀⠀⠀.⠀⠀⠀⠀.⠀⠀⠀⠀.⠀⠀⠀⠀.

Allas! my worthi maister honorable,⠀⠀⠀⠀⠀15
⠀⠀This landes verray tresor and richesse!

Dethe, by thi deth, hath harme irreparable
  Unto us doon; hir vengeable duresse
  Despoiled hath this land of the swetnesse
    Of rethorik, for un-to Tullius   20
    Was never man so lyk a-monges us.

Also who was hier in philosophie
  To Aristotle, in our tonge, but thow?
The steppes of Virgile in poesie
  Thow folwedist eeke, men wot wel y-now.   25
  That combre-world that the, my maistir, slow,
    Would I slayne were! Deth was to hastyf,
    To renne on the and reve the thi lyf.

Deth hath but smal consideracioun
  Unto the vertuous, I have espied;   30
No more, as shewith the probacioun,
  Than to a vicious maistir losel tried.
  A-mong an heep every man is maistried
    With hire, as wel the porre as is the riche;
    Lered and lewde eeke standen al y-liche.   35

She myghte han taried hir vengeance awhile,
  Til that some man had egal to the be.
Nay, lat be that! sche knew wel that this yle
  May never man forth brynge lyk to the,
  And hir office needes do mot she: 40
    God bad hir do so, I truste as for the beste.
    O maister, maister, God thi soule reste!
1400.

JOHN LYDGATE

LONDON LYCKPENY

To London once my steppes I bent,
  Where trouth in no wyse should be faynt.
To-Westmynster-ward I forthwith went,
  To a man of law to make complaynt:
  I sayd, "For Marys love, that holy saynt,   5

Pyty the poore that wold proceede!"
But for lack of mony I cold not spede.

And as I thrust the prese amonge,
   By froward chaunce my hood was gone;
Yet for all that I stayd not longe,   10
     Tyll to the Kynges Bench I was come:
     Before the judge I kneled anon,
And prayd hym for Gods sake to take heede;
But for lack of mony I myght not speede.

Beneth hem sat clarkes, a great rout,   15
   Which fast dyd wryte by one assent:
There stoode up one and cryed about,
   "Rychard, Robert, and John of Kent!"
     I wyst not well what this man ment,
He cryed so thycke there in dede;   20
But he that lackt mony myght not spede.

Unto the Common Place I yode thoo,
   Where sat one with a sylken hoode;
I dyd hym reverence, for I ought to do so,
     And told my case as well as I coode,   25
     How my goodes were defrauded me by falshood:
I gat not a mum of his mouth for my meed,
And for lack of mony I myght not spede.

Unto the Rolles I gat me from thence,
   Before the clarkes of the Chauncerye,   30
Where many I found earnyng of pence;
     But none at all once regarded mee.
     I gave them my playnt uppon my knee:
They lyked it well, when they had it reade;
But, lackyng mony, I could not be sped.   35

In Westmynster Hall I found out one
   Which went in a long gown of raye:
I crowched and kneled before hym anon;
     For Maryes love, of help I hym praye.
     "I wot not what thou meanest," gan he say;   40
To get me thence he dyd me bede:
For lack of mony I cold not speed.

Within this hall nether rich nor yett poore
    Wold do for me ought, although I shold dye.
Which seing, I gat me out of the doore,   45
    Where Flemynges began on me for to cry,
  "Master, what will you copen or by?
Fyne felt hattes, or spectacles to reede?
Lay down your sylver, and here you may speede."

Then to Westmynster Gate I presently went,   50
    When the sonne was at hyghe pryme.
Cookes to me they tooke good entente,
    And proferred me bread, with ale and wyne,
    Rybbes of befe, both fat and ful fyne;
A fayre cloth they gan for to sprede: 55
But, wantyng mony, I myght not then speede.

Then unto London I dyd me hye;
    Of all the land it beareth the pryse.
"Hot pescodes!" one began to crye;
    "Strabery rype!" and "cherryes in the ryse!"   60
    One bad me come nere and by some spyce;
Peper and safforne they gan me bede:
But for lack of mony I myght not spede.

Then to the Chepe I gan me drawne,
    Where mutch people I saw for to stand.   65
One ofred me velvet, sylke, and lawne;
    An other he taketh me by the hande:
  "Here is Parys thred, the fynest in the land."
I never was used to such thynges in dede,
And, wantyng mony, I myght not speed.   70

Then went I forth by London stone,
    Thoroughout all Canwyke streete:
Drapers mutch cloth me offred anone.
    Then met I one cryed "Hot shepes feete!"
    One cryde "Makerell!" "Ryshes grene!" an other
      gan greete;   75
On bad me by a hood to cover my head.
But for want of mony I myght not be sped.

Then I hyed me into Est Chepe:
   One cryes "Rybbes of befe!" and many a pye;
Pewter pottes they clattered on a heape: 80
   There was harpe, pype, and mynstralsye;
   "Yea, by Cock!" "Nay, by Cock!" some began crye;
Some songe of Jenken and Julyan for there mede.
But for lack of mony I myght not spede.

Then into Cornhyll anon I yode,   85
   Where was mutch stolen gere amonge:
I saw where honge myne owne hoode,
   That I had lost amonge the thronge;
   To by my own hood I thought it wronge;
I knew it well as I dyd my crede;   90
But for lack of mony I could not spede.

The taverner tooke me by the sleve;
   "Sir," sayth he, "wyll you our wyne assay?"
I answered, "That can not mutch me greve;
   A peny can do no more then it may."   95
   I drank a pynt, and for it dyd paye;
Yet sore a-hungerd from thence I yede,
And, wantyng mony, I cold not spede.

Then hyed I me to Belyngsgate,
   And one cryed, "Hoo! go we hence!"   100
I prayd a barge-man, for Gods sake,
   That he wold spare me my expence.
   "Thou scapst not here," quod he, "under two pence;
I lyst not yet bestow my almes dede."
Thus, lackyng mony, I could not speede.   105

Then I convayd me into Kent,
   For of the law wold I meddle no more;
Because no man to me tooke entent,
   I dyght me to do as I dyd before.
   Now Jesus, that in Bethlem was bore,   110
Save London, and send trew lawyers there mede!
For who-so wantes mony with them shall not spede!

Between 1399 and 1413?

JAMES I OF SCOTLAND

FROM

THE KINGIS QUAIR

Bewailing in my chamber thus allone,
    Despeired of all joye and remedye,
For-tirit of my thoght, and wo-begone,
    Unto the wyndow gan I walk in hye,
    To se the warld and folk that went forby: 5
As for the tyme, though I of mirthis fude
Myght have no more, to luke it did me gude.

Now was there maid fast by the touris wall
    A gardyn faire, and in the corneris set
Ane herbere grene, with wandis long and small   10
    Railit about; and so with treis set
    Was all the place, and hawthorn hegis knet,
That lyf was non walking there forby
That myght within scarse ony wight aspye.

So thik the bewis and the leves grene   15
    Beschadit all the aleyes that there were,
And myddis every herbere myght be sene
    The scharpe grene suete jenepere,
    Growing so faire with branchis here and there,
That, as it semyt to a lyf without,   20
The bewis spred the herbere all about.

And on the smalle grene twistis sat
    The lytill suete nyghtingale, and song
So loud and clere, the ympnis consecrat
    Off lufis use, now soft, now lowd among,   25
    That all the gardyng and the wallis rong
Ryght of thaire song, and of the copill next
Off thaire suete armony, and lo the text:

"Worschippe, ye that loveris bene, this May,
    For of your blisse the Kalendis are begonne,   30
And sing with us, 'Away, winter, away!
    Cum, somer, cum, the suete sesoun and sonne!'
    Awake for schame, that have your hevynnis wonne,

And amorously lift up your hedis all!
Thank Lufe, that list you to his merci call." 35

Quhen thai this song had song a lytill thrawe,
    Thai stent a quhile; and therewith, unaffraid,
As I beheld and kest myn eyne a-lawe,
    From beugh to beugh thay hippit and thai plaid,
    And freschly in thaire birdis kynd arraid 40
Thaire fetheris new, and fret thame in the sonne,
And thankit Lufe, that had thaire makis wonne.

This was the plane ditee of thaire note;
    And there-with-all unto my-self I thoght,
"Quhat lyf is this that makis birdis dote? 45
    Quhat may this be, how cummyth it of ought?
    Quhat nedith it to be so dere ybought?
It is nothing, trowe I, bot feynit chere,
And that men list to counterfeten chere."

Eft wald I think, "O Lord, quhat may this be, 50
    That Lufe is of so noble myght and kynde,
Lufing his folk? and suich prosperitee
    Is it of him as we in bukis fynd?
    May he oure hertes setten and unbynd?
Hath he upon oure hertis suich maistrye? 55
Or all this is bot feynyt fantasye!

"For gif he be of so grete excellence
    That he of every wight hath cure and charge,
Quhat have I gilt to him or doon offense,
    That I am thrall and birdis gone at large, 60
    Sen him to serve he myght set my corage?
And gif he be noght so, than may I seyne,
'Quhat makis folk to jangill of him in veyne?'

"Can I noght elles fynd bot gif that he
    Be lord, and as a god may lyve and regne, 65
To bynd and louse, and maken thrallis free,
    Than wold I pray his blisfull grace benigne
    To hable me unto his service digne,
And evermore for to be one of tho
Him trewly for to serve in wele and wo." 70

And there-with kest I doun myn eye ageyne,
    Quhare-as I sawe, walking under the toure,
Full secretly new cummyn hir to pleyne,
    The fairest or the freschest yonge floure
    That ever I sawe, me thoght, before that houre;   75
For quhich sodayn abate, anon astert
The blude of all my body to my hert.

And though I stude abaisit tho a lyte,
    No wonder was; for-quhy my wittis all
Were so overcom with plesance and delyte,   80
    Onely throu latting of myn eyen fall,
    That sudaynly my hert became hir thrall,
For ever, of free wyll—for of manace
There was no takyn in hir suete face.

And in my hede I drewe right hastily;   85
    And eft-sones I lent it forth ageyne,
And sawe hir walk, that verray womanly,
    With no wight mo, bot onely wommen tueyne.
    Than gan I studye in my-self and seyne,
"A, suete, ar ye a warldly creature,   90
Or hevinly thing in likenesse of nature?

"Or ar ye god Cupidis owin princesse,
    And cummyn are to louse me out of band?
Or ar ye verray Nature the goddesse,
    That have depaynted with your hevinly hand   95
    This gardyn full of flouris, as they stand?
Quhat sall I think, allace! quhat reverence
Sall I minister to your excellence?

"Gif ye a goddesse be, and that ye like
    To do me payne, I may it noght astert;   100
Gif ye be warldly wight, that dooth me sike,
    Quhy lest God mak you so, my derrest hert,
    To do a sely prisoner thus smert,
That lufis yow all, and wote of noght bot wo?
And therefor merci, suete, sen it is so."   105

    Quhen I a lytill thrawe had maid my moon,
    Bewailling myn infortune and my chance,

Unknawin how or quhat was best to doon,
   So ferre i-fallyng into lufis dance,
   That sodeynly my wit, my contenance,   110
My hert, my will, my nature, and my mynd,
Was changit clene ryght in an-othir kind.

Off hir array the form gif I sall write,
   Toward hir goldin haire and rich atyre
In fret-wyse couchit was with perllis quhite   115
   And grete balas lemyng as the fyre,
   With mony ane emeraut and faire saphire;
And on hir hede a chaplet fresch of hewe,
Off plumys partit rede and quhite and blewe,

Full of quaking spangis bryght as gold,   120
   Forgit of schap like to the amorettis,
So new, so fresch, so plesant to behold,
   The plumys eke like to the floure-jonettis,
   And othir of schap like to the round crokettis;
And, above all this, there was, wele I wote,   125
Beautee eneuch to mak a world to dote.

About hir nek, quhite as the fyre amaille,
   A gudely cheyne of smale orfeverye,
Quhareby there hang a ruby, without faille,
   Lyke to ane herte schapin verily,   130
   That, as a sperk of lowe, so wantonly
Semyt birnyng upon hir quhyte throte.
Now gif there was gud partye, God it wote.

And forto walk that fresche Mayes morowe,
   An huke sche had upon hir tissew quhite,   135
That gudeliare had noght bene sene toforowe,
   As I suppose; and girt sche was a lyte.
   Thus halflyng louse for haste, to suich delyte
It was to see hir youth in gudelihede
That for rudenes to speke thereof I drede.   140

In hir was youth, beautee, with humble aport,
   Bountee, richesse, and wommanly facture,
God better wote than my pen can report:
   Wisedome, largesse, estate, and connyng sure
   In every poynt so guydit hir mesure,   145

In a word, in dede, in schap, in contenance,
That Nature myght no more hir childe avance.

Throw quhich anon I knew and understude
    Wele that sche was a warldly creature;
On quhom to rest myn eye, so mich gude   150
    It did my wofull hert, I yow assure,
    That it was to me joye without mesure.
And at the last my luke unto the hevin
I threwe furthwith, and said thir versis sevin:

"O Venus clere, of goddis stellifyit,   155
    To quhom I yelde homage and sacrifise,
Fro this day forth your grace be magnifyit,
    That me ressavit have in suich a wise,
    To lyve under your law and do servise!
Now help me furth, and for your merci lede   160
My hert to rest, that deis nere for drede!"

Quhen I with gude entent this orisoun
    Thus endid had, I stynt a lytill stound;
And eft myn eye full pitously adoun
    I kest, behalding unto hir lytill hound,   165
    That with his bellis playit on the ground:
Than wold I say, and sigh there-with a lyte,
"A! wele were him that now were in thy plyte!"

An-othir quhile the lytill nyghtingale,
    That sat apon the twiggis, wold I chide,   170
And say ryght thus: "Quhare are thy notis smale,
    That thou of love has song this morowe-tyde?
    Seis thou noght hire that sittis the besyde?
For Venus sake, the blisfull goddesse clere,
Sing on agane, and mak my lady chere.   175

"And eke I pray—for all the paynes grete
    That, for the love of Proigne, thy sister dere,
Thou sufferit quhilom, quhen thy brestis wete
    Were with the teres of thyne eyen clere
    All bludy ronne, that pitee was to here   180
The crueltee of that unknyghtly dede,
Quhare was fro the bereft thy maidenhede—

"Lift up thyne hert, and sing with gude entent;
    And in thy notis suete the treson telle
That to thy sister, trewe and innocent,   185
    Was kythit by hir husband false and fell;
    For quhois gilt, as it is worthy wel,
Chide thir hubandis that are false, I say,
And bid thame mend, in the twenty devil way.

"O lytill wrecch, allace, maist thou noght se   190
    Quho commyth yond? Is it now tyme to wring?
Quhat sory thoght is fallin upon the?
    Opyn thy throte; hastow no lest to sing?
    Allace! sen thou of reson had felyng,
Now, suete bird, say ones to me 'pepe';   195
I dee for wo; me think thou gynnis slepe.

"Hastow no mynde of lufe? quhare is thy make?
    Or artow seke, or smyt with jelousye?
Or is sche dede, or hath sche the forsake?
    Quhat is the cause of thy malancolye,   200
    That thou no more list maken melodye?
Sluggart, for schame! lo here thy goldin houre,
That worth were hale all thy lyvis laboure!

"Gyf thou suld sing wele ever in thy lyve,
    Here is, in fay, the tyme and eke the space.   205
Quhat wostow than? sum bird mau cum and stryve
    In song with the, the maistry to purchace.
    Suld thou than cesse, it were grete schame, allace!
And here, to wyn gree happily for ever,
Here is the tyme to syng, or ellis never."   210

I thoght eke thus: "Gif I my handis clap,
    Or gif I cast, than will sche flee away;
And gif I hald my pes, than will sche nap;
    And gif I crye, sche wate noght quhat I say:
    Thus quhat is best wate I noght be this day.   215
Bot blawe, wynd, blawe, and do the levis schake,
That sum twig may wag, and mak hir to wake."

With that anon ryght sche toke up a sang;
    Quhare come anon mo birdis and alight:

Bot than to here the mirth was tham amang,　　220
　　Over that, to, to see the suete sicht
　　Off hyr ymage, my spirit was so light
Me thoght I flawe for joye without arest,
So were my wittis boundin all to fest.

And to the notis of the philomene,　　225
　　Quhilkis sche sang, the ditee there I maid
Direct to hire that was my hertis quene,
　　Withoutin quhom no songis may me glade;
　　And to that sanct, there walking in the schade,
My bedis thus, with humble hert entere,　　230
Devotly than I said on this manere:

"Quhen sall your merci rew upon your man,
　　Quhois service is yit uncouth unto yow?
Sen, quhen ye go, ther is noght ellis than.
　　Bot, hert, quhere as the body may noght throu,　　235
　　Folow thy hevin! quho suld be glad bot thou
That suich a gyde to folow has undertake?
Were it throu hell, the way thou noght forsake!"

And efter this the birdis everichone
　　Tuke up an othir sang full loud and clere,　　240
And with a voce said, "Wele is us begone,
　　That with oure makis are togider here;
　　We proyne and play without dout and dangere,
All clothit in a soyte full fresch and newe,
In lufis service besy, glad, and trewe.　　245

"And ye, fresche May, ay mercifull to bridis,
　　Now welcum be ye, floure of monethis all;
For noght onely your grace upon us bydis,
　　Bot all the warld to witnes this we call,
　　That strowit hath so playnly over all　　250
With newe fresche suete and tender grene,
Oure lyf, oure lust, oure governoure, oure quene."

This was thair song, as semyt me full heye,
　　With full mony uncouth suete note and schill.
And therewith-all that faire upward hir eye　　255
　　Wold cast amang, as it was Goddis will,
　　Quhare I myght se, standing allane full still,

The faire facture that Nature, for maistrye,
In hir visage wroght had full lufingly.

And quhen sche walkit had a lytill thrawe 260
    Under the suete grene bewis bent,
Hir faire fresche face, as quhite as ony snawe,
    Scho turnyt has, and furth hir wayis went.
    Bot tho began myn axis and turment,
To sene hir part, and folowe I na myght; 265
Me thoght the day was turnyt into nyght.

1423?

ROBERT HENRYSON

FROM

THE TESTAMENT OF CRESSEID

This duleful sentence Saturne tuik on hand,
And passit doun quhair cairfull Cresseid lay;
And on hir heid he laid ane frostie wand,
Than lawfullie on this wyse can he say:
"Thy greit fairnes, and al thy bewtie gay, 5
Thy wantoun blude, and eik thy goldin hair,
Heir I exclude fra the for evermair.

"I change thy mirth into melancholy,
Quhilk is the mother of all pensivenes;
Thy moisture and thy heit, in cald and dry; 10
Thyne insolence, thy play and wantones,
To greit diseis; thy pomp and thy riches,
In mortall neid; and greit penuritie
Thow suffer sall, and as ane beggar die."

O cruell Saturne, fraward and angrie, 15
Hard is thy dome and to malitious!
On fair Cresseid quhy hes thow na mercie,
Quhilk was sa sweit, gentill, and amorous?
Withdraw thy sentence, and be gracious
As thow was never; so shawis thow thy deid, 20
Ane wraikfull sentence gevin on fair Cresseid.

Than Cynthia, quhen Saturne past away,
Out of hir sait discendit down belyve,
And red ane bill on Cresseid quhair scho lay,
Contening this sentence diffinityve: 25
"Fra heil of body I the now depryve,
And to thy seiknes sal be na recure,
Bot in dolour thy dayis to indure.

"Thy cristall ene minglit with blude I mak;
Thy voice sa cleir unplesand, hoir, and hace;   30
Thy lusty lyre ouirspred with spottis blak,
And lumpis haw appeirand in thy face.
Quhair thow cummis ilk man sall fle the place;
This sall thow go begging fra hous to hous,
With cop and clapper, lyk ane lazarous."   35

This doolie dreame, this uglye visioun,
Brocht to ane end, Cresseid fra it awoik,
And all that court and convocatioun
Vanischit away. Than rais scho up and tuik
Ane poleist glas, and hir shaddow culd luik;   40
And quhen scho saw hir face sa deformait,
Gif scho in hart was wa aneuch, God wait!

Weiping full sair, "Lo, quhat it is," quod sche,
"With fraward langage for to mufe and steir
Our craibit goddis; and sa is sene on me!   45
My blaspheming now have I bocht full deir;
All eirdlie joy and mirth I set areir.
Allace, this day! Allace, this wofull tyde,
Quhen I began with my goddis for to chyde!"

Be this was said, ane chyld come fra the hall   50
To warne Cresseid the supper was reddy;
First knokkit at the dure, and syne culd call,
"Madame, your father biddis you cum in hy;
He hes merwell so lang on grouf ye ly,
And sayis, 'Your prayers bene to lang sum deill;   55
The goddis wait all your intent full weill.' "

Quod scho, "Fair chylde, ga to my father deir,
And pray him cum to speik with me anone."
And sa he did, and said, "Douchter, quhat cheir?"

"Allace!" quod scho, "father, my mirth is gone!"   60
"How sa?" quod he; and scho can all expone,
As I have tauld, the vengeance and the wraik,
For hir trepas, Cupide on hir culd tak.

He luikit on hir uglye lipper face,
The quhilk befor was quhite as lillie-flour: 65
Wringand his handis, oftymes he said, Allace,
That he had levit to se that wofull hour!
For he knew weill that thair was na succour
To hir seiknes, and that dowblit his pane.
Thus was thair cair aneuch betuix thame twane.   70

Quhen thay togidder murnit had full lang,
Quod Cresseid, "Father, I wald not be kend;
Thairfoir in secreit wyse ye let me gang
Unto yone hospitall at the tounis end;
And thidder sum meit, for cheritie, me send   75
To leif upon; for all mirth in this eird
Is fra me gane—sic is my wickit weird."

Than in' ane mantill and ane bawer hat,
With cop and clapper, wonder prively,
He opnit ane secreit yet, and out thair at   80
Convoyit hir, that na man suld espy,
Unto ane village half ane myle thairby;
Delyverit hir in at the spittail-hous,
And daylie sent hir part of his almous.

Sum knew hir weill, and sum had na knawledge   85
Of hir, becaus scho was sa deformait
With bylis blak, ouirspred in hir visage,
And hir fair colour faidit and alterait.
Yit thay presumit, for hir hie regrait
And still murning, scho was of nobill kin;   90
With better will thairfoir they tuik hir in.

The day passit, and Phebus went to rest;
The cloudis blak ouirquhelmit all the sky.
God wait gif Cresseid was ane sorrowful gest,
Seeing that uncouth fair and harbery.   95
But meit or drink scho dressit hir to ly

In ane dark corner of the hous allone;
And on this wyse, weiping, scho maid hir mone:

"O sop of sorrow sonken into cair!
　O cative Cresseid! for now and ever-mair　　　　100
　　Gane is thy joy and all thy mirth in eird;
Of all blyithnes now art thou blaiknit bair;
Thair is na salve may saif the of thy sair!
　　Fell is thy fortoun, wickit is thy weird;
　　　Thy blys is baneist, and thy baill on breird!　　105
Under the eirth God gif I gravin wer,
　　Quhar nane of Grece nor yit of Troy micht
　　　heird!" . . . .

Thus chydand with her drerie destenye,
Weiping, scho woik the nicht fra end to end;
Bot all in vane: hir dule, hir cairfull cry　　　　110
Micht nocht remeid, nor yit hir murning mend.
Ane lipper lady rais, and till hir wend,
And said, "Quhy spurnis thou aganis the wall,
To sla thyself, and mend nathing at all?

"Sen that thy weiping dowbillis bot thy wo,　　　　115
I counsall the mak vertew of ane neid,
To leir to clap thy clapper to and fro,
And live efter the law of lipper leid."
Thair was na buit, bot forth with thame scho yeid
Fra place to place, quhill cauld and hounger sair　　120
Compellit hir to be ane rank beggair.

That samin tyme, of Troy the garnisoun,
Quhilk had to chiftane worthy Troylus,
Throw jeopardy of weir had strikken down
Knichtis of Grece in number marvellous.　　　　125
With greit tryumphe and laude victorious
Agane to Troy richt royallie they raid
The way quhair Cresseid with the lipper baid.

Seing that companie, thai come all with ane stevin,
Thay gaif ane cry, and schuik coppis gude speid;　　130
Said, "Worthie lordis, for Goddis lufe of hevin
To us lipper part of your almous deid!"
Than to thair cry nobill Troylus tuik heid;

Having pietie, neir by the place can pas
Quhair Cresseid sat, not witting quhat scho was.　　135

Than upon him scho kest up baith her ene,
And with ane blenk it come into his thocht
That he sumtime hir face befoir had sene;
Bot scho was in sic plye he knew hir nocht.
Yit than hir luik into his mynd it brocht　　140
The sweit visage and amorous blenking
Of fair Cresseid, sumtyme his awin darling.

Na wonder was, suppois in mynd that he
Tuik hir figure sa sone, and lo! now, quhy;
The idole of ane thing in cace may be　　145
Sa deip imprentit in the fantasy
That it deludis the wittis outwardly,
And sa appeiris in forme and lyke estait
Within the mynd as it was figurait.

Ane spark of lufe than till his hart culd spring,　　150
And kendlit all his bodie in ane fyre;
With hait fewir ane sweit and trimbling
Him tuik, quhill he was reddie to expyre;
To beir his scheild his breist began to tyre;
Within ane quhyle he changit mony hew,　　155
And nevertheles not ane ane-uther knew.

For knichtlie pietie and memoriall
Of fair Cresseid, ane gyrdill can he tak,
Ane purs of gold, and mony gay jowall,
And in the skirt of Cresseid doun can swak;　　160
Than raid away, and not ane word [he] spak,
Pensiwe in hart, quhill he come to the toun,
And for greit cair oft-syis almaist fell doun.

The lipper folk to Cresseid than can draw,
To se the equall distribution　　165
Of the almous; bot quhen the gold thay saw,
Ilk ane to uther prewelie can roun
And said, "Yone lord hes mair affectioun,
However it be, unto yone lazarous
Than to us all; we knaw be his almous."　　170

"Quhat lord is yone?" quod scho—"have ye na feill—
Hes done to us so greit humanitie?"
"Yes," quod a lipper man, "I knaw him weill;
Schir Troylus it is, gentill and fre."
Quhen Cresseid understude that it was he,   175
Stiffer than steill thair stert ane bitter stound
Throwout hir hart, and fell doun to the ground.

Quhen scho, ouircome with siching sair and sad,
With mony cairfull cry and cald, "Ochane!
Now is my breist with stormie stoundis stad,   180
Wrappit in wo, ane wretch full will of wane!"
Than swounit scho oft or scho culd refrane,
And ever in hir swouning cryit scho thus:
"O fals Cresseid, and trew knicht Troilus!

"Thy lufe, thy lawtie, and thy gentilnes   185
I countit small in my prosperitie,
Sa elevait I was in wantones,
And clam upon the fickill quheill sa hie.
All faith and lufe, I promissit to the,
Was in the self fickill and frivolous.   190
"O fals Cresseid, and trew knicht Troilus!

"For lufe of me thow keipt gude continence,
Honest and chaist in conversatioun;
Of all wemen protectour and defence
Thou was, and helpit thair opinioun: 19.
My mynd, in fleschlie foull affectioun,
Was inclynit to lustis lecherous.
Fy! fals Cresseid! O trew knicht Troylus!

"Lovers, be war, and tak gude heid about
Quhome that ye lufe, for quhome ye suffer paine: 20
I lat you wit thair is richt few thairout
Quhome ye may traist, to have trew lufe agane;
Preif quhen ye will, your labour is in vaine.
Thairfoir I reid ye tak thame as ye find,
For they ar sad as widdercock in wind.   20

"Becaus I knaw the greit unstabilnes,
Brukkil as glas, into my-self I say,

Traisting in uther als greit unfaithfulnes,
Als unconstant, and als untrew of fay.
Thocht sum be trew, I wait richt few are thay.   210
Quha findis treuth lat him his lady ruse;
Nane but my-self, as now, I will accuse."

Quhen this was said, with paper scho sat doun,
And on this maneir maid hir testament:
"Heir I beteiche my corps and carioun   215
With wormis and with taidis to be rent.
My cop and clapper, and myne ornament,
And all my gold, the lipper folk sall have,
Quhen I am deid, to burie me in grave.

"This royall ring, set with this rubie reid,   220
Quhilk Troylus in drowrie to me send,
To him agane I leif it quhen I am deid,
To mak my cairfull deid unto him kend.
Thus I conclude schortlie, and mak ane end.
My spreit I leif to Diane, quhair scho dwellis,   225
To walk with hir in waist woddis and wellis.

"O Diomeid! thou hes baith broche and belt
Quhilk Troylus gave me in takning
Of his trew lufe!"—And with that word scho swelt.
And sone ane lipper man tuik of the ring,   230
Syne buryit hir withouttin tarying.
To Troylus furthwith the ring he bair,
And of Cresseid the deith he can declair.

Quhen he had hard hir greit infirmitie,
Hir legacie and lamentatioun,   235
And how scho endit in sic povertie,
He swelt for wo, and fell doun in ane swoun;
For greit sorrow his hart to brist was boun;
Siching full sadlie, said, "I can no moir;
Scho was untrew, and wo is me thairfoir!"   240

Sum said he maid ane tomb of merbell gray,
And wrait hir name and superscriptioun,
And laid it on hir grave, quhair that scho lay,
In goldin letteris, conteining this ressoun:

"Lo, fair ladyis! Cresseid of Troyis toun,   24.
Sumtyme countit the flour of womanheid,
Under this stane, lait lipper, lyis deid!"

Now, worthie wemen, in this ballet schort,
Made for your worschip and instructioun,
Of cheritie I monische and exhort,   25.
Ming not your lufe with fals deceptioun.
Beir in your mynd this schort conclusioun
Of fair Cresseid, as I have said befoir.
Sen scho is deid, I speik of hir no moir.

About 1460?   1532.

WILLIAM DUNBAR

SANCT SALVATOUR, SEND SILVER SORROW

Sanct Salvatour, send silver sorrow!
It grevis me both evin and morrow,
Chasing fra me all cheritie;
It makis me all blythness to borrow;
My panefull purss so pricliss me.

Quhen I wald blythlie ballattis breif,
Langour thairto givis me no leif;
War nocht gud howp my hart uphie,
My verry corpis for cair wald cleif;
My panefull purss so prikillis me.

Quhen I sett me to sing or dance,
Or go to plesand pastance,
Than pansing of penuritie
Revis that fra my remembrance;
My panefull purss so prikillis me.

Quhen men that hes purssis in tone
Passis to drynk or to disjone,
Than mon I keip ane gravetie,

And say that I will fast quhill none;
My panefull purss so pricliss me.   20

My purss is maid of sic ane skyn,
Thair will na corss byd it within;
Fra it as fra the Feynd thay fle,
Quha evir tyne, quha evir win;
My panefull purss so pricliss me.   25

Had I ane man of ony natioun
Culd mak on it ane conjuratioun,
To gar silver ay in it be,
The Devill suld haif no dominatioun
With pyne to gar it prickill me.   30

I haif inquyrit in mony a place,
For help and confort in this cace;
And all men sayis, my Lord, that ye
Can best remeid for this malice,
That with sic panis prickillis me.   35

About 1503?

FROM
THE GOLDYN TARGE

Ryght as the stern of day begouth to schyne,
Quhen gone to bed war Vesper and Lucyne,
   I raise, and by a rosere did me rest.
Up sprang the goldyn candill matutyne,
With clere depurit bemes cristallyne,   5
   Glading the mery foulis in thair nest;
   Or Phebus was in purpur cape revest,
Up raise the lark, the hevyns menstrale fyne
   In May, in till a morow myrthfullest.

Full angellike thir birdis sang thair houris   10
Within thair courtyns grene, in to thair bouris,
   Apparalit quhite and red, wyth blomes suete:
Anamalit was the felde wyth all colouris;
The perly droppis schake in silvir schouris,
   Quhill all in balme did branch and levis flete: 15
   To part fra Phebus did Aurora grete;

Hir cristall teris I saw hyng on the flouris,
    Quhilk he for lufe all drank up with his hete. . . . .

Quhat throu the mery foulys armony,
And throu the ryveris sounn rycht ran me by,   20
    On Fflorais mantill I slepit as I lay:
Quhare sone in to my dremes fantasy
I saw approch, agayn the orient sky,
    A saill als quhite as blossum upon spray,
    Wyth merse of gold, brycht as the stern of day;   25
Quhilk tendit to the land full lustily,
    As falcounn swift desyrouse of hir pray.

And hard on burd unto the blomyt medis,
Amang the grene rispis and the redis,
    Arrivit sche, quhar fro anonn thare landis   30
Ane hundreth ladyes, lusty in to wedis,
Als fresch as flouris that in May up spredis,
    In kirtillis grene, withoutyn kell or bandis;
    Thair brycht hairis hang gletering on the strandis
In tressis clere, wyppit wyth goldyn thredis;   35
    With pappis quhite, and mydlis small as wandis. . . . .

Full lustily thir ladyes all in fere
Enterit within this park of most plesere,
    Quhare that I lay our-helit wyth levis ronk.
The mery foulis, blisfullest of chere,   40
Salust Nature, me thoucht, on thair manere;
    And ewiry blome on branch, and eke on bonk,
    Opnyt and spred thair balmy levis donk,
Full low enclynyng to thair quene so clere,
    Quham of thair nobill norising thay thonk.   45

Syne to dame Flora, on the samyn wyse,
Thay saluse, and thay thank a thousand syse;
    And to dame Wenus, lufis mychti quene,
Thay sang ballettis in lufe, as was the gyse,
With amourouse notis lusty to devise,   50
    As thay that had lufe in thair hertis grene;
    Thair hony throtis, opnyt fro the splene,
With werblis suete did perse the hevinly skyes,
    Quhill loud resownyt the firmament serene. . . . . :

And ewiry one of thir, in grene arayit, 55
On harp or lute full merily thai playit,
   And sang ballettis with michty notis clere;
Ladyes to dance full sobirly assayit,
Endlang the lusty rywir so thai mayit:
    Thair observance rycht hevynly was to here. 60
    Than crap I throu the levis and drew nere,
Quhare that I was richt sudaynly affrayit,
    All throu a luke, quhilk I have boucht full dere.

And schortly for to speke, be lufis quene
I was aspyit: scho bad hir archearis kene 65
   Go me arrest, and thay no time delayit.
Than ladyes fair lete fall thair mantillis grene,
With bowis big in tressit hairis schene.
    All sudaynly thay had a felde arayit,
    And yit rycht gretly was I noucht affrayit; 70
The party was so plesand for to sene,
    A wonder lusty bikkir me assayit.

And first of all, with bow in hand ybent,
Come dame Beautee, rycht as scho wald me schent;
   Syne folowit all hir dameselis yfere, 75
With mony diverse aufull instrument,
Unto the pres: Fair Having wyth hir went,
    Fyne Portrature, Plesance, and lusty Chere.
    Than come Resoun, with schelde of gold so clere,
In plate and maille, as Mars armypotent; 80
Defendit me that nobil chevallere. . . . .

Unto the pres persewit Hie Degree;
Hir folowit ay Estate and Dignitee,
   Comparisoun, Honour, and Noble Array,
Will, Wantonnes, Renoun, and Libertee, 85
Richesse, Fredomm, and eke Nobilitee.
    Wit ye thay did thair baner hye display;
    A cloud of arowis as hayle schour lousit thay,
And schot, quhill wastit was thair artilye;
    Syne went abak reboytit of thair pray. 90

Quhen Venus had persavit this rebute,
Dissymilance scho bad go mak persute,
   At all powere to perse the Goldyn Targe;

And scho, that was of doubilnes the rute,
Askit hir choise of archeris in refute: 9!
    Wenus the best bad hir go wale at large.
    Scho tuke Presence plicht ankers of the barge,
And Fair Callyng, that wele a flayn coud schute,
    And Cherising for to complete hir charge.

Dame Hamelynes scho tuke in company,   10(
That hardy was, and hende in archery,
    And broucht dame Beautee to the felde agayn.
With all the choise of Venus chevalry
Thay come, and bikkerit unabaisitly:
    The schour of arowis rappit on as rayn.   10.
    Perilouse Presence, that mony syre has slayne,
The bataill broucht on bordour hard us by;
    The salt was all the sarar, suth to sayn.

Thik was the schote of grundyn dartis kene;
Bot Resoun, with the Scheld of Gold so schene,   11
    Warly defendit quho so ewir assayit;
The aufull stoure he manly did sustene,
Quhill Presence kest a pulder in his ene,
    And than as drunkyn man he all forvayit:
Quhen he was blynd the fule wyth hym thay playit,   11
And banyst hym amang the bewis grene;
    That sory sicht me sudaynly affrayit.

Than was I woundit to the deth wele nere,
And yoldyn as a wofull prisonnere
    To lady Beautee, in a moment space;   12
Me thoucht scho semyt lustiar of chere,
Efter that Resoun tynt had his eyne clere,
    Than of before, and lufliare of face.
    Quhy was thou blyndit, Resoun? quhi, allace!
And gert ane hell my paradise appere,   1:
    And mercy seme quhare that I fand no grace.

Dissymulance was besy me to sile,
And Fair Calling did oft apon me smyle,
    And Cherising me fed wyth wordis fair;
New Acquyntance enbracit me a quhile,   1,

And favouryt me, quhill men mycht go a myle,
  Syne tuk hir leve—I saw hir nevir mare.
  Than saw I Dangere toward me repair;
I coud eschew hir presence be no wyle;
  On syde scho lukit wyth ane fremyt fare;   135

And at the last, departing, coud hir dresse,
And me delyverit unto Hevynesse
  For to remayne, and scho in cure me tuke.
Be this the Lord of Wyndis, wyth wodenes,
God Eolus, his bugill blew, I gesse,   140
  That with the blast the levis all to-schuke:
  And sudaynly, in the space of a luke,
All was hyne went; thare was bot wildernes,
  Thare was no more bot birdis, bank, and bruke.

In twynkling of ane eye to schip thai went,   145
And swyth up saile unto the top thai stent,
  And with swift course atour the flude thay frak.
Thay fyrit gunnis wyth powder violent,
Till that the reke raise to the firmament;
  The rochis all resownyt wyth the rak,   150
  For reird it semyt that the raynbow brak;
Wyth spirit affrayde apon my fete I sprent
  Amang the clewis, so carefull was the crak.

And as I did awake of my sueving,
The joyfull birdis merily did syng   155
  For myrth of Phebus tendir bemes schene;
Suete war the vapouris, soft the morowing,
Halesum the vale depaynt wyth flouris ying;
  The air attemperit, sobir, and amene;
  In quhite and rede was all the felde besene,   160
Throu Naturis nobil fresch anamalyng,
  In mirthfull May, of ewiry moneth quene.

1503?   **1508.**

THE DANCE OF THE SEVIN DEIDLY SYNNIS

    Off Februar the fyiftene nycht,
    Full lang befoir the dayis lycht,
      I lay in till a trance;

And then I saw baith hevin and hell:
Me thocht, amangis the feyndis fell,   5
   Mahoun gart cry ane dance

Off schrewis that wer nevir schrevin,
Aganiss the feist of Fasternis evin,
   To mak thair observance;
He bad gallandis ga graith a gyiss,   10
And kast up gamountis in the skyiss,
   That last came out of France.

"Lat se," quod he, "now quha begynnis?"
With that the fowll Sevin Deidly Synnis
   Begowth to leip at anis.   15
And first of all in dance wes Pryd,
With hair wyld bak and bonet on syd,
   Lyk to mak vaistie wanis;

And round abowt him, as a quheill,
Hang all in rumpillis to the heill   20
   His kethat for the nanis.
Mony prowd trumpour with him trippit
Throw skaldand fyre; ay as they skippit
   Thay gyrnd with hiddouss granis.

Heilie harlottis on hawtane wyiss   25
Come in with mony sindrie gyiss,
   Bot yit luche nevir Mahoun;
Quhill preistis come in with bair schevin nekkis,
Than all the feyndis lewche and maid gekkis,
   Blak Belly and Bawsy Brown.   30

Than Yre come in with sturt and stryfe;
His hand wes ay upoun his knyfe,
   He brandeist lyk a beir.
Bostaris, braggaris, and barganeris,
Eftir him passit in to pairis,   35
   All bodin in feir of weir,

In jakkis and scryppis and bonettis of steill;
Thair leggis wer chenyeit to the heill.
   Ffrawart was thair affeir:
Sum upon udir with brandis beft;   40

Sum jaggit uthiris to the heft
   With knyvis that scherp cowd scheir.

Nixt in the dance followit Invy,
Fild full of feid and fellony,
   Hid malyce and dispyte;   45
Ffor pryvie hatrent that tratour trymlit.
Him followit mony freik dissymlit,
   With fenyeit wirdis quhyte;

And flattereris in to menis facis;
And bakbyttaris of sindry racis,   50
   To ley that had delyte;
And rownaris of fals lesingis;
Allace! that courtis of noble kingis
   Of thame can nevir be quyte.

Nixt him in dans come Cuvatyce,   55
Rute of all evill and grund of vyce,
   That nevir cowd be content.
Catyvis, wrechis, and okkeraris,
Hud-pykis, hurdaris, and gadderaris,
   All with that warlo went: 60

Out of thair throttis thay schot on udder
Hett moltin gold, me thocht a fudder,
   As fyreflawcht maist fervent;
Ay as thay tomit thame of schot,
Ffeyndis fild thame new up to the thrott   65
   With gold of allkin prent.

Syne Sweirnes, at the secound bidding,
Com lyk a sow out of a midding;
   Full slepy wes his grunzie.
Mony sweir bumbard belly-huddroun,   70
Mony slute daw and slepy duddroun,
   Him serwit ay with sounzie.

He drew thame furth in till a chenzie,
And Belliall, with a brydill renzie,
   Evir lascht thame on the lunzie.   75
In dance thay war so slaw of feit
Thay gaif thame in the fyre a heit,
   And maid thame quicker of counzie.

Than Lichery, that lathly corss,
Berand lyk a bagit horss,   80
    And Ydilness did him leid.
Thair wes with him ane ugly sort,
And mony stynkand fowll tramort,
    That had in syn bene deid. . . . .

Than the fowll monstir Glutteny,
Off wame unsasiable and gredy,
    To dance he did him dress.
Him followit mony fowll drunckart,
With can and collep, cop and quart,   95
    In surffet and excess.

Full mony a waistless wallydrag,
With wamiss unweildable, did furth wag,
    In creische that did incress.
"Drynk!" ay thay cryit, with mony a gaip: 100
The feyndis gaif thame hait leid to laip;
    Thair lovery wes na less.

Na menstrallis playit to thame but dowt;
Ffor glemen thair wer haldin owt,
    Be day and eik by nycht,   105
Except a menstrall that slew a man—
Swa till his heretage he wan,
    And entirt be breif of richt.

Than cryd Mahoun for a Heleand padzane;
Syne ran a feynd to feche Makfadzane,   110
    Ffar northwart in a nuke:
Be he the correnoch had done schout,
Erschemen so gadderit him abowt,
    In hell grit rowme thay tuke.

Thae tarmegantis, with tag and tatter,   115
Ffull lowd in Ersche begowth to clatter,
    And rowp lyk revin and ruke:
The Devill sa devit wes with thair yell
That in the depest pot of hell
    He smorit thame with smuke.   120

1507?

GAWIN DOUGLAS

FROM

THE PROLOUG OF THE XII BUK OF ENEADOS

The twynklyng stremowris of the orient
Sched purpour sprangis with gold and asure ment,
Persand the sabill barmkyn nocturnall,
Bet doun the skyis clowdy mantill wall.
Eous the steid, with ruby harnys red,   5
Abuf the sey lyftis furth hys hed,
Of cullour soyr, and sumdeill broun as berry,
Forto alichtyn and glaid our emyspery,
The flambe owtbrastyng at his noyss-thyrlys,
So fast Pheton with the quhyp hym quhyrlys,   10
To roll Appollo hys faderis goldyn char,
That schrowdith all the hevynnys and the ayr:
Quhill schortly, with the blesand torch of day,
Abilgheit in hys lemand fresch array,
Furth of hys palyce ryall ischit Phebus,   15
With goldyn croun and vissage gloryus,
Crysp haris brycht as chrisolyte or topace,
For quhais hew mycht nane behald hys face;
The fyry sparkis brastyng from hys eyn,
To purge the ayr and gylt the tendyr greyn,   20
Defundand from hys sege etheryall
Glaid influent aspectis celicall;
Before hys regale hie magnificens
Mysty vapour upspryngand, sweit as sens,
In smoky soppys of donk dewis wak,   25
Moich hailsum stovys ourheldand the slak;
The aureat fanys of hys trone soverane
With glytrand glans ourspred the occiane,
The large fludis lemand all of lycht
Bot with a blenk of hys supernale sycht.   30
Forto behald it was a glore to se
The stablit wyndis and the cawmyt see,
The soft sesson, the firmament sereyn,
The lowne illumynat ayr, and fyrth ameyn;
The sylver-scalyt fyschis on the greit   35
Ourthwort cleir stremys sprynkland for the heyt,

With fynnys schynand broun as synopar,
And chyssell talys, stowrand heir and thar;
The new cullour alychtnyng all the landis,
Forgane thir stannyris schane the beriall strandis,   40
Quhil the reflex of the diurnal bemys
The beyn bonkis kest ful of variant glemys.
And lusty Flora dyd hyr blomys spreid
Under the feit of Phebus sulghart steid;
The swardit soyll enbroud with selcouth hewys;   45
Wod and forest obumbrat with thar bewys,
Quhois blisfull branschis porturat on the grund;
With schaddoys schene schew rochis rubicund;
Towris, turrettis, kyrnellis, pynnaclys hie
Of kyrkis, castellis, and ilke fair cite,   50
Stude payntit, every fyall, fayn, and stage,
Apon the plane grund, by thar awyn umbrage.
Of Eolus north blastis havand no dreid,
The sulghe spred her braid bosum on breid,
Zephyrus confortabill inspiratioun   55
Fortill ressave law in hyr barm adoun;
The cornys croppis and the beris new brerd
With glaidsum garmont revestyng the erd:
So thik the plantis sprang in every peyce,
The feildis ferleis of thar fructuus fleyce.   60

1513.

SIR DAVID LYNDSAY

FROM
THE DREME

THE PROLOG

In to the Calendis of Januarie,
   Quhen fresche Phebus, be movyng circulair,
Frome Capricorne wes enterit in Aquarie,
   With blastis that the branchis maid full bair,
   The snaw and sleit perturbit all the air,   5
And flemit Flora frome every bank and bus
Throuch supporte of the austeir Eolus.

Efter that I the larg wynteris nycht
    Had lyne walking in to my bed, allone,
Throuch hevy thocht, that no way sleip I mycht,   10
    Rememberyng of divers thyngis gone,
    ~So up I rose and clethit me anone.
Be this fair Tytane, with his lemis lycht,
Ouer all the land had spred his baner brycht.

With cloke and hude I dressit me belyve,   15
    With dowbyll schone, and myttanis on my handis:
Howbeit the air was rycht penetratyve,
    Yit fure I furth, lansing ouirthorte the landis,
    Toward the see, to schorte me on the sandis,
Because unblomit was baith bank and braye.   20
And so, as I was passing be the waye,

I met dame Flora, in dule weid dissagysit,
    Quhilk in to May wes dulce and delectabyll;
With stalwart stormis hir sweitnes wes supprisit;
    Hir hevynlie hewis war turnit in to sabyll,   25
    Quhilkis umquhile war to luffaris amiabyll.
Fled frome the froste, the tender flouris I saw
Under dame Naturis mantyll lurking law.

The small fowlis in flokkis saw I flee,
    To Nature makand greit lamentatioun: 30
Thay lychtit doun besyde me, on ane tree;
    Of thair complaynt I had compassioun;
    And, with ane pieteous exclamatioun,
Thay said, "Blyssit be Somer, with his flouris!
And waryit be thow, Wynter, with thy schouris!"   35

"Allace, Aurora!" the syllie larke can crye,
    "Quhare hes thou left thy balmy liquour sweit,
That us rejosit, we mounting in the skye?
    Thy sylver droppis ar turnit in to sleit.
    O fair Phebus, quhare is thy hoilsum heit?   40
Quhy tholis thow thy hevinlie plesand face
With mystie vapouris to be obscurit, allace!

"Quhar art thow, May, with June thy syster schene,
    Weill bordourit with dasyis of delyte?

And gentyll Julie, with thy mantyll grene,   45
    Enamilit with rosis red and quhyte?
    Now auld and cauld Januar, in dispyte,
Reiffis frome us all pastyme and plesour:
Allace! quhat gentyll hart may this indure?

"Ouersylit ar with cloudis odious   50
    The goldin skyis of the orient;
Changeyng in sorrow our sang melodious,
    Quhilk we had wount to sing, with gude intent,
    Resoundand to the hevinnis firmament:
Bot now our daye is changeit in to nycht."   55
With that thay rais, and flew furth of my sycht.

Pensyve in hart, passing full soberlie,
    Unto the see fordward I fure anone:
The see was furth, the sand wes smooth and drye.
    Then up and doun I musit myne allone,   60
    Tyll that I spyit ane lyttill cave of stone,
Heych in ane craig; upwart I did approche,
But tarying, and clam up in the roche;

And purposit, for passing of the tyme,
    Me to defende from ociositie,   65
With pen and paper to register in ryme
    Sum mery mater of antiquitie.
    Bot Idelnes, ground of iniquitie,
Scho maid so dull my spreitis, me within,
That I wyste nocht at quhat end to begin,   70

But satt styll in that cove, quhare I mycht see
    The wolteryng of the wallis, up and doun;
And this fals warldis instabilytie
    Unto that see makkand comparisoun,
    And of this warldis wracheit variatioun   75
To thame that fixis all thair hole intent,
Consideryng quho most had suld most repent.

So with my hude my hede I happit warme,
    And in my cloke I fauldit boith my feit;
I thocht my corps with cauld suld tak no harme;   80
    My mittanis held my handis weill in heit;
    The skowland craig me coverit frome the sleit:

Thare styll I satt, my bonis for to rest,
Tyll Morpheus with sleip my spreit opprest.

So, throw the bousteous blastis of Eolus,   85
   And throw my walkyng on the nycht before,
And throw the seyis movyng marvellous,
   Be Neptunus, with mony route and rore,
   Constrainit I was to sleip, withouttin more:
And quhat I dremit, in conclusioun   90
I sall you tell, ane marvellous visioun.

About 1528?   1552.

STEPHEN HAWES

FROM

THE PASTIME OF PLEASURE

HOW GRAUNDE AMOURE WAS RECEYVED OF LA BELLE PUCELL

Whan she it knewe, than ryght incontynent
She called to her Peace and dame Mercy,
With Justyce, and Reason the lady excellent,
Pleasaunce, Grace, with good dame Memory,
To weyte upon her full ententyfly: 5
Me to receyve with all solempne joye,
Adowne her chambre she wente on her waye.

And in meane whyle the gentyll porteres,
Called Countenaunce, on my way then me ledde,
Into the basse courte of grete wydnes,   10
Where all of golde there was a conduyte hede,
With many dragons enameled with reed,
Whiche dyde spoute oute the dulcet lycoure,
Lyke cristall clere, with aromatyke odoure.

Alofte the basse toure foure ymages stode,   15
Whiche blewe the claryons well and wonderly.
Alofte the toures the golden fanes good
Dyde with the wynde make full swete armony;
Them for to here it was grete melody.
The golden toures with crystall clarefyed   20
Aboute were glased moost clerely purefyed.

And the gravell whereupon we wente,
Full lyke the golde that is mooʒt pure and fyne,
Withouten spotte of blacke encombremente,
Aboute our fete it dyde ryghte clerely shyne: 25
It semed more lyke a place celestyne
Than an erthely mansyon whiche shall away
By longe tyme and proces an other day.

And towarde me I dyde se than comynge
La Belle Pucell, the moost fayre creature 30
Of ony fayre erthely persone lyvynge,
Whiche with me mette with chere so demure.
Of the shynynge golde was all her vesture.
I dyde my duty, and ones or twyes ywys
Her lyppes softe I dyde full swetely kys. 35

"Aha!" quod she, "that I am very fayne
That you are come, for I have thought longe
Sythen the tyme that we parted in twayne,
And for my sake you have had often wronge;
But your courage so hardy and stronge 40
Hath caused you for to be vyctoryous
Of your enmyes so moche contraryous."

With her praty honde, whyte as ony lyly,
She dyde me lede into a ryall hall,
With knottes kerved full ryght craftely, 45
The wyndowes fayre glased with crystall;
And all aboute, upon the golden wall,
There was enameled, with fygures curyous,
The syege of Troye so harde and dolorous.

The flore was paved with precyous stones; 50
And the rofe of mervaylous geometry,
Of the swete sypres wrought for the nones,
Encensynge oute the yll odours mysty.
Amyddes the rofe there shone full wonderly
A poynted dyamonde of mervaylous bygnes, 55
With many other grete stones of ryches.

So up we wente to a chambre fayre,
A place of pleasure and delectacyon,
Strowed with flowres flagraunte of ayre,

Without ony spotte of perturbacyon.   60
I behelde ryght well the operacyon
Of the mervaylous rofe set full of rubyes,
And tynst with saphers and many turkeys.

The walles were hanged with golden aras,
Whiche treated well of the syege of Thebes;   65
And yet all aboute us depured was
The crystallyne wyndowes of grete bryghtnes.
I can nothynge extende the goodlynes
Of this palays, for it is impossyble
To shewe all that unto me [was] vysyble.   70

But La Belle Pucell full ryght gentylly
Dyde syt adoune by a wyndowes syde,
And caused me also full swetely
By her to sytte at that gentyll tyde.
"Welcome!" she sayde: "ye shall with me abyde,   75
After your sorowe to lyve in joye and blysse;
You shall have that ye have deserved ywys."

Her redolente wordes of swete influence
Degouted vapoure moost aromatyke,
And made conversyon of my complacence;   80
Her depured and her lusty rethoryke
My courage reformed, that was so lunatyke,
My sorowe defeted, and my mynde dyde modefy,
And my dolourous herte began to pacyfy.

All thus in love we gan to devyse,   85
For eche of other were ryght joyous.
Than at the last, in a mervaylous wyse,
Full sodaynly there came unto us
Lytell Cupyde with his moder Venus,
Whiche was well cladde in a fayre mantyll blewe,   90
With golden hertes that were perst anewe.

And rounde aboute us she her mantyll cast,
Sayenge that she and her sonne Cupyde
Wolde us conjoyne in maryage in hast:
"And to lete knowe all your courte so wyde,   95
Sende you Perseveraunce before to provyde,

To warne your ladyes for to be redy
To morowe betyme, ryght well and solemply."

We answered bothe our hertes were in one,
Sayenge that we dyde ryght well agre,   100
For all our foes were added and gone.
Ryght gladde I was that joyfull day to se.
And than anone, with grete humylyte,
La Bell Pucell to a fayre chambre bryght
Dyde me than brynge for to rest all nyght.   105

And she toke her leve; I kyst her lovely.
I wente to bedde; but I coude not slepe,
For I thought so moche upon her inwardly
Her moost swete lokes into my herte dyde crepe,
Percynge it through with a wounde so depe: 110
For Nature thought every houre a day
Tyll to my lady I sholde my dette well paye.

About 1506.   **1509.**

HOWE REMEMBRAUNCE MADE HIS EPYTAPHY ON HIS GRAVE

The good dame Mercy, with dame Charyte,
My body buryed full ryght humbly,
In a fayre temple of olde antyquyte,
Where was for me a dyryge devoutely,
And with many a masse full ryght solempnely;   5
And over my grave, to be in memory,
Remembraunce made this lytell epytaphy: . . . .

"O mortall folke, you may beholde and se
How I lye here, somtyme a myghty knyght.
The ende of joye and all prosperyte   10
Is Dethe at last, through his course and myght:
After the day there cometh the derke nyght;
For though the day be never so longe,
At last the belles ryngeth to evensonge.

"And I my selfe, called La Graunde Amoure,   15
Sekynge adventure in the worldly glory,
For to attayne the ryches and honoure,

Dyde thynke full lytell that I sholde here ly,
Tyll Dethe dyde mate me full ryght pryvely.
Lo what I am, and whereto you must!   20
Lyke as I am, so shall you be all dust.

"Than in your mynde inwardely dyspyse
The bryttle worlde, so full of doublenes,
With the vyle flesshe, and ryght soone aryse
Out of your slepe of mortall hevynes;   25
Subdue the Devyll with grace and mekenes,
That, after your lyfe frayle and transytory,
You may than lyve in joye perdurably."

About 1506.   1509.

JOHN SKELTON

FROM

WHY COME YE NAT TO COURT

Ones yet agayne
Of you I wolde frayne,
Why come ye nat to court?—
To whyche court?
To the Kynges courte,   5
Or to Hampton Court?—
Nay, to the Kynges court!
The Kynges courte
Shulde have the excellence;
But Hampton Court   10
Hath the pre-emynence,
And Yorkes Place,
With my lordes grace,
To whose magnifycence
Is all the conflewence,   15
Sutys and supplycacyons,
Embassades of all nacyons.
Strawe for lawe canon!
Or for the lawe common!
Or for lawe cyvyll!   20
It shall be as he wyll:

Stop at law tancrete,
An obstract or a concrete;
Be it soure, be it swete,
His wysdome is so dyscrete   25
That, in a fume or an hete,
"Wardeyn of the Flete,
Set hym fast by the fete!"
And of his royall powre
Whan him lyst to lowre,   30
Than "Have him to the Towre,
Saunz aulter remedy!
Have hym forthe by and by
To the Marshalsy
Or to the Kynges Benche!"   35
He dyggeth so in the trenche
Of the court royall,
That he ruleth them all.
So he dothe undermynde,
And suche sleyghtes dothe fynde,   40
That the Kynges mynde
By hym is subverted,
And so streatly coarted
In credensynge his tales
That all is but nutshales   45
That any other sayth,
He hath in him suche fayth.
    Now, yet all this myght be
Suffred and taken in gre,
If that that he wrought   50
To any good ende were brought;
But all he bringeth to nought,
By God, That me dere bought!
He bereth the Kyng on hand,
That he must pyll his lande,   55
To make his cofers ryche;
But he laythe all in the dyche,
And useth suche abusyoun
That in the conclusyoun
All commeth to confusyon.   60
Perceyve the cause why!
To tell the trouth playnly,

He is so ambicyous,
So shamles, and so vicyous,
And so supersticyous,   65
And so moche oblivyous
From whens that he came,
That he falleth into a *caeciam:*
Whiche, truly to expresse,
Is a forgetfulnesse,   70
Or wylfull blyndnesse,
Wherwith the Sodomites
Lost theyr inward syghtes;
The Gommoryans also
Were brought to deedly wo,   75
As Scrypture recordis.
"A caecitate cordis,"
In the Latyne synge we,
"Libera nos, Domine!"
But this madde Amalecke,   80
Lyke to a Mamelek,
He regardeth lordes
No more than potshordes;
He is in suche elacyon
Of his exaltacyon,   85
And the supportacyon
Of our soverayne lorde,
That, God to recorde,
He ruleth all at wyll,
Without reason or skyll: 90
How be it the primordyall
Of his wretched originall,
And his base progeny,
And his gresy genealogy,
He came of the sank royall   95
That was cast out of a bochers stall.

About 1522.

BALLADS

ST. STEPHEN AND HEROD

Seynt Stevene was a clerk in Kyng Herowdes halle,
And servyd him of bred and cloth, as every kyng befalle.

Stevyn out of kechone cam, wyth boris hed on honde:
He saw a sterre was fayr and brygt over Bedlem stonde.

He kyst adoun the boris hed, and went in to the halle: 5
"I forsak the, Kyng Herowdes, and thi werkes alle.

"I forsak the, Kyng Herowdes, and thi werkes alle;
Ther is a chyld in Bedlem born is beter than we alle."

"Quat eylyt the, Stevene? Quat is the befalle?
Lakkyt the eyther mete or drynk in Kyng Herowdes halle?"   10

"Lakit me neyther mete ne drynk in Kyng Herowdes halle:
Ther is a chyld in Bedlem born is beter than we alle."

"Quat eylyt the, Stevyn? Art thu wod, or thu gynnyst to brede?
Lakkyt the eyther gold or fe, or ony ryche wede?"

"Lakyt me neyther gold ne fe, ne non ryche wede: 15
Ther is a chyld in Bedlem born xal helpyn us at our nede."

"That is al so soth, Stevyn, al so soth, iwys,
As this capoun crowe xal that lyth here in myn dysh."

That word was not so sone seyd, that word in that halle,
The capoun crew "Cristus natus est!" among the lordes alle.   20

"Rysyt up, myn turmentowres! be to and al be on;
And ledyt Stevyn out of this town, and stonyt hym wyth ston!"

Tokyn he Stevene, and stonyd hym in the way;
And therfore is his evyn on Crystes owyn day.

FROM

A GEST OF ROBYN HODE

THE VII. FYTTE

The kynge came to Notynghame,
    With knyghtes in grete araye,
For to take that gentyll knyght
    And Robyn Hode, and yf he may.

He asked men of that countrè   5
    After Robyn Hode,
And after that gentyll knyght,
    That was so bolde and stout.

Whan they had tolde hym the case,
 Our kynge understode ther tale,   10
And seased in his honde
 The knyghtès londès all.

All the passe of Lancasshyre
 He went both ferre and nere,
Tyll he came to Plomton Parke;   15
 He faylyd many of his dere.

There our kynge was wont to se
 Herdès many one,
He coud unneth fynde one dere
 That bare ony good horne.   20

The kynge was wonder wroth withall,
 And swore by the Trynytè,
"I wolde I had Robyn Hode,
 With eyen I myght hym se.

"And he that wolde smyte of the knyghtès hede, 25
 And brynge it to me,
He shall have the knyghtès londes,
 Syr Rycharde at the Le.

"I gyve it hym with my charter,
 And sele it with my honde,   30
To have and holde for ever more,
 In all mery Englonde."

Than bespake a fayre olde knyght,
 That was treue in his fay:
"A, my leegè Lorde the Kynge,   35
 One worde I shall you say.

"There is no man in this countrè
 May have the knyghtès londes,
Whyle Robyn Hode may ryde or gone
 And bere a bowe in his hondes.   40

"That he ne shall lese his hede,
 That is the best ball in his hode.
Give it no man, my Lorde the Kynge,
 That ye wyll any good."

Half a yere dwelled our comly kynge   45
    In Notyngham, and well more:
Coude he not here of Robyn Hode,
    In what countrè that he were.

But alway went good Robyn
    By halke and eke by hyll,   50
And alway slewe the kyngès dere,
    And welt them at his wyll.

Than bespake a proude fostere,
    That stode by our kyngès kne:
"Yf ye wyll see good Robyn,   55
    Ye must do after me.

"Take fyve of the best knyghtes
    That be in your lede,
And walke downe by yon abbay,
    And gete you monkès wede.   60

"And I wyll be your ledès-man,
    And lede you the way;
And or ye come to Notyngham,
    Myn hede then dare I lay

"That ye shall mete with good Robyn,   65
    On lyve yf that he be;
Or ye come to Notyngham,
    With eyen ye shall hym se."

Full hastely our kynge was dyght,
    So were his knyghtès fyve,   70
Everych of them in monkès wede,
    And hasted them thyder blyve.

Our kynge was grete above his cole,
    A brode hat on his crowne;
Ryght as he were abbot-lyke,   75
    They rode up in-to the towne.

Styf botès our kynge had on,
    Forsoth as I you say;
He rode syngynge to grenè wode;
    The covent was clothed in graye.   80

His male-hors and his gretè somers
   Folowed our kynge behynde,
Tyll they came to grenè wode,
   A myle under the lynde.

There they met with good Robyn,   85
   Stondynge on the waye,
And so dyde many a bolde archere,
   For soth as I you say.

Robyn toke the kyngès hors,
   Hastely in that stede,   90
And sayd, "Syr abbot, by your leve,
   A whyle ye must abyde.

"We be yemen of this foreste,
   Under the grene-wode tre:
We lyve by our kyngès dere;   95
   Other shyft have not wee.

"And ye have chyrches and rentès both,
   And gold full gretè plentè:
Gyve us some of your spendynge,
   For Saynte Charytè."   100

Than bespake our cumly kynge,
   Anone than sayd he:
"I brought no more to grenè-wode
   But forty pounde with me.

"I have layne at Notyngham,   105
   This fourtynyght, with our kynge,
And spent I have full moche good
   On many a grete lordynge.

"And I have but forty pounde,
   No more than have I me;   110
But yf I had an hondred pounde,
   I wolde vouch it safe on the."

Robyn toke the forty pounde,
   And departed it in two partye;
Halfendell he gave his mery men,   115
   And bad them mery to be,

Full curteysly Robyn gan say,
   "Syr, have this for your spendyng:
We shall mete another day."
   "Gramercy," than sayd our kynge.   120

"But well the greteth Edwarde, our kynge,
   And sent to the his seale,
And byddeth the com to Notyngham,
   Both to mete and mele."

He toke out the brodè targe,   125
   And sone he lete hym se;
Robyn coud his courteysy,
   And set hym on his kne.

"I love no man in all the worlde
   So well as I do my kynge: 130
Welcome is my lordès seale;
   And, monke, for thy tydynge,

"Syr abbot, for thy tydynges,
   To day thou shalt dyne with me,
For the love of my kynge,   135
   Under my trystell-tre."

Forth he lad our comly kynge,
   Full fayre by the honde.
Many a dere there was slayne,
   And full fast dyghtande.   140

Robyn toke a full grete horne,
   And loude he gan blowe:
Seven score of wyght yonge men
   Came redy on a rowe;

All they kneled on theyr kne,   145
   Full fayre before Robyn.
The kynge sayd hym selfe untyll,
   And swore by Saynt Austyn,

"Here is a wonder semely sight:
   Me thynketh, by Goddès pyne,   150
His men are more at his byddynge
   Then my men be at myn."

Full hastely was theyr dyner idyght,
   And therto gan they gone.
They served our kynge with al theyr myght,   155
   Both Robyn and Lytell Johan:

Anone before our kynge was set
   The fattè venyson,
The good whyte brede, the good rede wyne,
   And therto the fyne ale and browne.   160

"Make good chere," said Robyn,
   "Abbot, for charytè;
And for this ylkè tydynge
   Blyssed mote thou be.

"Now shalte thou se what lyfe we lede,   165
   Or thou hens wende;
Than thou may enfourme our kynge,
   Whan ye togyder lende."

Up they stertè all in hast,
   Theyr bowes were smartly bent: 170
Our kynge was never so sore agast;
   He wende to have be shente.

Two yerdes there were up set;
   Thereto gan they gange:
By fyfty pase, our kynge sayd,   175
   The merkès were to longe.

On every syde a rose-garlonde,
   They shot under the lyne:
"Whoso fayleth of the rose-garlonde," sayd Robyn,
   "His takyll he shall tyne,   180

"And yelde it to his mayster,
   Be it never so fyne
(For no man wyll I spare,
   So drynke I ale or wyne),

"And bere a buffet on his hede,   185
   I-wys ryght all bare."
And all that fell in Robyns lote,
   He smote them wonder sare.

Twyse Robyn shot aboute,
 And ever he cleved the wande;   190
And so dyde good Gylberte
 With the whytè hande.

Lytell Johan and good Scathelocke,
 For nothynge wolde they spare;
When they fayled of the garlonde,   195
 Robyn smote them full sore.

At the last shot that Robyn shot,
 For all his frendès fare,
Yet he fayled of the garlonde
 Thre fyngers and mare.   200

Than bespake good Gylberte,
 And thus he gan say:
"Mayster," he sayd, "your takyll is lost;
 Stande forth and take your pay."

"If it be so," sayd Robyn,   205
 "That may no better be,
Syr abbot, I delyver the myn arowe;
 I pray the, syr, serve thou me."

"It falleth nct for myn ordre," sayd our kynge,
 "Robyn, by thy leve,   210
For to smyte no good yeman,
 For doute I sholde hym greve."

"Smyte on boldely," sayd Robyn;
 "I give the largè leve."
Anone our kynge, with that worde,   215
 He folde up his sleve,

And sych a buffet he gave Robyn
 To grounde he yede full nere.
"I make myn avowe to God," sayd Robyn,
 "Thou arte a stalworthe frere.   220

"There is pith in thyn arme," sayd Robyn,
 "I trowe thou canst well shete."
Thus our kynge and Robyn Hode
 Togeder gan they mete.

Robyn behelde our comly kynge 225
    Wystly in the face;
So dyde Syr Rycharde at the Le,
    And kneled downe in that place;

And so dyde all the wylde outlawes,
    Whan they se them knele: 230
"My Lorde the Kynge of Englonde,
    Now I knowe you well!"

"Mercy then, Robyn," sayd our kynge,
    "Under your trystyll-tre,
Of thy goodnesse and thy grace, 235
    For my men and me!"

"Yes, for God," sayd Robyn,
    "And also God me save!
I aske mercy, my Lorde the Kynge,
    And for my men I crave." 240

"Yes, for God," than sayd our kynge;
    "And therto sent I me,
With that thou leve the grenè-wode,
    And all thy company,

"And come home, syr, to my courte, 245
    And there dwell with me."
"I make myn avowe to God," sayd Robyn,
    "And ryght so shall it be.

"I wyll come to your courte,
    Your servyse for to se, 250
And brynge with me of my men
    Seven score and thre.

"But me lyke well your servyse,
    I wyll come agayne full soone,
And shote at the donnè dere, 255
    As I am wonte to done."

THE VIII. FYTTE

"Haste thou ony grene cloth," sayd our kynge,
    "That thou wylte sell nowe to me?"
"Ye, for God," sayd Robyn;
    "Thyrty yerdes and thre."

"Robyn," sayd our kynge, 5
  "Now pray I the,
Sell me some of that cloth,
  To me and my meynè."

"Yes, for God," then sayd Robyn,
  "Or elles I were a fole; 10
Another day ye wyll me clothe,
  I trowe, ayenst the Yole."

The kynge kest of his colè then;
  A grene garment he dyde on,
And every knyght also, iwys, 15
  Another had full sone.

Whan they were clothed in Lyncolne grene,
  They keste away theyr graye:
"Now we shall to Notyngham,"
  All thus our kynge gan say. 20

They bente theyr bowes, and forth they went,
  Shotynge all in-fere,
Towarde the towne of Notyngham,
  Outlawes as they were.

Our kynge and Robyn rode togyder, 25
  For soth as I you say;
And they shote plucke-buffet,
  As they went by the way.

And many a buffet our kynge wan
  Of Robyn Hode that day; 30
And nothynge spared good Robyn
  Our kynge in his pay.

"So God me helpè," sayd our kynge,
  "Thy game is nought to lere;
I sholde not get a shote of the, 35
  Though I shote all this yere."

All the people of Notyngham
  They stode and behelde;
They sawe nothynge but mantels of grene
  That covered all the felde. 40

Than every man to other gan say,
  "I drede our kynge be slone:
Come Robyn Hode to the towne, i-wys
  On lyve he lefte never one."

Full hastely they began to fle,   45
  Both yemen and knaves;
And olde wyves that myght evyll goo,
  They hypped on theyr staves.

The kynge loughe full fast,
  And commaunded theym agayne: 50
When they se our comly kynge,
  I-wys they were full fayne.

They ete and dranke, and made them glad,
  And sange with notès hye.
Then bespake our comly kynge   55
  To Syr Richarde at the Lee:

He gave hym there his londe agayne;
  A good man he bad hym be.
Robyn thanked our comly kynge,
  And set hym on his kne.   60

Had Robyn dwelled in the kyngès courte
  But twelve monethes and thre,
That he had spent an hondred pounde
  And all his mennes fe.

In every place where Robyn came   65
  Ever more he layde downe,
Both for knyghtès and for squyres
  To gete hym grete renowne.

By than the yere was all agone
  He had no man but twayne,   70
Lytell Johan and good Scathelocke,
  With hym all for to gone.

Robyn sawe yonge men shote
  Full fayre upon a day:
"Alas!" than sayd good Robyn,   75
  "My welthe is went away.

"Somtyme I was an archere good,
    A styffe and eke a stronge;
I was compted the best archere
    That was in mery Englonde.   80

"Alas!" then sayd good Robyn,
    "Alas and well a woo!
Yf I dwele lenger with the kynge,
    Sorowe wyll me sloo."

Forth than went Robyn Hode   85
    Tyll he came to our kynge:
"My Lorde the Kynge of Englonde,
    Graunte me myn askynge!

"I made a chapell in Bernysdale,
    That semely is to se;   90
It is of Mary Magdaleyne,
    And thereto wolde I be.

"I myght never in this seven nyght
    No tyme to slepe ne wynke,
Nother all these seven dayes   95
    Nother ete ne drynke.

"Me longeth sore to Bernysdale;
    I may not be therfro:
Barefote and wolwarde I have hyght
    Thyder for to go."   100

"Yf it be so," than sayd our kynge,
    "It may no better be;
Seven nyght I gyve the leve,
    No lengre, to dwell fro me."

"Gramercy, lorde," then sayd Robyn,   105
    And set hym on his kne:
He toke his leve full courteysly;
    To grene wode then went he.

Whan he came to grenè wode,
    In a mery mornynge,   110
There he herde the notès small
    Of byrdès mery syngynge.

"It is ferre gone," sayd Robyn,
 "That I was last here:
Me lyste a lytell for to shote   115
 At the donnè dere."

Robyn slewe a full grete harte;
 His horne than gan he blow,
That all the outlawes of that forest
 That horne coud they knowe,   120

And gadred them togyder,
 In a lytell throwe.
Seven score of wyght yonge men
 Came redy on a rowe,

And fayre dyde of theyr hodes,   125
 And set them on theyr kne:
"Welcome," they sayd, "our mayster,
 Under this grene-wode tre!"

Robyn dwelled in grenè wode
 Twenty yere and two;   130
For all drede of Edwarde our kynge,
 Agayne wolde he not goo.

Yet he was begyled, i-wys,
 Through a wycked woman,
The pryoresse of Kyrkèsly,   135
 That nye was of hys kynne,

For the love of a knyght,
 Syr Roger of Donkesly,
That was her ownè speciall.
 Full evyll mote they the!   140

They toke togyder theyr counsell
 Robyn Hode for to sle,
And how they myght best do that dede,
 His banis for to be.

Than bespake good Robyn,   145
 In place where as he stode:
"To morow I muste to Kyrkesly,
 Craftely to be leten blode."

Syr Roger of Donkestere,
   By the pryoresse he lay;   15•
And there they betrayed good Robyn Hode,
   Through theyr falsè playe.

Cryst have mercy on his soule,
   That dyed on the rode!
For he was a good outlawe,   15!
   And dyde pore men moch god.

THE HUNTING OF THE CHEVIOT

The Persè owt off Northombarlonde,
   And a vowe to God mayd he
That he wold hunte in the mowntayns
   Off Chyviat within days thre,
In the magger of doughtè Dogles
   And all that ever with him be;

The fattiste hartes in all Cheviat
   He sayd he wold kyll, and cary them away.
"Be my feth," sayd the dougheti Doglas agayn,
   "I wyll let that hontyng yf that I may."   1•

Then the Persè owt off Banborowe cam;
   With him a myghtee meany,
With fifteen hondrith archares bold off blood and bone
   The wear chosen owt of shyars thre.

This begane on a Monday at morn,   1
   In Cheviat the hillys so he:
The chylde may rue that ys un-born;
   It wos the more pittè.

The dryvars thorowe the woodès went,
   For to reas the dear;
Bomen byckarte uppone the bent   2
   With ther browd aros cleare.

Then the wyld thorowe the woodès went,
   On every sydè shear;
Greahondès thorowe the grevis glent,   2
   For to kyll thear dear.

This begane in Chyviat the hyls abone,
    Yerly on a Monnyn-day;
Be that it drewe to the oware off none,
    A hondrith fat hartès dcd ther lay.   30

The blewe a mort uppone the bent,
    The semblyde on sydis shear;
To the quyrry then the Persè went,
    To se the bryttlynge off the deare.

He sayd, "It was the Duglas promys   35
    This day to met me hear;
But I wyste he wolde faylle, verament."
    A great oth the Persè swear.

At the laste a squyar off Northomberlonde
    Lokyde at his hand full ny: 40
He was war a the doughetie Doglas commynge;
    With him a myghttè meany,

Both with spear, bylle, and brande;
    Yt was a myghtti sight to se;
Hardyar men, both off hart nor hande,   45
    Wear not in Cristiantè.

The wear twenti hondrith spear-men good,
    Withoute any feale;
The wear borne along be the watter a Twyde,
    Yth bowndès of Tividale.   50

"Leave of the brytlyng of the dear," he sayd,
    "And to your boys lock ye tayk good hede;
For never sithe ye wear on your mothars borne
    Had ye never so mickle nede."

The dougheti Dogglas on a stede,   55
    He rode alle his men beforne;
His armor glytteryde as dyd a glede:
    A boldar barne was never born.

"Tell me whos men ye ar," he says,
    "Or whos men that ye be: 60
Who gave youe leave to hunte in this Chyviat chays,
    In the spyt of myn and of me?"

The first mane that ever him an answear mayd,
    Yt was the good Lord Persè:
"We wyll not tell the whoys men we ar," he says,   6[
    "Nor whos men that we be;
But we wyll hounte hear in this chays,
    In the spyt of thyne and of the.

"The fattiste hartès in all Chyviat
    We have kyld, and cast to carry them away.   7(
"Be my troth," sayd the doughetè Dogglas agayn,
    "Therfor the ton of us shall de this day."

Then sayd the doughtè Doglas
    Unto the Lord Persè:
"To kyll alle thes giltles men,   7[
    Alas, it wear great pittè!

"But, Persè, thowe art a lord of lande;
    I am a yerle callyd within my contrè:
Let all our men uppone a parti stande,
    And do the battell off the and of me."   8(

"Nowe Cristes cors on his crowne," sayd the Lord Persè
    "Who-so-ever ther-to says nay;
Be my troth, doughttè Doglas," he says,
    "Thow shalt never se that day.

"Nethar in Ynglonde, Skottlonde, nar France,   8[
    Nor for no man of a woman born,
But, and fortune be my chance,
    I dar met him, on man for on."

Then bespayke a squyar off Northombarlonde,
    Richard Wytharyngton was his nam: 9(
"It shall never be told in Sothe-Ynglonde," he says,
    "To Kyng Herry the Fourth, for sham.

"I wat youe byn greate lordès twaw;
    I am a poor squyar of lande:
I wylle never se my captayne fyght on a fylde,   9[
    And stande my selffe and loocke on;
But whylle I may my weppone welde,
    I wylle not fayle both hart and hande."

That day, that day, that dredfull day!
    The first fit here I fynde;   100
And youe wyll here any mor a the hountyng a the
      Chyviat,
    Yet ys ther mor behynde.

The Yngglyshe men hade ther bowys yebent,
    Ther hartes wer good yenoughe;
The first off arros that the shote off,   105
    Seven skore spear-men the sloughe.

Yet byddys the Yerle Doglas uppon the bent,
    A captayne good yenoughe;
And that was sene verament,
    For he wrought hom both woo and wouche.   110

The Dogglas partyd his ost in thre,
    Lyk a cheffe cheften off pryde:
With suar spears off myghttè tre,
    The cum in on every syde;

Thrughe our Yngglyshe archery   115
    Gave many a wounde fulle wyde;
Many a doughetè the garde to dy,
    Which ganyde them no pryde.

The Ynglyshe men let ther boys be,
    And pulde owt brandes that wer brighte: 120
It was a hevy syght to se
    Bryght swordes on basnites lyght.

Thorowe ryche male and myneyeple,
    Many sterne the strocke done streght;
Many a freyke that was fulle fre   125
    Ther undar foot dyd lyght.

At last the Duglas and the Persè met,
    Lyk to captayns of myght and of mayne:
The swapte togethar tylle the both swat,
    With swordes that wear of fyn myllan.   130

Thes worthè freckys for to fyght,
    Ther-to the wear fulle fayne,
Tylle the bloode owte off thear basnetes ṣprente,
    As ever dyd heal or rayn.

"Yelde the, Persè," sayde the Doglas,   13
   "And i feth I shalle the brynge
Wher thowe shalte have a yerls wagis
   Of Jamy our Skottish kynge.

"Thoue shalte have thy ransom fre,
   I hight the hear this thinge;   14
For the manfullyste man yet art thowe
   That ever I conqueryd in filde fighttynge."

"Nay," sayd the Lord Persè,
   "I tolde it the beforne,
That I wolde never yeldyde be   14
   To no man of a woman born."

With that ther cam an arrowe hastely,
   Forthe off a myghttè wane;
Hit hathe strekene the Yerle Duglas
   In at the brest-bane.   15

Thorowe lyvar and longès bathe
   The sharpe arrowe ys gane,
That never after in all his lyffe-days
   He spayke mo wordès but ane:
That was, "Fyghte ye, my myrry men, whyllys ye
     may,   15
   For my lyff-days ben gan."

The Persè leanyde on his brande,
   And sawe the Duglas de;
He tooke the dede mane by the hande,
   And sayd, "Wo ys me for the!   16

"To have savyde thy lyffe, I wolde have partyde with
   My landes for years thre,
For a better man, of hart nare of hande,
   Was nat in all the north contrè."

Off all that se a Skottishe knyght,   16
   Was callyd Ser Hewe the Monggombyrry:
He sawe the Duglas to the deth was dyght;
   He spendyd a spear, a trusti trè.

He rod uppone a corsiare
    Throughe a hondrith archery;   170
He never stynttyde, nar never blane,
    Tylle he cam to the good Lord Persè.

He set uppone the Lorde Persè
    A dynte that was full soare;
With a suar spear of a myghttè tre   175
    Clean thorow the body he the Persè ber,

A the tothar syde that a man myght se
    A large cloth-yard and mare.
Towe bettar captayns wear nat in Cristiantè
    Then that day slan wear ther.   180

An archar off Northomberlonde
    Say slean was the Lord Persè:
He bar a bende bowe in his hand,
    Was made off trusti tre.

An arow, that a cloth-yarde was lang,   185
    To the harde stele halyde he;
A dynt that was both sad and soar
    He sat on Ser Hewe the Monggombyrry.

The dynt yt was both sad and sar,
    That he of Monggomberry sete;   190
The swane-fethars that his arrowe bar,
    With his hart-blood the wear wete.

Ther was never a freake wone foot wolde fle,
    But still in stour dyd stand,
Heawyng on yche othar, whylle the myghte dre,   195
    With many a balfull brande.

This battell begane in Chyviat
    An owar befor the none;
And when even-songe bell was rang,
    The battell was nat half done.   200

The tocke . . . . on ethar hande
    Be the lyght off the mone;
Many hade no strenght for to stande,
    In Chyviat the hillys abon.

Of fifteen hondrith archars of Ynglonde   205
  Went away but seventi and thre;
Of twenti hondrith spear-men of Skotlonde,
  But even five and fifti.

But all wear slayne Cheviat within;
  The hade no strengthe to stand on hy: 210
The chylde may rue that ys unborne;
  It was the mor pittè.

Thear was slayne, withe the Lord Persè,
  Sir Johan of Agerstone,
Ser Rogar, the hinde Hartly,   215
  Ser Wyllyam, the bolde Hearone.

Ser Jorg, the worthè Loumlè,
  A knyghte of great renowen,
Ser Raff, the ryche Rugbe,
  With dyntes wear beaten dowene.   220

For Wetharryngton my harte was wo,
  That ever he slayne shulde be;
For when both his leggis wear hewyne in to,
  Yet he knyled and fought on hys kny.

Ther was slayne, with the dougheti Duglas,   225
  Ser Hewe the Monggombyrry,
Ser Davy Lwdale, that worthè was;
  His sistars son was he.

Ser Charls a Murrè in that place,
  That never a foot wolde fle;   230
Ser Hewe Maxwelle, a lorde he was,
  With the Doglas dyd he dey.

So on the morrowe the mayde them byears
  Off birch and hasell so gray:
Many wedous, with wepyng tears,   235
  Cam to fache ther makys away.

Tivydale may carpe off care,
  Northombarlond may mayk great mon,
For towe such captayns as slayne wear thear
  On the march-parti shall never be non.   240

Word ys commen to Eddenburrowe,
    To Jamy the Skottische kynge,
That dougheti Duglas, lyff-tenant of the marches,
    He lay slean Chyviot within.

His handdès dyd he weal and wryng;   245
    He sayd, "Alas, and woe ys me!
Such an othar captayn Skotland within,"
    He sayd, "ye-feth shuld never be."

Worde ys commyn to lovly Londone,
    Till the fourth Harry our kynge,   250
That Lord Persè, leyff-tenante of the marchis,
    He lay slayne Chyviat within.

"God have merci on his solle," sayde Kyng Harry,
    "Good Lord, yf Thy will it be!
I have a hondrith captayns in Ynglonde," he sayd,   255
    "As good as ever was he;
But, Persè, and I brook my lyffe,
    Thy deth well quyte shall be."

As our noble kynge mayd his avowe,
    Lyke a noble prince of renowen,   260
For the deth of the Lord Persè
    He dyde the battell of Hombyll-down;

Wher syx and thrittè Skottishe knyghtes
    On a day wear beaten down:
Glendale glytteryde on ther armor bryght,   265
    Over castille, towar, and town.

This was the hontynge off the Cheviat,
    That tear begane this spurn:
Old men that knowen the grownde well yenoughe
    Call it the battell of Otterburn.   270

At Otterburn begane this spurne
    Uppone a Monnynday:
Ther was the doughtè Doglas slean;
    The Persè never went away.

Ther was never a tym on the marche-partès   275
    Sen the Doglas and the Persè met,
But yt ys mervele and the rede blude ronne not,
    As the reane doys in the stret.

Jhesue Crist our balys bete,
  And to the blys us brynge!   280
Thus was the hountynge of the Chivyat:
  God send us alle good endyng!

JOHNIE COCK

Johny he has risen up i the morn,
  Calls for water to wash his hands;
But little knew he that his bloody hounds
  Were bound in iron bands, bands,
  Were bound in iron bands.   5

Johny's mother has gotten word o that,
  And care-bed she has taen:
"O Johny, for my benison,
  I beg you 'l stay at hame;
For the wine so red and the well-baken bread,   10
  My Johny shall want nane.

"There are seven forsters at Pickeram Side,
  At Pickeram where they dwell;
And for a drop of thy heart's bluid
  They wad ride the fords of hell."   15

Johny he 's gotten word of that,
  And he 's turnd wondrous keen;
He 's put off the red scarlett,
  And he 's put on the Lincolm green.

With a sheaf of arrows by his side,   20
  And a bent bow in his hand,
He 's mounted on a prancing steed,
  And he has ridden fast oer the strand.

He 's up i Braidhouplee, and down i Bradyslee,
  And under a buss o broom;   25
And there he found a good dun deer,
  Feeding in a buss of ling.

Johny shot, and the dun deer lap,
  And she lap wondrous wide,
Until they came to the wan water,   30
  And he stemd her of her pride.

He 'as taen out the little pen-knife
    ('T was full three quarters long),
And he has taen out of that dun deer
    The liver bot and the tongue.   35

They eat of the flesh, and they drank of the blood,
    And the blood it was so sweet,
Which caused Johny and his bloody hounds
    To fall in a deep sleep.

By then came an old palmer,   40
    And an ill death may he die!
For he 's away to Pickram Side
    As fast as he can drie.

"What news, what 'news?" says the seven forsters;
    "What news have ye brought to me?"   45
"I have noe news," the palmer said,
    "But what I saw with my eye.

"High up i Bradyslee, low down i Bradisslee,
    And under a buss of scroggs,
O there I spied a well-wight man,   50
    Sleeping among his dogs.

"His coat it was of light Lincolm,
    And his breeches of the same,
His shoes of the American leather,
    And gold buckles tying them."   55

Up bespake the seven forsters,
    Up bespake they ane and a':
"O that is Johny o Cockleys Well,
    And near him we will draw."

O, the first y stroke that they gae him,   60
    They struck him off by the knee.
Then up bespake his sister's son:
    "O the next 'll gar him die!"

"O some they count ye well-wight men,
    But I do count ye nane;   65
For you might well ha wakend me,
    And askd gin I wad be taen.

"The wildest wolf in aw this wood
　　Wad not ha done so by me:
She'd ha wet her foot ith wan water, 70
　　And sprinkled it oer my brae;
And if that wad not ha wakend me.
　　She wad ha gone and let me be.

"O bows of yew, if ye be true,
　　In London, where ye were bought, 75
Fingers five, get up belive!
　　Manhuid shall fail me nought."

He has killd the seven forsters,
　　He has killd them all but ane;
And that wan scarce to Pickeram Side, 80
　　To carry the bode-words hame.

"Is there never a boy in a' this wood
　　That will tell what I can say;
That will go to Cockleys Well,
　　Tell my mither to fetch me away?" 85

There was a boy into that wood,
　　That carried the tidings away;
And many ae was the well-wight man
　　At the fetching o Johny away.

JOCK O THE SIDE

Peeter a Whifeild he hath slaine,
　　And John a Side he is tane,
And John is bound both hand and foote,
　　And to the New Castle he is gone.

But tydinges came to the Sybill o the Side, 5
　　By the water-side as shee rann;
Shee tooke her kirtle by the hem,
　　And fast shee runn to Mangerton.

　　　·　　·　　·　　·　　·　　·　　·

　　The lord was sett downe at his meate; 10
When these tydings shee did him tell,
　　Never a morsell might he eate.

But lords the wrunge their fingars white,
    Ladyes did pull themselves by the haire,
Crying, "Alas and weladay!   15
    For John o the Side wee shall never see more.

"But wee 'le goe sell our droves of kine,
    And after them our oxen sell,
And after them our troopes of sheepe,
    But wee will loose him out of the New Castell." 20

But then bespake him Hobby Noble,
    And spoke these words wonderous hye:
Sayes, "Give me five men to my selfe,
    And I 'le feitch John o the Side to thee."

"Yea, thou 'st have five, Hobby Noble,   25
    Of the best that are in this countrye;
I 'le give thee five thousand, Hobby Noble,
    That walke in Tyvidale, trulye."

"Nay, I 'le have but five," saies Hobby Noble,
    "That shall walke away with mee: 30
Wee will ryde like noe men of warr,
    But like poore badgers wee wilbe."

They stuffet up all their baggs with straw,
    And their steeds barefoot must bee:
"Come on, my bretheren," sayes Hobby Noble,   35
    "Come on your wayes, and goe with mee!"

And when they came to Culerton ford,
    The water was up, they cold it not goe;
And then they were ware of a good old man,
    How his boy and hee were at the plowe.   40

"But stand you still," sayes Hobby Noble,
    "Stand you still heere at this shore,
And I will ryde to yonder old man,
    And see where the gate it lyes ore.

"But Christ you save, father!" quoth hee,   45
    "Crist both you save and see!
Where is the way over this fford?
    For Christ's sake tell itt mee!"

"But I have dwelled heere three-score yeere,
   Soe have I done three-score and three;
I never sawe man nor horsse goe ore,
   Except itt were a horse of tree."   50

"But fare thou well, thou good old man!
   The devill in hell I leave with thee;
Noe better comfort heere this night   55
   Thow gives my bretheren heere and me."

But when he came to his brether againe,
   And told this tydings full of woe,
And then they found a well good gate,
   They might ryde ore by two and two.   60

And when they were come over the fforde,
   All safe gotten att the last,
"Thankes be to God!" sayes Hobby Nobble,
   "The worst of our perill is past."

And then they came into Howbrame wood,   65
   And there then they found a tree,
And cutt itt downe then by the roote;
   The lenght was thirty ffoote and three.

And four of them did take the planke,
   As light as it had beene a fflee,   70
And carryed itt to the New Castle,
   Where as John a Side did lye.

And some did climbe up by the walls,
   And some did climbe up by the tree,
Untill they came upp to the top of the castle,   75
   Where John made his moane trulye.

He sayd, "God be with thee, Sybill o the Side!
   My owne mother thou art," quoth hee;
"If thou knew this night I were here,
   A woe woman then woldest thou bee.   80

"And fare you well, Lord Mangerton!
   And ever I say God be with thee!
For if you knew this night I were heere,
   You wold sell your land for to loose mee.

"And far: thou well, Much, millers sonne! 85
    Much, millars sonne, I say;
Thou has beene better att merke midnight
    Then ever thou was att noone o the day.

"And fare thou well, my good Lord Clough!
    Thou art thy ffathers sonne and heire; 90
Thou never saw him in all thy liffe
    But with him durst thou breake a speare.

"Wee are brothers childer nine or ten,
    And sisters children ten or eleven:
We never came to the feild to fight 95
    But the worst of us was counted a man."

But then bespake him Hoby Noble,
    And spake these words unto him:
Saies, "Sleepest thou, wakest thou, John o the Side,
    Or art thou this castle within?" 100

"But who is there," quoth John oth Side,
    "That knowes my name soe right and free?"
"I am a bastard-brother of thine;
    This night I am comen for to loose thee."

"Now nay, now nay," quoth John o the Side; 105
    "Itt ffeares me sore that will not bee;
Ffor a pecke of gold and silver," John sayd,
    "In faith, this night, will not loose mee."

But then bespake him Hobby Noble,
    And till his brother thus sayd hee: 110
Sayes, "Four shall take this matter in hand,
    And two shall tent our geldings ffree."

Four did breake one dore without,
    Then John brake five himsell;
But when they came to the iron dore, 115
    It smote twelve upon the bell.

"Itt ffeares me sore," sayd Much the miller,
    "That heere taken wee all shalbee!"
"But goe away, bretheren," sayd John a Side;
    "For ever, alas! this will not bee." 120

"But ffye upon thee!" sayd Hobby Noble;
    "Much the miller, fye upon thee!
It sore feares me," said Hobby Noble,
    "Man that thou wilt never bee."

But then he had Fflanders files two or three,   125
    And hee fyled downe that iron dore,
And tooke John out of the New Castle,
    And sayd, "Looke thou never come heere more!"

When he had him fforth of the New Castle,
    "Away with me, John, thou shalt ryde!"   130
But ever, alas! itt cold not bee,
    For John cold neither sitt nor stryde.

But then he had sheets two or three,
    And bound Johns boults fast to his ffeete,
And sett him on a well good steede;   135
    Himselfe on another by him seete.

Then Hobby Noble smiled and loughe,
    And spoke these worde in mickle pryde:
"Thou sitts soe finely on thy geldinge
    That, John, thou rydes like a bryde."   140

And when they came thorrow Howbrame towne,
    Johns horsse there stumbled at a stone:
"Out and alas!" cryed Much the miller,
    "John, thou 'le make us all be tane!"

"But fye upon thee!" saies Hobby Noble,   145
    "Much the millar, fye on thee!
I know full well," sayes Hobby Noble,
    "Man that thou wilt never bee."

And when the came into Howbrame wood,
    He had Fflanders files two or three   150
To file Johns bolts beside his ffeete,
    That hee might ryde more easilye.

Sayes, "John, now leape over a steede!"
    And John then hee lope over five:
"I know well," sayes Hobby Noble,   155
    "John, thy ffellow is not alive."

Then he brought him home to Mangerton:
    The lord then he was att his meate;
But when John o the Side he there did see,
    For faine hee cold noe more eate.   160

He sayes, "Blest be thou, Hobby Noble,
    That ever thou wast man borne!
Thou hast feitched us home good John oth Side,
    That was now cleane ffrom us gone."

SIR PATRICK SPENS

The king sits in Dumferling toune,
    Drinking the blude-reid wine:
"O, whar will I get guid sailor,
    To sail this schip of mine?"

Up and spak an eldern knicht,   5
    Sat at the kings richt kne:
"Sir Patrick Spence is the best sailoɪ
    That sails upon the se."

The king has written a braid letter
    And signd it wi his hand,   10
And sent it to Sir Patrick Spence,
    Was walking on the sand.

The first line that Sir Patrick red,
    A loud lauch lauchèd he;
The next line that Sir Patrick red,   15
    The teir blinded his ee.

"O, wha is this has don this deid,
    This ill deid don to me,
To send me out this time o' the yeir,
    To sail upon the se?   20

"Mak hast, mak haste, my mirry men all;
    Our guid schip sails the morne."
"O, say na sae, my master deir,
    For I feir a deadlie storme.

"Late, late yestreen I saw the new moone,   25
    Wi the auld moone in hir arme;
And I feir, I feir, my deir master,
    That we will cum to harme."

O, our Scots nobles wer richt laith
    To weet their cork-heild schoone;   30
Bot lang owre a' the play wer playd,
    Thair hats they swam aboone.

O, lang, lang may their ladies sit,
    Wi thair fans into their hand,
Or eir they se Sir Patrick Spence   35
    Cum sailing to the land.

O, lang, lang may the ladies stand,
    Wi thair gold kems in their hair,
Waiting for thair ain deir lords,
    For they 'll se thame na mair.   40

Haf owre, haf owre to Aberdour,
    It 's fiftie fadom deip,
And thair lies guid Sir Patrick Spence
    Wi the Scots lords at his feit.

SIR HUGH, OR THE JEW'S DAUGHTER

Four and twenty bonny boys
    Were playing at the ba;
And by it came him sweet Sir Hugh,
    And he playd oer them a'.

He kickd the ba with his right foot,   5
    And catchd it wi his knee;
And throuch-and-thro the Jew's window
    He gard the bonny ba flee.

He 's doen him to the Jew's castell,
    And walkd it round about;   10
And there he saw the Jew's daughter
    At the window looking out.

"Throw down the ba, ye Jew's daughter,
    Throw down the ba to me!"
"Never a bit," says the Jew's daughter,   15
    "Till up to me come ye."

"How will I come up? How can I come up?
    How can I come to thee?
For as ye did to my auld father,
    The same ye'll do to me."   20

She's gane till her father's garden,
    And pu'd an apple, red and green:
'T was a' to wyle him, sweet Sir Hugh,
    And to entice him in.

She's led him in through ae dark door,   25
    And sae has she thro nine;
She's laid him on a dressing-table,
    And stickit him like a swine.

And first came out the thick, thick blood,
    And syne came out the thin,   30
And syne came out the bonny heart's blood:
    There was nae mair within.

She's rowd him in a cake o lead,
    Bade him lie still and sleep;
She's thrown him in Our Lady's draw-well,   35
    Was fifty fathom deep.

When bells were rung, and mass was sung,
    And a' the bairns came hame,
When every lady gat hame her son,
    The Lady Maisry gat nane.   40

She's taen her mantle her about,
    Her coffer by the hand,
And she's gane out to seek her son,
    And wanderd oer the land.

She's doen her to the Jew's castell,   45
    Where a' were fast asleep:
"Gin ye be there, my sweet Sir Hugh,
    I pray you to me speak,"

She 's doen her to the Jew's garden,
   Thought he had been gathering fruit: 50
"Gin ye be there, my sweet Sir Hugh,
   I pray you to me speak."

She neard Our Lady's deep draw-well,
   Was fifty fathom deep:
"Whareer ye be, my sweet Sir Hugh,   55
   I pray you to me speak."

"Gae hame, gae hame, my mither dear,
   Prepare my winding sheet;
And at the back o merry Lincoln
   The morn I will you meet."   60

Now Lady Maisry is gane hame,
   Made him a winding sheet;
And at the back o merry Lincoln
   The dead corpse did her meet.

And a' the bells o merry Lincoln   65
   Without men's hands were rung,
And a' the books o merry Lincoln
   Were read without man's tongue,
And neer was such a burial
   Sin Adam's days begun.   70

THE THREE RAVENS

There were three ravens sat on a tree,
   Downe a downe, hay down, hay downe;
There were three ravens sat on a tree,
   With a downe;
There were three ravens sat on a tree,   5
They were as blacke as they might be,
   With a downe derrie, derrie, derrie, downe, downe.

The one of them said to his mate,
"Where shall we our breakefast take?"

"Downe in yonder greene field   10
There lies a knight slain under his shield.

"His hounds they lie downe at his feete,
So well they can their master keepe.

"His haukes they flie so eagerly
There's no fowle dare him come nie."   15

Downe there comes a fallow doe,
As great with yong as she might goe.

She lift up his bloudy hed,
And kist his wounds that were so red.

She got him up upon her backe,   20
And carried him to earthen lake.

She buried him before the prime;
She was dead herselfe ere even-song time.

God send every gentleman
Such haukes, such hounds, and such a leman.   25

EDWARD

"Why dois your brand sae drap wi bluid,
          Edward, Edward?
Why dois your brand sae drap wi bluid,
          And why sae sad gang yee, O?"
"O, I hae killed my hauke sae guid,   5
          Mither, mither;
O, I hae killed my hauke sae guid,
          And I had nae mair bot hee, O."

Your haukis bluid was nevir sae reid,
          Edward, Edward;   10
Your haukis bluid was nevir sae reid,
          My deir son, I tell thee, O."
"O, I hae killed my reid-roan steid,
          Mither, mither;
O, I hae killed my reid-roan steid,   15
          That erst was sae fair and frie, O."

"Your steid was auld, and ye hae gat mair,
          Edward, Edward;

Your steid was auld, and ye hae gat mair:
    Sum other dule ye drie, O."   20
"O, I hae killed my fadir deir,
       Mither, mither!
O, I hae killed my fadir deir!
    Alas, and wae is mee, O!"

"And whatten penance wul ye drie, for that,   25
       Edward, Edward?
And whatten penance will ye drie, for that?
    My deir son, now tell me, O."
"Ile set my feit in yonder boat,
       Mither, mither;   30
Ile set my feit in yonder boat,
    And Ile fare ovir the sea, O."

"And what wul ye doe wi your towirs and your ha,
       Edward, Edward?
And what wul ye doe wi your towirs and your ha, 35
    That were sae fair to see, O?"
"Ile let thame stand tul they doun fa,
       Mither, mither;
Ile let thame stand tul they doun fa,
    For here nevir mair maun I bee, O."   40

"And what wul ye leive to your bairns and your wife,
       Edward, Edward?
And what wul ye leive to your bairns and your wife,
    Whan ye gang ovir the sea, O?"
"The warldis room; late them beg thrae life,   45
       Mither, mither!
The warldis room; late them beg thrae life,
    For thame nevir mair wul I see, O."

"And what wul ye leive to your ain mither dear,
       Edward, Edward?   50
And what wul ye leive to your ain mither dear?
    My deir son, now tell me, O."
"The curse of hell frae me sall ye beir,
       Mither, mither!
The curse of hell frae me sall ye beir,   55
    Sic counseils ye gave to me, O."

THE TWA SISTERS

There was twa sisters in a bowr
  (Edinburgh, Edinburgh);
There was twa sisters in a bowr
  (Stirling for ay);
There was twa sisters in a bowr: 5
There came a knight to be their wooer
  (Bonny Saint Johnston stands upon Tay).

He courted the eldest wi glove an ring,
But he lovd the youngest above a' thing.

He courted the eldest wi brotch an knife,   10
But lovd the youngest as his life.

The eldest she was vexed sair,
An much envi'd her sister fair.

Into her bowr she could not rest:
Wi grief an spite she almos brast.   15

Upon a morning fair an clear,
She cried upon her sister dear:

"O sister, come to yon sea stran,
An see our father's ships come to lan."

She's taen her by the milk-white han,   20
An led her down to yon sea stran.

The youngest stood upon a stane:
The eldest came an threw her in.

She tooke her by the middle sma,
An dashd her bonny back to the jaw.   25

"O sister, sister, tak my han,
An Ise mack you heir to a' my lan!

"O sister, sister, tak my middle,
An yes get my goud and my gouden girdle!

"O sister, sister, save my life,   30
An I swear Ise never be nae man's wife!"

"Foul fa the han that I should tacke!
It twind me an my wardles make.

"Your cherry cheeks an yallow hair
Gars me gae maiden for evermair."   35

Sometimes she sank, an sometimes she swam,
Till she came down yon bonny mill-dam.

O, out it came the miller's son,
An saw the fair maid swimmin in:

"O father, father, draw your dam!   40
Here's either a mermaid or a swan."

The miller quickly drew the dam,
And there he found a drownd woman.

You coudna see her yallow hair
For gold and pearle that were so rare.   45

You coudna see her middle sma
For gouden girdle that was sae braw.

You coudna see her fingers white
For gouden rings that was sae gryte.

An by there came a harper fine,   50
That harped to the king at dine.

When he did look that lady upon,
He sighd and made a heavy moan.

He's taen three locks o her yallow hair,
An wi them strung his harp sae fair.   55

The first tune he did play and sing,
Was "Farewell to my father, the King."

The nextin tune that he playd syne,
Was "Farewell to my mother, the Queen."

The lasten tune that he playd then,   60
Was "Wae to my sister, fair Ellen."

THE CRUEL BROTHER

A gentleman cam oure the sea
    (Fine flowers in the valley),
And he has courted ladies three
    (With the light green and the yellow).

One o them was clad in red: 5
He asked if she wad be his bride.

One o them was clad in green:
He asked if she wad be his queen.

The last o them was clad in white:
He asked if she wad be his heart's delight.   10

"Ye may ga ask my father, the King;
Sae maun ye ask my mither, the Queen;

"Sae maun ye ask my sister Anne;
And dinna forget my brither John."

He has asked her father, the King;   15
And sae did he her mither, the Queen;

And he has asked her sister Anne;
But he has forgot her brother John.

Her father led her through the ha;
Her mither danced afore them a';   20

Her sister Anne led her through the closs;
Her brither John set her on her horse.

It's then he drew a little penknife,
And he reft the fair maid o her life.

"Ride up, ride up," said the foremost man;   25
"I think our bride comes hooly on."

"Ride up, ride up," said the second man;
"I think our bride looks pale and wan."

Up than cam the gay bridegroom,
And straucht unto the bride he cam.   30

"Does your side-saddle sit awry?
Or does your steed . . . .

"Or does the rain run in your glove?
Or wad ye chuse anither love?"

"The rain runs not in my glove,   35
Nor will I e'er chuse anither love.

"But O an I war at Saint Evron's well,
There I wad licht, and drink my fill!

"Oh an I war at Saint Evron's closs,
There I wad licht, and bait my horse!"   40

Whan she cam to Saint Evron's well,
She dought na licht to drink her fill.

Whan she cam to Saint Evron's closs,
The bonny bride fell aff her horse.

"What will ye leave to your father, the King?"   45
"The milk-white steed that I ride on."

"What will ye leave to your mother, the Queen?"
"The bluidy robes that I have on."

"What will ye leave to your sister Anne?"
"My gude lord, to be wedded on."   50

"What will ye leave to your brither John?"
"The gallows-pin to hang him on."

"What will ye leave to your brither's wife?"
"Grief and sorrow a' the days o her life."

"What will ye leave to your brither's bairns?"   55
"The meal-pock to hang oure the arms."

Now does she neither sigh nor groan:
She lies aneath yon marble stone.

BABYLON, OR THE BONNIE BANKS O FORDIE

There were three ladies lived in a bower,
    Eh vow bonnie,
And they went out to pull a flower
    On the bonnie banks o Fordie.

They hadna pu'ed a flower but ane,   5
When up started to them a banisht man.

He's taen the first sister by her hand,
And he's turned her round and made her stand.

"It's whether will ye be a rank robber's wife,
Or will ye die by my wee pen-knife?"   10

"It's I'll not be a rank robber's wife,
But I'll rather die by your wee pen-knife."

He's killed this may, and he's laid her by
For to bear the red rose company.

He's taken the second ane by the hand,   15
And he's turned her round and made her stand.

"It's whether will ye be a rank robber's wife,
Or will ye die by my wee pen-knife?"

"I'll not be a rank robber's wife,
But I'll rather die by your wee pen-knife."   20

He's killed this may, and he's laid her by
For to bear the red rose company.

He's taken the youngest ane by the hand,
And he's turned her round and made her stand;

Says, "Will ye be a rank robber's wife,   25
Or will ye die by my wee pen-knife?"

"I'll not be a rank robber's wife,
Nor will I die by your wee pen-knife;

"For I hae a brother in this wood,
And gin ye kill me, it's he'll kill thee."   30

"What's thy brother's name? Come tell to me."
"My brother's name is Baby Lon."

"O sister, sister, what have I done!
O, have I done this ill to thee!

"O, since I've done this evil deed,   35
Good sall never be seen o me."

He's taken out his wee pen-knife,
And he's twyned himsel o his ain sweet life.

SWEET WILLIAM'S GHOST

There came a ghost to Margret's door,
  With many a grievous groan;
And ay he tirled at the pin,
  But answer made she none.

"Is that my father Philip,   5
  Or is't my brother John?
Or is't my true-love, Willy,
  From Scotland new come home?"

"'T is not thy father Philip,
  Nor yet thy brother John;   10
But 't is thy true-love, Willy,
  From Scotland new come home.

"O sweet Margret, O dear Margret,
  I pray thee speak to me;
Give me my faith and troth, Margret,   15
  As I gave it to thee."

"Thy faith and troth thou's never get,
  Nor yet will I thee lend,
Till that thou come within my bower
  And kiss my cheek and chin."   20

"If I shoud come within thy bower,
  I am no earthly man;
And shoud I kiss thy rosy lips,
  Thy days will not be lang.

"O sweet Margret, O dear Margret,   25
  I pray thee speak to me;
Give me my faith and troth, Margret,
  As I gave it to thee."

"Thy faith and troth thou's never get,
  Nor yet will I thee lend,   30
Till you take me to yon kirk
  And wed me with a ring."

"My bones are buried in yon kirk-yard,
  Afar beyond the sea,
And it is but my spirit, Margret,   35
  That's now speaking to thee."

She stretchd out her lilly-white hand,
  And, for to do her best,
"Hae, there's your faith and troth, Willy;
  God send your soul good rest!"   40

Now she has kilted her robes of green
  A piece below her knee,
And a' the live-lang winter night
  The dead corp followed she.

"Is there any room at your head, Willy,   45
  Or any room at your feet,
Or any room at your side, Willy,
  Wherein that I may creep?"

"There's no room at my head, Margret,
  There's no room at my feet,   50
There's no room at my side, Margret,
  My coffin's made so meet."

Then up and crew the red, red cock,
  And up then crew the gray:
"'T is time, 't is time, my dear Margret,   55
  That you were going away."

No more the ghost to Margret said,
  But with a grievous groan
Evanishd in a cloud of mist,
  And left her all alone.   60

"O stay, my only true-love, stay!"
  The constant Margret cry'd:
Wan grew her cheeks, she closd her een,
  Stretchd her soft limbs, and dy'd.

LORD THOMAS AND FAIR ANNET

Lord Thomas and Fair Annet
  Sate a' day on a hill;
Whan night was cum, and sun was sett
  They had not talkt their fill.

Lord Thomas said a word in jest,   5
  Fair Annet took it ill:
"A, I will nevir wed a wife
  Against my ain friends' will."

"Gif ye wull nevir wed a wife,
  A wife wull neir wed yee."   10
Sae he is hame to tell his mither,
  And knelt upon his knee.

"O rede, O rede, mither," he says,
  "A gude rede gie to mee:
O sall I tak the nut-browne bride,   15
  And let Faire Annet bee?"

"The nut-browne bride haes gowd and gear,
  Fair Annet she has gat nane;
And the little beauty Fair Annet haes,
  O it wull soon be gane."   20

And he has till his brother gane:
  "Now, brother, rede ye mee;
A, sall I marrie the nut-browne bride,
  And let Fair Annet bee?"

"The nut-browne bride has oxen, brother,   25
  The nut-browne bride has kye:
I wad hae ye marrie the nut-browne bride,
  And cast Fair Annet bye."

"Her oxen may dye i the house, billie,
  And her kye into the byre;   30
And I sall hae nothing to mysell
  Bot a fat fadge by the fyre."

And he has till his sister gane:
  "Now, sister, rede ye mee;
O sall I marrie the nut-browne bride,   35
  And set Fair Annet free?"

"I'se rede ye tak Fair Annet, Thomas,
  And let the browne bride alane,
Lest ye sould sigh, and say 'Alace,
  What is this we brought hame!'"   40

"No, I will tak my mither's counsel,
    And marrie me owt o hand;
And I will tak the nut-browne bride:
    Fair Annet may leive the land."

Up then rose Fair Annet's father,   45
    Twa hours or it wer day,
And he is gane into the bower
    Wherein Fair Annet lay.

"Rise up, rise up, Fair Annet," he says;
    "Put on your silken sheene: 50
Let us gae to St. Marie's kirke,
    And see that rich weddeen."

"My maides, gae to my dressing-roome,
    And dress to me my hair;
Whaireir yee laid a plait before,   55
    See yee lay ten times mair.

"My maides, gae to my dressing-room,
    And dress to me my smock;
The one half is o the holland fine,
    The other o needle-work."   60

The horse Fair Annet rade upon,
    He amblit like the wind;
Wi siller he was shod before,
    Wi burning gowd behind.

Four and twenty siller bells   65
    Wer a' tyed till his mane;
And yae tift o the norland wind,
    They tinkled ane by ane.

Four and twenty gay gude knichts
    Rade by Fair Annet's side,   70
And four and twenty fair ladies,
    As gin she had bin a bride.

And whan she cam to Marie's kirk,
    She sat on Marie's stean:
The cleading that Fair Annet had on,   75
    It skinkled in their een.

And whan she cam into the kirk,
　　She shimmerd like the sun;
The belt that was about her waist
　　Was a' wi pearles bedone.　　　　　　　　　80

She sat her by the nut-browne bride;
　　And her een they wer sae clear,
Lord Thomas he clean forgat the bride
　　Whan Fair Annet drew near.

He had a rose into his hand;　　　　　　　　85
　　He gae it kisses three,
And, reaching by the nut-browne bride,
　　Laid it on Fair Annet's knee.

Up than spak the nut-browne bride;
　　She spak wi meikle spite:　　　　　　　　90
"And whair gat ye that rose-water,
　　That does mak yee sae white?"

"O I did get the rose-water
　　Whair ye wull neir get nane,
For I did get that very rose-water　　　　　95
　　Into my mither's wame."

The bride she drew a long bodkin
　　Frae out her gay head-gear,
And strake Fair Annet unto the heart,
　　That word spak nevir mair.　　　　　　　100

Lord Thomas he saw Fair Annet wex pale,
　　And marvelit what mote bee;
But whan he saw her dear heart's blude,
　　A' wood-wroth wexed hee.

He drew his dagger, that was sae sharp,　　105
　　That was sae sharp and meet,
And drave it into the nut-browne bride,
　　That fell deid at his feit.

"Now stay for me, dear Annet!" he sed;
　　"Now stay, my dear!" he cry'd;　　　　　110
Then strake the dagger untill his heart,
　　And fell deid by her side.

Lord Thomas was buried without kirk-wa,
    Fair Annet within the quiere;
And o the tane thair grew a birk,   115
    The other a bonny briere.

And ay they grew, and ay they threw,
    As they wad faine be neare;
And by this ye may ken right weil
    They were twa luvers deare.   120

KEMP OWYNE

Her mother died when she was young,
    Which gave her cause to make great moan:
Her father married the warst woman
    That ever lived in Christendom.

She served her with foot and hand,   5
    In every thing that she could dee;
Till once, in an unlucky time,
    She threw her in ower Craigy's sea;

Says, "Lie you there, dove Isabel,
    And all my sorrows lie with thee,   10
Till Kemp Owyne come ower the sea,
    And borrow you with kisses three:
Let all the warld do what they will,
    Oh, borrowed shall you never be."

Her breath grew strang, her hair grew lang,   15
    And twisted thrice about the tree;
And all the people, far and near,
    Thought that a savage beast was she.

These news did come to Kemp Owyne,
    Where he lived far beyond the sea;   20
He hasted him to Craigy's sea,
    And on the savage beast lookd he.

Her breath was strang, her hair was lang,
    And twisted was about the tree;
And with a swing she came about: 25
    "Come to Craigy's sea, and kiss with me.

"Here is a royal belt," she cried,
  "That I have found in the green sea;
And while your body it is on,
  Drawn shall your blood never be:
But if you touch me, tail or fin,
  I vow my belt your death shall be."

He stepped in, gave her a kiss;
  The royal belt he brought him wi.
Her breath was strang, her hair was lang,
  And twisted twice about the tree;
And with a swing she came about:
  "Come to Craigy's sea, and kiss with me.

"Here is a royal ring," she said,
  "That I have found in the green sea;
And while your finger it is on,
  Drawn shall your blood never be:
But if you touch me, tail or fin,
  I swear my ring your death shall be."

He stepped in, gave her a kiss;
  The royal ring he brought him wi.
Her breath was strang, her hair was lang,
  And twisted ance about the tree;
And with a swing she came about:
  "Come to Craigy's sea, and kiss with me.

"Here is a royal brand," she said,
  "That I have found in the green sea;
And while your body it is on,
  Drawn shall your blood never be:
But if you touch me, tail or fin,
  I swear my brand your death shall be."

He stepped in, gave her a kiss;
  The royal brand he brought him wi.
Her breath was sweet, her hair grew short,
  And twisted nane about the tree;
And smilingly she came about,
  As fair a woman as fair could be.

THOMAS RYMER

True Thomas lay oer yond grassy bank;
    And he beheld a ladie gay,
A ladie that was brisk and bold,
    Come riding oer the fernie brae.

Her skirt was of the grass-green silk,   5
    Her mantle of the velvet fine;
At ilka tett of her horse's mane
    Hung fifty silver bells and nine.

True Thomas he took off his hat,
    And bowed him low down till his knee: 10
"All hail, thou mighty Queen of Heaven!
    For your peer on earth I never did see."

"O no, O no, True Thomas," she says,
    "That name does not belong to me;
I am but the queen of fair Elfland,   15
    And I'm come here for to visit thee.

.   .   .   .

"But ye maun go wi me now, Thomas;
    True Thomas, ye maun go wi me,
For ye maun serve me seven years,
    Thro weel or wae as may chance to be."   20

She turned about her milk-white steed,
    And took True Thomas up behind;
And aye wheneer her bridle rang,
    The steed flew swifter than the wind.

For forty days and forty nights   25
    He wade thro red blude to the knee;
And he saw neither sun nor moon,
    But heard the roaring of the sea.

O, they rade on and further on,
    Until they came to a garden green: 30
"Light down, light down, ye ladie free;
    Some of that fruit let me pull to thee."

"O no, O no, True Thomas," she says,
    "That fruit maun not be touched by thee,
For a' the plagues that are in hell   35
    Light on the fruit of this countrie.

"But I have a loaf here in my lap,
    Likewise a bottle of claret wine;
And now, ere we go farther on,
    We'll rest a while, and ye may dine."   40

When he had eaten and drunk his fill,
    "Lay down your head upon my knee,"
The lady sayd, "ere we climb yon hill,
    And I will show you fairlies three.

"O see not ye yon narrow road,   45
    So thick beset wi thorns and briers?
That is the path of righteousness,
    Tho after it but few enquires.

"And see not ye that braid braid road,
    That lies across yon lillie leven?   50
That is the path of wickedness,
    Tho some call it the road to heaven.

"And see not ye that bonny road,
    Which winds about the fernie brae?
That is the road to fair Elfland,   55
    Where you and I this night maun gae.

"But Thomas, ye maun hold your tongue,
    Whatever you may hear or see;
For gin ae word you should chance to speak,
    You will neer get back to your ain countrie."   60

He has gotten a coat of the even cloth,
    And a pair of shoes of velvet green;
And till seven years were past and gone,
    True Thomas on earth was never seen.

THE WEE WEE MAN

As I was wa'king all alone,
  Between a water and a wa,
And there I spy'd a wee wee man,
  And he was the least that ere I saw.

His legs were scarce a shathmont's length,   5
  And thick and thimber was his thigh;
Between his brows there was a span,
  And between his shoulders there was three.

He took up a meikle stane,
  And he flang't as far as I could see: 10
Though I had been a Wallace wight,
  I couldna liften't to my knee.

"O wee wee man, but thou be strang!
  O, tell me where thy dwelling be."
"My dwelling's down at yon bonny bower;   15
  O, will you go with me and see?"

On we lap, and awa we rade,
  Till we came to yon bonny green;
We lighted down for to bait our horse,
  And out there came a lady fine.   20

Four and twenty at her back,
  And they were a' clad out in green:
Though the King of Scotland had been there,
  The warst o' them might hae been his queen.

On we lap, and awa we rade,   25
  Till we came to yon bonny ha,
Whare the roof was o the beaten gould,
  And the floor was o the cristal a'.

When we came to the stair-foot,
  Ladies were dancing, jimp and sma;   30
But in the twinkling of an eye
  My wee wee man was clean awa.

MARY HAMILTON

Word's gane to the kitchen,
    And word's gane to the ha,
That Marie Hamilton gangs wi bairn
    To the hichest Stewart of a'. . . . .

She's tyed it in her apron,
    And she's thrown it in the sea;
Says, "Sink ye, swim ye, bonny wee babe,
    You'l neer get mair o me."

Down then cam the auld Queen,
    Goud tassels tying her hair:
"O Marie, where's the bonny wee babe
    That I heard greet sae sair?"

"There never was a babe intill my room;
    As little designs to be;
It was but a touch o my sair side,
    Come oer my fair bodie."

"O Marie, put on your robes o black,
    Or else your robes o brown,
For ye maun gang wi me the night,
    To see fair Edinbro town."

"I winna put on my robes o black,
    Nor yet my robes o brown;
But I'll put on my robes o white,
    To shine through Edinbro town."

When she gaed up the Cannogate,
    She laughd loud laughters three;
But whan she cam down the Cannogate,
    The tear blinded her ee.

When she gaed up the Parliament stair,
    The heel cam aff her shee;
And lang or she cam down again
    She was condemnd to dee.

When she cam down the Cannogate,
    The Cannogate sae free,

Many a ladie lookd oer her window,
   Weeping for this ladie.   40

"Ye need nae weep for me," she says,
   "Ye need nae weep for me;
For had I not slain mine own sweet babe,
   This death I wadna dee.

"Bring me a bottle of wine," she says,   45
   "The best that eer ye hae,
That I may drink to my weil-wishers,
   And they may drink to me.

"Here's a health to the jolly sailors
   That sail upon the main;
Let them never let on to my father and mother   50
   But what I'm coming hame.

"Here's a health to the jolly sailors
   That sail upon the sea;
Let them never let on to my father and mother   55
   That I cam here to dee.

"Oh little did my mother think,
   The day she cradled me,
What lands I was to travel through,
   What death I was to dee.   60

"Oh little did my father think,
   The day he held up me,
What lands I was to travel through,
   What death I was to dee.

"Last night I washd the Queen's feet,   65
   And gently laid her down;
And a' the thanks I've gotten the nicht,
   To be hanged in Edinbro town!

"Last nicht there was four Maries,
   The nicht there'll be but three;
There was Marie Seton, and Marie Beton,   70
   And Marie Carmichael, and me."

BONNIE GEORGE CAMPBELL

High upon Highlands,
  And low upon Tay,
Bonnie George Campbell
  Rade out on a day.

Saddle⁷ and bridled   5
  And gallant rade he:
Hame cam his guid horse,
  But never cam he.

Out cam his auld mither,
  Greeting fu' sair;   10
And out cam his bonnie bride,
  Riving her hair.

Saddled and bridled
  And booted rade he:
Toom hame cam the saddle,   15
  But never cam he.

"My meadow lies green,
  And my corn is unshorn,
My barn is to build,
  And my babe is unborn."   20

Saddled and bridled
  And booted rade he:
Toom hame cam the saddle,
  But never cam he.

MIRACLE PLAYS

THE DELUGE

God. I, God, that all the world have wrought,
Heaven and earth, and all of nought,
I see my people in deede and thought
  Are sett fowle in sinne.
My ghost shall not lenge in man,

That through fleshie liking is my fone,
But till VI skore yeares be gone,
    To loke if they will blynne.

Manne that I made I will destroy,
Beast, worme, and fowle to flie;   10
For one earthe they doe me nye,
    The folke that are theron.
Hit harmes me so hartfullie,
The malyce that doth nowe multeply,
That sore it greveth me inwardlie   15
    That ever I made manne.

Therfore, Noe, my servant free,
That righteous man art, as I see,
A shipp sone thou shall make the
    Of trees drye and lighte.   20
Little chambers therein thou make;
And bynding sliche also thou take,
With-in and out thou ne slake
    To anoynte it through all thy mighte.

300 cubytes it shall be long,   25
And 50 of breadeth, to mak it stronge;
Of heighte 50: the mete thou fonge,
    Thus measure it about.
One wyndow worch through thy wytte;
One cubyte of length and breadeth make it: 30
Upon the side a dore shall sit
    For to come in and out.

Eating places thou make also,
Three roofed chambers, one or two;
For with water I thinke to flow   35
    Man that I can make.
Destroyed all the world shalbe,
Save thou; thy wife, thy sonnes three,
And all there wives also with thee
    Shall saved be for thy sake.   40

Noe. Ah, Lord! I thanke The lowd and still,
That to me art in such will,

And spares me and my house to spill,
　　As now I sothlie fynde.
Thy bydding, Lord, I shall fulfill,　　　　　　　　　45
And never more The greeve ne grill,
That suche grace hast sent me till
　　Among all mankinde.

Have done, yow men and women all!
Helpe for ought that may befall　　　　　　　　　50
To worke this shipp, chamber and hall,
　　As God hath bydden us doe.
Sem. Father, I am already bowne:
Anne axe I have, by my crowne,
As sharpe as any in all this towne,　　　　　　　55
　　For to goe there to.

Ham. I have a hatchet wonder-kene
To byte well, as may be seene;
A better grownden, as I weene,
　　Is not in all this towne.　　　　　　　　　　60
Japhet. And I can well make a pyn,
And with this hammer knock yt in;
Goe and worche without more dynne,
　　And I am ready bowne.

Uxor Noe. And we shall bring tymber to,　　　　65
For wee mon nothing els doe;
Women be weake to underfoe
　　Any great travayle.
Uxor Sem. Here is a good hackstock;
On this yow maye hew and knock.　　　　　　　70
Shall non be idle in this flock,
　　Ne now may no man fayle.

Uxor Ham. And I will goe to gather sliche,
The ship for to cleane and piche;
Anoynted yt must be every stich,　　　　　　　　75
　　Board, tree, and pyn.
Uxor Japhet. And I will gather chippes here
To make a fire for yow in feere,
And for to dight your dynner
　　Against yow come in.　　　　　　　　　　　80

Tunc faciunt signa, quasi laborarent cum diversis instrumentis.

 Noe. Now in the name of God I will begin
 To make the shippe that we shall in,
 That we be ready for to swym
  At the cominge of the flood.
 These bordes I joyne here together,   85
 To kepe us safe from the wedder,
 That we may row both hither and thider,
  And safe be from this floode.

 Of this tree will I make the mast,
 Tyde with gables that will last,   90
 With a sayle-yarde for each blast,
  And each thinge in ther kinde;
 With topcastle and bewsprytt,
 With coardes and ropes I have all meete,
 To sayle forth at the next weete.   95
  This shipp is at an ende.

*Tunc Noe iterum cum tota familia faciunt signa laborandi
cum diversis instrumentis.*

 Wife, in this castle we shall be keped:
 My childer and thou, I wold, in leaped.
 Uxor Noe. In faith, Noe, I had as lief thou sleppit;
  For all thy frankish fare   100
 I will not doe after thy red.
 Noe. Good wife, doe now as I the bydd!
 Uxor Noe. By Christ! not or I see more neede,
  Though thou stand all the day and stare.

 Noe. Lord, that women be crabbed aye,   105
 And never are meke, that dare I saye.
 This is well sene by me to daye,
  In witnes of yow each one.
 Good wife, let be all this beere
 That thou makes in this place here;   110
 For all they wene thou art master—
  And so thou art, by St. John!

 Deus. Noe, take thou thy meanye,
 And in the shippe hye that yow be,

For none so righteous man to me   115
    Is now on earth lyvinge.
Of cleane beastes with thee thou take
Seaven and seaven, or thou slake,
Hee and shee, make to make;
    Be lyve in that thou bringe   120

Of beastes uncleane two and two,
Male and female, without moe;
Of cleane fowles seaven alsoe,
    The hee and shee together;
Of fowles uncleane two and no more,   125
As I of beastes said before;
That shalbe saved throughe my lore,
    Against I send the wedder.

Of all meates that must be eaten
Into the ship loke there be getten,   130
For that no way may be foryeten;
    And doe all this bydeene,
To sustayne man and beast therein,
Aye till the water cease and blyn.
This world is filled full of synne,   135
    And that is now well sene.

Seaven dayes be yet coming,
You shall have space them in to bringe.
After that is my lyking
    Mankinde for to nye: 140
40 dayes and 40 nightes
Rayne shall fall for ther unrightes;
And that I have made through my mightes
    Now think I to destroye.

Noe. Lord, at Your byddinge I am bayne,   145
Sith non other grace will gayne;
Hit will fulfill fayne,
    For gratious I Thee fynde.
A 100 wynters and 20
This shipp making taried have I,   150
If through amendment any mercye
    Wolde fall unto mankinde.

Have done, you men and women all!
Hye you lest this water fall,
That each beast were in his stall,   155
    And into the ship broughte:
Of cleane beastes seaven shalbe,
Of uncleane two; this God bade me.
This floode is nye, well may we see,
    Therfore tary you noughte.   160

*Tunc Noe introibit archam, et familia sua dabit et recitabit
omnia animalia depicta in cartis; et, postquam unusquis-
que suam locutus est partem, ibit in archam, uxore Noe
excepta; et animalia depicta cum verbis concordare de-
bent; et sic incipiet primus filius:*

Sem. Syr, here are lyons, libardes in;
Horses, mares, oxen, and swyne,
Geates, calves, sheepe, and kine
    Here sitten thou may see.
Ham. Camels, asses men may finde,   165
Bucke, doe, harte, and hynde;
And beastes of all manner kinde
    Here bene, as thinkes mee.

Japhet. Take here cattes and doggs to,
Otter, fox, fulmart also;   170
Hares hopping gaylie can goe,
    Have cowle here for to eate.
Uxor Noe. And here are beares, wolfes sett,
Apes, owles, marmoset,
Weesells, squirrels, and firret;   175
    Here they eaten their meate.

Uxor Sem. Yet more beastes are in this howse:
Here cattis maken it full crowse;
Here a rotten, here a mowse;
    They stand nye together.   180
Uxor Ham. And here are fowles, les and more:
Hearnes, cranes, and byttour,
Swans, peacockes, and them before
    Meate for this wedder.

Uxor Japhet. Here are cockes, kites, crowes,   185
Rookes, ravens, many rowes,
Duckes, curlewes: who ever knowes
    Eache one in his kinde?
And here are doves, diggs, drakes;
Redshankes runninge through the lakes;   190
And each fowle that ledden makes
    In this shipp men may finde.

Noe. Wife, come in! why standes thou here?
Thou art ever froward, that dare I sweare.
Come in, on Gods half! tyme yt were,   195
    For feare lest that we drowne.
Uxor Noe. Yea, sir, set up your sayle
And rowe forth with evill heale!
For, without any fayle,
    I will not out of this towne: 200

But I have my gossips everichon,
One foote further I will not gone;
They shall not drowne, by St. John,
    And I may save their lyfe!
They loved me full well, by Christ!   205
But thou wilt let them in thy chist,
Els rowe forth, Noe, whether thou list,
    And get thee a new wife.

Noe. Sem, sonne, loe, thy mother is wraw.
For sooth such another I do not know.   210
Sem. Father, I shall fett her in, I trow,
    Without any fayle.
Mother, my father after thee send,
And bydds the into yonder ship wend.
Loke up and se the wynde,   215
    For we be readye to sayle.

Uxor Noe. Sonne, goe again to him and say
I will not come therein to daye.
Noe. Come in, wife, in 20 devills waye,
    Or els stand there without.   220
Ham. Shall wee all fet her in?

Noe. Yea, sonnes, in Christs blessinge and myne:
I would yow hyde yow betyme,
   For of this floode I am in doubte.

The Good Gossopes. The flood comes in, full fleetinge
    faste; 225
   On every side it spredeth full fare;
For feare of drowning I am agast!
   Good gossip, let us draw neare,
And let us drinke or we depart,
   For often tymes we have done soe; 230
For at a draught thou drinkes a quarte,
   And so will I doe or I goe.

Japhet. Mother, we praye you altogether,
For we are here your owne childer,
Come into the ship for feare of the wedder, 235
   For His love That you boughte.
Uxor Noe. That will I not, for all your call,
But I have my gossopes all.
Sem. In feith, mother, yet you shall,
   Whether you will or not. 240

Tunc ibit.

Noe. Welcome, wife, into this boate.
Uxor Noe. And have thou that for thy mote!

Et dat alapam vita?

Noe. A! ha! mary, this is hote;
   It is good to be still.
A! children, me thinkes my boate remeves; 245
Our tarying here hugelie me greves;
Over the lande the water spredes:
   God doe as He will!

Ah, great God, That art so good,
That worchis not Thie will is wood. 250
Now all this world is on a flood,
   As I see well in sighte.
This window I will shut anon,

And into my chamber will I gone
Till this water, so greate one,   255
   Be slaked throughe Thy mighte.

*Tunc Noe claudet fenestram archae; et per modicum spatium
infra tectum cantent psalmum "Save mee, O God"; et
aperiens fenestram et respiciens:*

Now 40 dayes are fullie gone,
Send a raven I will anone,
If ought-were earth, tree, or stone
   Be drye in any place.   260
And if this foule come not againe,
It is a signe, soth to sayne,
That drye it is on hill or playne,
   And God hath done some grace.

Tunc dimittet corvum, et capiens columbam in manibus dicat:

Ah Lord, wherever this raven be   265
Somewhere is drye, well I see;
But yet a dove, by my lewtye,
   After I will sende:
Thou wilt turne againe to me,
For of all fowles that may flye   270
   Thou art most meke and hend.

*Tunc emittet columbam, et erit in nave alia columba ferens
olivam in ore quam dimittet ex malo per funem in manus
Noe; et postea dicat Noe:*

Ah Lord, blessed be Thou aye,
That me hast comfort thus to-day!
By this sight I may well saye
   This flood beginnes to cease: 275
My sweete dove to me brought hase
A branch of olyve from some place;
This betokeneth God has done us some grace
   And is a signe of peace.

Ah Lord, honoured most Thou be!   280
All earthe dryes, now I see;
But yet, tyll Thou comaunde me,
   Hence will I not hye.

All this water is awaye;
Therfore, as sone as I maye,   285
Sacryfice I shall doe, in faye,
  To Thee devoutlye.

Deus. Noe, take thy wife anone,
And thy children every one;
Out of the shippe thou shalt gone,   290
  And they all with thee.
Beastes and all that can flie
Out anone they shall hye,
On earth to grow and multeplye:
  I will that yt be soe.   295

Noe. Lord, I thanke The through Thy mighte!
Thy bidding shall be done in height,
And as fast as I may dighte
  I will doe The honoure,
And to Thee offer sacrifice;   300
Therfore comes in all wise,
For of these beastes that bene Hise
  Offer I will this stower.

*Tunc egrediens archam cum tota familia sua accipiet animalia
sua et volucres et offeret ea et mactabit.*

Lord, God in majestye,
That such grace hast graunted me,   305
Where all was lorne, save to be,
  Therfore now I am bowne,
My wife, my childer, my meanye,
With sacrifice to honoure Thee
With beastes, fowles, as Thou may see,   310
  I offer here right sone.

Deus. Noe, to me thou arte full able,
And thy sacrifice acceptable.
For I have fownd thee trew and stable,
  On the now must I myn: 315
Warry earth will I no more
For mans synne, that greves me sore—
For of youth man full yore
  Has byn enclyned to syne.

You shall now grow and multeply, 320
And earth againe you edefie.
Each beast and fowle that may flie
   Shall be afrayd of you:
And fishe in sea that may flytte
Shall susteyne yow, I yow behite; 325
To eate of them yow ne lett,
   That cleane bene you may knowe.

Thereas you have eaten before
Grasse and rootes, sith you were bore,
Of cleane beastes now, les and more, 330
   I geve you leave to eate,
Safe bloode and flesh, bothe in feare,
Of wrong dead carren that is here;
Eate not of that in no manere,
   For that aye you shall let. 335

Manslaughter also you shall flee,
For that is not pleasant to me:
That shedes bloode, he or shee,
   Ought-where amongst mankinde,
That blood foule sheede shalbe 340
And vengence have, that men shall se;
Therfore beware now, all yee,
   You fall not in that synne.

A forwarde now with thie I make,
And all thy seede for thy sake, 345
Of suche vengeance for to slake;
   For now I have my will.
Here I behet the a heaste
That man, woman, fowle, ne beaste,
With water, while the world shall last, 350
   I wil no more spill.

My bowe betwene you and me
In the firmament shall bee,
By verey token that you may see
   That such vengeance shall cease; 355
That man ne woman shall never more

Be wasted by water as is before:
But for syn that greveth me sore,
   Therfore this vengeance was.

Where cloudes in the welkin bene, 360
That ilke bowe shall be sene
In tokeninge that my wrath and tene
   Shall never this wroken be.
The stringe is turned toward you
And toward me is bent the bowe, 365
That such wedder shall never showe;
   And this behett I thee.

My blessing now I geve the here,
To thee, Noe, my servant dere,
For vengeance shall no more appeare. 370
And now fare well, my darling deere.

ABRAHAM'S SACRIFICE

Introitus Abrahe, etc.

Abraham. Most myghty Makere of sunne and of mone,
   Kyng of kynges and Lord over alle,
Allemyghty God in hevyn trone,
   I The honowre and evyr more xal!
My Lord, my God! to The I kalle; 5
   With herty wylle, Lord, I The pray;
I synfulle lyff lete me nevyr falle,
   But lete me leve evyr to Thi pay!

Abraham my name is kydde,
   And patryarke of age ful olde; 10
And yit be the grace of God is bredde,
   In myn olde age, a chylde fulle bolde.
Ysaac, lo! here his name is tolde,
   My swete sone that stondyth me by;
Amonges alle chylderyn that walkyn on wolde 15
   A lovelyer chylde is non trewly.

I thanke God with hert welle mylde
   Of His gret mercy and of His hey grace,

And pryncepaly ffor my suete chylde,
    That xal to me do gret solace.   20
Now, suete sone, ffayre fare thi fface;
    Fful hertyly do I love the:
Ffor trewe herty love now in this place,
    My swete childe, com, kysse now me.

Ysaac. At youre byddynge your mouthe I kys.   25
    With lowly hert I yow pray,
Youre fadyrly love lete me nevyr mysse,
    But blysse me, your chylde, bothe nyght and day.
Abraham. Almyghty God, That best may,
    His dere blyssyng He graunt the!   30
And my blyssyng thou have alle way,
    In what place that evyr thou be.

Now, Ysaac, my sone so suete,
    Almyghty God loke thou honoure,
Wiche That made bothe drye and wete,   35
    Shynyng sunne and scharpe schoure.
Thu art my suete childe, and *par amoure*
    Fful wele in herte do I the love:
Loke that thin herte, in hevyn toure
    Be sett to serve oure Lord God above.   40

In thi yonge lerne God to plese,
    And God xal quyte the weyl thi mede:
Now, suete sone, of wordys these
    With alle thin hert thou take good hede.
Now fare weyl, sone; God be thin spede!   45
    Evyn here at hom thou me abyde:
I must go walkyn, ffor I have nede;
    I come agen withinne a tyde.

Ysaac. I pray to God, Ffadyr of myght,
    That He yow spede in alle your waye!   50
From shame and shenshipp, day and nyht,
    God mote yow kepe in your jornay.
Abraham. Now fare weylle, sone! I the pray
    Evyr in thin hert loke God thou wynde,
Hym to serve, bothe nyght and day.   55
    I pray to God sende the good mynde.

Ther may no man love bettyr his childe
  Than Isaac is lovyd of me:
Almyghty God, mercyful and mylde,
  Ffor my swete son I wurchyp The!   60
I thank The, Lord, with hert ful fre,
  Ffor this fayr frute Thou hast me sent:
Now gracyous God, wher so he be,
  To save my sone evyr more be bent!

Dere Lord, I pray to The also,   65
  Me to save for Thi servvaunte;
And sende me grace nevyr for to do
  Thyng that xulde be to Thi displesaunte.
Bothe ffor me and for myn infaunte,
  I pray The, Lord God, us to help!   70
Thy gracyous goodnes Thou us grawnt,
  And save Thi servaunt from helle qwelp!

Angelus. Abraham, how! Abraham,
  Lyst and herke weylle onto me!
Abraham. Al redy, sere, here I am;   75
  Telle me your wylle what that it be.
Angelus. Almyghty God thus doth bydde the:
  Ysaac thi sone anon thou take,
And loke hym thou slee anoon, lete se;
  And sacrafice to God hym make.   80

Thy welbelovyd childe thou must now kylle;
  To God thou offyr hym, as I say,
Evyn upon yon hey hylle,
  That I the shewe here in the way.
Tarye not be nyght nor day,   85
  But smertly thi gate thou goo:
Upon yon hille thou knele and pray
  To God, and kylle the childe ther and scloo!

Abraham. Now Goddys comaundement must nedys
    be done;
  Alle His wyl is wourthy to be wrought;   90
But yitt the fadyr to scle the sone,
  Grett care it causyth in my thought.

In byttyr bale now am I brought
   My swete childe with knyf to kylle;
But yit my sorwe avaylith ryght nowth,   95
   For nedys I must werke Goddys wylle.

With evy hert I walke and wende,
   My childys deth now for to be;
Now must the fadyr his suete sone schende:
   Alas! for ruthe it is pete!   100
My swete sone, come hedyr to me;
   How, Isaac, my sone dere,
Com to thi ffadyr, my childe so fre,
   Ffor we must wende to-gedyr in fere.

Isaac. Alle redy, fadyr, evyn at your wylle,   105
   And at your byddyng I am yow by;
With yow to walk ovyr dale and hille,
   At youre callyng I am redy.
To the fadyr evyr most comly,
   It ovyth the childe evyr buxom to be: 110
I wyl obey, ful hertyly,
   To alle thyng that ye bydde me.

Abraham. Now, son, in thi necke this fagot thou take,
   And this fyre bere in thinne honde,
Ffor we must now sacrefyse go make,   115
   Evyn aftyr the wylle of Goddys sonde.
Take this brennyng bronde,
   My swete childe, and lete us go.—
Ther may no man that levyth in londe
   Have more sorwe than I have wo!   120

Ysaac. Ffayr fadyr, ye go ryght stylle;
   I pray yow, fadyr, speke onto me.
Abraham. Mi gode childe, what is thi wylle?
   Telle me thyn hert, I pray to the.
Ysaac. Ffadyr, fyre and wood here is plente,   125
   But I kan se no sacryfice;
What ye xulde offre fayn wold I se,
   That it were don at the best avyse.

Abraham. God xal that ordeyn, That sytt in hevynne,
   My swete sone, ffor this offryng*   130
A derrere sacryfice may no man nempne
   Than this xal be, my dere derlyng.
Ysaac. Lat be, good fadyr, your sad wepynge!
   Your hevy cher agrevyth me sore:
Telle me, fadyr, your grett mornyng,   135
   And I xal seke sum help therfore.

Abraham. Alas, dere sone! for nedys must me
   Evyn here the kylle, as God hath sent;
Thyn owyn fadyr thi deth must be—
   Alas! that evyr this bowe was bent!   140
With this fyre bryght thou must be brent;
   An aungelle seyd to me ryght so.
Alas, my chylde! thou xalt be shent!
   Thi careful fadyr must be thi ffo!

Ysaac. Almyghty God, of His grett mercye,   145
   Fful hertyly I thanke The sertayne!
At Goddys byddyng here for to dye,
   I obeye me here for to be sclayne.
I pray yow, fadyr, be glad and fayne,
   Trewly to werke Goddys wylle: 150
Take good comforte to yow agayn,
   And have no dowte your childe to kylle.

Ffor Godys byddyng forsothe it is,
   That I of yow my deth schulde take:
Agens God ye don amys,   155
   Hys byddyng yf ye xuld forsake.
Yowre owyn dampnacion xulde ye bake,
   If ye me kepe from this reed:
With your swerd my deth ye make,
   And werk evyrmore the wylle of God.   160

Abraham. The wylle of God must nedys be done;
   To werke His wylle I seyd nevyr nay:
But yit the ffadyr to sle the sone,
   My hert doth clynge and cleve as clay!

Ysaac. Yitt werke Goddys wylle, fadyr, I yow pray, 165
    And sle me here anoon forthe ryght;
And turne fro me your face away,
    Myne heed whan that ye xul of smyght.

Abraham. Alas, dere childe! I may not chese;
    I must nedys my swete sone kylle!   170
My dere derlyng now must me lese;
    Myn owyn sybb blood now xal I spylle!
Yitt this dede or I fulfylle,
    My swete sone, thi mouth I kys.
Ysaac. Al redy, fadyr! evyn at your wylle   175
    I do your byddyng, as reson is.

Abraham. Alas, dere sone! here is no grace,
    But nedis ded now must thou be!
With this kerchere I kvre thi face:
    In the tyme that I sle the,   180
Thy lovely vesage wold I not se,
    Not for alle this werdlys good!
With this swerd, that sore grevyth me,
    My childe I sle and spylle his blood!

Angelus. Abraham! Abraham! thou fadyr fre!   185
    Abraham. I am here redy: what is your wylle?
Angelus. Extende thin hand in no degre!
    I bydde thou hym not kylle!
Here do I se by ryght good skylle
    Allemyghty God that thou dost drede,   190
For thou sparyst nat thi sone to spylle:
    God wylle aqwhyte the welle thi mede!

Abraham. I thank my God in hevyn above,
    And Hym honowre fir this grett grace!
And that my Lord me thus doth prove,   195
    I wylle Hym wurchep in every place!
My childys lyff is my solace;
    I thank myn God evyr for his lyff!
In sacrifice here or I hens pace,
    I sle this shepe with this same knyff.   200

Now this shepe is deed and slayn,
    With this fyre it xal be brent.
Of Isaac my sone I am ful fayn,
    That my swete childe xal not be shent.
This place I name, with good entent,   205
    The hille of Godys vesytacion;
Ffor hedyr God hath to us sent
    His comforte, aftyr grett trybulacion.

Angelus. Herke, Abraham, and take good heyd!
    By Hymself God hath thus sworne,   210
Ffor that thou woldyst a done this dede,
    He wylle the blysse bothe evyn and morne.
Ffor thi dere childe thou woldyst have lorn,
    At Goddys byddyng, as I the telle,
God hath sent the word beforn   215
    Thi seed xal multyplye wher so thou duelle.

As sterres in hevyn byn many and fele,
    So xal thi seed encrese and growe;
Thou xalt ovyrcome, in welthe and wele,
    Alle thi fomen reknyd be rowe;   220
As sond in the se doth ebbe and flowe,
    Hath cheselys many unnumerabylle,
So xal thi sede, thou mayst me trowe,
    Encres and be evyr prophytabylle.

Ffor to my speche thou dedyst obeye,   225
    Thyn enmyes portes thou shalt possede;
And alle men on erthe, as I the seye,
    Thei xal be blyssed in thi sede.
Almyghty God thus the wylle mede,
    Ffor that good wylle that thou ast done;   230
Therfore thank God, in word and dede,
    Bothe thou thiself and Ysaac thi sone.

Abraham. A! my Lord God to wurchep on kne now I
    falle!
    I thank The, Lord, of Thi mercy!
Now, my swete childe, to God thou kalle,   235
    And thank we that Lord now hertyly!

Isaac. With lowly hert to God I crye:
　　I am His servvant bothe day and nyght!
I thank The, Lord, in hevyn so hyghe,
　　With hert, with thought, with mayn, with myght! 240

Abraham. Gramercy, Lord, and Kyng of grace!
　　Gramercy, Lord over lordys alle!
Now my joye returnyth his trace,
　　I thank The, Lorde, in hevyn Thin halle!
Isaac. Ovyr alle kynges crownyd Kyng, I The kalle! 245
　　At Thi byddyng to dye with knyff,
I was fful buxum, evyn as Thi thralle:
　　Lord, now I thank The, Thou grauntyst me lyff.

Abraham. Now we have wurchepyd oure blyssyd
　　　　Lorde,
　　On grounde knelyng upon oure kne;　　　　　250
Now lete us tweyn, sone, ben of on acorde,
　　And goo walke hom into oure countre.
Ysaac. Ffadyr, as ye wylle so xal it be;
　　I am redy with yow to gon;
I xal yow folwe with hert fulle fre;　　　　　255
　　Alle that ye bydde me sone xal be don.

Abraham. Now God, alle thyng of nowth That made,
　　Evyr wurcheppyd He be on watyr and londe!
His gret honowre may nevyr more fade,
　　In felde nor town, se nor on sonde!　　　　260
As althyng, Lord, Thou hast in honde,
　　So save us alle, wher so we be;
Whethyr we syttyn, walk, or stonde,
　　Evyr on Thin handwerke Thou have pyte!

MORALITY PLAYS

EVERYMAN

Messenger. I pray you all gyve your audyence,
And here this mater with reverence,
By fygure a morall playe.
The somonynge of Everyman called it is,

That of our lyves and endynge shewes 5
How transytory we be all daye.
This matter is wonders precyous,
But the entent of it is more gracyous
And swete to bere awaye.
The story sayth, "Man, in the begynnynge 10
Loke well and take good heed to the endynge,
Be you never so gay;
Ye thynke synne in the begynnynge full swete,
Whiche in the ende causeth the soule to wepe,
Whan the body lyeth in claye." 15
Here shall you se how Felawshyp and Jolyte
Bothe, Strengthe, Pleasure, and Beaute,
Wyll fade from the as floure in Maye.
For ye shall here how our Heven Kynge
Calleth Everyman to a general rekenynge. 20
Gyve audyence and here what He doth saye.

God speketh.

I perceyve here, in my majeste,
How that all creatures be to me unkynde,
Lyvynge without drede in worldely prosperyte.
Of ghostly syght the people be so blynde, 25
Drowned in synne, they know me not for theyr God.
In worldely ryches is all theyr mynde;
They fere not my ryghtwysnes, the sharpe rood.
My lawe that I shewed whan I for them dyed
They forgete clene, and shedynge of my blode rede: 30
I hanged bytwene two, it can not be denyed;
To gete them lyfe I suffred to be deed;
I heled theyr fete; with thornes hurt was my heed.
I coude do nomore than I dyde, truely,
And nowe I se the people do clene forsake me: 35
They use the seven deedly synnes dampnable,
As pryde, coveytyse, wrathe, and lechery,
Now in the worlde be made commendable.
And thus they leve of aungelles the hevenly company,
Every man lyveth so after his owne pleasure; 40
And yet of theyr lyfe they be nothynge sure.
I se the more that I them forbere
The worse they be fro yere to yere;

All that lyveth appayreth faste.
Therfore I wyll in all the haste   45
Have a rekenynge of every mannes persone;
For, and I leve the people thus alone
In theyr lyfe and wycked tempestes,
Veryly they wyll become moche worse than beestes:
For now one wolde by envy another up ete;   50
Charyte they do all clene forgete.
I hoped well that every man
In my glory sholde make his mansyon,
And therto I had them all electe;
But now I se, like traytours dejecte,   55
They thanke me not for the pleasure that I to them ment,
Nor yet for theyr beynge that I them have lent.
I profered the people grete multytude of mercy,
And fewe there be that asketh it hertly;
They be so combred with worldly ryches   60
That nedes on them I must do justyce,
On every man lyvynge without fere.—
Where art thou, Deth, thou mighty messengere?
    Dethe. Almyghty God, I am here at Your wyll,
Your commaundement to fulfyll.   65
    God. Go thou to Everyman,
And shewe hym, in my name,
A pylgrymage he must on hym take,
Whiche he in no wyse may escape;
And that he brynge with hym a sure rekenynge,   70
Without delay or ony taryenge.
    Dethe. Lorde, I wyll in the worlde go renne over all,
And cruelly out serche bothe grete and small.
Every man wyll I beset that lyveth beestly,
Out of Goddes lawes, and dredeth not foly;   75
He that loveth rychesse I wyll stryke with my darte,
His syght to blynde, and fro heven to departe,
Excepte that almes be his good frende,
In hell for to dwell, worlde without ende.
Loo, yonder I se Everyman walkynge;   80
Full lytell he thynketh on my comynge!
His mynde is on flesshely lustes and his treasure,
And grete payne it shall cause hym to endure
Before the Lorde, Heven Kynge.—

Everyman, stande styll! Whyder arte thou goynge,   85
Thus gayly? hast thou thy Maker forgete?
    Everyman. Why asketh thou?
Woldst thou wete?
    Dethe. Ye, syr, I wyll shewe you:
In grete hast I am sende to the   90
Fro God, out of His mageste.
    Everyman. What, sente to me?
    Dethe. Ye, certaynly.
Thoughe thou have forgete Hym here,
He thynketh on the in the hevenly spere,   95
As, or we departe, thou shalte knowe.
    Everyman. What desyreth God of me?
    Dethe. That shall I shewe the:
A rekenynge He wyll nedes have,
Without ony lenger respyte.   10c
    Everyman. To gyve a rekenynge longer layser I crave;
This blinde mater troubleth my wytte.
    Dethe. On the thou must take a longe journey;
Therfore thy boke of counte with the thou brynge,
For turne agayne thou can not by no waye;   105
And loke thou be sure of thy rekenynge,
For before God thou shalte answere and shewe
Thy many badde dedes and good but a fewe,
How thou hast spente thy lyfe, and in what wyse,
Before the chefe Lorde of paradyse.   11ᴏ
Have ado we were in that waye,
For, wete thou well, thou shalte make none attournay.
    Everyman. Full unredy I am suche rekenynge to gyve.
I knowe the not: what messenger arte thou?
    Dethe. I am Dethe, that no man dredeth.   115
For every man I reste, and no man spareth,
For it is Goddes commaundement
That all to me sholde be obedyent.
    Everyman. O Dethe, thou comest whan I had the
      leest in mynde.
In thy power it lyeth me to save: 120
Yet of my good wyl I gyve the, yf thou wyl be kynde,
Ye, a thousande pounde shalte thou have,
And dyfferre this mater tyll another daye.
    Dethe. Everyman, it may not be by no waye.

I set not by golde, sylver, nor rychesse, 125
Ne by pope, emperour, kynge, duke, ne prynces;
For, and I wolde receyve gyftes grete,
All the worlde I might gete:
But my custome is clene contrary.
I gyve the no respyte; come hens, and not tary. 130
 Everyman. Alas, shall I have no lenger respyte?
I may saye, Dethe geveth no warnynge.
To thynke on the, it maketh my herte seke,
For all unredy is my boke of rekenynge:
But XII yere and I myght have abydynge, 135
My countynge boke I wolde make so clere
That my rekenynge I sholde not nede to fere.
Wherfore, Dethe, I praye the, for Goddes mercy,
Spare me tyll I be provyded of remedy.
 Dethe. The avayleth not to crye, wepe, and praye: 140
But hast the lyghtly that thou were gone that journaye;
And preve thy frendes yf thou can;
For, wete thou well, the tyde abydeth no man,
And in the worlde eche lyvynge creature
For Adams synne must dye of nature. 145
 Everyman. Dethe, yf I sholde this pylgrymage take,
And my rekenynge suerly make,
Shewe me, for Saynt Charyte,
Sholde I not come agayne shortly?
 Dethe. No, Everyman, and thou be ones there, 150
Thou mayst never more come here,
Trust me veryly.
 Everyman. O gracyous God in the hye sete celestyall,
Have mercy on me in this moost nede!—
Shall I have no company fro this vale terrestryall 155
Of myne acqueynce that way me to lede?
 Dethe. Ye, if ony be so hardy,
That wolde go with the and bere the company.
Hye the that thou were gone to Goddes magnyfycence,
Thy rekenynge to gyve before His presence. 160
What, wenest thou thy lyve is gyven the,
And thy worldely goodes also?
 Everyman. I had wende so, veryle.
 Dethe. Nay, nay, it was but lende the;
For, as soone as thou arte go, 165

Another a whyle shall have it, and than go ther fro
Even as thou hast done.
Everyman, thou arte made: thou hast thy wyttes fyve,
And here on erthe wyll not amende thy lyve;
For sodenely I do come.   170
    Everyman. O wretched caytyfe, wheder shall I flee,
That I myght scape this endles sorowe!—
Now, gentyll Deth, spare me tyll to morowe,
That I may amende me
With good advysement.   175
    Dethe. Naye, therto I wyll not consent,
Nor no man wyll I respyte,
But to the herte sodeynly I shall smyte
Without ony advysement.
And now out of thy syght I wyll me hy: 180
Se thou make the redy shortely,
For thou mayst saye, "This is the daye
That no man lyvynge may scape awaye."
    Everyman. Alas, I may well wepe with syghes
      depe:
Now have I no maner of company   185
To helpe me in my journey and me to kepe,
And also my wrytynge is full unredy.
How shall I do now for to excuse me?
I wolde to God I had never be gete!
To my soule a full grete profyte it had be,   190
For now I fere paynes huge and grete.
The tyme passeth: Lorde helpe, That all wrought!
For though I mourne it avayleth nought.
The day passeth and is almoost ago;
I wote not well what for to do.   195
To whome were I best my complaynt to make?
What and I to Felawshyp therof spake,
And shewed hym of this sodeyne chaunce?
For in hym is all myne affyaunce,
We have in the worlde so many a daye   200
Be good frendes in sporte and playe.
I se hym yonder certaynely;
I trust that he wyll bere me company,
Therfore to hym wyll I speke to ese my sorowe.—
Well mette, good Felawshyp, and good morowe.   205

Felawshyp. Everyman, good morowe by this daye.
Syr, why lokest thou so pyteously?
If ony thynge be amysse I praye the me saye,
That I may helpe to remedy.
    Everyman. Ye, good Felawshyp, ye,   210
I am in greate jeoparde.
    Felawshyp. My true frende, shewe to me your mynde;
I wyll not forsake the to thy lyves ende,
In the way of good company.
    Everyman. That was well spoken and lovyngly.   215
    Felawshyp. Syr, I must nedes knowe your hevynesse;
I have pyte to se you in ony dystresse.
If ony have you wronged, ye shall revenged be,
Though I on the grounde be slayne for the,
Though that I knowe before that I sholde dye.   220
    Everyman. Veryly, Felawshyp, gramercy.
    Felawshyp. Tusshe, by thy thankes I set not a strawe;
Shewe me your grefe, and saye no more.
    Everyman. If I my herte sholde to you breke,
And than you to tourne your mynde fro me,   225
And wolde not me comforte whan ye here me speke,
Then sholde I ten tymes soryer be.
    Felawshyp. Syr, I saye as I wyll do in dede.
    Everyman. Than be you a good frende at nede;
I have founde you true herebefore.   230
    Felawshyp. And so ye shall evermore;
For in fayth and thou go to hell,
I wyll not forsake the by the waye.
    Everyman. Ye speke lyke a good frende; I byleve
        you well.
I shall deserve it and I maye.   235
    Felawshyp. I speke of no deservynge, by this daye;
For he that wyll saye and nothynge do,
Is not worthy with good company to go:
Therfore shewe me the grefe of your mynde,
As to your frende moost lovynge and kynde.   240
    Everyman. I shall shewe you how it is:
Commaunded I am to go a journaye,
A longe waye, harde and daungerous,
And gyve a strayte counte without delaye
Before the hye judge Adonay;   245

Wherfore I pray you bere me company,
As ye have promysed, in this journaye.

    Felawshyp. That is mater in dede: promyse is duty;
But and I sholde take suche a vyage on me,
I knowe it well it shulde be to my payne;   250
Also it make me aferde certayne.
But let us take counsell here as well as we can,
For your wordes wolde fere a stronge man.

    Everyman. Why, ye sayd yf I had nede,
Ye wolde me never forsake, quycke ne deed,   255
Thoughe it were to hell truely.

    Felawship. So I sayd, certaynely;
But suche pleasures be set asyde, the sothe to saye;
And also, yf we toke suche a journaye,
Whan sholde we come agayne?   260

    Everyman. Naye, never agayne tyll the daye of dome.

    Felawship. In fayth, than wyll not I come there.
Who hath you these tydynges brought?

    Everyman. In dede, Deth was with me here.

    Felawship. Now, by God That alle hathe bought,   265
If Deth were the messenger,
For no man that is lyvynge to daye
I wyll not go that lothe journaye—
Not for the fader that bygate me.

    Everyman. Ye promysed other wyse, parde.   270

    Felawshyp. I wote well I say so, truely;
And yet yf thou wylte ete and drinke and make good chere,
Or haunt to women the lusty company,
I wolde not forsake you, whyle the day is clere,
Trust me veryly.   275

    Everyman. Ye, therto ye wolde be redy:
To go to myrthe, solas, and playe
Your mynde wyll soner apply
Than to bere me company in my longe journaye.

    Felawship. Now in good fayth I wyll not that waye;   280
But and thou wyll murder, or ony man kyll,
In that I wyll helpe the with a good wyll.

    Everyman. O that is a symple advyse in dede!
Gentyll felawe, helpe me in my necessyte!
We have loved longe, and now I nede;   285
And now, gentyll Felawshyp, remember me!

Felawshyp. Wheder ye have loved me or no,
By Saynt John I wyll not with the go.
   Everyman. Yet I pray the, take the labour and do so
     moche for me,
To brynge me forwarde, for Saynt Charyte,   29
And comforte me tyll I come without the towne.
   Felawshyp. Nay, and thou wolde gyve me a newe
     gowne,
I wyll not a fote with the go;
But and thou had taryed, I wolde not have lefte the so.
And, as now, God spede the in thy journaye,   29
For from the I wyll departe as fast as I maye.
   Everyman. Wheder a waye, Felawshyp? wyll thou
     forsake me?
   Felawship. Ye, by my faye! To God I betake the.
   Everyman. Farewell, good Felawshyp; for the my
     herte is sore:
Adewe for ever, I shall se the no more.   30
   Felawship. In fayth, Everyman, fare well now at
     the ende;
For you I wyll remembre that partynge is mournynge.
   Everyman. Alacke! shall we thus departe in dede?
A, Lady, helpe, without ony more comforte!
Lo, Felawshyp forsaketh me in my moost nede: 3
For helpe in this worlde wheder shall I resorte?
Felawshyp herebefore with me wolde mery make;
And now lytell sorowe for me dooth he take.
It is sayd, in prosperyte men frendes may fynde,
Whiche in adversyte be full unkynde.   3
Now wheder for socoure shall I flee,
Syth that Felawshyp hath forsaken me?
To my kynnesmen I wyll, truely,
Prayenge them to helpe me in my necessyte;
I byleve that they wyll do so,   3
For kynde wyll crepe where it may not go.
I wyll go saye, for yonder I se them go.—
Where be ye now, my frendes and kynnesmen?
   Kynrede. Here be we now at your commaundement:
Cosyn, I praye you, shewe us your entent   3
In ony wise, and not spare.
   Cosyn. Ye, Everyman; and to us declare

If ye be dysposed to go ony whyder,
For, wete you well, wyll lyve and dye to gyder.

  Kynrede. In welth and wo we wyll with you holde,   325
For over his kynne a man may be bolde.

  Everyman. Gramercy, my frendes and kynnesmen
      kynde.
Now shall I shewe you the grefe of my mynde:
I was commaunded by a messenger,
That is a hye kynges chefe offycer;   330
He bad me go a pylgrymage to my payne,
And I knowe well I shall never come agayne;
Also I must gyve a rekenynge strayte,
For I have a grete enemy that hath me in wayte,
Whiche entendeth me for to hynder.   335

  Kynrede. What acounte is that whiche ye must render?
That wolde I knowe.

  Everyman. Of all my workes I must shewe,
How I have lyved, and my dayes spent;
Also of yll dedes that I have used   340
In my tyme syth lyfe was me lent,
And of all vertues that I have refused:
Therfore I praye you, go thyder with me
To helpe to make myn accounte, for Saint Charyte.

  Cosyn. What, to go thyder? Is that the mater?   345
Nay, Everyman, I had lever fast brede and water,
All this fyve yere and more.

  Everyman. Alas, that ever I was bore!
For now shall I never be mery,
If that you forsake me.   350

  Kynrede. A, syr; what, ye be a mery man:
Take good herte to you, and make no mone;
But one thynge I warne you, by Saynt Anne,
As for me ye shall go alone.

  Everyman. My Cosyn, wyll you not with me go?   355

  Cosyn. No, by Our Lady, I have the crampe in my to:
Trust not to me; for, so God me spede,
I wyll deceyve you in your moost nede.

  Kynrede. It avayleth not us to tyse.
Ye shall have my mayde, with all my herte: 360
She loveth to go to feestes there to be nyse,
And to daunce, and abrode to sterte;

I wyll gyve her leve to helpe you in that journey,
If that you and she may agree.

    Everyman. Now shewe me the very effecte of your
        mynde: 365
Wyll you go with me, or abyde behynde?

    Kynrede. Abyde behynde! ye, that wyll I and I maye;
Therfore farewell tyll another daye.

    Everyman. Howe sholde I be mery or gladde?
For fayre promyses men to me make; 370
But when I have moost nede, they me forsake.
I am deceyved; that maketh me sadde.

    Cosyn. Cosyn Everyman, farewell now;
For, veryly, I wyll not go with you:
Also of myne owne unredy rekenynge 375
I have to accounte, therfore I make taryenge.
Now God kepe the, for now I go.

    Everyman. A, Jesus, is all come hereto?
Lo, fayre wordes maketh fooles fayne;
They promyse, and nothynge wyll do certayne. 380
My kynnesmen promysed me faythfully,
For to abyde with me stedfastly;
And now fast awaye do they flee.
Even so Felawship promysed me.
What frende were best me of to provyde? 385
I lose my time here longer to abyde,
Yet in my mynde a thynge there is:
All my lyfe I have loved ryches;
If that my Good now helpe me myght,
He wolde make my herte full lyght; 390
I wyll speke to him in this distresse.—
Where arte thou, my Gooddes and Ryches?

    Goodes. Who calleth me? Everyman? what, hast
        thou haste?
I lye here in corners trussed and pyled so hye,
And in chestes I am locked so fast, 395
Also sacked in bagges, thou mayst se with thyn eye,
I can not styre; in packes lowe I lye:
What wolde ye have, lightly me saye.

    Everyman. Come hyder, Good, in al the hast thou
        may,
For of counseyll I must desyre the. 400

Goodes. Syr, and ye in the worlde have sorowe or
    adversyte,
That can I helpe you to remedy shortly.
    Everyman. It is another dysease that greveth me;
In this worlde it is not, I tell the so.
I am sent for an other way to go, 405
To gyve a strayte counte generall
Before the hyest Jupyter of all:
And all my lyfe I have had joye and pleasure in the,
Therfore I pray the go with me;
For, paraventure, thou mayst before God Almighty 410
My rekenynge helpe to clene and puryfye,
For it is sayd ever amonge
That money maketh all ryght that is wronge.
    Goodes. Nay, Everyman, I synge an other songe:
I folowe no man in suche vyages, 415
For and I wente with the,
Thou sholdes fare moche the worse for me;
For bycause on me thou dyd set thy mynde,
Thy rekenynge I have made blotted and blynde,
That thyne accounte thou can not make truly; 420
And that hast thou for the love of me.
    Everyman. That wolde greve me full sore,
Whan I sholde come to that ferefull answere:
Up, let us go thyther togyder.
    Goodes. Nay, not so; I am to brytell, I may not
    endure: 425
I wyll folowe no man one fote, be ye sure.
    Everyman. Alas, I have the loved, and had grete
    pleasure
All my lyfe dayes on good and treasure.
    Goodes. That is to thy dampnacyon, without lesynge,
For my love is contrary to the love everlastynge; 430
But yf thou had me loved moderately durynge,
As to the poore gyve parte of me,
Than sholdest thou not in this dolour be,
Nor in this grete sorowe and care.
    Everyman. Lo, now was I deceyved or I was ware, 435
And all I may wyte my spendynge of tyme.
    Goodes. What, wenest thou that I am thyne?
    Everyman. I had went so.

Goodes. Naye, Everyman, I saye no:
As for a whyle I was lente the;　　　　　　　44
A season thou hast had me in prosperyte.
My condycyon is mannes soule to kyll;
If I save one, a thousande I do spyll.
Wenest thou that I wyll folowe the?
Nay, fro this worlde not, veryle.　　　　　　44

　　Everyman. I had wende otherwyse.

　　Goodes. Therfore to thy soule Good is a thefe;
For whan thou arte deed, this is my gyse:
Another to deceyve in this same wyse
As I have done the, and all to his soules reprefe.　　45

　　Everyman. O false Good, cursed thou be,
Thou traytour to God, that hast deceyved me,
And caught me in thy snare.

　　Goodes. Mary, thou brought thy selfe in care,
Wherof I am gladde;　　　　　　　45
I must nedes laugh, I can not be sadde.

　　Everyman. A, Good, thou hast had long my hertely love
I gave the that whiche sholde be the Lordes above:
But wylte thou not go with me in dede?
I pray the trouth to saye.　　　　　　46

　　Goodes. No, so God me spede;
Therfore fare well, and have good daye.

　　Everyman. O, to whome I make my mone?
For, to go with me in that hevy journaye,
Fyrst Felawshyp sayd he wolde with me gone;　　46
His wordes were very pleasaunt and gaye,
But afterwarde he lefte me alone.
Than spake I to my kynnesmen all in despayre,
And also they gave me wordes fayre,
They lacked no fayre spekynge;　　　　　　47
But all forsake me in the endynge.
Than wente I to my Goodes, that I loved best,
In hope to have comforte, but there had I leest;
For my Goodes sharpely dyd me tell
That he bryngeth many in to hell.　　　　　　47
Than of my selfe I was ashamed,
And so I am worthy to be blamed;
Thus may I well my selfe hate.
Of whome shall I now conseyll take?

I thynke that I shall never spede   480
Tyll that I go to my Good Dede.
But, alas, she is so weke
That she can nother go nor speke:
Yet will I venter on her now.—
My Good Dedes, where be you?   485
    Good Dedes. Here I lye, colde in the grounde;
Thy synnes hath me sore bounde
That I can nat stere.
    Everyman. O Good Dedes, I stande in fere:
I must you pray of counseyll,   490
For helpe now sholde come ryght well.
    Good Dedes. Everyman, I have understandynge
That ye be somoned acounte to make
Before Myssyas, of Jherusalem kynge;
And you do by me, that journay with you wyll I take. 495
    Everyman. Therfore I come to you my moone to make:
I praye you that ye wyll go with me.
    Good Dedes. I wolde full fayne, but I can not stand,
      veryly.
    Everyman. Why, is there ony thynge on you fall?
    Good Dedes. Ye, syr, I may thanke you of all: 500
Yf ye had parfytely chered me,
Your boke of counte full redy had be.
Loke, the bokes of your workes and dedes eke,
A, se how they lye under the fete,
To your soules hevynes.   505
    Everyman. Our Lorde Jesus helpe me!
For one letter here I can not se.
    Good Dedes. There is a blynde rekenynge in tyme
      of dystres!
    Everyman. Good Dedes, I praye you helpe me in this
      nede,
Or elles I am for ever dampned in dede;   510
Therfore helpe me to make rekenynge
Before the Redemer of all thynge,
That Kynge is and was and ever shall.
    Good Dedes. Everyman, I am sory of your fall,
And fayne wolde I helpe you and I were able.   515
    Everyman. Good Dedes, your counseyll I pray you
      gyve me.

Good Dedes. That shall I do veryly:
Thoughe that on my fete I may not go,
I have a syster that shall with you also,
Called Knowlege, whiche shall with you abyde,   520
To helpe you to make that dredeful rekenynge.
   Knowlege. Everyman, I wyll go with thee and be
     thy gyde,
In thy moost nede to go by thy syde.
   Everyman. In good condycyon I am now in every
     thynge,
And am hole content with this good thynge,   525
Thanked by God my Creature.
   Good Dedes. And whan He hath brought you there
Where thou shalte hele the of thy smarte,
Than go you with your rekenynge and your good dedes
     togyder
For to make you joyfull at herte   530
Before the blessyd Trynyte.
   Everyman. My Good Dedes, gramercy;
I am well content certaynly
With your wordes swete.
   Knowlege. Now go we togyder lovyngly   535
To Confessyon, that clensynge ryvere.
   Everyman. For joy I wepe: I wolde we were there;
But, I pray you, gyve me cognycyon
Where dwelleth that holy man, Confessyon?
   Knowlege. In the house of salvacyon;   540
We shall fynde hym in that place,
That shall us comforte by Goddes grace.—
Lo, this is Confessyon: knele downe and aske mercy;
For he is in good conceyte with God Almyghty.
   Everyman. O gloryous fountayne that all unclenenes
     doth claryfy,   545
Wasshe fro me the spottes of vyce unclene,
That on me no synne may be sene!
I come, with Knowlege, for my redempcyon,
Redempte with herte and full contrycyon;
For I am commaunded a pylgrymage to take,   550
And grete accountes before God to make.
Now I pray you, Shryfte, moder of salvacyon,
Helpe my good dedes for my pyteous exclamacyon!

Confessyon. I knowe your sorowe well, Everyman:
Bycause with Knowlege ye come to me,   555
I wyll you comforte as well as I can;
And a precyous jewell I wyll gyve the,
Called penaunce, voyce voyder of adversyte;
Therwith shall your body chastysed be
With abstynence and perseveraunce in Goddes servyce.   560
Here shall you receyve that scourge of me,
Whiche is penaunce stronge that ye must endure,
To remembre thy Savyour was scourged for the
With sharpe scourges, and suffred it pacyently:
So must thou or thou scape that paynful pylgrymage.   565
Knowlege, kepe hym in this vyage,
And by that tyme Good Dedes wyll be with the.
But in ony wyse be seker of mercy,
For your tyme draweth fast; and ye wyll saved be,
Aske God mercy, and He wyll graunte truely: 570
Whan with the scourge of penaunce man doth hym bynde,
The oyle of forgyvenes than shall he fynde.

    Everyman. Thanked be God for His gracyous werke;
For now I wyll my penaunce begyn:
This hath rejoysed and lyghted my herte,   575
Though the knottes be paynfull and harde within.

      Knowlege. Everyman, loke your penaunce that ye
      fulfyll,
What payne that ever it to you be;
And Knowlege shall gyve you counseyll at wyll,
How your accounte ye shall make clerely.   580

    Everyman. O eternal God, O hevenly Fygure,
O Way of Ryghtwysnes, O goodly Vysyon,
Whiche descended downe in a vyrgyn pure
Bycause He wolde Everyman redeme
(Whiche Adam forfayted by his dysobedyence),   585
O blessyd Godheed electe and hye devyne,
Forgyve my grevous offence!
Here I crye The mercy in this presence!
O ghostly Treasure, O Raunsomer and Redemer
Of all the worlde, Hope and Conduyter,   590
Myrrour of Joye, Foundatour of Mercy,
Whiche enlumyneth heven and erth therby,
Here my clamorous complaynt, though it late be!

Receyve my prayers! unworthy in this hevy lyfe
Though I be, a synner most abhomynable,   595
Yet let my name be wryten in Moyses table!—
O Mary, praye to the Maker of all thynge
Me for to helpe at my endynge,
And save me fro the power of my enemy;
For Deth assayleth me strongly!   600
And, Lady, that I may be meane of thy prayer
Of your Sones glory to be partynere,
Of your Sones glory to be partynere,
I beseche you, helpe my soule to save!—
Knowlege, gyve me the scourge of penaunce;   605
My flesshe therewith shall gyve acqueyntance.
I wyll now begyn, yf God gyve me grace.
    Knowlege. Everyman, God gyve you tyme and space:
Thus I bequeth you in the handes of our Savyour;
Now may you make your rekenynge sure.   610
    Everyman. In the name of the holy Trynyte,
My body sore punysshyd shall be.
Take this, body, for the synne of the flesshe!
Also thou delytest to go gay and freshe,
And in the way of dampnacyon thou dyd me brynge,   615
Therfore suffre now strokes of punysshynge!
Now of penaunce I wyll wade the water clere,
To save me from purgatory, that sharpe fyre.
    Good Dedes. I thanke God, now I can walke and
        go,
And am delyvered of my sykenesse and wo: 620
Therfore with Everyman I wyll go, and not spare;
His good workes I wyll helpe hym to declare.
    Knowlege. Now, Everyman, be mery and glad:
Your Good Dedes cometh now, ye may not be sad;
Now is your Good Dedes hole and sounde,   625
Goynge upryght upon the grounde.
    Everyman. My herte is lyght, and shalbe evermore;
Now wyll I smyte faster than I dyde before.
    Good Dedes. Everyman, pylgryme, my specyall frende,
Blessyd be thou without ende;   630
For the is preparate the eternal glory.
Ye have me made hole and sounde,
Therfor I wyll byde by the in every stounde.

Everyman. Welcome, my Good Dedes! Now I here
    thy voyce,
I wepe for very swetenes of love.   635
    Knowlege. Be no more sad, but ever rejoyce;
God seeth thy lyvynge in His trone above.
Put on this garment, to thy behove,
Whiche is wette with your teres,
Or elles before God you may it mysse   640
Whan ye to your journeys ende come shall.
    Everyman. Gentyll Knowlege, what do you it call?
    Knowlege. It is a garment of sorowe;
Fro payne it wyll you borowe:
Contrycyon it is,   645
That getteth forgyveness;
He pleaseth God passynge well.
    Good Dedes. Everyman, wyll you were it for your
    hele?
    Everyman. Now blessyd be Jesu, Maryes Sone,
For nowe have I on true contrycyon;   650
And lette us go now without taryenge.
Good Dedes, have we clere our rekenynge?
    Good Dedes. Ye, in dede, I have them here.
    Everyman. Than I trust we nede not fere.
Now, frendes, let us not parte in twayne.   655
    Knowlege. Nay, Everyman, that wyll we not, certayne.
    Good Dedes. Yet must thou leade with the
Thre persones of grete myght.
    Everyman. Who sholde they be?
    Good Dedes. Dyscrecyon and Strength they hyght;   660
And thy Beaute may not abyde behynde.
    Knowlege. Also ye must call to mynde
Your Fyve Wyttes as for your counseylours.
    Good Dedes. You must have them ready at all houres.
    Everyman. Howe shall I gette them hyder?   665
    Knowlege. You must call them all togyder,
And they wyll here you incontynent.
    Everyman. My frendes, come hyder and be present—
Dyscrecyon, Strengthe, my Fyve Wyttes, and Beaute.
    Beaute. Here at your wyll we be all redy;   670
What wyll ye that we sholde do?
    Good Dedes. That ye wolde with Everyman go,

And helpe hym in his pylgrymage.
Advyse you; wyll ye with him or not in that vyage?
   Strength. We wyll brynge hym all thyder,   675
To his helpe and comforte, ye may beleve me.
   Dyscrecyon. So wyll we go with hym all togyder.
   Everyman. Almyghty God, loved myght Thou be!
I gyve The laude that I have hyder brought
Strength, Dyscrecyon, Beaute, and Fyve Wyttes; lacke
    I nought: 680
And my Good Dedes, with Knowlege clere,
All be in my company at my wyll here;
I desyre no more to my besynes.
   Strengthe. And I, Strength, wyll by you stande in
    dystres,
Though thou wolde in batayle fyght on the grounde.   685
   Fyve Wittes. And though it were thrugh the worlde
    rounde,
We wyll not departe for swete ne soure.
   Beaute. No more wyll I, unto dethes houre,
What-so-ever therof befall.
   Dyscrecyon. Everyman, advyse you, fyrst of all;   690
Go with a good advysement and delyberacyon.
We all gyve you vertuous monycyon,
That all shall be well.
   Everyman. My frendes, harken what I wyll tell:
I praye God rewarde you in His heven spere.   690
Now herken, all that be here,
For I wyll make my testament
Here before you all present:
In almes, halfe my good I wyll gyve with my handes
    twayne,
In the way of charyte, with good entent;   700
And the other halfe styll shall remayne,
In queth to be retourned there it ought to be.
This I do in despyte of the fende of hell,
To go quyte out of his perell
Ever after and this daye.   705
   Knowlege. Everyman, herken what I saye:
Go to Presthode, I you advyse,
And receyve of him in ony wyse
The holy sacrament and oyntement togyder;

Than shortly se ye tourne agayne hyder. 710
We wyll all abyde you here.
  Fyve Wittes. Ye, Everyman, hye you that ye redy were :
There is no emperour, kynge, duke, ne baron
That of God hath commycyon
As hath the leest preest in the worlde beygne ; 715
For of the blessyd sacramentes pure and benygne
He bereth the keyes, and thereof hath the cure
For mannes redempcyon, it is ever sure,
Whiche God for our soules medycyne
Gave us out of His herte with grete payne, 720
Here in this transytory lyfe for the and me.
The blessyd sacramentes, VII there be :
Baptym, confyrmacyon, with preesthode good,
And the sacrament of Goddes precyous flesshe and blod,
Maryage, the holy extreme unccyon, and penaunce ; 725
These seven be good to have in remembraunce,
Gracyous sacramentes of hye devynyte.
  Everyman. Fayne wolde I receyve that holy body,
And mekely to my ghostly fader I wyll go.
  Fyve Wyttes. Everyman, that is the best that ye can
    do. 730
God, wyll you to salvacyon brynge,
For preesthode excedeth all other thynge :
To us holy Scrypture they do teche,
And converteth man fro synne, heven to reche ;
God hath to them more power gyven 735
Than to ony aungell that is in heven ;
With v wordes he may consecrate
Goddes body in flesshe and blode to make,
And handeleth his Maker bytwene his handes ;
The preest byndeth and unbyndeth all bandes 740
Bothe in erthe and in heven.—
Thou mynystres all the sacramentes seven ;
Though we kysse thy fete, thou were worthy ;
Thou arte surgyon that cureth synne deedly ;
No remedy we fynde, under God, 745
Bute all onely preesthode.—
Everyman, God gave preest that dygnyte,
And setteth them in His stede amonge us to be ;
Thus be they above aungelles in degree.

Knowlege. If preestes be good, it is so, suerly.   750
But whan Jesu hanged on the crosse, with grete smarte,
There He gave out of His blessyd herte
The same sacrament in grete tourment;
He solde them not to us, that Lorde omnypotent:
Therfore Saynt Peter, the apostell, dothe saye   755
That Jesus curse hath all they
Whiche God theyr Savyour do by or sell,
Or they for ony money do take or tell.
Synfull preestes gyveth the synners example bad:
Theyr chyldren sytteth by other mennes fyres, I have
          harde;   760
And some haunteth womens company,
With unclene lyfe as lustes of lechery;
These be with synne made blynde.
     Fyve Wyttes. I trust to God no suche may we fynde:
Therfore let us preesthode honour,   765
And folowe theyr doctryne for our soules socoure;
We be theyr shepe, and they shepeherdes be,
By whome we all be kept in suerte.—
Peas! for yonder I see Everyman come,
Whiche hath made true satysfaccyon.   770
     Good Dedes. Me thynke, it is he in dede.
     Everyman. Now Jesu be your alder spede!
I have receyved the sacrament of my redempcyon,
And than myne extreme unccyon.
Blessyd be all they that counseyled me to take it!   775
And now, frendes, let us go without longer respyte;
I thanke God that ye have taryed so longe.
Now set eche of you on this rodde your honde,
And shortely folowe me:
I go before there I wolde be.   780
God be your gyde!
     Strength. Everyman, we will nat fro you go
Tyll ye have gone this vyage longe.
     Dyscrecyon. I, Dyscrecyon, wyll byde by you also.
     Knowlege. And though this pylgrymage be never so
          stronge   785
I wyll never parte you fro.
     Strength. Everyman, I wyll be as sure by the
As ever I dyde by Judas Machabee.

Everyman. Alas, I am so faynt I may not stande;
My lymmes under me doth folde.   790
Frendes, let us nat tourne agayne to this lande,
Not for all the worldes golde,
For in to this cave must I crepe,
And tourne to earth, and there to slepe.
  Beaute. What, in to this grave, alas!   795
  Everyman. Ye, there shall ye consume, more and lesse!
  Beaute. And what, sholde I smoder here?
  Everyman. Ye, by my fayth, and never more appere!
In this worlde lyve no more we shall,
But in heven before the hyest Lorde of all.   800
  Beaute. I crosse out all this! adewe, by Saynt Johan!
I take my tappe in my lappe, and am gone.
  Everyman. What, Beaute, whyder wyll ye?
  Beaute. Peas! I am defe; I loke not behynde me,
Not and thou woldest gyve me all the golde in thy chest. 805
  Everyman. Alas! wherto may I truste?
Beaute gothe fast awaye fro me;
She promysed with me to lyve and dye.
  Strength. Everyman, I wyll the also forsake and denye;
Thy game lyketh me not at all.   810
  Everyman. Why, than ye wyll forsake me all!
Swete Strength, tary a lytell space.
  Strengthe. Nay, sir; by the rode of grace,
I wyll hye me from the fast,
Though thou wepe to thy herte to brast.   815
  Everyman. Ye wolde ever byde by me, ye sayd.
  Strength. Ye, I have you ferre ynoughe conveyde:
Ye be olde ynoughe, I understande,
Your pylgrymage to take on hande.
I repent me that I hyder came.   820
  Everyman. Strength, you to dysplease I am to blame;
Wyll ye breke promyse that is dette?
  Strength. In fayth, I care not.
Thou arte but a foole to complayne;
You spende your speche, and wast your brayne.   825
Go, thryst the in to the grounde.
  Everyman. I had wende surer I shulde you have founde:
He that trusteth in his Strength,
She hym deceyveth at the length.

Bothe Strength and Beaute forsaketh me,   830
Yet they promysed me fayre and lovyngly.
 Dyscrecyon. Everyman, I wyll after Strength be gone;
As for me, I will leve you alone.
 Everyman. Why, Dyscrecyon, wyll ye forsake me?
 Dyscrecyon. Ye, in fayth, I wyll go fro the;   835
For whan Strength goth before,
I folowe after ever more.
 Everyman. Yet, I pray the, for the love of the Trynyte,
Loke in my grave ones pyteously.
 Dyscrecyon. Nay, so nye wyll I not come.   840
Fare well, everychone.
 Everyman. O, all thynge fayleth, save God alone—
Beaute, Strength, and Dyscrecyon;
For whan Deth bloweth his blast,
They all renne fro me full fast.   845
 Fyve Wyttes. Everyman, my leve now of the I take;
I wyll folowe the other, for here I the forsake.
 Everyman. Alas! than may I wayle and wepe,
For I toke you for my best frende.
 Fyve Wyttes. I wyll no lenger the kepe.   850
Now fare well, and there an ende.
 Everyman. O Jesu, helpe! all hath forsaken me.
 Good Dedes. Nay, Everyman, I wyll byde with the;
I wyll not forsake the in dede.
Thou shalt fynde me a good frende at nede.   855
 Everyman. Gramercy, Good Dedes, now may I true
  frendes se:
They have forsaken me everychone;
I loved them better than my Good Dedes alone.
Knowlege, wyll ye forsake me also?
 Knowlege. Ye, Everyman, when ye to Deth shall go,   860
But not yet for no maner of daunger.
 Everyman. Gramercy, Knowlege, with all my herte.
 Knowlege. Nay, yet I wyll not from hens departe
Tyll I se where ye shall be come.
 Everyman. Me thynke, alas, that I must be gone   865
To make my rekenynge, and my dettes paye,
For I se my tyme is nye spent awaye.
Take example, all ye that this do here or se,
How they that I love best do forsake me,

Excepte my Good Dedes that bydeth truely.   870
    Good Dedes. All erthly thynges is but vanyte:
Beaute, Strength, and Dyscrecyon do man forsake;
Folysshe frendes and kynnesmen, that fayre spake,
All fleeth save Good Dedes, and that am I.
    Everyman. Have mercy on me, God moost myghty! 875
And stande by me, thou moder and mayde, holy Mary!
    Good Dedes. Fere not; I wyll speke for the.
    Everyman. Here I crye God mercy.
    Good Dedes. Shorte our ende and mynysshe our
      payne!
Let us go and never come agayne.   880
    Everyman. In to Thy handes, Lorde, my soule I
      commende:
Receyve it, Lorde, that it be not lost!
As Thou me boughtest, so me defende,
And save me from the fendes boost,
That I may appere with that blessyd hoost   885
That shall be saved at the day of dome!
In manus Tuas, of myghtes moost,
For ever *commendo spiritum meum.*
    Knowlege. Nowe hath he suffred that we all shall
      endure:
The Good Dedes shall make all sure.   890
Now hath he made endynge:
Me thynketh that I here aungelles synge,
And make grete joy and melody,
Where every mannes soule receyved shall be.
    The Aungell. Come, excellente electe spouse to Jesu! 895
Here above thou shalte go,
Bycause of thy synguler vertue:
Now the soule is taken the body fro,
Thy rekenynge is crystall clere.
Now shalte thou into the hevenly spere,   900
Unto the whiche all ye shall come
That lyveth well before the daye of dome.
    Doctour. This morall men may have in mynde:
Ye herers, take it of worth, olde and yonge,
And forsake Pryde, for he disceyveth you in the ende; 905
And remembre Beaute, Five Wyttes, Strength, and
      Dyscrecyon,

They all at the last do Everyman forsake,
Save his Good Dedes there dothe he take.
But beware: and they be small,
Before God he hath no helpe at all;   910
None excuse may be there for Everyman!
Alas! how shall he do than?
For after deth amendes may no man make,
For than mercy and pyte doth hym forsake;
If his rekenynge be not clere whan he doth come,   915
God wyll saye, "Ite, maledicti, in ignem eternum!"
And he that hath his accounte hole and sounde,
Hye in heven he shall be crounde.
Unto whiche place God brynge us all thyder,
That we may lyve body and soule togyder!   920
Therto helpe the Trynyte!
"Amen," saye ye, for Saynt Charyte.

FROM

THE MARIAGE OF WITT AND WISDOME

THE FIRST SCENE

Enter Severitie and his wife Indulgence, and their sonne Wit.
    Severitie. My sonne, drawe neare; give eare to me,
      And marke the cause aright
    For which I call the to this place:
      Lett all thy whole delight
    Be still in serving God aright,   5
      And treading vertues trace,
    And labour learning for to gett,
      Whilste thou hast time and space.
    I now have brought the on the way
      The thing for to attaine,   10
    Which, sonne, if thou mightst hap to hit,
      Wil turne unto thy gaine.
    Thou knowest how chargiable a thing
      Thy learning is to me;
    Thou knowest also the care I take   15
      For to provide for the;
    And now since that thyne age drawes on
      To natures riper state,

My purpose is and full intent
    To find for the a mate,   20
With whome thou mayest dispend the rest
    Of this thy life to come,
And joye as I thy father have
    With this, thy mother, done.
Indulgence. Indeed, good husband, that were good: 25
    We have no more but he;
My hart, me thinks, wold be at rest
    Him matched for to see.
But yet, my deare Severitie,
    Be headfull for your life,   30
That she be able for to live
    That he shall take to wyfe.
Severitie. Well, as for that I shall for-se;
    For why I knowe right well
That she whome I doe meane is rich,   35
    And highly doth excell.
Wherefore, sonne Witt, marke well my tale:
    Dame Wisdome is the wight
Whome you shall laboure to espouse
    With all your maine and might;   40
And if that she will be your wyfe,
    Looke what I leave behind,
You shall possesse it full and whole,
    According unto kind;
But if you find some worser haunt,   45
    And hap to run by rote,
I promisse the, before these folke,
    Thoust never cost me grote.
Witt. Deare father, for your grave advice
    Right humble thanks I give,   50
Entending to obay your charge
    So long as I shall live.
Now if that Witt with Wisdome may
    Be linked fast in love,
Then Witt shall think him-selfe right blest   55
    Of God That sits above!
Indulgence. Well said, good Witt, and hold the there.
    I tell the this before:

Indulgence, when thou maried art,
  Hath better pence in store.   60
Severitie. Such pampring mothers doe more harme
  Then ere thay can doe good.
Indulgence. If you had felt the paine we feel,
  You then wold change your mood.
Severitie. You showe that you the mother are   65
  Of this the outward man,
And not of mind; for if you ware,
  You wold be carefull then
To give him counsell how to use
  Him-selfe for to aspire   70
To Wisdomes frendship and her loove,
  The which we doe desire.
Indulgence. Alas, good sir! Why, harken, Wit,
  What counsell I can give;
When as thou commest to Wisdoms house,   75
  Then mayest thou it appreve:
Take heade that thou art nete and fine,
  And go straight bolt uppright,
And cast a chearfull looke on her,
  Smiling at the first sight.   80
And when thou commest to talke with her,
  Forgett not for to praise
Her house, herselfe, and all her things,
  And still be glad to please.
Be diligent to doe for her;   8.
  Be pleasant in her sight;
Say as she sayeth, allthough that she
  Doe say the crowe is white;
And if she have minde to oght,
  ⸱ Allthough it cost red gould,   90
Provide it for her, and thou mayest be
  More welcome and more bolde.
Severitie. Se, se, what counsell you can give!
  You showe your nature plaine.
This counsell liketh Wit right well,   95
  And maketh him al-to faine.
But, sirra, if thou list to thrive,
  Marke well what I shall say;

That Wisdome may become your wife,
    This is the redy waye :   100
Applie your booke, and still beware
    Of Idlenes, I say,
For he an enimy hath bin
    To Vertue many a day.
Beweare of Ircksomnis, I say,   105
    Which is a monster fell,
And neare to Lady Wisdomes house
    Doth alwayes use to dwell;
For he will have a fling at you,
    And so will Idlenes.   110
Therefore beware of these two folks,
    And God will sure you blesse.
Wit. As dutie doth requier in me,
    I thank you humbly
For these your fatherly precepts,   115
    And purpose earnestly
For to observe that you command,
    And these my foes to watch,
Least they perhaps, ere I be ware,
    Me in their snares shuld catch.   120
Indulgence. Well, yet before the goest, hold heare
    My blessing in a cloute :
Well fare the mother at a neede;
    Stand to thy tackling stout.
Wit. Mother, I thank you hartily,   125
    And you, father, likwise;
And both your blessings heare I crave
    In this my enterprise.
Bothe. God blesse the, Wit, our sonne,
    And send the good successe.   130
Wit. I thank you both, and pray to God
    To send to you no lesse !
            [Exeunt Severitie and Indulgence.]
God grant this my purpose may
    Come unto good effect.
Well, now I must aboute this geare;   135
    I must it not forgett.
                  [Exit.]

THE SECOND SCENE

Enter Idleness, the vice.

Idlenes. A, sirra, my masters,
    How fare you at this blessed day?
What, I ween, all this compony
    Are come to se a play!
What lackest the, good fellow?   5
    Didest the nere se man before?
Here is a gazing! I am the best man in the compony,
    When there is no more.
As for my properties I am sure
    You knowe them of old: 10
I can eate tell I sweate, and worke
    Tell I am a-cold;
I am allwayes troubled with the litherlurden,
    I love so to linger;
I am so lasy the mosse groweth   15
    An inch thick on the top of my finger!
But if you list to knowe my name,
    I wis I am too well knowen to some men:
My name is Idlenes, the flower
    Of the frying-pan!   20
My mother had two whelps at one litter,
    Both borne in Lent;
So we ware both put into a mussellbote,
    And came sailing in a sowes eare over sea into Kent.
My brother Ercsomnis and I catch the dogge;   25
    Being disposed to make mery,
We gott us both doune to Harlowe-bery.
But what is that to the purpose,
    Perhapes you wold knowe?
Give me leave but a littell,   30
    And I will you showe.
My name is Idelnes,
    As I tould you before,
And my mother Ignorance sent me hether.
    I pray the, sirra, what more?   35
Marry, my masters, she sent me
    The counterfait cranke for to play,
And to leade Witt, Severities sone,
    Out of the waye:

He should make a marrige with Wisdome, 40
   In all hast, as thay talke.
But stay thare awhile;
   Soft fier makes swete malt:
I must be firme to bring him out of his
   Broune stodie, on this fashion; 45
I will turne my name from Idlenes
   To Honest Recreation,
And then I will bring him to be
   Mistris Wantonnes man,
And, afaith, then he is in for a berd, 50
   Get out how he can!
But soft yet, my masters; who is within?
Open the dore and pull out the pin.
      Wantones entreth, and sayeth:
What, Dol, I say, open the dore!
   Who is in the streate? 55
What, Mr. Idlenes! lay a straw
   Under your feete.
I pray you, and me may aske you,
   What wind brought you hether?
Idelnes. A littell wind, I warrant you; 60
   I am as light as any fether!
But harke the.
Wantonis.   What! it is not so:
   Will he come indeade?
Idelnes. Nay, if I say the word,
   Thou mayest believe as thy creed. 65
But when he comes, you must
   Be curtious, I tell you,
And you shall find him as gentell as a faulcon,
   Every fooles fellowe. . . . .   [*Exit Wantonness.*]
      Enter Wit.
Wit. My father he hath charged me 70
   The thing to take in hand,
Which seames to me to be so hard
   It cannot well be scand;
For I have toyled in my booke,
   Where Wisdome much is praysed, 75
But she is so hard to find
   That I am nothing eased.

I wold I had bin set to blowe,
  Or to some other trade,
And then I might some leasure find,   80
  And better shift have made:
But nowe I swinke and sweate in vaine;
  My labour hath no end;
And moping in my study still
  My youthfull yeares I spend.   85
Wold God that I might hap to hit
  Upon some good resort,
Some pleasant pastime for to find,
  And use some better sporte.
Idlenes. Mary, no better; I am even as fitt   90
  For that purpose as a rope for a theefe.
And you will be lusty, cry "hay!"
  Amongst knaves I am the cheefe.
Witt. What, good fellow, art thou?
  What is thy name?   95
Idlenes. In faith I am Ipse, he,
  Even the very same. . . . .
Wit. Thou art a mery fellowe and wise,
  And if thou kepe thy-selfe warme.
Idlenes. In faith, I have a mother-wit,   100
  But I think no harme.
Wit. I pray the, what is thy name?
  To me it declare.
Idlenes. Nay, I am no nigard of my name,
  For that I will not spare.   105
Ha! by the masse, I could have told
  You even now!
What a short-brained villain am I!
  I am as wise as my mothers sowe.
I pray you, sir, what is my name?   110
  Cannot you tell?
Is there any here that knowes where
  My godfather doth dwell?
Gentellmen, if you will tarry
  While I goe look;   115
I am sure my name is
  In the church booke.

Wit. I prethy, come of, and tell me
  Thy name with redynis.
Idlenes. Faith, if you will neades knowe,   120
  My name is Idelnes.
Wit. Mary, fie on the, knave!
  I mene not thy compony.
Idlenes. What, because I spoke in jest
  Will you take it so angerly?   125
For my name is Honest Recreation.
  I let you well to witt
There is not in all the world
  A companion for you more fitt.
Wit. And if thy name be Honest Recreation,   130
  Thou art as welcome as any in this laund.
Idlenes. Yea, mary, is it!
  Wit. Why, then, give me thy hand.
Idlenes. In faith, I thank you. You are come
  Of a gentell birth,   135
And therefore I will bring you acquainted
  With a gentellwoman called Modest Mirth.
Wit. Yea, mary, with all my hart, and God have
    mercy. . . . .
Idlenes. Gentellman, here is the gentellewoman.
  Kisse her, I say; I am a horson els!   140
If I had knowne you wold not a kist her,
  I wold have kist her myselfe.
Wit. Gentellwoman, this shalbe to desier you
  Of more acquaintance.
Wantonnes. Sir, a ought I may pleasure you,   145
  I will give atendence.
To have many suters my lot dooth befall,
But yet me think I lyk you best of all.
Idelnes. Yea, she might have had many men
  Of knavery and of stellth.   150
Wantones. What saist thou?
Idlnes.   Mary, you might have had
  Many men of bravery and wellth;
But yet me thinkes there cannot be
  A match more fit
Then between Mistres Modest Mirth   155
  And you, Master Wit.

Wantones. That is well sayed.
Idlnes.   Yea, and that will be
   A redy carriage to the rope.
Wantones. What sayest thou?
Idelnis.   That will be
   A spety marige, I hope.   160
Wantones. By my troth, I am so wery I must nedes
     sit down;
   My legges will not hold.
Witt. Then will I sit down by you,
   If I may be so bold.
Idlenis. Heare is love, sir reverence;   165
   This geare is even fitt.
Oh, here is a hed hath a counting-house-
   Full of witt.
Wit. I am sure you are cuninge in musick;
   And therefore, if you please   170
Sing us a songe.
Wantonis.   That will I,
   If it were for your ease.

Here shall Wantonis sing this song to the tune of "Attend the, goe
   playe the," and, having sung him asleepe upon her lappe, let
   him snort; then let her set a fooles bable on his hed, and
   colling his face; and Idlenis shall steale away his purse from
   him, and goe his wayes.

The Song

Lye still, and heare nest the;
Good Witt, lye and rest the,
And in my lap take thou thy sleepe.   175
Since Idlenis brought the,
And now I have caught the,
I charge the let care away creepe.

So now that he sleepes full soundly,
Now purpose I roundly,   180
Trick this pretty doddy,
And make him a noddy,
And make him a noddy!

Since he was unstable,
He now wares a bable,   185

Since Idlenis led him away;
And now of a scollar
I will make him a colliar,
Since Wantonis beareth the swaye.

Well, now I have him chaunged,   190
I neades must be rainging;
I now must goe pack me,
For my gossops will lack me,
For my gossops will lack me!

   Enter Good Nurture, speaking this:
I mervell where my schollard Wit   195
  Is now of late become.
I feare least with il compony
  He happen for to run:
For I, Good Nurture, commonly
  Among all men am counted;   200
But Witt, by this his straying so,
  I feare hath me renounced.
Severitie, his father, sure
  Is grave and wise withall,
But yet his mother's pampring   205
  Will bring his sonne to thrall.
Here he stayeth, stumbling at Wit as he lyeth asleep.
Why, how now! how! what wight is this
  On whome we now have hit?
Softe, let me se: this same is he;
  Yea, truly, this is Wit!   210
    Here he awaketh him.
What, Wit, I say! arise for shame!
  O, God! where hast thou bin?
The compony made the a foole
  That thou of late wast in.
Here he riseth, rubbing his eyes, and saying:
O, arrant strumpet that she was   215
  That ran me in this case!
Good Nurture. Nay, rather thou art much to blame
  To be with such in place.
Here he washeth his face and taketh off the bable.
Come on, I say; amend this geere;
  Beware of all temptation.   220

Your wearinis for to refresh,
   Take Honest Recreation.
    He delivereth him Honest Recreation.
Wit. I thank you, Mr. Nurture, much
   For this your gentelnis,
And will doe your commandiments   225
   Henceforth with willingnis.
Good Nurture. God grant you may; and sirra, you
   Await upon him still.   *[Exit.]*
Witt. I thank you, sir, with all my hart,
   For this your greate good will.   230
One jourvy more I meane to make:
   I think I was acurst;
God grant the second time may be
   More happy then the first!   *[Thay both goe out.]*

.   .   .   .

THE FIFTE SCENE
Enter Fancie.

Fancie. Like as the rowling stone, we se,
   Doth never gather mosse;
And gold, with other metels mixt,
   Must neades be full of drosse;
So likwise I, which commonly   5
   Dame Fancy have to name,
Amongest the wise am hated much,
   And suffer mickle blame,
Because that, waving heare and there,
   I never stedfast stand,   10
Whereby the depth of learnings lore
   I cannot understand.
But Wit perhaps will me imbrace,
   As I will use the matter:
For whie? I meane to counterfait,   15
   And smoothly for to flatter,
And say I am a messinger
   From Lady Wisdome sent;
To se if that wil be a meane
   To bring him to my bent.   20
But se where he doth come.

Enter Wit.

Wit. Like as the silly mariner,
    Amidst the waving sea,
Doth clime the top of mightie mast
    Full oft both night and day,   25
But yet at last, when happily
    He come from ship to shore,
He seakes to saile againe as fresh
    As erst he did before;
So likwise I, which have escapte   30
    The brunts which I have done,
Am even as fresh to venter now
    As when I first begun:
A new adventure this I seek,
    Not having run my race.   35
But who is this whome I behold
    For to appeere in place?
Fancy. God save you, gentell Mr. Witt,
    And send you good successe!
Wit. Faire dame, I thank you hartily,   40
    And wish in you no lesse.
What, may one be bolde to aske
    Your name without offence?
Fancy. Yea, sir, with good will that you may,
    And eke my whole pretence: 45
My name is Fancy; and the cause
    Of this my coming now
From Lady Wisdome is to showe
    A message unto you.
Wit. Then are ye welcome unto me,   50
    For Lady Wisdomes sake.
Fancy. Here is the letter which she bad
    Me unto you to take.

Here he receveth the letter, and readeth it to himselfe.

Wit. My ladyes will herein is this,
    That you should goe with me   55
Unto a place with her to meete,
    As here she doth decree.
Fancy. Even so, good sir; even when you will,
    I doe the same allowe:

Goe you before in at the dore,   60
   And I will follow you.

Here Wit going in, one shall pull him by the arme, whereupon he
shall cry on this manner:

Wit. Alas, I am betrayed!
   This sight makes me agast!
Fancy. Nay, nay, no force, sir!
   I charge you [bind] him fast.   65
Now, Wit, if that thou list
   To match thyselfe with me,
Thou shalt be free as ere thou wast,
   And now released be.
Wit. Alas, I am not so;   70
   Dame Wisdome hath my hart.
Fancy. Then shalt thou lye there still, i-wis,
   Untill thou feelst the smart.   [*Exeunt.*]

. . . .

THE EIGHTH SCENE

Enter Good Nurture.

Good Nurture. To them whose shoulders doe supporte
   The charge of tender youth,
One greefe falls on anothers neck,
   And youth will have his rueth.
Since first I gan to nurture Wit,   5
   Full many cares hath past,
But when he had slain Ircksomnis,
   I thought me safe at last:
But now I se the very end
   Of that my late distresse   10
Is a begining unto greefe
   Which wilbe nothing lesse;
For when I thought that Wit of late
   To Wisdomes house had gone,
He came not there, but God knowes where   15
   This retchlesse Witt is run.
Ne knowe I where to seeke him now;
   Whereby I learne with paine
There is no greefe so far gone past
   But may returne againe.   20

Here Wit cryeth out in prison, and sayeth this:

The silly bird once caught in net,
   If she escape alive,
Will come no more so nye the snare
   Her fredome to deprive,
But rather she will leave her haunt   25
   The which she used before;
But I, alas! when steede is stolen,
   Doo shut the stable dore:
For, being often caught before,
   Yet could I not refraine;   30
More foolish then the witlis birde,
   I came to hand againe.
Alas! the chaines oppresse me sore
   Wherewith I now am lad,
But yet the paine doth pinch me more   35
   Wherein my hart is clad!
O, mightie Jove, now grant that some
   Good man may passe this place,
By whose good helpe I might be brought
   Out of this wofull case!   40
Good Nurture. What noyse is this? what pitious
    plaints
   Are sounding in my eare?
My hart doth give me it is Wit,
   The which I now do heare.
      He commeth nere the prison.
I will drawe nere and see   45
What wight art thou, which doost lament
   And thus dost pine in paine.
Wit. My name is Witt. My greefe is greate;
   How should I then refraine?
Good Nurture. What, Wit! how camest thou heare? 50
   O God! what chaunce is this?
Wit. Dame Fancy brought me in this case;
   I know I did amis.
Good Nurture. What, Fancy? Where is she?
   Oh, that I once might catch her!   55
Wit. Wold God you could, or else some one,
   That able weare to matche her;
But she no soner heard your voyce,
   There standing at the dore,

Then she with all her folks hath fled,   60
    And will be seene no more:
But I, poore sowle, ly here in chaines.
Here entreth and releaseth him Good Nurture.
Good Nurture. Once more I have releast the of thy
    paines.
Wit. Your most unworthy schollard
    Gives to you immortall thanks.   65
Good Nurture. I pray you now take better heed
    You play no more such pranckes.
Pluck up your spirits: your marige day
    Is come even at hand,
Tomorrow Wisdome shall you wed,   70
    I let you understand.
Wit. Right so as you think good,
    I shall contented be.
Good Nurture. Then let us goe for to prepare;
    Come on, I say, with me!   75
                              [Exeunt.]

. . . .

THE TENTH SCENE

Enter Severitie and Wit.

Severitie. Well now, son Witt, the proofe is plaine:
    The cloudes were nere so black
But the brightnis of the sun
    At last might put them back;
The wind did never blowe so much,   5
    Wherewith the bark was tore,
But that the wether was so calme
    To bring the ship to shore.
The danger now is past:
    Addresse thyselfe with speede   10
To meete with Wisdome, thy deere wyfe,
    As we before decreede.
Wit. It shalbe done as dutie binds,
    And as I bounden stand.
But se, good father! now behold,   15
    Dame Wisdome is at hand.

Enter Good Nurture and Wisdome; and Wisdome and Wit singeth
this song:

 Wisdome. My joye hath overgrowen my greefe;
  My cure is past;
 For Fortune hath bin my relefe
  Now at last!   20
 Tantara tara tantara,
  My husband is at hand!
 His comly grace appeeres in place,
  As I doe understand.
 Wit. My lady, thrise welcome to me,   25
  Mine onely joy!
 The gentellnis, God give it the
  Without annoy.
 Tantara tara tantara,
  Welcome, my worthy wyfe!   30
 Thou art my parte; thine is my hart,
  My blessed lim of life!
 Wisdome. As dutie doth bind according to kind,
  I thanke ye much:
 Thy wife for the will spend her life;   35
  She will not gruch.
 Tantara tara tantara,
  The summe of all my blisse!
 The welcomest wight, my cheefe delight,
  That shalbe and that is!   40
 Wit. Let me thy comly corpes imbrace,
  Dere Wisdome, now!
 Wisdome. Good Wit, I alwaies loved the place
  To be with you:
 Tantara tara tantara,   45
  Thou hast my hart in hold.
 Wit. Ne doe I faine, but tell the plaine
  I am thy owne, behold.

     Here endeth the song.

 Good Nurture. Well, now I am right glad
  To se you both well met.   50
 Severitie. And so am I, with all my hart,
  That thay so sure are set.
 Both. We thank ye both right humbly;

Wit. And wish to mary speedyly:
Wisdome. For why? allthough the turtle long
   Ware parted from her mate,
Wit. Now, God be thanked, thay are met
   In good and happy state.
The Lord be thanked for His grace,
   Which gave the unto me!
Then welcome; nothing in heven or earth
   More welcommer can be.
Wisdome. And you to me, dere Wit.
Severitie. Come, now the time requires
   That we departe away
To celebrate the nuptiales
   With joy, this wedding-day!
Wit. Goe you before, my father deare,
   And you, good master, straight;
And then both I and Wisdome to
   Upon you will awaite.   *[Goe forth al*

JOHN HEYWOOD

THE FOURE PP

   Palmer. Now God be here, Who kepeth this plac
Now, by my fayth, I cry you mercy;
Of reason I must sew for grace,
My rudnes sheweth me now so homely.
Wherof your pardon axt and wonne,
I sew now, as curtsey doth me bynde,
To tell this whiche shall be begonne
In order as may come beste in mynde.
I am a palmer, as you se,
Which of my life muche part hath spent
In many a farre and fayre cuntre,
As pylgrimes do of good intent.
At Jerusalem have I bene
Before Christes blessed sepulture;
The Mount of Calvary have I sene,
A holy place, ye may be sure;
To Josaphat and Olyvete

On fote, God wote, I wente ryght bare—
Many a salt teare dyde I sweete
Before this carkes wolde come thare;   20
Yet have I been at Rome also,
And gone the stacions all arowe,
Saynt Peters shryne and many mo
Then, yf I tolde, all ye do know—
Except that there be any suche   25
That hath bene there, and dilygently
Hath taken hede and marked muche,
Then can they speke as muche as I.
Then at the Roodes also I was;
And rounde about to Amias;   30
At Saynt Toncomber; and Saynt Tronion;
At Saynt Bothulph; and Saynt Anne of Bucston;
On the hilles of Armony, where I sawe Noes arke;
With holy Job; and Saynt George in Suthwarke;
At Waltam; and at Walsingam;   35
And at the good roode of Dagnam;
At Saynt Corneles; at Saynt James in Gales;
And at Saynt Winefrides well in Wales;
At Our Lady of Boston; at Saint Edmundes-bery;
And streyght to Saynt Patrikes Purgatory;   40
At Rydibone; and at the bloud of Hayles,
Where pilgrimes paynes right muche avayles;
At Saynt Davis; and at Saynt Denis;
At Sainte Mathewe; and Saynt Marke in Venis;
At Mayster John Shorne; at Canterbury;   45
The great God of Katewade; at Kynge Herry;
At Saynt Saviours; at Our Lady of Sothwell;
At Crome; at Wylsdom; and at Muswell;
At Saynte Rycharde; and at Saynte Roke;
And at Our Lady that standeth in the oke.   50
To these with other many one
Devoutly have I prayed and gone,
Praying to them to pray for me
Unto the Blissed Trinitie;
By whose prayers and my dayly payne   55
I truste the soner to obtayne
For my salvacion grace and mercy,
For be ye sure I thynke surelye

Who seketh sayntes for Cristes sake—
And namely suche as payne do take   60
On fote to punyshe their frayle body—
Shall therby merite more hyely
Then by any thynge done by man.
> *Pardoner.* And whan ye have gone as farre as
> you can,
For all your labour and ghostly entent   65
Yet welcome home as wyse as ye went!
> *Palmer.* Why, syr, dispise ye pylgrymage?
> *Pardoner.* Nay, fore God, syr, then dyd I rage
I thyncke ye ryght well occupyed
To seke these sayntes on every syde.   70
Also your payne I not disprayse it,
But yet I dyscommende your wyt;
And, or we go, even so shall ye,
Yf you in this wyll answere mee:
I praye you, shewe what the cause is   75
Ye went al these pylgrymages.
> *Palmer.* Forsoth this lyfe I dyd begyn
To ryd the bondage of my syn,
For which these sayntes rehersed or this
I have both sought and sene, I wis,   80
Besechyng them to be recorde
Of all my payne unto the Lorde,
That gyveth all remyssyon
Upon eche mannes contricion;
And by theyr good mediacion,   85
Upon myne humble submyssion,
I trust to have in very dede
For my soule helth the better speede.
> *Pardoner.* Now is your owne confession lyckely
To make your-selfe a fole quickely,   90
For I perceyve ye woulde obtayne
No nother thynge for all your payne
But onely grace your soule to save.
Now marke in this what wyt ye have
To seke so farre, and helpe so nye: 95
Even here at home is remedye,
For at your dore my-selfe doth dwell,
Who could have saved your soule as well

As all your wyde wanderyng shall do,
Though ye went thrise to Jericho.   100
Now, syns ye myght have spedde at home,
What have ye won by ronning to Rome?
   Palmer. If this be true that ye have moved,
Then is my wytte in-dede reproved;
But let us heare first what ye are.   105
    Pardoner. Truely I am a pardoner.
    Palmer. Truely a pardoner—that may be trewe;
But a trewe pardoner doth not ensew!
Ryght selde is it seene or never
That trewth and pardoners dwell together;   110
For, be your pardons never so great,
Yet them to enlarge ye wyll not let
With suche lyes that ofte tymes, Chryste wot,
Ye seme to have that ye have not.
Wherfore I went my-selfe to the selfe thynge   115
In every place, and, without faynynge,
Had as muche pardon there assuredly
As ye can promyse me here doutfully.
How-be-it I thynke ye do but scoffe;
But if ye had all the pardon ye speke of,   120
And no whyt of pardon graunted
In any place where I have haunted,
Yet of my laboure I nothyng repent.
God hath respect howe eche tyme is spent,
And, as in His knowledge all is regarded,   125
So by His goodnes all is rewarded.
    Pardoner. By the fyrst part of this last tale
It semeth ye come to late from the ale,
For reason on your syd so farre doth faile
That ye leve resonyng and begyn to rayle;   130
Wherin ye forget your owne part clerely,
For ye be as untrewe as I;
And in one poynt ye are beyonde me,
For ye may lye by aucthoritie—
And all that hath wandred so farre   135
That no man can be theyr controller.
And wher ye esteme your laboure so much,
I saye yet agayne my pardons be suche
That, yf there were a thousand soules on a hepe,

I wolde brynge them al to heaven as good chepe   14●
As ye have brought your-selfe on pylgrimage
In the least quarter of your vyage,
Which is farre a this side heaven, by God!
There your labour and pardon is od,
With small coste and without any payne   14
These pardons bryngeth them to heaven playne:
Geve me but a peny or two pence,
And as sone as the soule departeth hens,
In halfe a houre, or three quarters at moste,
The soule is in heaven with the Holy Ghoste.   15●

    Poticarye. Sende ye any soules to heaven by
      water?
    Pardoner. Yf we do, syr, what is the mater?
    Potycary. By God, I have a drye soule shulde
      thyther!
I pray you let our soules go to heaven togyther.
So busy you twayne be in soule helth,   15
May not a potycary come in by stelth?
Yes, that I wyll, by Saynte Antony!
And, by the leve of this company,
Prove ye false knaves both, or we go,
In parte of your sayinges, as this, lo: 16
Thou by thy travayle thinkest heaven to get;
And thou by pardons and reliques countest no let
To sende thyne owne soule to heaven sure,
And all other whom thou lyste to procure:
Yf I toke an action, then were they blanke;   16
For lyke theves the knaves rob away my thank.
All soules in heaven havinge relefe,
Shall they thank your craftes? nay, thank myne chefe
No soule, ye knowe, entreth heaven gate
Tyll from the body he be seperate;   17
And whome have ye knowne die honestli
Without helpe of the poticary?
Nay, all that commeth to our handlinge—
Except ye hap to come to hangynge;
That way, parchaunce, ye shall not mister   17
To go to heaven without a glyster!
But, be ye sure, I wolde be wo
Yf ye should chaunce to begyle me so.

As good to lye with me a-nyght
As hange abrode in the mone lyght!   180
There is no choyse to flie my hande
But, as I sayde, into the bande.
Syns of our soules the multytude
I sende to heaven, when all is vewed,
Who should but I, then, all-together   185
Have thanke of al their comming thither?
    Pardoner. Yf ye kylde a thousande in an houre
      space,
When come they to heaven, dying from state of grace?
    Poticary. If a thousande pardons about your
      necks were tied,
When come they to heaven yf they never dyed?   190
    Palmer. Longe lyfe after good workes in-dede
Doth hynder mannes receit of mede,
And death before one dewty done
May make us thynke we dye to sone;
Yet better tary a thynge, then have it,   195
Then go to sone and vaynly crave it.
    Pardoner. The longer ye dwell in communicacion,
The lesse shall ye lyke this ymaginacion;
For ye maye perceyve even at the fyrste chop
Your tale is trapt in such a stop   200
That, at the leaste, ye seme worse then we.
    Poticary. By the masse, I holde us nought all
      three!
    Pedler. By Our Lady, then have I gone wronge;
And yet to be here I thought longe!
    Poticary. Brother, ye have gone wronge no,
      whyt.   205
I prayse your fortune and your wyt,
That can derecte you so discretely
To plante you in this company:
Thou [a] palmer, and thou a pardoner,
I a poticary.
    Pedler. And I a pedler.   210
    Potycary. Now on my fayth full well watched!
Where the devyll were we foure hatched?
    Pedler. That maketh no mater, syns we be
      matched.

I could be mery yf that I catched
Some money for part of the ware in my packe.			215
   Potycary. What the devyll hast thou there at thy
     backe?
   Pedler. Why, doest thou not know that every pedler
In every trifull must be a medler?
Specially in womens triflynges;
Those use we chieflye above all thynges:			220
Which thynges to se if ye be disposed,
Beholde what ware here is disclosed.
This gere sheweth it-selfe in suche bewte
That eche man thinketh it sayeth, "Come, by me!"
Loke; where your-selfe can lyke to be choser,			225
Your-selfe shall make pryce though I be loser!
Is here nothyng for me father palmer?
Have ye not a wanton in a corner
For all your walkynge to holy places?
By Chryst, I have herde of as straung cases!			230
Who lyveth in love or love wolde wynne,
Even at this packe he muste begynne;
Where is right many a proper token,
Of which by name parte shalbe spoken:
Gloves, pinnes, combes, glasses unspotted,			235
Pomanders, hookes, and lases knotted,
Broches, rynges, and all manner bedes,
Lace, rounde and flat, for womens heades,
Nedels, thred, thimbels, sheres, and al suche knackes,
(Where lovers be, no suche thynges lackes),			240
Sipers, swathbondes, ribandes, and sleve-laces,
Gyrdels, knyves, purses, and pyncaces.

.   .   .   .

   Pedler. Let womens matters passe, and marke
     myne!
What-ever theyr poyntes be, these pointes be fine.		280
Wherfore, yf ye be wyllyng to bye,
Ley downe money! come of quickelye!
   Palmer. Nay, by me trouth, we be lyke friers:
We are but beggers, we be no byers.
   Pardoner. Syr, you may showe your ware for
     your mynde,					285
But I thynke ye shall no profit fynde.

Pedler. Wel, though this journey acquite no cost,
Yet thinke I not my labour loste;
For, by the fayth of my bodye,
I lyke full well this companye. 290
Up shall this packe, for it is playne
I came not hither all for gayne.
Who may not playe one daye in a weke,
May thincke his thrift farre to seke!
Devise what pastyme ye thinke best, 295
And make ye sure to fynde me prest.

Poticarye. Why, be ye so universall
That ye can do what-so-ever ye shall?

Pedler. Sir, yf ye lyst to appose me,
What I can do then shall ye see. 300

Poticary. Then tel me this: be ye parfit in drink-
ing?

Pedler. Parfyt in drynkyng as may be wysht bi
thinking!

Poticarye. Then after your drinking how fal ye to
winking?

Pedler. Syr, after drynkinge, while the shot is
tinkynge,
Some heades be swiming, but mine wil be sinking, 305
And upon drinkyng myne eyes wyll be pinkynge,
For wynkyng to drynkynge is alwaye linkynge.

Poticarye. Then drynke and slepe ye can well do.
But yf ye were desyred therto,
I pray you, tell me, can ye synge? 310

Pedler. Syr, I have some syghte in syngynge.

Potycary. But is your breste any-thynge swete?

Pedler. What-ever my brest be, mi voice is mete.

Poticary. That answere sheweth you a ryght
syngyng man.
Now what is your wyll, good father, than? 315

Palmer. What helpeth wyll where is no skyll?

Pardoner. And what helpeth skil wher is no wyl?

Poticary. For wyll or skyll, what helpeth it
Wher froward knaves be lacking wit?
Leve of this curiosytie; 320
And who that lyst, synge after me!

Here they synge.

Pedler. This lyketh me well, so mot I the!
   Pardoner. So helpe me God, it lyketh not me!
Where company is met and wel agreed,
Good pastime doth right wel in-dede;   325
But who can syt in dalyaunce
Men syt in suche a varyaunce
As we were set or ye came in?
Which strife this man did first beginne,
Allegyng that suche men as use   330
For love of God, and not refuse,
On fote to goe from place to place
A pylgrimage, calling for grace,
Shall in that payne with penitence
Obtayne discharge of conscyence,—   335
Comparyng that lyfe for the best
Enduccion to our endlesse reste.
Upon these words our matter grew;
For, yf he coulde avowe them trewe,
As good to be a gardener   340
As for to be a pardoner.
But when I heard hym so farre wide,
I then approched and replyed,
Sayinge this: that this indulgence,
Havynge the forsayde penitence,   345
Deschargeth man of all offence
With much more profite then this pretence.
I aske but two pence at the moste—
I-wys, this is not very great coste,—
And from all payne, without dyspayre,—   350
My soule for his,—kepe even his chayre,
And when he dyeth he may be sure
To come to heaven even at pleasure.
And more then heaven he may not get,
How farre so-ever he lyst to jet.   355
Then is his payne more then his wit
To walke to heaven, synce he may sytte!
Syr, as we were in this contencion,
In came this dawe with his invention,
Revilyng us, hym-selfe avauntynge,   360
That all the soules to heaven ascending
Are mooste bounde to the potycarye,

Because he helpeth moost men to dye;
Before which death he sayeth, in-dede,
No soule in heaven can have his meede.   365
    Pedler. Why, dooe potycaryes kyll menne?
    Poticary. By God, menne say so now and then!
    Pedler. And I thought you wolde not have mist
To make men lyve as long as ye lyst.
    Potycary. As long as we lest? nay, as long as they
        can!   370
    Pedler. So myght we lyve wythout you than.
    Potycary. Yea, but it is necessary
For to have a potycary;
For when ye fele your conscience redye,
I can send you to heaven very quickly.   375
Wherfore, concernyng our matter here,
Above these twayne I am best, clere;
And, yf ye lyste to take me so,
I am content you and no mo
Shall be our judge as in this case,   380
Which of us thre shal take the beste place.
    Pedler. I neyther wyll judge the beste nor
        worst;
For, be ye blyste or be ye curste,
Ye knowe it is no whit my sleyghte
To be a judge in matters of wayghte.   385
It behoveth no pedlers nor proctours
To take on them judgment as doctours.
But if your myndes be only set
To worke for soule helth, ye be wel met;
For eche of you somwhat doth shew   390
That souls toward heven bi you do grow;
Then, if ye can so well agree
To continue together all three
And all you three obey one wyll,
Then all your mindes you may fulfyll: 395
As, yf ye came all to one man
Who shuld goe pilgrimage more then he can?
In that ye, palmer, as debyte,
May clerely dyscharge him, parde;
And for al other sins, once had contricion,   400
Your pardon geveth him full remyssion;

And then ye, maister poticary,
May sende hym to heaven by-and-by.

    Poticary. If he taste of this boxe nye about the
      prime,
By the masse, he is in heaven or evensonge tyme! 405
My crafte is suche that I can ryght well
Sende my frindes to heaven and my-selfe to hell.
But, syrs, marke this man, for he is wise
Who coulde devyse suche a devise;
For yf we three may be as one,   410
Then be we lordes everichone;
Betwene us all coulde not be miste
To save the soules of whome we lyste.
But, for good order, at a worde,
Twayne of us must waite on the third;   415
And unto that I doo agre,
For both you twayne shall wait on me.

    Pardoner. What chaunce is this that such an elfe
Commaund to knaves, beside him-selfe?
Nay, nay, my frende, that wyll not be;   420
I am to good to wayte on thee!

    Palmer. By Our Lady, and I wolde be lothe
To waite on the better of you bothe!

    Pedler. Yet be ye sure, for all this doute,
This wayting must be brought about.   425
Men cannot prosper, wilfully led;
All thynge decayeth where is no hed.
Wherfore, doubtles, marke what I saye:
To one of you three twayne muste obey;
And, sins ye cannot agree in voyce   430
Who shalbe hed, there is no choyse
But to devyse some maner thynge
Wherein ye all be lyke connynge;
And in the same who can do best,
The other twayne to make them preste   435
In every thyng of his intente
Holly to be at commaundymente.
And nowe I have founde one maystry
That ye can do indefferentli,
And is nother sellynge nor byinge,   440
But even onely very lyinge;

And all ye three can lye as well
As can the falsest devyll in hell.
And though afore ye herde me grudge
In greater matters to be your judge,   445
Yet in lyinge I can some skyll,
And yf I shall be judge I wyll;
And, be ye sure, without flattery,
Where my conscience fyndeth the maystry,
There shall my judgement strayght be founde,   450
Though I myghte wynne a thousande pounde.
      Palmer. Syr, for lyinge, though I can do it,
Yet am I loth for to go to it.
      Pedler. Ye have no cause to feare, beholde,
For ye may be uncontrolled.   455
And ye in this have good advauntage,
For lying in your common usage.
And you in lyinge be well spedde,
For al your craft doth stande in falshed.
Ye nede not care who shall begyn,   460
For eche of you may hope to wyn.
Now speake, all thre, even as ye fynde:
Be ye agreed to followe my mynde?
      Palmer. Yea, by my trouth, I am content.
      Pardoner. Now, in good fayth, and I assent.   465
      Potycary. Yf I denyed, I were a nodye,
For all is myne, by Goddes body!
            Here the poticary hoppeth.
      Palmer. Here were a hopper to hop for the
            rynge!
But, syr, this gere goth not by hoppynge.
      Potycary. Syr, in this hoppynge I wyll hop
            so well   470
That my tonge shall hop as well as my hele;
Upon whiche hoppyng I hope, and not doute it,
To hop so that ye shall hop without it.
      Palmer. Syr, I wyll neyther boste ne braule,
But take suche fortune as may fall;   475
And if ye wyn this maistrye,
I wyll obey you quietly.
And sure I thynke that quietnesse
In any man is great rychesse,

In any manner companye,   480
To rule or to be ruled indifferently.
   Pardoner. By that boste thou semest a begger
     in-dede.
What can thy quietnesse helpe us at nede?
If we shulde sterve, thou hast not, I thynke,
One peny to by us one potte of drinke.   485
Nay, yf rychesse might rule the roste,
Beholde what cause I have to boste!
Lo, here be pardons halfe a dosyn;
For ghostly ryches they have no cosyn;
And, moreover, to me they brynge   490
Suffycient succour for my lyvynge.
And here be relikes of suche a kynde
As in this worlde no man can fynde.
Knele downe, all three, and when ye leve kyssynge,
Who lyst to offer shall have me blessynge!   495
Frendes, here shall ye se even anone
Of All-Halowes the blessed jaw-bone:
Kysse yt hardly, with good devocion!
   Poticary. This kysse shall brynge us muche promo-
     cion.—
Fough! by Sainte Saviour, I never kyst a
     wars!   500
For, by Al-Halowes, me thynketh
That Al-Halowes breth stynketh.
   Palmer. Ye judge Al-Halowes breth unknowen;
If any breth stynke, it is your owne.   505
   Poticary. I know myne own breth from Al-
     Halowes,
Or els it were tyme to kysse the gallowes.
   Pardoner. Nay, sirs, beholde, here may ye se
The great-tooe of the Trinitie:
Who to this tooe any money voweth,   510
And once may role it in his mouth,
All his lyfe after, I undertake,
He shalbe ryd of the toth-ake.
   Poticarye. I praye you tourne that relyke aboute!
Other the Trinitie had the goute,   515
Or else, because it is three tooes in one,
God made it muche as thre tooes alone. . . . .

  Pardoner. Marke well this relyke; here is a
   whipper!
My frinde unfayned, here is a slypper   525
Of one of the Seven Slepers, be sure.
Doutlesse thys kys shal do you great pleasure,
For all these two dayes it shall so ease you
That none other savours shall displease you.
  Poticarye. All these two dayes! nay, all these two
   yeare!   530
For all the savours that may come heare
Can be no worse. . . . ,
  Pedler. Syr, me thynketh your devocion is but
   small.
  Pardoner. Smal? mary, me thinketh he hath none
   at all!   535
  Poticarye. What the devyll care I what ye thinke?
Shall I prayse relikes when they stinke?
  Pardoner. Here is an eye-toth of the Great Turke:
Whose eyes be ones set on this pece of worke
May happely lese part of his eye-syght,   540
But not all tyl he be blynde out-ryght.
  Potycary. What-so-ever any other man seeth,
I have no devocion to Turkes teeth;
For although I never sawe a greater,
Yet me thinketh I have sene many beter.   545
  Pardoner. Here is a boxe full of humble-bees
That stonge Eve as she sat on her knees
Tastyng the frute to her forbidden:
Who kisseth the bees within this hidden
Shall have as muche pardon, of ryght,   550
As for anye relyke he kist thys nyght.
  Palmer. Syr, I wyll kysse them, with all my harte.
  Potycary. Kysse them agayne, and take my parte,
For I am not worthy—nay, let be;
Those bees that stonge Eve shall not sting me! 555
  Pardoner. Good frendes, I have yett here-in this
   glasse,
Whiche on the drinke at the wedding was
Of Adam and Eve undoutedly;
Yf ye honour this relike devoutly,
All-though ye thurst no whit the lesse,   560

Yet shall ye drinke the more doubtlesse;
After whiche drynkyng ye shalbe as mete
To stande on your head as on your fete.
    Potycary. Ye, mary, now I can you thanke;
In presens of this the reste be blanke.   565
Wold God this relike had come rather!
Kysse that relycke well, good father!
Suche is the payne that ye palmers take
To kysse the pardon-bowle for the drynke sake.
O holy yest, that loketh full sowre and stale,   570
For Goddes bodye, helpe me to a cup of ale!
The more I beholde thee, the more I thurste;
The oftener I kysse, the more I lyke to burste!
But syns I kisse thee so devoutlye,
Hire me, and helpe me with drinke till I die!—   575
What, so muche prayinge and so lytel spede?
    Pardoner. Ye, for God knoweth when it is nede
To send folkes drinke, but, by Saint Antoni,
I wene He hath sent you to much al-readie.
    Poticary. If I have never the more for thee,   580
Then be the relikes no riches to me
Nor to thy-selfe, except they be
More beneficiall then I can se.
Richer is one boxe of thys treacle
Then all thy relikes that do no myracle.   585
Yf thou haddest prayed but halfe so muche to me
As I have prayed to thy relykes and thee,
Nothinge concernyng myne occupacion
But streyght should have wrought on operacion.
And as in value I passe you an ace.   590
Here lieth much riches in a lyttle space:
I have a boxe of rubarde here,
Whiche is as deynty as it is dere;
So helpe me God and hollydam,
Of this I wolde not geve a dram   595
To the best frende I have in Englandes grounde
Though he wolde geve me xx pounde;
For though the stomacke do it abhor,
It pourgeth you clene from the color,
And maketh your stomake sore to walter,   600
That ye shall never come to the halter.

Pedler. Then is that medecine a soverain thyng
To preserve a man from hangyng.
    Poticary. Yf ye wyll taste but thys crome that
      ye se,
Yf ye be hanged, never trust me!   605
Here have I diapompholicus,
A spetial ointment, as doctours discusse;
For a fistela or a canker
Thys oyntment is even shot-anker,
For this medicine helpeth one and other,   610
Or bringeth them in case that they nede no other.
Here is a syrapus de Bizansys;
A lyttell thynge is ynough of thys,
For even the weyght of one scrippull
Shall make you stronge as a crippull.   615
Here be other; as diosfialios,
Diagalanga, and sticados,
Blanka manna, diospoliticon,
Mercury sublime, and metridaticon,
Pelitory, and arsefetita,   620
Cassy, and coloquintita.
These be the thynges that breke all stryfe
Betwene mannes sickness and his lyfe;
From all payne these shall you delyver,
And set you even at rest for-ever.   625
Here is a medezine—no mo like the same!—
Which commenly is called thus by name:
Alikakabus or alkakengy;
A good thynge for dogges that be mangy.
Such be these medecines that I can   630
Helpe a dogge as well as a man.
Not one thynge here particulerly
But worketh universally,
For it doth me as much good when I sel yt
As all the byers that taste it or smell it.   635
Now, since my medecines be so speciall,
And in operacion so generall,
And redy to worke when-so-ever they shal,
So that in ryches I am principall,
Yf any reward may entreat ye,   640
I beseche your maship be good to me,

And ye shall have a boxe of marmelade
So fyne that ye mai digge it with a spade.

    Pedler. Syr, I thanke you, but your rewarde
Is not the thynge that I regarde;   645
I must and wyl be indifferent:
Wherfore procede in your entent.

    Potycarie. Now, yf I wyste this wishe no synne,
I wolde to God I might begynne!

    Pardoner. I am content that thou lye fyrste.   650

    Palmer. Even so am I; and say thy worst!
Now let us heare of all thy lyes
The greatest lye thou mayst devyse,
And in the fewest wordes thou can.

    Poticary. Forsoth, ye be a honest man.   655

    Palmer. There sayd ye muche, but yet no lye.

    Pardoner. Now lye ye both, by Our Ladye:
Thou lyest in boste of his honestye,
And he hath lyed in affirmyng thee.

    Poticary. Yf we both lye and ye say trewe,   660
Then of these lyes your part adewe!
And yf ye wyn, make none avaunte;
For ye are sure of one yll servaunte.
Ye may perceyve by the wordes he gave
He taketh your mashyp but for a knave.   665
But who tolde trewe or lyed in-dede,
That wyl I knowe or we procede:
Syr, after that I fyrste beganne
To prayse you for an honest man,
When ye affyrmed it for no lye,   670
(Now, by your faith, speake even trewlye),
Thought you your affyrmation trewe?

    Palmer. Ye, mary, I; for I wolde ye knewe
I thynke my-selfe an honeste man.

    Potycary. What thought you in the contrary
         than?   675

    Pardoner. In that I sayde the contrary,
I thyncke from trouth I dyd not vary.

    Poticary. And what of my wordes?

    Pardoner.   I thought ye lyed.

    Poticary. And so thought I, by God That dyed!
Nowe have you twayne eche for him-selfe layde   680

That none hath lyed but both trusayed;
And of us twayne none hath denyed,
But both affyrmeth, that I have lyed:
Now, sins [ye] both your trouth confesse,
And that we both my lye so wytnes 685
That twaine of us thre in one agree,—
And that the lyer the wynner must bee,—
Who coulde provyde suche evidence
As I have done in this pretence?
Me thynketh this matter sufficient 690
To cause you to geve judgement
And to geve me the maistrye,
For ye perceive these knaves can not lie.

    Palmer. Thoughe nother of us as yet had lyed,
Yet what we can do is untryed; 695
For yet we have devysed nothynge,
But answered you and geven hearynge.

    Pedler. Therfore I have devised one waye
Wherby all three your myndes maye saye;
For eche of you one tale shall tell, 700
And whiche of you telleth most mervaile
And moste unlyke to be true,
Shall moste prevayle, what-ever ensewe.

   .   .   .   .

    Pardoner. Well, syr, marke what I can say.
I have bene a pardoner many a day,
And done greater cures gostely
Then ever he dyd bodely:
Namely this one which ye shall heare, 775
Of one departed within this seven yere;
A friende of myne, and lykewyse I
To her agayne was as fryendly;
Who fell sycke so sodeynly
That deade she was even by-and-by, 780
And never spake with priest nor clarke,
Nor had no whit of his holy warke.
For I was thens, it coulde not be;
Yet harde I saye she asked for me. .
But when I bethought me how this chaunced, 785
And that I have to heaven avaunced
So many soules to me but straungers

And coulde not kepe my frynde from daungers,
But she to dye so daungerously,
For her soule helth specyally,   790
That was the thynge that greved me so
That nothynge colde release my woe
Tyll I had tryed even out of hande
In what estate her soule dyd stande;
For whiche tryall, shorte tale to make,   795
I toke this journey for her sake.
Geve eare, for here begynneth the story.
From hence I wente to purgatory,
And toke with me this geare in my fyste,
Wherby I may do there what I lyste.   800
I knocked, and was let in quickely;
But, Lord, how low the soules made curtsy!
And I to every soule agayne
Dyd geve a becke them to retayne,
And asked them this question than: 805
Yf that the soule of suche a woman
Dyd late amonge them there appere.
Wherto they sayd, "Shee came not here."
Then fearde I muche it was not well;
"Alas," thought I, "she is in hell!"   810
For with her lyfe I was so acqueinted
That sure I thought she was not saynted.
With this it chaunced me to snese:
"Chryst helpe!" quoth a soule that laye for his fees.
"Those wordes," quoth I, "thou shalte not lease." 815
Then with these pardons of all degrees
I payed his tole, and set hym so quight
That streyght to heaven he toke his flyght.
And I from thens to hell that nyght,
To healpe this woman yf I myght,   820
Not as who sayth by auctorite
But by the waye of entreate.
And fyrst to the devyll that kept the gate
I came, and spake after this rate:
"All hayle, syr devyl!" and made lowe curtesy. 825
"Welcome!" quoth he thus smilyngly.
He knew me well, and I at last
Remembred hym sins long tyme past;

For, as good hap wold have it chaunce,
This devyl and I were of old acquentance,   830
For ofte in the play of Corpus Cristi
He hath played the devill at Coventry.
By his acquentance and my behavoure
He shewed to me ryght frendly favoure.
And, to make me retourne the shorter,   835
I sayd to this devyl: "Good maister porter,
For all olde love, if it lye in your poure,
Helpe me to speke with my lorde and your."
"Be sure," quoth he, "no tonge can tell
What time thou couldest have com so wel,   840
For thys daye Lucifer fell;
Whiche is our festivall in hell.
Nothinge unreasonable craved thys day
That shall in hell have any naye.
But yet beware thou come not in   845
Tyll tyme thou mayst thy pasporte wyn;
Wherfore stande styll, and I wyl wyt
Yf I can get thy save-condyt."
He taryed not, but shortely gat it,
Under seale and the Dyvyls hand at it,   850
In ample wyse, as ye shall here;
Thus it began: "Lucifer,
By the power of God chife devyll of hell,
To all the devyls that there do dwel,
And every of them, we sende gretynge,   855
Under streyght charge and commaundynge,
That they aidinge and assystent be
To suche a pardoner"—and named me,—
"So that he may at lyberte
Passe save without his jeopardye   860
Tyll that he be from us extincte
And clerely out of helles precincte;
And, his pardons to kepe in savegarde,
We wyll they lye in the porters warde.
Geven in the fornes of our palays,   865
In our hye court of matters of malys,
Such a day and yere of our raine."
"God save the Devyll!" quoth I, "for playne,
I trust this wryting to be sure."

"Then put thy trust," quoth he, "in eure,   870
Syns thou arte sure to take no harme."
This devyl and I walked arme in arme
So farre tyll he had brought me thyther
Where all the devyls of hell together
Stode in aray in suche apparayle   875
As for that day there metely fell:
Their hornes well gylte, their clowes full cleane,
Theyr tayles well kempte, and, as I wene,
With sothery butter their bodyes anoynted;
I never sawe devyls so well appoynted.   880
The maister devyll sat in his jacket,
And all the soules were playing at racket:
None other rackettes they had in hande
Save every soule a good fyre-brande;
Wherwith they played so pretely   885
That Lucifer laughed merely,
And all the resedew of the fendes
Dyd laugh full well togytther lyke frendes.
But of my frende I sawe no whyt,
Nor durst not aske for her as yet.   890
Anone all this route was brought in sylens,
And I by an usher brought in presens.
Then to Lucyfer lowe as I coulde
I kneled; whiche he so well alowed
That thus he beckt, and, by Saynt Antony,   895
He smyled on me well-favoredly,
Bendyng his browes, as brode as barne-durres,
Shakyng his eares, as ruged as burres,
Rolyng his eyes, as rounde as II bushels,
Flastyng the fyre out of his nosethrels,   900
Gnashyng his teath so vaingloriousle
That me thought time to fall to flattery;
Wherwith I tolde, as I shall tell:
"O plesaunt pecture! O prince of hell,
Feutred in fashion abominable!   905
And syns that is inestimable
For me to prayse the worthyly,
I leve of prayse, as unworthy
To geve the prayse, besechyng thee
To heare my sute and then to be   910

So good to graunt the thyng I crave;
And, to be shorte, this wolde I have—
The soule of one which hither's flitted
Delivered hens and to me remitted.
And in this doinge, though all be not quit, 915
Yet in some parte I shall deserve it;
As thus: I am a pardoner,
And over soules as controller
Through-out the erth my power doth stand,
Where many a soule lyeth on my hand, 920
That spede in matters as I use them,
As I receyve them or refuse them;
Wherby, what tyme thy pleasure is
Ye shall requyre any parte of this,
The least devyl here that can come thyther 925
Shal chose a soule and bring him hyther."
"Ho! ho!" quod the Devyll, "we are well pleased.
What is his name thou woldest have eased?"
"Nay," quoth I, "be it good or evyll,
My commyng is for a she-devyll." 930
"What calste her?" quoth he, "thou horsen!"
"Forsoth," quoth I, "Margery Coorson."
"Now, by our honour," sayd Lucyfer,
"No devyll in hel shall with-holde her;
And yf thou woldst have twenty mo, 935
Were not for justice, they should go,
For all the devyls within this den
Have more to do with to women
Then with al the charge we have besyde.
Wherfore, yf thou our frende wyl be tryed, 940
Aply thy pardons to women so
That unto us there come no mo."
To do my best I promysed by othe;
Which I have kept, for, as the fayth goth,
At these dayes to heaven I do procure 945
Ten women to one man, be sure.
Then of Lucifer my leave I tooke,
And streyght unto the maister cooke;
I was had into the kytchen,
For Margeryes offyce was therin. 950
And or the meat were half rosted in-dede,

I toke her then fro the spyt for spede.   960
But when she sawe this brought to pas,
To tell the joy wherin she was,
And of all the devyls, for joy how they
Dyd rore at her delyvery,
And howe the chaynes in hell dyd ringe,   965
And how all the soules therin dyd synge,
And how we were brought to the gate,
And howe we toke our leve therat,
Be suer lake of tyme suffereth nat
To rehearse the xx part of that: 970
Wherfore, this tale to conclude brefely,
Thys woman thanked me chefely
That she was ryd of this endles death;
And so we departed on New Market Heath.
And yf any man do minde her,   975
Who liste to seke her ther shall he fynde her!
  Pedler. Syr, ye have sought her wonders well;
And where ye found her, as ye tell,
To here the chaunce ye found in hell,
I fynde ye were in great parell.   980
  Palmer. His tale is all much parellous,
But part is much more mervaylous;
As where he sayde the devyls complayn
That women put them to such payne
By theyr condicions so croked and crabbed,   985
Frowardly fashioned, so wayward and wrabbed,
So farre in devision, and sturryng suche stryfe,
That all the devyls be wery of theyr lyfe.
Thus in effect he told for trouth;
Wherby muche marvell to me ensueth,   990
That women in hel suche shrewes can be
And here so gentyll, as farre as I se.
Yet have I sene many a myle
And many a woman in the whyle;
Not one good citye, towne, nor borough   995
In Cristendome but I have bene thorough;
And this I wolde ye should understand:
I have sene women five hondred thousande,

  .   .   .   .

And ofte with them have longe time taried;   1000

Yet in all places where I have bene,
Of all the women that I have sene,
I never saw nor knew, in my conscience,
Any one woman oute of pacience.

    Poticary. By the masse, there is a greate lye! 1005
    Pardoner. I never heard a greater, by Our Lady!
    Pedler. A greater? nay, know ye any so great?
    Palmer. Syr, whether that I lose or get,
For my part judgement shall be prayed.
    Pardoner. And I desyre as he hath sayde. 1010
    Poticary. Procede, and ye shal be obeyed.
    Pedler. Then shall not judgement be delayde.
Of all these three, if eche mannes tale
In Poules Churche Yard were set on sale
In some mannes hand that hath the sleight, 1015
He should sure sel these tales by weyght;
For as they wey so be they worth.
But which weyeth best, to that now· forth!
Syr, al the tale that ye dyd tell
I beare in mynde; and yours as well; 1020
And, as ye saw the matter metely,
So lyed ye both well and discretely. . . . .
Yet, by these ten bones, I could ryght well
Ten tymes soner all that have beleved
Then the tenth parte of that he hath meved.

    Poticary. Two knaves before i lacketh ii knaves
        of fyve; 1035
Then one, and then one, and both knaves a-lyve;
Then two, and then two, and thre at a cast;
Thou knave, and thou knave, and thou knave, at last!
Nay, knave, yf ye tri me by nomber,
I wyll as knavyshly you accomber. 1040
Your mynd is all on your prevy tythe,
For all in ten me thynketh your wit lyethe.
Now ten tymes I besech Hym That hie sittes
Thy wyves x commandements maye serche thy v
        wittes; . . . .
And twenty times ten thys wysh I wold,
That thou hadst ben hanged at ten yere old,
For thou goest about to make me a slave—

I wyll thou know I am a gentyll knave!   1050
And here is an-other shall take my parte.
   Pardoner. Nay, fyrst I beshrew your knaves harte
Or I take parte in your knavery!
I wyll speake fayre, by Our Lady!
Syr, I beseche your maship to be   1055
As good as ye can be to me.
   Pedler. I wolde be glade to do you good
And him also, be he never so wode;
But dout you nat I wyl now do
The thynge my consciens ledeth me to.   1060
Both your tales I take farre impossible
Yet take I his farther incredible.
Not onely the thynge it-selfe alloweth it,
But also the boldenes therof avoweth it.
I knowe not where your tale to try,   1065
Nor yours but in hell or purgatory;
But his boldnes hath faced a lye
That may be tryed even in this company—
As, if ye lyst, to take this order:
Amonge the women in this border,   1070
Take three of the yongest and thre of the eldest,
Three of the hotest and three of the coldest,
Thre of the wysest and three of the shrewdest,
Thre of the chastest and thre of the lewdest,
Three of the lowest and thre of the hyghest,   1075
Three of the farthest and thre of the nyest,
Three of the fayrest and thre of the maddest,
Three of the foulest and thre of the saddest;
And when all these threes be had a-sunder,
Of eche three two justly by nomber   1080
Shall be founde shrewes—excepte this fall,
That ye hap to fynde them shrewes all.
Hym-selfe for trouth all this doth knowe,
And ofte hath tryed some of this rowe;
And yet he swereth by his conscience   1085
He never sawe woman breke pacience.
Wherfore, consydered with true entent
His lye to be so evydente,
And to appeare so evydently
That both you affyrmed it a lye,   1090

And that my consciens so depely
So depe hath sought this thynge to trye,
And tryed it with mynde indifferent,
Thus I awarde, by waye of judgement,
Of all the lyes ye all have spent   1095
His lye to be most excellent.

   Palmer. Syr, though ye were bound of equite
To do as ye have done to me,
Yet do I thanke you of your paine,
And wyll requite some part agayne.   1100

   Pardoner. Marye, syr, ye can no lesse do
But thanke him as much as it cometh to;
And so will I do for my part:
Now a vengeaunce on thy knaves hart!
I never knew pedler a judge before   1105
Nor never wil trust pedlynge-knave more!—
What dost thou there, thou horeson nody?

   Poticary. By the masse, lerne to make curtsye.
Curtsy before, and curtsy behynd hym,
And then on ech side, the devill blind hym!   1110
Nay, when I have it perfitly,
Ye shall have the devyl and al of curtsy!
But it is not sone lerned, brother,
One knave to make curtsy to another;
Yet, when I am angry, that is the worste,   1115
I shal cal my mayster knave at the fyrste.

   Palmer. Then would some maister perhappes
     clout ye,
But as for me ye nede not dout ye;
For I had lever be without ye
Then have suche besines about ye.   1120

   Pardoner. So helpe me God, so were ye better!
What should a begger be a jetter?
Yt were no whit your honestye
To have us twaine jet after ye.

   Poticary. Syr, be ye sure he telleth you true; 1125
Yf we should wayt, this would ensewe:
It would be sayde, trust me at a worde,
Two knaves made curtsy to the thyrde.

   Pedler. Now, by my trouth, to speke my mynde,
Sins they be so loth to be assined,   1130

To let them lose I thynke it best,
And so shal ye lyve best in rest.
    Palmer. Syr, I am not on them so fonde
To compel them to kepe theyr bonde;
And syns ye lyst not to waite on me,   1135
I clerely of waytinge discharge ye.
    Pardoner. Mary, syr, I hartely thanke you.
    Poticary. And I lykewyse, I make God avow.
    Pedler. Now be ye all even as ye begone;
No man hath lost nor no man hath wone.   1140
Yet in the debate wherewith ye began,
By way of advise I will speke as I can.
I do perceyve that pilgrimage
Is chiefe the thinge ye have in usage;
Wherto, in effecte, for the love of Christ   1145
Ye have, or should have, bene entist;
And who so doth with such intente
Doth wel declare his tyme well spente.
And so do ye in your pretence,
Yf ye procure this indulgence   1150
Unto your neyghbours charitably
For love of them in God only.
All thys may be ryght well applied
To shewe you both wel occupyed;
For though you walke not bothe one way,   1155
Yet, walkyng thus, this dare I saye:
That both your walkes come to one ende.
And so for all that do pretende,
By ayde of Goddes grace, to ensewe
Any manner kynde of vertue: 1160
As some great almoyse for to geve,
Some in wylfull povertie to lyve,
Some to make hye-wayes and such other warkes,
And some to maintayne priestes and clerkes
To synge and say the sarvyes apoynted.   1165
These, with all other vertues well marked,
All-though they be of sondry kyndes,
Yet be they not used with sondry myndes;
But as God onely doth all those move,
So every man, onely for His love,   1170
With love and drede obediently

Worketh in these vertues uniformely.
Thus every vertue, yf we lyst to scan,
Is pleasant to God and thankeful to man;
And who that by grace of the Holy Ghoste   1175
To any one vertue is moved moste,
That man, by that grace, that one applye,
And therin serve God moste plentyfully!
Yet not that one so farre wyde to wreste,
So lykyng the same to mislyke the rest;   1180
For who so wresteth his worke is in vayne.
And even in that case I perceyve you twayne,
Lykinge your vertue in suche wyse
That eche others vertue you do despise.
Who walketh this way for God wold fynd hym, 1185
The farther they seke Him, the farther behynd Hym.
One kynde of vertue to despyse another
Is lyke as the syster myght hange the brother.

    Poticarye. For feare leaste suche parels to me
      myght fall,
I thanke God I use no vertue at all!   1190

    Pedler. That is of all the very worste waye;
For more harde it is, as I have herde saye,
To begyn vertue where none is pretended
Then, where it is begon, the abuse to be amended.
How-be-it, ye be not al to begynne;   1195
One sygne of vertue ye are entred in;
As this: I suppose ye dyd say true
In that ye sayd ye use no vertue;
In the which wordes I dare well reporte
Ye are well beloved of all this sorte,   1200
By your raylyng here openly
At pardons and reliques so leudly.

    Potycarie. In that I thynke my faut not great,
For all that he hath I know counterfete.

    Pedler. For his and all other that ye knowe
      fayned   1205
Ye be nother councelled nor constrayned
To any suche thynge in any case
To geve any reverence in any suche place.
But where ye dout the truth, not knowynge,
Belevynge the best, good may be growinge;   1210

In judgynge the best, no harme at the least;
In judginge the worste, no good at the best.
But best in these thynges it semeth to me
To take no judgement uppon yee;
But as the Churche doeth judge or take them,   1215
So do ye receyve or forsake them;
And so, be sure, ye cannot erre,
But may be a fruitfull folower.
    Poticarye. Go ye before, and, as I am a true man,
I wyll folowe as faste as I can.   1220
    Pardoner. And so wyll I; for he hath sayde so
      wel,
Reason wolde we should folow his counsel.

Palmer. Then to our reason God geve us His grace,
    That we may folow with faith so fermly
His commaundimentes, that we may purchase   1225
    His love, and so consequently
    To beleve His Churche fast and faythfully;
So that we may, according to His promyse,
Be kept out of errour in any wyse.

And all that hath escaped us here by negligence, 1230
    We clerely revoke and forsake it.
To passe the tyme in this without offence,
    Was the cause why the maker dyd make it;
    And so we humbly beseche you take it;
Besechynge Our Lorde to prosper you all   1235
In the fayth of His Churche Universall!

1530?   About 1545.

NOTES

NOTES

OLD ENGLISH POEMS

(1) BEOWULF. Lines 189–498, 662–852, 1232–1650, 1787–1919, 2200–2820, 3120–82 The translation is based on the text of Wyatt's edition. The poem probably took its present form about the beginning of the eighth century, but the materials of which it is composed are much older. The opening lines of the first passage translated are as follows:

> Swa ða mæl-ceare   maga Healfdenes
> singala seað;   ne mihte snotor hæleð
> wean onwendan;   wæs þæt gewin to swyð,
> laþ ond longsum,   þe on ða leode becom,
> nyd-wracu niþ-grim,   niht-bealwa mæst.
> Þæt fram ham gefrægn   Higelaces þegn,
> god mid Geatum,   Grendles dæda;
> se wæs mon-cynnes   mægenes strengest
> on þæm dæge   þysses lifes,
> æþele ond eacen.   Het him yð-lidan
> godne gegyrwan;   cwæð, he guð-cyning
> ofer swan-rade   secean wolde,
> mærne þeoden,   þa him wæs manna þearf.

(1) *The Cleansing of Heorot.* The scene of the action is Denmark. Hrothgar, the Danish king, had built a great hall called Heorot; here he and his thanes feasted, while the gleeman sang to the music of the harp. But Grendel, a monster of the fens, offspring of Cain, ravaged Heorot, slaying many thanes as they lay asleep after the feast; and for twelve years the hall had stood desolate by night. At this point the selection begins. ¶ 1. *Healfdene's son:* Hrothgar. ¶ 5. *thane of Hygelac:* Beowulf, nephew of Hygelac; Hygelac, king of the Geats, was a historical character, who died about 520 A.D. in the invasion of "Friesland" referred to later in the poem. ¶ 6. *Geats:* a people living in the south of Sweden; perhaps the Jutes. ¶ 25. *Weder-folk:* Beowulf and his men; "Weders" is one name for the Geats. ¶ 29. *Scyldings:* the Danish royal house, also the Danish people; from "Scyld," the name of the founder of the dynasty.

(3) 3. *Wedermark:* the land of the Weders, or Geats. ¶ 7. *Boar-likenesses:* images of boars on the crests of the helmets. *cheek-guards:* helmets. ¶ 38. *Wendlas:* perhaps Vandals.

(5) 4. *eotens:* giants. *nickers:* water-demons. ¶ 20. *Hrethmen:* Danes; literally, "triumph-men.

(6) 40. *gave them webs of war-speed:* i. e., wove for them a destiny or success in war.

(10) 18. *Ring-Danes:* Danes wearing ring-mail; an allusion to their warlike character.

(11) 5. *Ingwines:* a name for the Danes.

(14) 11. *prince of rings:* prince who distributes rings, or treasure.

(17) 21. *spear-holt:* spear-shaft, spear. ¶ 39. *ring-bark:* ship with rings on its prow.

(19) *The Fight with the Dragon.* ¶ 1–5. The wars and quarrels between the Geats and their neighbors referred to in this part of *Beowulf* (the fights of Hæthcyn and Heardred against the Swedes, the story of the Swedish exiles Eanmund and Eadgils, and the expedition of Hygelac against the West Frisians, Franks and Hugs) doubtless formed the subjects of other long tales, similar to *Beowulf*, with which the hearers were perfectly familiar; now that the tales are lost it is impossible to make from these tangled references any clear or precise account of what happened. *Heardred:* son of Hygelac, whom he succeeded as king of the Geats. *Battle-Scylfings:* the Scylfings were the Swedish royal family; the name was also used for the Swedish people. *nephew of Hereric:* Heardred. ¶ 10–14, 19–21. The MS is defective here. The words in brackets are translations of conjectural emendations.

343

(25) 34. *Wægmundings:* the family to which Beowulf and Wiglaf belonged.

(29) 5. *Whale's Ness:* the name of a headland. ¶ 36–38. The MS is defective here The words in brackets are translations of conjectural emendations.

(30) CHARMS. The Old.English *Charms* are clearly survivals from a very early time when the Angles and Saxons were heathen. The "mighty women" of the second charm here given are the Valkyrie of Northern mythology, one of whose spears is supposed to have caused the "stitch." ¶ 33. *wounded with iron strongly:* i. e., hammered heavily.

(31) THE FRISIAN WIFE. From the Gnomic Verses in the *Exeter Book*, some of which are very ancient.

(31) RIDDLE. From the so-called *Riddles of Cynewulf*, the authorship of which is now considered doubtful; most of the riddles belong, however, to Cynewulf's age, the eighth century. ¶ 4. *wall's roof:* the horizon.

(31) THE WANDERER. Probably of the eighth century.

(33) 6. *wall-place:* the earth.

(33) THE BANISHED WIFE'S LAMENT. Probably of the eighth century.

(34) CÆDMON'S HYMN. The earliest of the extant religious poems in Old English The verses are at the end of the Moore MS of Bede's *Ecclesiastical History*, and must have been written there about the year 737.

(34) THE PHOENIX. Lines 1–84. The poem was written in the eighth century and probably by Cynewulf. The first half, including the passage here translated, is based upon a Latin poem, *Carmen de Phœnice*, by Lactantius (fl.300 A.D.).

(36) GENESIS. Lines 338–441 of the so-called *Genesis B*, which belongs to the second half of the ninth century.

(38) 16. The MS is here defective, and the words in brackets have been added in the present translation to complete the sentence.

(38) JUDITH. The poem is of the last half of the ninth century or the beginning of the tenth. The author is unknown, but evidently belonged to the school of Cynewulf. The fragment that has survived is only the last part of a poem apparently covering the whole story of Judith as told in the Old Testament Apocrypha. Nebuchadnezzar, king of Assyria sent a great army against the land of the Jews because they had refused to help him in his war with the Medes. The advance of the army on Jerusalem was stayed at the city of Bethulia which commanded the passes in the hill country: and the Assyrians encamped in the plain and besieged the city. At the end of four and thirty days the distress of the Bethulians was intense; the people demanded that the city be surrendered, and the rulers with great difficulty persuaded them to wait five days more for deliverance at the hand of Jehovah. At this crisis arose Judith, a widow, "exceedingly beautiful to behold," and called the rulers before her and said, "Hear me, and I will do a thing which shall go down to all generations." She revealed to them a part of her plan and bade them hold the city till her return. That night she went forth, with her maid, and entered the camp of the Assyrians. To the guards who took her she said, "I am a daughter of the Hebrews, and I flee away from their presence, because they are about to be given you to be consumed; and I am coming into the presence of Holofernes the chief captain of your host, to declare words of truth; and I will show before him a way whereby he shall go and win all the hill country, and there shall not be lacking of his men one person nor one life." Holofernes was captivated by her beauty, and sought from the first to betray her; but she craftily protected herself, and also won the privilege of leaving the camp every night to pray. On the fourth day Holofernes made a feast, and here the extant portion of the poem begins.

(44) THE BATTLE OF MALDON. The poem is a fragment, being incomplete both at the beginning and at the end. It is based upon a historical event, an invasion of the east coast of England by Danish Vikings, in 991, and their defeat of Earl Byrhtnoth and his forces at Maldon. In the narrative the terms "earl," "prince," "Æthelred's thane," "stronghold of heroes," "lord of warriors," etc., always refer to Byrhtnoth. The warriors whose names are given are all on Byrhtnoth's side; the Vikings were all strangers to the narrator.

EARLY MIDDLE ENGLISH POEMS

(49) POEMA MORALE. Lines 1–27, 90–101, 224–31, 244–51, 352–72. *Poema Morale=* "Moral Poem"; the title is often given as "Moral Ode." With the exceptions noted below, the text is that of the Jesus College MS as edited for the Early English Text Society.

(50) 14. *The=*he who. ¶ 15. *hit=*it; the antecedent is the preceding clause, not "lust." ¶ 21. *eye=*awe. *mon=*to man. The sense of the whole line is, Man stands more in awe of man than of Christ. ¶ 22, 26. *The=*he who. ¶ 28–33. These lines are from the Trinity College MS, taking the place of seven rather confused lines in the Jesus College MS. ¶ 28, 30. *the=*who. ¶ 43. *that=*those that. ¶ 46. *blysse:* the reading of the Trinity College MS. ¶ 49. *Avene* . *Sture:* the rivers Avon and Stour; probably those in Hampshire, not those in Warwickshire. ¶ 51. *that=*to whom.

(51) 53. Understand "to whom" before "was." *thenche:* understand "evil' as the object. ¶ 57. *other=*each other. ¶ 63. *bever:* the reading of the Trinity College MS. ¶ 68. *godes=*of good. *nys Him nowiht with-ute=*there is nothing that He is without. ¶ 69. *godes=*of good. *wone=*want, lack.

(51) THE BRUT. The text is that of the Cottonian MSS, Otho, C. xiii, as edited by Sir Frederic Madden, including his emendations in the footnotes. The MS is fragmentary in places, and the lines have not been numbered; but the selection here given corresponds to ll. 13,785–14,064 in the Cottonian MSS, Caligula, A. ix—a longer version. The title of the poem is derived from the name of the legendary first king of Britain, Brut, grandson of Aeneas. The selection describes the coming to Britain of a band of Angles, in the fifth century A.D., and the aid they gave the British king, Vortiger, against the Picts ("Peutes"), a barbarous people living in the north of the island, survivors of the earliest inhabitants.

(52) 35. *Alemaine:* Germany (from "Alemanni," the name of an early Teutonic tribe); the term is here used for a wide territory, including the region south of Denmark from which the Angles came.

(54) 90. *Thonre:* Thor, god of "thunder."

(55) 142. *Umbre=*Humber; an estuary on the northeastern coast of Britain.

(56) A BESTIARY. Lines 1–52. The text is that of the Early English Text Society edition. *Natura leonis=*"nature of the lion." *Significacio prime nature=*"meaning of the first nature." ¶ 12. *he:* the hunter. *is=*them; the antecedent is "fet-steppes," l. 7.

(57) 39. *manne=*of men.

(57) THE OWL AND THE NIGHTINGALE. Lines 1–94, 253–64, 315–52. The text is that of Morris and Skeat, in their *Specimens of Early English*, from the MSS.

(58) 21–23. *he=*it; the antecedent is "drem." ¶ 28. *thare=*of the. ¶ 31. *thare=* the. ¶ 34. *Me:* indirect object after "wers." ¶ 43. *gret:* swollen with wrath.

(59) 56. *bare:* exposed, unprotected. ¶ 65. *fugel-kunne:* indirect object after "loth." ¶ 70. *Hire thonkes=*of her own thoughts, i. e., willingly. ¶ 85. *The=*that. ¶ 94. *on:* to be taken with "fode."

(60) 110. *heo=*it; the antecedent is "stefne." ¶ 128. *he=*it, the antecedent is "crei." ¶ 130. *Thas=*of the. ¶ 134. *heo=*it; the antecedent is "murhthe."

(61) 138, 139. *he=*it; the antecedent is "song.' ¶ 141. *Alvred:* King Alfred the Great; the so-called *Proverbs of Alfred* was a popular work at this time.

(61) CURSOR MUNDI. Lines 1237–1432. The text is that of the Trinity College MS as edited for the Early English Text Society, except for a few readings from the other MSS. *Cursor Mundi=*"Course of the World."

(63) 81. *Fison=*Phison, or Pison. *Gison=*Gihon. *Tigre=*Tigris. *Eufrate=* Euphrates. Cf. Gen. 2:11–14.

(64) 114. *Kaym=*Cain.

(65) 188. *Noe=*Noah.

(66) 192. *Moyses=*Moses

(66) THE PEARL. Lines 1–120, 157–276, 301–60, 1153–76. The text is that of the

Early English Text Society edition, except for some of Gollancz' emendations. The longest omitted passage (lines 361–1152) consists chiefly of a religious homily put into the mouth of the maiden. ¶ 2. *to clanly clos:* "'Too cleanly enclosed,' i. e., for earthly existence."—Gollancz.

(67) 41. *hit*=itself.

(69) 129. *con shere*=has refined.

(70) 162. *upon*=open.

(71) 188. *in hit mesure:* in its measure, adequately. ¶ 200. *in wommon lore:* in the way that women are taught.

(72) 236. " It is proved to be a pearl of price."

(73) 277. *noght bot doel dystresse:* sorrow naught but distress. ¶ 289. *Deme Dryghtyn, ever Hym adyte:* let the Lord decree, ever let Him ordain.

(74) 298. *of lyghtly leme:* i. e., *lyghtly leme of,* " may lightly glint away."—Gollancz. Osgood translates "lurez" as "frowns," and "leme" as "drive." ¶ 306. *take me halte:* "Strike me halt, or maimed."—Gollancz.

(74) THE PROVERBS OF HENDYNG. Lines 79–110. The text is that of the Harleian MS, as edited by Morris and Skeat in their *Specimens of Early English.*

(75) 2c. *Be thou*=if thou art. ¶ 21. *me*=men. ¶ 22. *Gest thou nout*=thou wilt not go.

(76) ALYSOUN. The text is that of the Harleian MS as edited by T. Wright, in *Specimens of Lyric Poetry,* for the Percy Society. ¶ 7, 15, 17. *he*=she (O. E. "heo," she).

(77) 37. *under gore*=under clothes, i. e., alive.

(77) SPRINGTIME. The text comes from the same source as the preceding poem.

(78) 22. *mo*=more, many others ¶ 29. *Deores:* supply " come " as predicate. ¶ 34. "If I shall feel the need of joy from one of them.

(79) THE VIRGIN'S SONG TO HER BABY CHRIST. The text is that of the Harleian MS as edited by F. J. Furnivall, in *Political, Religious, and Love Poems,* for the Early English Text Society.

MIDDLE ENGLISH METRICAL ROMANCES

(79) THE LAY OF HAVELOK THE DANE. Lines 537–662. The text is that of Morris and Skeat in their *Specimens of Early English.* The romance is a translation of a French poem, *Le Lai d'Havelok le Danois,* which probably was based upon a lost Anglo-Saxon original. The story in brief is as follows. In the time of Athelwold, king of England, Birkabeyn, king of Denmark, died and left his three children in the care of his friend Godard, who was appointed regent. Godard shut up the children in a castle, and usurped the throne; before long he cut the throats of the two daughters, and ordered a fisherman, Grim, to drown the son, Havelok, in the sea. The incidents in the selection followed. Grim then fled with the royal child to England, and settled in the place which was afterward named Grimsby in his honor. When Havelok came of age he returned to Denmark, and by a series of incredibly heroic achievements regained the throne of his father.

(80) 31, 32. Skeat suggests a change of order, to get a rhyme: "And caste the knave so harde adoun That he crakede there hise croun." ¶ 36. *That*=so that.

(81) 63. *He*=they.

(83) SYR GAWAYN AND THE GRENE KNYGHT. Lines 130–466, 2160–2478. The text is that of the Early English Text Society edition, except that a few emendations suggested in the footnotes of that edition have been incorporated in the text. The romance opens with the description of a New Year banquet at the court of the legendary King Arthur, where occur the incidents narrated in the first selection. The middle portion of the story—here omitted—is briefly as follows. When New Year's day again approaches, Gawayn sets off upon his horse Gringolet in search of the Green Chapel. He comes at last to a great castle, whose lord assures him that the chapel is near by and induces him to stay at the castle until the appointed day arrives. Gawayn and his host make an agreement that every night each will give the

other what he has got during the day. Several days pass. Each morning the lord of the castle goes hunting, and during his absence his wife makes love to Gawayn. The knight yields so far as to accept a kiss from her each day; but at night, when the lord returns and gives Gawayn the game he has killed, Gawayn gives him the kiss. On the last day of his stay, the lady prevails upon the knight to accept a girdle, and this he does not give to her husband. On New Year's morning Gawayn sets out for the Green Chapel, and has the experiences described in the second selection.

(83) *The Stranger at King Arthur's Court.*

(89) 235. *the kyng wyth croun:* i. e., the crowned king.

(91) *Sir Gawayn at the Green Chapel.*

(92) 12. *a launde:* supply "saw" as the governing word. ¶ 30. *Wowayn*=Gawayn.

(93) 46–48. The sense is obscure. Miss Weston translates, "I trow that gear is preparing for the knight who will meet me here." *me*=my. *Bi rote:* the meaning is doubtful; Morris gives " cheerfully, confidently."

(95) 129. *Haf at the:* i. e., I have a stroke at thee, so take care.

(98) 258. *Salamon*=Solomon. ¶ 259. *Dalyda*=Delilah. *Davyth*=David. ¶ 260. *Barsabe*=Bathsheba.

(99) 301. *Gaynour:* Guinevere, Arthur's queen. ¶ 306. *Tyntagelle*=Tintagel; in Cornwall. *Uter*=Uther, the father of Arthur.

JOHN GOWER

(100) CONFESSIO AMANTIS. Book II. 291–372. *Confessio Amantis*=" Confession of a Lover." The text is that of the Early English Text Society edition.

WILLIAM LANGLAND

(102) PIERS THE PLOWMAN. The text is that of 1377 (the so-called B text), as edited by W. W. Skeat for the Early English Text Society. ¶ 5. *Malverne hulles:* in the west of England. ¶ 14. *toure.* Cf. Langland's explanation, in Passus I. 12–14:

> "The toure up the toft," quod she, "Treuthe is there-inne,
> And wolde that ye wroughte as His word techeth;
> For he is Fader of Feith, fourmed yow alle."

¶ 15. *dongeon.* Cf. Passus I. 59–64:

> "That dongeoun in the dale, that dredful is of sighte,
> What may it be to mene, madame, I yow biseche?"
> "That is the Castle of Care: who-so cometh therinne
> May banne that he borne was to body or to soule.
> Therinne wonieth a wighte that Wronge is yhote,
> Fader of Falshed, and founded it hym-selve."

(103) 17. *felde.* Cf. Matt. 13:38: "The field is the world." The tower, the dale, and the field thus include the whole universe—heaven, hell, and earth. ¶ 37. "Yet" should be understood before "han." ¶ 38. *That Poule precheth.* Apparently the reference is to II Thess. 3:10: "If any would not work, neither should he eat." ¶ 39. *Qui turpiloquium loquitur*=" he who speaks slander." ¶ 44. *roberdes knaves:* lawless vagabonds (literally, " Robert's knaves or men"; by some regarded as originally Robin Hood's followers). ¶ 46. *Pilgrymes and palmers.* Pilgrims were people who made pilgrimages to some sacred spot and then returned home to their usual occupations. Palmers were originally pilgrims to the Holy Land, who brought back palms as symbols of victory; but the term came to be applied to professional, or chronic, pilgrims, whatever the shrines they visited; cf. *The Foure PP*, ll. 9 ff., p. 312. ¶ 47. *Seynt James:* his shrine in Galicia, Spain, was popular with pilgrims. ¶ 54. *Walsyngham:* an English village, near Norwich, where was a celebrated shrine of the Virgin.

(104) 58. *foure ordres:* the Carmelites (white friars), Augustines (Austin friars), Jacobins or Dominicans (black friars), and Franciscans or Minorites (gray friars); they were all mendicant orders. ¶ 68. *pardoner:* cf. the Prologue to *The Canterbury Tales*, ll. 669 ff.

p. 143. ¶ 84. *pestilence tyme:* probably the reference is to the Black Death, the first and greatest of the pestilences of the fourteenth century, which occurred in 1348–49; others followed in 1361–62, 1369, and 1375–76. ¶ 85, 86. Cf. the Prologue to *The Canterbury Tales*, ll. 507–10, p. 139, and the note, p. 352. ¶ 87. *bachelers:* novices in the church. *doctours:* i. e., teachers, doctors of divinity. ¶ 93, 94. The sense is that these ecclesiastics served in the courts of chancery and the exchequer, claiming for the king the debts due him from the various wards of the city and also waifs and strays.

(105) 99. *consistorie:* usually a church council, but here the assembly at the Last Judgment. ¶ 101. See Matt. 16:18, 19. ¶ 103. *foure vertues:* prudence, temperance, fortitude, and justice. ¶ 104. *closyng gatis:* the poet makes a play upon "cardinals," which is derived from Latin "cardo," a hinge. ¶ 126. *so*=so that. *leute*=loyalty; i. e., thy liegemen. *lovye*=may love. ¶ 130. *thal:* i. e., that which. ¶ 132–38. The first four words are supposed to be spoken by the king, to whom the angel then replies. The whole passage may be translated thus: "'I am king, I am prince.' Perhaps neither, hereafter. O thou who administerest the special laws of Christ the King, that thou mayst do this the better be merciful as well as just! Naked justice craves to be clothed by thee with mercy. What sort of grain thou wishest to reap, such sow! If justice is made naked, may naked justice be meted to thee: if mercy is sown, mayst thou reap mercy!'

(106) 139. *Goliardeys:* the word is based upon "Golias," the name of an imaginary bishop, the fictitious author of certain anonymous Latin poems of the twelfth century that express sentiments similar to those here put into the mouth of Goliardeys. ¶ 141, 142. The sense of the Latin, including the play upon "rex" and "regere," may be rendered thus: "Since a ruler is said to get his name from the fact that he rules, he has the name without the thing unless he is zealous to maintain the laws." ¶ 145. "The king's precepts are to us the chains of the law." ¶ 146–209. The poet here applies the fable of belling the cat to political conditions of the day: the old King Edward III (the cat) was hated and feared; his grandson Richard, the heir apparent, was but a child (the kitten); and there was much discontent among the common people high and low (the rats and the mice), which culminated a few years later in Wat Tyler's rebellion, in 1381.

(107) 191. See Eccles. 10:16: "Woe to thee, O land, when thy king is a child!" ¶ 199 *Nere*=were it not for. ¶ 203. *costed:* i. e., would have cost.

(108) 224. *Dieu vous save, dame Emme*="God save you, dame Emma"; apparently a line from a low song. ¶ 228. *Oseye*=Alsace, in Germany. *Gascoigne*=Gascony, in France. ¶ 229. *Ryne*=Rhine. *Rochel:* a river and district in France.

GEOFFREY CHAUCER

(108) The text follows closely the best MSS, as published by the Chaucer Society; readings from the poorer MSS have been substituted where the better MSS are clearly corrupt and a few emendations by modern editors have been adopted.

(108) THE BOOK OF THE DUCHESSE. Lines 291–442. The text is based on the Fairfax MS. The poem is in honor of the Duchess Blanche, wife of the Duke of Lancaster (John of Gaunt), who died in September, 1369. The selection—which gives no idea of the scope of the poem as a whole—is here printed as an example of Chaucer's descriptions of Nature in his first period.

(109) 20. *Tewnes*=Tunis. ¶ 38. *Ector*=Hector, the Trojan hero. ¶ 39. *Lamedon*= Laomedon, the father of Priam. ¶ 40. *Medea:* the daughter of Aëtes, in whose kingdom was the Golden Fleece, guarded by a sleepless dragon; when the Argonauts came there she fell in love with their leader, Jason, by her magic arts aided him to secure the Fleece, and then fled with him. ¶ 41. *Eleyne*=Helen, the love of Paris and cause of the Trojan War. *Lavyne* =Lavinia; the second wife of Æneas and daughter of Latinus, king of Latium. ¶ 43. *lex and glose:* the walls are likened to the pages of a book, in which the text occupies the center and the gloss, or commentary, the margin; the sense is, therefore, that the walls were covered

all over with scenes from *The Romance of the Rose.* ¶ 44. *Romaunce of the Rose:* the famous French allegorical poem, of the latter half of the thirteenth century; Chaucer translated it.

(110) 72. *relayes:* i. e., reserve packs of hounds. ¶ 78. *themperour Octovyen:* "A favorite character of Carolingian legend," and here "probably a flattering allegory for the King" (A.W. Ward).

(111) 118. *seven:* an allusion to the seven planets—all that were then known.

(112) 145. *Argus*=Algus. "Algus" is from Old French "algorisme," a French adaptation "from the Arabic 'al-Khowaragmi,' .... surname of the Arab mathematician Abu Ja'far Mohammed Ben Musa, who flourished early in the ninth century, and through the translation of whose work on algebra the Arabic numerals became generally known in Europe" (*A New English Dictionary*).

(112) THE HOUS OF FAME. Book II. 21–160, 452–545; Book III. 20–110, 266–328. The text is based on the Fairfax MS. In Book I, after an introduction and an invocation, the poet describes a dream, in which he found himself in the temple of Venus and saw painted on the wall the adventures of Æneas; coming out of the temple into a large field, he dreamed that he spied, close by the sun, a huge eagle all of gold, that began to descend; at this point, after a few introductory lines to Book II, the selection begins.

(113) 34. *oon:* apparently the dreamer's sharp-tongued wife; cf. ll. 37, 38. Chaucer's marriage is supposed to have been unhappy.

(114) 58. *Joves:* a peculiar form of "Jove," due (says Skeat) to the influence of the Old French nominative, as in "Jacques." ¶ 60. *Ennok*=Enoch; see Gen. 5:24. *Elye*=Elias, or Elijah; see II Kings 2:11. ¶ 61. *Romulus:* the Roman legend was that the founder of Rome did not die but was carried up to heaven by his father, Mars. *Ganymede:* a beautiful youth, whom the eagle of Zeus carried to Olympus to be the cup-bearer of the gods. ¶ 88. *Cupido*=Cupid. ¶ 90. *goddesse:* the word is Skeat's conjecture. ¶ 95. *cadence:* perhaps rhythmic prose, in distinction from rhyme; it might more naturally mean unrhymed verse, but it is not known that Chaucer wrote any.

(115) 108. The sense is, "And in helping people who serve Cupid."

(116) 146. *ayerishe bestes:* the signs of the zodiac, as the Ram, the Bull, etc. ¶ 153. *Boesse*=Boece, or Boethius (470?–525), whose *De Consolatione Philosophiae* ("Of the Consolation of Philosophy"), partly in verse, was a favorite work in the Middle Ages; Chaucer translated it; the passage referred to is in Book IV, Metre i. ¶ 166. *Marcyan*=Martianus Minneus Felix Capella (fifth century A.D.), a satirist, author of *De Nuptiis Philologiae et Mercurii* ("Of the Nuptials of Philology and Mercury"); it includes treatises on the Seven Sciences, and "gives a hint of the true system of astronomy" (Gilman). ¶ 167. *Anteclaudian:* "Anticlaudianus" is a Latin poem by Alanus ab Insulis (1114?–1202?), which contains descriptions of the regions of the air.

(117) 185. *Ravene:* the constellation Corvus. *eyther Bere:* the constellations Ursa Major and Ursa Minor, or the Great Bear and the Little Bear. ¶ 186. *Arionis harpe:* the constellation Lyra. Arion was a musician of early Greek myth. ¶ 187. *Castor, Polux:* the sons of Leda, wooed by Zeus disguised as a swan; they became the constellation Gemini. *Delphyne:* the constellation Delphinus, or Dolphin. ¶ 188. *Athalantes*=Atlas' (from "Atlante," ablative case of "Atlas"). *doughtres sevene:* the constellation of the Pleiades. ¶ 203. *Seynt Julyane:* Julian was the patron saint of hospitality; cf. the Prologue to *The Canterbury Tales*, ll. 339, 340, p. 135. ¶215. *Peter:* i. e., by St. Peter.

(118) 256. *Seynt Thomas:* Thomas à Becket, at Canterbury, in the county of Kent.

(120) 308. *Gyle*=Giles. ¶331. *Sit:* infinitive, depending on "saugh," l. 334. ¶ 337–62. Cf. the *Æneid*, iv. 173 ff.

(121) 355. See Rev. 4:6.

(122) 384. Hercules put on a shirt which had been smeared with the poisonous blood of the Centaur Nessus.

(122) THE LEGEND OF GOOD WOMEN. Lines 1–202 of the later version. The text is based on the Fairfax MS. ¶ 16. *Bernarde:* St. Bernard was famed for his learning.

(124) 72. An allusion to a famous and long-maintained dispute as to whether the leaf or the flower deserved the greater honor; cf. the poem, "The Flower and the Leaf," formerly attributed to Chaucer.

(125) 114. *Agenores doghtre:* Europa, daughter of Agenor, the mythical founder of the Phoenician race; she was loved by Zeus, who, in the shape of a bull, swam with her on his back to Crete.

(127) THE CANTERBURY TALES. The text is based on the Ellesmere MS, and follows it closely.

(127) *The Prologue.* ¶ 7. The sun is called "young" because it has run through only the first sign of the zodiac, Aries, or the Ram. ¶ 8. *halfe cours:* the second half of the sign of the Ram lies in the month of April. The pilgrims met, then, about the middle of the month; the Prologue to "The Tale of the Man of Lawe," ll. 1–6, fixes the date more exactly as the sixteenth. ¶ 17. *martir:* Thomas à Becket, archbishop of Canterbury, who was killed in the cathedral at Canterbury, in 1170; his shrine was long visited by hosts of pilgrims. ¶ 20. *Southwerk:* a suburb of London, south of the Thames. *Tabard:* the name of an inn.

(128) 51. *Alisaundre:* Alexandria, in Egypt. ¶52. *hadde the bord bigonne:* had been honored with a seat at the head of the table. ¶ 53. *Pruce:* Prussia. ¶ 54. *Lettow:* Lithuania. *Ruce:* Russia. ¶ 56. *Gernade:* Granada. ¶ 57. *Algezir:* Algeciras, a Moorish city, taken by the Christians in 1344. *Belmarye:* a Moorish kingdom in Africa. ¶ 58. *Lyeys:* Layas, a town in Armenia; it was wrested from the Turks about 1367. *Satalye:* Adalia, a seaport of Asia Minor. ¶ 59. *Grete See:* the Mediterranean. ¶ 62. *Tramyssene:* Tramessen, a Moorish kingdom in Algeria. ¶ 65. *Palatye:* in Asia Minor; "one of the lordships held by Christian knights after the Turkish conquests" (Tyrwhitt).

(129) 87. *as of so litel space:* i. e., considering the short time. ¶ 88. *lady=*lady's. ¶ 101. *he:* i. e., the knight.

(130) 111. *bracer:* a leathern covering for the forearm (French "bras," arm; cf. "bracelet"). "A bracer serveth for two causes, one to save his arme from the strype [=stroke] of the strynge and his doublet from wearynge."—Ascham, *Toxophilus*, Book II. ¶ 115. *Cristofre:* a figure of St. Christopher, worn as a brooch for good luck. ¶ 118. *Prioresse:* the head of a priory of nuns. ¶ 120. *Seinte Loy:* St. Eligius (Old French "Eloy"), the patron saint of goldsmiths, farriers, etc. ¶ 124–26. "There is nothing to show that Chaucer intended a sneer; he merely states a fact, viz., that the prioress spoke the usual Anglo-French of the English court, of the English law-courts, and of the English ecclesiastics of the higher rank."—Skeat. On the other hand, the whole sketch of the prioress is satirical.

(131) 159. *gauded al with grene:* i. e., the larger and more ornamental beads, called gauds, were green. ¶ 161. *crowned:* surmounted by a crown. "The crowned 'A' is supposed to represent *Amor*, or charity, the greatest of all the Christian virtues."—Skeat. ¶ 162 "*Amor vincit omnia*": "Love conquers all things"; a quotation, with transposition of the first and the last word, from Virgil, *Eclogues*, x. 69. ¶ 173. *Seint Maure . . . . Seint Beneit:* St. Maur, St. Benedict; their "rule" was the earliest form of monastic discipline in the Roman Church. ¶ 179. *rechelees:* Harleian MS, "cloisterlees." ¶ 187. *Austyn:* St. Augustine (354–430), the church father; in the monastic order modeled on his ideas and named after him, very strict discipline was maintained.

(132) 192. *no cost:* in no way. ¶ 209. *lymytour:* a friar who had permission to beg within the limits of a certain district. ¶ 210. *ordres foure:* see note on "Piers the Plowman," l. 58, p. 347. ¶ 216. *frankeleyns:* freeholders, "landowners of free but not noble birth and ranking next below the gentry" (*A New English Dictionary*). ¶ 220. *he was licentiat:* i. e., he had received a license from the Pope to forgive all kinds of sins; a curate had to refer certain cases to his bishop.

(133) 254. "*In principio*": the first two words of John's gospel in the Vulgate; limitours were accustomed to quote Scripture as they made their rounds. ¶ 258. *love-dayes:*

"Days fixed for settling differences by umpire, without having recourse to law or violence The ecclesiastics seem generally to have had the principal share in the management of these transactions."—Wright.

(134) 276. *kept:* i. e., guarded from pirates. *for*=for fear of. ¶ 277. *Middelburgh:* a port in the Netherlands. *Orewelle:* formerly the name of a port at the mouth of the river Orwell, in England, just across the Channel from Middelburgh. ¶ 285. *Clerk:* usually a cleric, or clergyman (Latin "clericus"), but here a student preparing for the church. *Oxenford:* Oxford. ¶ 286. *logyk:* the logic of Aristotle, as developed by the schoolmen, was the chief study in the universities of the Middle Ages. ¶ 291. *benefice:* a "living" in the church. ¶ 297, 298. There is a playful allusion to the fact that alchemists were sometimes called philosophers; the clerk was not that kind of philosopher, and, instead of searching in books to learn how to change the baser metals into gold, he changed his gold into books. ¶ 310. *parvys:* "The church-porch, or portico of St. Paul's, where the lawyers were wont to meet for consultation."—Morris.

(135) 315. *patente:* a document conferring certain restricted rights or privileges. *pleyn commissioun:* a warrant or other instrument conferring full authority. ¶ 318–20. "The learned sergeant was clever enough to untie any entail and pass the property as estate in fee simple."—W. H. H. Kelke, *Notes and Queries*, 5 S., vi. 487. ¶ 323. *In termes:* i. e., in the proper language. ¶ 324. *Kyng William:* William the Conqueror, who became king of England in 1066. ¶ 331. *Frankeleyn:* see note on l. 216. ¶ 333. According to mediaeval physiology a person's temperament, or bodily habit ("complexioun"), was determined by the proportion of the four "humors"—blood, phlegm, yellow bile, black bile; one in whom the first predominated had a "sanguine" temperament. ¶ 340. *Seint Julian:* Saint Julian was the patron saint of hospitality and good cheer.

(136) 353. *table dormant:* literally "table sleeping"; the sense is that his table stood always undisturbed, instead of being taken away after each meal as was common. ¶ 355. *sessiouns:* sessions of court. ¶ 363, 364. *lyveree . . . . fraternitee:* the trade guilds were allowed to wear a distinctive dress. ¶ 366. *chaped:* having chapes, or metal caps, at the tip of the sheath. "Tradesmen and mechanics were prohibited from using knives adorned with silver, gold, or precious stones; so that Chaucer's pilgrims were of a superior estate."—Skeat. ¶ 377, 378. "It was the manner in times past, upon festival evens, called *vigiliae*, for parishioners to meet in their church-houses, or church-yards, and there to have a drinking-fit for the time. . . . . Hither came the wives in comely manner; and they which were of the better sort had their mantles carried with them, as well for show as to keep them from cold at table."—Speght. *al bifore:* before all the others. ¶ 381. *poudre-marchant tart:* a tart flavoring powder. *galyngale:* an aromatic root much used in cooking. ¶ 384. *mortreux:* "A kind of soup or pottage, made either of bread and milk or of various kinds of meat."— *A New English Dictionary*. ¶ 387. *blankmanger:* "A dish composed usually of fowl, but also of other meat, minced with cream, rice, almonds, sugar, eggs, etc."—*A New English Dictionary*. ¶ 389. *Dertemouthe:* Dartmouth, in the southwestern extremity of England; then a seaport of some importance. ¶ 390. *as he couthe:* sailors are notoriously bad horsemen.

(137) 397. *Burdeux-ward:* the neighborhood of Bordeaux, the center of the French wine-trade. ¶ 400. The meaning is that he threw his prisoners overboard. ¶ 403. *lodemenage*=pilotage. ¶ 404. *Hulle:* Hull, a thriving seaport on the east coast of England. *Cartage:* Carthage, the famous seaport on the north coast of Africa. ¶ 408. *Gootlond:* Gottland, an island in the Baltic Sea. *cape of Fynystere:* on the northwest coast of Spain. ¶ 414. *astronomye:* i. e., astrology. ¶ 415–18. The sense is, He watched over the welfare of his patient largely by observing the fortunate astrological hours, knowing well how to determine the favorable moment for making images by means of which he could help the sick man. The expression is clearer in Chaucer's *Hous of Fame*, III. 175–80:

> And clerkes eek, which conne wel
> Al this magyke naturel,

That craftely don hir ententes,
To make, in certeyn ascendentes,
Images, lo, through which magyk
To make a man ben hool or syk.

¶ 417. *ascendent*=ascendant; an astrological term, meaning "the point of the ecliptic, or degree of the zodiac, which at any moment . . . . is just rising above the eastern horizon" (*A New English Dictionary*); there was supposed to be an ascendant most favorable for each event or undertaking. ¶ 420. According to mediaeval medicine, founded largely on the teaching of Galen, the health of the body depended upon the proper mixture of these four elements, an excess of any one causing certain diseases. ¶ 429-34. Esculapius was the Greek god of healing. Dioscorides was a Greek medical writer of the first century A.D. "Rufus was a Greek physician . . . . of the age of Trajan; Haly, Serapion, and Avicen were Arabian physicians and astronomers of the eleventh century; Rhasis was a Spanish Arab of the tenth century; and Averroes was a Moorish scholar who flourished in Morocco in the twelfth century. Johannes Damascenus was also an Arab physician, ... probably of the ninth century; Constantinus Afer, a native of Carthage, ... lived at the end of the eleventh century: Bernardus Gordonius, professor of medicine at Montpellier, appears to have been Chaucer's contemporary; John Gatisden was a distinguished physician of Oxford in the earlier half of the fourteenth century; Gilbertyn is supposed by Warton to be the celebrated Gilbertus Anglicus."—Wright. (Gilbertus Anglicus wrote a compendium of medicine, about 1290.) Hippocrates ("Ypocras"), the "Father of Medicine," was a Greek of the fifth century B.C. Galen (130-200? A.D.), the second great name in the history of Greek medicine, was the foremost medical authority in the Middle Ages.

(138) 442. *pestilence:* England was visited by pestilence several times in the fourteenth century, the last time in 1376. ¶ 443. *For*=because. *cordial:* a medicine; it was believed that liquid gold was a remedy for some diseases. ¶ 447, 448. "The West of England, and especially the neighborhood of Bath, ... was celebrated till a comparatively recent period, as the district of cloth-making. Ypres and Ghent were the great clothing-marts on the continent."—Wright. ¶ 450. *offrynge:* the offering of gifts before sacred relics, especially on Relic Sunday. ¶ 465. *Boloigne:* there was a famous shrine of the Virgin Mary in Boulogne. ¶ 466. *Galice:* Galicia, in Spain, where was a shrine of St. James. *Coloigne:* the bones of the three Wise Men of the East were supposed to be preserved at Cologne. ¶ 472, *foot-mantel:* an outer skirt, to keep the gown clean.

(139) 486. *cursen:* "Refusal to pay tithes was punishable with the lesser excommunication."—Bell. ¶ 489. *his offryng:* voluntary contributions to him, in distinction from the compulsory tithes. ¶ 503. *if a preest take keepe:* i. e., if it is the office of every priest to take care of his flock. ¶ 507. The sense is, He did not hire a curate to care for his parish. ¶ 510. *chaunterie:* an endowment for the support of priests to sing mass for the soul of the founder or other specified persons; also the company of priests enjoying the endowment. ¶ 511. *bretherhed:* brotherhood or company of monks; some of the monasteries were very rich and luxurious.

(140) 526. *spiced*=seasoned, over-nice, corrupt; the last is the meaning here. ¶ 548. *ram:* "This was the usual prize at wrestling-matches."—Morris.

(141) 563. *he hadde a thombe of gold:* the phrase originally meant that a miller had a fine sense of touch and could tell accurately the fineness of the meal by rubbing it between his thumb and finger; such a miller could grow rich by his skill, and need not cheat. ¶ 567. *Maunciple:* an officer who bought the provisions for a college or (as here) of an inn-of-court where lawyers lived. *temple:* an inn-of-court; so called from the Temple, in London, once the headquarters of the Knights Templars, and afterward converted into an inn-of-court. ¶ 570. *by taille:* i. e., on credit (French "tailler," to cut; cf. "tally," a score kept by cutting notches in a stick). ¶ 586. *sette hir aller cappe:* over-reached, cheated, them all. ¶ 587. *Reve:* a steward of an estate.

(142) 623. *Somnour:* an officer who summoned persons before the ecclesiastical courts,

(143) 643. *"Watte":* a proper name. ¶ 646. *"Questio quid juris":* one of the law terms that he had picked up; it means, "The question is, what is the law?" ¶ 652. *a fynch eek coude he pulle:* he could also swindle an unsuspecting person; cf. "pluck a pigeon." ¶ 662. *significavit=* "it has been signified"; the first word of a writ issued against an excommunicated person. ¶ 667. *ale-stake:* a pole projecting horizontally from a tavern, on which was often hung a garland.

(144) 685. *vernycle:* "A diminutive of 'Veronike,' (Veronica), a copy in miniature of the picture of Christ, which is supposed to have been miraculously imprinted upon a handkerchief preserved in the church of St. Peter at Rome."—Tyrwhitt. ¶ 692. *Berwik:* in the north of England on the Scottish border. *Ware:* in the south of England. ¶ 695. *Lady=* Lady's. ¶ 710. *offertorie:* "An anthem sung or said in the mass, ... while the offerings of the people are being received."—*A New English Dictionary.*

(145) 741. *Plato seith.* Chaucer's authority is Boethius, *De Consolatione Philosophiae,* Book III, Prose 12: "Sin thou hast lerned by the sentence of Plato that 'nedes the wordes moten be cosines to the thinges of which theys peken.' "—Chaucer's translation. ¶ 754. *Chepe:* Cheapside, a business street in London.

(146) 781. *fader=* father's. ¶ 785. *make it wys:* make it a subject of deliberation. ¶ 791. *shorte with our weye:* shorten our way with. ¶ 799. *oure aller cost:* the cost of us all.

(147) 810. *swore:* understand "we" as subject. ¶ 826. *wateryng of Seint Thomas:* a watering-place about two miles from London, on the Canterbury road.

(148) *The Nonne Preestes Tale.* The tale of one of the priests who accompanied the prioress; see "The Prologue," l. 164, p. 131. It is based upon a fable in verse, "Dou Coc et dou Werpil," by Marie de France (13th century), and upon the metrical romance, *Roman de Renart,* chap. 5. ¶ 12. *sooty:* early cottages often had no chimneys. *bour . . . . halle:* the words strictly mean the private apartments and the large assembly room of a castle or manor; Chaucer playfully uses them here for the two rooms of the "narrow cottage," in one of which slept the widow and her daughters, while the cock and his wives perched in the other (see l. 64).

(149) 35–38. "The cock knew each ascension of the equinoctial, and crew at each; that is, he crew every hour, as 15° of the equinoctial make an hour."—Skeat. *ascencioun:* ascending degree. *equinoxial:* "The celestial equator; so called because, when the sun is on it, the days and nights are of equal length in all parts of the world."—*A New English Dictionary.*

(150) 104. *fume:* "A noxious vapor supposed formerly to rise from the stomach to the brain."—*A New English Dictionary. complecciouns:* see note on "The Prologue," l. 333, p. 351.

(151) 105. *humours:* the fluids of the body, especially blood, phlegm, yellow bile, and black bile; mediaeval physiology made much of them in explaining health and disease; see note just cited. ¶ 108. *rede colera:* red bile; the same as yellow bile, one of the "humors" (see note just cited). ¶ 120. *Caton=* Cato: the supposed author of a work in Latin verse, *De Moribus* ("Of Morals"), very popular in the Middle Ages; it has been attributed to Seneca and to Boethius; the story referred to is in Book ii, Dist. 32. ¶ 123. *as:* an expletive, used to introduce the imperative sentence. ¶ 128. *toun=* enclosure, yard (O. E. "tun"). ¶ 135. See notes on l. 108 and on "The Prologue," l. 333, p. 351. ¶ 139. *terciane:* a tertian fever, so called because it recurs every third day. ¶ 143. *centaure:* centaury, a medicinal plant; so called because its virtues were supposed to have been discovered by Chiron, the centaur.

(152) 148. *fader=* father's. ¶ 156. *thee=* prosper. ¶ 164. *Oon of the gretteste auctours:* Cicero, *De divinatione,* lib. i, cap. 27, and Valerius Maximus, lib. i, cap. 7, sect. 10, both tell the story; Chaucer apparently means the former (cf. note on ll. 244, 245).

(154) 244, 245. Cicero tells this story in the work cited in the note on l. 164, but earlier in the same chapter, not in a later one.

(155) 290. Kenelm became king of Mercia, the midland region of early England, in

819, at the age of seven; he was murdered by an agent of his sister Quendrida, who desired the throne. He dreamt that a fair and noble tree stood before his bed; it reached to the stars, and shone bright with blossoms and fruit; he climbed the tree, and while he stood upon it one of his best friends felled it to the ground, and the young king became a bird and flew to heaven. (See the life of Kenelm, in *Early English Poems*, ed. by F. J. Furnivall, and published with the transactions of the Philological Society, 1858.) ¶ 303. *Macrobeus:* a writer of the fifth century A.D.; he wrote a commentary on Cicero's *Somnium Scipionis* ("Scipio's Dream").

(156) 310. *Joseph:* see Gen., chaps. 37, 40, 41. ¶ 318. *Lyde*=Lydia. ¶ 321–28. The story is told by Dares Phrygius, *De excidio Trojae Historia*, cap. 24. ¶ 343. "*In principio*": the first two words of John's gospel in the Vulgate. ¶ 344. A Latin proverb, meaning "Woman is man's confusion."

(157) 367, 368. The year, Old Style, began on March 25; and it was a belief of the early fathers that the first day of creation was March 18. ¶ 369, 370. One would suppose, at first that Chaucer meant that thirty-two days had passed since the beginning of March, i. e., that it was now April 2; but ll. 374, 375 show that it was May 3, for that is the day on which the sun would have passed the twenty-first degree in the sign Taurus. ¶ 377. *pryme:* apparently here nine A.M., or the end of the first quarter of a day of twelve hours beginning at 6 A.M. ¶ 392. *Launcelot de Lake:* the romance of King Arthur's greatest knight, Sir Launcelot of the Lake.

(158) 402. *undern:* "The time of the mid-day meal."—Skeat. ¶ 407. *Scariot:* Judas Iscariot. *Genylon:* the traitor who caused the defeat of Charlemagne's rear-guard and the death of Roland at Roncesvalles. ¶ 408. *Synon:* the crafty Greek who helped to persuade the Trojans to bring the wooden horse inside the walls; see the *Æneid*, ii. 57–259. ¶ 421 *Augustyn:* St. Augustine, the church father. ¶ 422. *Boece*=Boethius; see note on "The Hous of Fame," l. 153, p. 349. *Bradwardyn:* professor of divinity in Oxford University; he died in 1349.

(159) 451. *Phisiologus:* a mediaeval Latin poem on animals; see p. 56 for a selection from an English translation.

(160) 492. *daun Burnel the Asse:* not an author, but a story in a mediaeval Latin poem. ¶ 496. *lese his benefice:* the cock forbore to crow at the usual time, and the priest awoke too late on the morning when he was to have been ordained. ¶ 509. *Ecclesiaste.* The apocryphal book Ecclesiasticus, 12:16: "And the enemy will speak sweetly with his lips, and in his heart take counsel how to overthrow thee into a pit."

(161) 527–32. Chaucer is slyly ridiculing a poem by Geoffrey de Vinsauf on the death of Richard I. ¶ 543. *Hasdrubales:* Hasdrubal, king of Carthage, and his wife killed themselves when the Romans took Carthage in 146 B.C.

(162) 574. *Jakke Straw:* a leader in Wat Tyler's rebellion, in 1381.

(163) 612. *thee*=prosper. ¶ 621. *Seint Paul seith:* see II Tim. 3:16. ¶ 625. *my lord:* a marginal note in the Ellesmere MS reads, "Scilicet dominus Archiepiscopus Cantuariensis"; the reference, therefore, is doubtless to William Courtenay, who was archbishop of Canterbury at the time the tale was written.

(163) TRUTH. The text of ll. 1–21 is based on the Ellesmere MS; that of the envoy, on Additional MS 10340. ¶ 9. *hyr:* Fortune.

(164) THE COMPLAYNT OF CHAUCER TO HIS PURSE. The text is based on the Fairfax MS. ¶ 4. *but*=unless. ¶ 5. *Me were as leef be:* it were as agreeable to me to be; or, I had as soon be.

(165) 22. *conquerour:* Henry IV, who came to the throne in 1399. *Brutes:* Brut was a legendary early king of Britain. *Albyoun*=Albion; Britain.

THOMAS HOCCLEVE

(165) MI MAISTER CHAUCER. From *The Regement of Princes*, ll. 1961–74, 2079–2107. The text is that of the Early English Text Society edition. ¶ 4. *science*=knowledge.

(166) 20. *Tullius:* Marcus Tullius Cicero.

JOHN LYDGATE

(166) LONDON LYCKPENY. The text is that of the Harleian MS, as edited by W. W. Skeat in his *Specimens of English Literature*. It is doubtful if the poem is really by Lydgate, but it has long been attributed to him. *Lyckpeny:* "Some call London a lick-peny . . . . because of feastings, with other occasions of expence and allurements, which cause so many unthrifts among countrey gentlemen and others, who flock into her in such excessive multitudes."—James Howell's *Londinopolis*, 1657.

(167) 11. *Kynges Bench:* a law court. ¶ 18. *Rychard, Robert, and John:* sample names of country gentlemen who were wasting their substance in lawsuits in London. ¶ 22. *Common Place:* court of Common Pleas. ¶ 23. *sylken hoode:* sergeants-at-law, or pleaders, wore silk hoods. ¶ 29. *Rolles:* the Court of Chancery. ¶ 36. *Westmynster Hall:* here sat Parliament.

(168) 46. *Flemynges:* Flemish tradesmen abounded in London at this time. ¶ 51. *hyghe pryme:* nine A.M.; cf. note on "The Nonne Preestes Tale," l. 377, p.157 . ¶ 57. *London:* i.e., the city proper; Westminster, where he has been hitherto, was outside the walls (cf. the reference to Westminster Gate, l. 50). ¶ 64. *Chepe:* Cheapside, one of the great business streets of London (O. E. "ceap," barter). ¶ 71. *London stone:* an old Roman milestone, from which distances from London were reckoned; it was in Canwick (Candlewick) Street, now Cannon Street, where it may still be seen, built into the wall of St. Swithin's Church; cf. *II Henry VI*, IV. vi.

(169) 83. *Jenken and Julyan:* these subjects of street ballads are obscure; *Julyan* may be St. Julian. ¶ 85. *Cornhyll;* Cornhill, a street. ¶ 99. *Belyngsgate:* Billingsgate, on the north bank of the Thames; now the site of the famous fishmarket. ¶ 106. *Kent:* the county southeast of London.

JAMES I OF SCOTLAND

(170) THE KINGIS QUAIR. Stanzas 30–67. The text is that of the Scottish Text Society edition, which is based on the unique MS of the poem in the Bodleian Library. The poem describes the love of the royal poet for Lady Jane Beaufort, whom he first saw walking in the garden while he was imprisoned in Windsor Castle, and whom he finally married. ¶ 27. *of:* Skeat's conjecture for "on" of the MS. *next:* i. e., which comes next, follows. ¶ 30. *Kalendis:* the Calends were the first day of any month in the Roman calendar, and hence the term came to be used as a general measure of time.

(173) 124. *round crokettis:* Skeat's conjecture for "floure-jonettis" of the MS.

(174) 168. *were him:* were it for him. ¶ 177. *Proigne*=Procne. She was the wife of Tereus, king of Thrace, who pretended that Procne was dead and married her sister Philomela; when the latter discovered the truth, Tereus cut out her tongue, but she wove the story of her wrongs into a robe and sent the robe to Procne; the sisters then took revenge upon the king by serving up his son to him at table; the gods finally changed them all into birds, Philomela into a nightingale.

(176) 241. *a*=one. *wele is us begone:* well has it happened to us.

ROBERT HENRYSON

(177) THE TESTAMENT OF CRESSEID. Stanzas 45–59, 66–86. The text is that of the Scottish Text Society edition which follows the Charteris edition of 1593. Cressida, a beautiful widow of Troy, daughter of the priest Calchas (who had left the city and gone over to the Greeks because he foreknew the fall of Troy), became the mistress of Troilus, a son of King Priam; she forsook him for the Greek hero Diomede, and afterward sank lower and lower; becoming resentful against Venus and Cupid, she was doomed by the gods to be changed into a leper, and the events narrated in the selection then follow. Henryson's poem is a continuation of Chaucer's *Troilus and Criseyda*, which ends with Cressida's faithlessness to Troilus.

(180) 118. *live:* Skeat's emendation; the MS has "leir."

(182) 190. *self*=same.

(183) 225. *Diane*=Diana.

(184) 245. *Troyis*=Troy's.

WILLIAM DUNBAR

(184) The text is that of the Scottish Text Society edition, except that the few suggested emendations have been incorporated.

(184) SANCT SALVATOUR, SEND SILVER SORROW. 1. *Sanct Salvatour:* St. Salvator. *send silver sorrow:* send sorrow to silver.

(185) 33. *my Lord:* the Scottish king

(185) THE GOLDYN TARGE. Stanzas 1, 2, 6, 7, 12, 13, 16-18, 21-29, ¶ 2. *Lucyne=* Lucina, the moon.

(186) 20. *rycht:* to be taken with "by." *ran:* understand "which" as subject. ¶ 21. *Fflorais*= Flora's. ¶ 44. *quene:* Nature, who is one of the ladies. ¶ 48. *Wenus*=Venus. ¶ 52. *splene:* the spleen was regarded as the seat of the affections.

(189) THE DANCE OF THE SEVIN DEIDLY SYNNIS. The deadly sins are those which, if unrepented of in this life, condemn the soul to eternal death in hell; they are thus distinguished from venial sins, which may be atoned for in purgatory.

(190) 6. *Mahoun:* the Devil. The word is a corruption of "Mahommed"; in the Middle Ages it was believed that Mahommed was worshiped as a god, and hence his name came to be used for any false god and even for the Devil. ¶ 8. *Fasternis evin:* the evening of Shrove Tuesday, the day before the beginning of the fast of Lent; it was often given to merry-making. ¶ 30. *Blak Belly and Bawsy Brown:* popular names of imps.

(191) 74. *Belliall*=Belial; he was an indolent devil (cf. *Paradise Lost*, II. 108-17).

(192) 109. *Heleand*=Highland. Dunbar, as a Lowlander, loved to satirize the Highlanders. ¶ 110. *Makfadzane*=Macfadyen; a Highland contemporary. ¶ 113. *Erschemen*= Ersemen; Highlanders, who spoke Erse, or Gaelic, the original language of the Scotch.

GAWIN DOUGLAS

(193) THE PROLOUG OF THE XII BUK OF ENEADOS. Lines 21-80. The text is that of W. W. Skeat in his *Specimens of English Literature*, from a MS in Trinity College, Cambridge. ¶ 5. *Eous:* one of the horses of the sun; cf. Greek ἠώς, dawn. ¶ 10. *Pheton* =Phaeton; he was the son of Apollo, and presumptuously essayed to drive the chariot of the sun-god. ¶ 15. *Phebus*=Phoebus.

(194) 45-47. *enbroud . . . . obumbrat . . . . porturat:* the copulatives "is" and "are" should be understood.

SIR DAVID LYNDSAY

(194) THE DREME. The text is that of D. Laing's edition of Lyndsay, which is based on the earliest editions. ¶ 1. *Calendis:* the first day of the month. ¶ 2, 3. The meaning is that the sun, in its apparent annual motion through the zodiac, had left the sign Capricorn and entered upon the sign Aquarius.

(195) 13. *Tytane:* Titan, the sun. Hyperion, god of the sun, was one of the Titans in the early Greek mythology.

STEPHEN HAWES

(197) THE PASTIME OF PLEASURE. Cap. xxxviii; cap. xlii, stanzas 1, 10-12. The text, by the courtesy of Professor A. K. Potter, is from his rotographs of the Earl of Dysart's unique copy of the 1509 edition.

(197) *How Graunde Amoure Was Receyved of La Belle Pucell.* Graunde Amoure,

after long discipline and encounters with many foes, reaches the "solemn mansion" of his lady love; at this point the selection begins.

(198) 45. *knottes:* carvings of intricate design. ¶ 51. *geometry:* i. e., geometrical design. ¶ 53. *mysty:* Hawes seems to have conceived of the odors as mists or exhalations.

(199) 63. *tynst:* probably a misprint for "tinct." ¶ 80. The sense seems to be, And changed my mood to a complacent one.

JOHN SKELTON

(201) WHY COME YE NAT TO COURT. Lines 396–491. The text is that of A. Dyce's edition of Skelton, which is based on the earliest editions. The selection attacks Cardinal Wolsey, then at the height of his power. ¶ 6. *Hampton Court:* the palatial residence of Wolsey. ¶ 12. *Yorkes Place:* the residence of Wolsey as archbishop of York. ¶ 18. *lawe canon:* the law of the ecclesiastical courts.

(202) 27. *Flete:* Fleet Prison, in Fleet Street. ¶ 31. *Towre:* the Tower of London, a state prison. ¶ 32. *Sauns aulter remedy*="without other remedy"; i. e., without means of avoiding imprisonment. ¶ 34. *Marshalsy:* the Marshalsea, both a prison and a law court; here the reference is to the court, where the prisoner from the Tower will be tried. ¶ 35. *Kynges Benche:* a law court. ¶ 54. *bereth .... on hand:* "Leads on to a belief, persuades."—Dyce.

(203) 72–76. See Gen., chap. 19. ¶ 77, 79. The quotation is from the Litany: "From blindness of heart deliver us, Lord!" ¶ 80. *Amalecke*=Amalekite; see I Sam., chap. 15. ¶ 81. *Mamelek*=Mameluke. The Mamelukes were mercenary soldiers in the employ of the Turks. ¶ 96. *bochers stall:* Wolsey was the son of a butcher.

BALLADS

(203) ST. STEPHEN AND HEROD. In a MS of about 1450; the ballad may itself be of the thirteenth century.

(204) 4. *Bedlem*=Bethlehem. ¶ 20. *Cristus natus est*—"Christ is born." ¶ 24. St. Stephen's Day is December 26, and the eve of it is therefore Christmas Day.

(204) A GEST OF ROBYN HODE. The whole ballad, which "may have been put together as early as 1400 or before" (Professor Child), combines several different adventures of Robin Hood and is doubtless based upon still older ballads. The earliest known reference to the Robin Hood ballads is in Langland's *Piers the Plowman* (the version of 1377) V. 400, 401, where Sloth says,

> I can noughte perfitly my Pater-noster, as the prest it syngeth,
> But I can rymes of Robyn Hood and Randolf, Erle of Chestre.

The two "fits," or parts, here printed were first published by Wynkyn de Worde, London, between 1492 and 1534. Robin Hood was not a historical character, but a popular idealization of an outlaw.

(204) *The vii. Fytte.* 1. *Notynghame*=Nottingham; it is near Sherwood Forest, the favorite haunt of Robin Hood. ¶ 3. *that gentyll knight:* Sir Richard at the Lee (cf. l. 28); he and Robin had befriended each other in extremities, and Robin had recently killed the sheriff in order to release the knight, imprisoned in his own castle.

(205) 42. *best ball in his hode:* a humorous expression for the head.

(208) 148. *Austyn:* Augustine.

(209) 177. Apparently the garland was hung on each wand as a target.

(211) 253. *But*=unless. *lyke*=please.

(211) *The viii. Fytte.*

(212) 17. *Lyncolne grene:* the best green cloth was formerly made in the town of Lincoln. It is supposed that foresters adopted this color in order that they might not be easily seen by the deer.

(213) 44. *lefte*=would leave. ¶ 50. *agayne:* supply "come"; some versions read "to come" instead of "agayne."

(214) 89. *Bernysdale*=Barnsdale; a woodland region in Yorkshire, another haunt of Robin Hood.

(216) THE HUNTING OF THE CHEVIOT. In the Ashmole MS, 1550 or later; the ballad was composed much earlier, as the language shows. It seems to have been founded upon an actual occurrence, the Battle of Otterburn (1388), although it does not give the facts so accurately as the ballad of that title. ¶ 1. *Persè:* Earl Percy, the famous Henry Hotspur, so called; he was warden of the marches, or border, between England and Scotland; he was not really killed until fifteen years later, at the battle of Shrewsbury (1403). *Northombarlonde:* an English county bordering on Scotland. ¶ 4. *Chyviat*=Cheviot. The Cheviot Hills are partly on the Scottish side of the border. ¶ 5. *Dogles*=Douglas; James Douglas, the second earl, who was killed at Otterburn by Percy. ¶ 11. *Banborowe*=Banborough.

(217) 49. *Twyde*=Tweed; a river forming a part of the boundary between England and Scotland. ¶ 50. *Tividale*=Teviotdale; the valley of the Teviot, which flows into the Tweed.

(218) 80. *do:* understand "let us" before it. ¶ 91. *Sothe-Ynglonde*=South England.

(220) 166. *Monggombyrry*=Montgomery. ¶ 168. Skeat reads, "a spear a trusti tre" ="a spear of trusty wood."

(221) 186. *stele:* i. e., the steel head. ¶ 188. *sat*=set. ¶ 201. Child suggests that the missing word in the MS is "rest"; Gummere, that the reading should be "The tocke them off," i. e., they retreated.

(222) 216. *Hearone*=Heron. ¶ 217. *Loumlè*=Lumley. ¶ 219. *Raff*=Ralph. ¶ 221. *Wetharryngton*=Witherington. ¶ 227. *Lwdale:* in later versions, "Lambwell." ¶ 229. *Murrè*=Murray.

(223) 241. *Eddenburrowe*=Edinburgh. ¶ 245. *weal and wryng:* Skeat suggests "wryng, and weal"="wring, and wail." ¶ 262. *Hombyll-down*=Homildon; here the English won a victory over the Scotch, in 1402, but it could not have been fought to avenge the death of Percy, for he took part in it and died a year later. ¶ 265. *Glendale:* the district in which Homildon is. ¶ 268. The line has not been satisfactorily explained. Skeat says, "This is said to be a proverb, meaning 'That tear, or pull, brought about this kick.'" Child suggests that the meaning is, "Alas, that e'er began this spurn," or that "possibly 'that tear' is for 'that there,' meaning simply 'there.'"

(224) JOHNIE COCK. In the Percy Papers, communicated by a Scotch lady in 1780. The ballad is certainly early in its origin, as appears from internal evidence.

(225) 33. *three quarters:* i. e., of a yard.

(226) 82, 86. *boy:* Child says this is evidently a corruption for "bird," which occurs in some versions.

(226) JOCK O THE SIDE. In the Percy MS, about 1650. There was a Jock (or John) of the Side, a marauder of the Scotch border, in the time of Mary Queen of Scots. ¶ 9. There is a line missing here in the MS.

(227) 28. *Tyvidale*=Teviotdale; the valley of the river Teviot, in southern Scotland.

(231) SIR PATRICK SPENS. In Percy's *Reliques*, 1765; based on MSS sent him from Scotland. The ballad may be founded on the historical incident that in 1281 many Scotch nobles were drowned on the return voyage from Norway, whither they had gone as escort to the daughter of their king, bride of the king of Norway. ¶ 1. *Dumferling*=Dunfermline; a town near Edinburgh, formerly containing a royal palace. ¶ 9. *braid letter:* a letter on a broad sheet.

(232) 32. The line means that they were over head in water. ¶ 41. *Aberdour:* a seaport near Dunfermline.

(232) SIR HUGH, OR THE JEW'S DAUGHTER. In Jamieson's *Popular Ballads*, 1806. The ballad is an old one, and is founded upon an incident reported to have occurred in the town of Lincoln in 1255.

(234) THE THREE RAVENS. In Ravenscroft's *Melismata*, 1611.

(235) EDWARD. In Percy's *Reliques*, 1765; communicated to him by a Scotch nob'e-man.

(237) THE TWA SISTERS. This version was made by Child from versions in several MSS (1783–1801) and Jamieson's *Popular Ballads*, 1806. ¶ 2, 4. *Edinburgh . . . . Stirling:* the sisters were royal princesses (see l. 57), and apparently for this reason the refrain mentions Edinburgh, the capital, and Stirling, formerly a favorite residence of the Scottish kings. ¶ 7. *Saint Johnston:* apparently the residence of the knight. *Tay:* a Scottish river, somewhat to the north of Stirling. ¶ 21. *sea stran:* cf. "mill-dam," l. 37; such naïve inconsistencies are characteristic of the old ballads.

(239) THE CRUEL BROTHER. In Kinloch's MSS; this ballad was communicated to him in 1827. ¶ 32. There are a few words missing here in the MS.

(240) BABYLON, OR THE BONNIE BANKS O FORDIE. In Motherwell's *Minstrelsy*, 1827.

(242)- SWEET WILLIAM'S GHOST. In Ramsay's *Tea-Table Miscellany*, 1740. ¶ 56–64. "These are clearly modern, but very likely represent original stanzas not remembered in form."—Sargent and Kittredge.

(243) LORD THOMAS AND FAIR ANNET. In Percy's *Reliques*, 1765; this ballad was sent him in MS from Scotland. An English version was printed in the latter part of the seventeenth century.

(245) 59. *holland:* linen; so called because the finest was then made in Holland.

(247) KEMP OWYNE. In Motherwell's *Minstrelsy*, 1827.

(249) THOMAS RYMER. In Tytler's Brown MS, sent him by a Mrs. Brown in 1800. The ballad is an old one, and is probably based on a poem, "Thomas of Erceldoune," of the fifteenth century. Thomas was an actual personage, of the thirteenth century; he was credited with prophetic powers, the gift of the queen of the elves, who had carried him off to elfland. ¶ 1. *True:* i. e., truthful in his prophecies. ¶ 16. There is a gap here in the MS.

(251) THE WEE, WEE MAN. In Herd's MSS, 1776. ¶ 11. *Wallace:* i. e., very strong; William Wallace (1274?–1305), the hero of Scotch history and romance, was of prodigious strength.

(252) MARY HAMILTON. In Sharpe's *Ballad Book*, 1824. "The ballad must . . . . have arisen between 1719 and 1764" (Child); it seems to be based on incidents connected with the court of Mary Queen of Scots and of Peter the Great of Russia. ¶ 3. *Marie Hamilton:* one of the ladies-in-waiting of Queen Mary. ¶ 4. *Stewart:* the Scotch king. ¶ 13. *auld Queen:* Queen Mary. ¶ 29. *Cannogate:* a main street of old Edinburgh; Holyrood Palace is at the lower end, and the Parliament House at the upper end.

(254) BONNIE GEORGE CAMPBELL. In Motherwell's *Minstrelsy*, 1827; a combination of several versions. ¶ 2. *Tay:* a river in Scotland, near the Highlands.

MIRACLE PLAYS

(254) THE DELUGE. From the Chester Plays. The text is that of the Early English Text Society edition. The MS on which this edition is based is dated 1607, and the earliest extant MS is only sixteen years earlier; the language, too, is comparatively modern; but the MSS "appear to be based on a text of the beginning of the fifteenth century," and "the composition of the cycle probably dates from some fifty or sixty years earlier"(Pollard). ¶ 5–8. Cf. Gen. 6:3.

(255) 8. *blynne*=cease, i. e., from sin. ¶ 17. *Noe*=Noah.

(256) 53. *Sem*=Shem. ¶ 65. *Uxor Noe*="wife of Noah." ¶ 80. Stage direction following this line: "Then they shall make motions as if they were working with various tools."

(257) 93. *topcastle:* a protected place at the masthead, from which missiles were thrown. ¶ 96. Stage direction following this line: "Then Noah and his whole family shall again make motions of working with various tools." ¶ 103. *By Christ:* such anachronisms as

this and the one in l. 112 are not uncommon in the miracle and morality plays. ¶ 108. *yow:* the spectators.

(259) 160. Stage direction following this line: "Then Noah shall enter the ark, and his family shall give him all the animals, represented by pictures, reciting their names; and after each one has spoken his part he shall go into the ark, Noah's wife excepted; and the pictures of the animals ought to coincide with their names; and the first son shall begin thus."

(261) 240. Stage direction following this line: "Then she shall go." ¶ 242. *that:* see the stage direction that follows: "And gives him a lively slap?" ¶ 250. *That=*he who.

(262) 256. Stage direction following this line: "Then Noah shall shut the window of the ark; and for a moderate space of time let them sing, within, the psalm 'Save me, O God'; and [then], opening the window and looking out, [Noah shall say]." ¶ 264. Stage direction following this line: "Then shall he send forth a raven, and, taking a dove in his hands, let him say." ¶ 271. Stage direction following this line: "Then he shall send out a dove, and there shall be in the ship another dove bearing an olive branch in her mouth, which [someone] shall send from the mast along a cord into the hands of Noah; and then let Noah say."

(263) 303. Stage direction following this line: "Then, going out of the ark with his whole family, he shall take the animals and birds, and shall offer them up and slay them."

(265) ABRAHAM'S SACRIFICE. From the Coventry Plays. The text is that of the old Shakespeare Society edition. Most of the MS of the Coventry Plays was written in 1468, and the cycle was probably composed early in the same century. ¶ *Introitus Abrahe, etc.=* "Enter Abraham and the others." ¶ 15. *wolde:* apparently an error for "molde," earth.

(266) 37. *par amoure=*"by love."

(267) 73. *Angelus=*"angel."

MORALITY PLAYS

(272) EVERYMAN. Except for a few emendations, the text is that of the Britwell Library copy of Skot's edition (published about 1529), as edited by Greg in *Materialen zur Kunde des älteren englischen Dramas.* The play is probably based on a Dutch original; the English version dates from the latter part of the fifteenth century. ¶ 3. *By fygure=*in form.

(273) 31. *two:* i. e., the two thieves at the Crucifixion.

(275) 111. *ado=*to do; literally, "at do." ¶ 112. *make none attournay:* have no deputy, or substitute.

(278) 245. *Adonay:* God (plural of Hebrew "Adon," lord).

(280) 290. *brynge me forwarde=*accompany me.

(281) 356. *Our Lady:* the Virgin Mary.

(284) 454. *Mary:* a mild oath by the Virgin; the same as "marry" in Shakspere.

(285) 494. *Myssyas=*Messiah. ¶ 495. *do by me=*act according to my advice. ¶ 500. *of=*for.

(286) 526. *by=*be. *Creature=*Creator.

(288) 601. *be meane=*by means.

(289) 663. *Fyve Wyttes:* the five senses.

(292) 788. *Judas Machabee=*Judas Maccabeus; the heroic leader of the Jews in their struggle against the Romans in the second century B.C. (see the book of the Maccabees in the Old Testament Apocrypha).

(293) 796. *more and lesse:* high and low, i. e., all people.

(295) 887, 888. *In manus Tuas . . . . commendo spiritum meum=*"Into Thy hands I commend my spirit"; see Luke 23:46. ¶ 904. *take it of worth=*value it.

(296) 916. "*Ite, maledicti, in ignem eternum*"="Go, ye cursed, into everlasting fire"; cf. Matt. 25:41.

(296) THE MARIAGE OF WITT AND WISDOME. The text is that of the old Shakespeare Society edition (from a unique MS), considerably emended. The play cannot be dated at

all precisely, but seems to belong to the age of Elizabeth. The first, fifth, and tenth scenes are here given entire; two short passages in the second scene are omitted, and 46 lines at the end of the eighth scene. *Witt*=mind, intelligence.

(300) *The Second Scene.* ¶ 37. *counterfait cranke:* "A rogue who feigned sickness in order to move compassion and get money."—*A New English Dictionary.* "Cranke" is thieves' slang; cf. German "krank," sick.

(301) 50. *in for a berd:* deluded, trapped.

(302) 90. *Mary:* the name of the Virgin, used as an exclamation or mild oath. ¶ 110. *sir:* one in the audience.

(310) *The Tenth Scene.*

(312) 55. *turtle:* the turtle-dove.

JOHN HEYWOOD

(312) THE FOURE PP. The basis of the text is a black-letter edition in the Bodleian Library, Oxford University. The edition is undated; but it was printed at London by William Copland, who was in the publishing business from 1547 to 1569. It has some of the readings of the edition of 1569, but on the whole is closer to the so-called first edition of 1545(?). Some of the readings of these last two editions, and some of Professor Manly's emendations, have been adopted in the present edition; in some other cases Manly's conjectures are confirmed by the Copland text. ¶ 1. The punctuati ⌐, which makes better sense than the traditional punctuation of the line, is Professor Manly's. ¶ 2. *you:* the audience; the palmer is alone on the stage. ¶ 17. *Josaphat:* the vale of Jehosaphat, outside the walls of Jerusalem; here stood a church to St. Stephen, the first martyr (see Acts, chaps. 6, 7). *Olyvete:* Mount Olivet.

(313) 22. *stacions:* "A station may be defined as the appointed visitation of some church, altar, shrine, or other the like ecclesiastical locale, for pious purposes and with certain spiritual graces annexed."—W. M. Rossetti. ¶ 29. *Roodes:* the islands of Rhodes in the Mediterranean; in the fourteenth century it was the headquarters of the Knights of St. John. ¶ 30. *Amias:* perhaps for Emmaus, near Jerusalem; see Luke 24:13. ¶ 31, 32. Shrines in Great Britain. ¶ 33. *Armony:* Armenia. Cf. Maundevile's *Voiage and Travaile* (1371), chap. 13: "And so passe men be this Ermonie, and entren the see of Persie. . . . . And there besyde is another Hille, that men clepen Ararathe [=Ararat], ... where Noes Schipp rested, and yit is upon that Montayne; and men may seen it a ferr in cleer Wedre; and that montayne is wel a 7 Myle highe." ¶ 34–43. British shrines, with the exceptions noted. 37. *Corneles:* a Roman saint, beheaded in 250 A.D., for refusing to sacrifice in the temple of Mars. *Gales:* Galicia, in Spain. ¶ 40. *Saynt Patrikes Purgatory:* a smoking pit in a wild region of Ireland. ¶ 41. *bloud of Hayles:* blood with miraculous powers, kept in a crystal vessel at the abbey of Hales, in Gloucestershire. ¶ 43. *Denis:* patron saint of France; his body was supposed to be enshrined in the Abbey of St. Denis, at Paris. ¶ 45–48. British shrines again. ¶ 45. *Shorne:* nothing is known of this saint; he certainly was not at Canterbury, where it was the shrine of Thomas à Becket that drew the pilgrims. (The punctuation of the line is Professor Manly's.) ¶ 46. *Katewade:* "Catwade Bridge is in Samford Hundred, in the country of Suffolk, where there may have been a famous chapel and rood."—Gilchrist. ¶ 49. *Rycharde:* perhaps the same Saint Richard that Drayton speaks of (*Poly-Olbion*, Song xxiv) as having died at Lucca, Italy, where his relics wrought many miracles. *Roke:* St. Roch; there was a church in his honor in Lombardy.

(314) 64. The pardoner evidently has entered while the palmer was speaking the last few lines.

(316) 140. *as good chepe:* in as good market, i. e., as cheaply. "Chepe," or " cheap"= market, buying and selling place (O. E. "ceap"). ¶ 144. *There*=where. *od*=at variance. ¶ 151. The poticary evidently has entered in time to hear the preceding sentence or two. ¶ 165. *toke an action:* equivalent to the modern legal phrase "bring an action"; cf. "rob," l. 166. ¶ 171. *honestli:* the reading of the Copland edition, confirming the conjecture of

Dodsley and other editors. ¶ 176. *glyster*=clyster, an injection; as given in early times it often did more harm than good.

(317) 182. *bande:* i. e., rope. ¶ 188. *from*=out of. ¶ 203. The pedler evidently has entered as the preceding line was being spoken.

(318) 227. *me*=my.

(319) 305. *swiming:* 1569 ed., "swynking.

(320) 342. *wide:* i. e., wide of the truth. ¶ 347. *pretence:* i. e., the claim of the palmer. ¶ 351. The punctuation, which puts sense into an obscure line, is Professor Manly's The meaning is that by the pardons of the pardoner (who will wager his soul on the result) a man may go to heaven easily, sitting in his chair as it were; cf. l. 347.

(321) 377. *clere*=clearly. ¶ 386. *proctours:* proctors, in English colleges, are disciplinary officers, not teachers. ¶ 387. *doctours:* the word is used in its original sense of "teachers" (Latin "docere," to teach). ¶ 398. *debyte:* a corruption of "depute," deputy. ¶ 401. *Your:* i. e., the pardoner's.

(322) 404. *prime:* 9 A.M. ¶ 418, 419. All the early editions assign these lines to the poticary; Dodsley made the correction. ¶ 427. *decayeth:* Manly's emendation; the early editions have "decayed." ¶ 432. *maner thynge:* manner of thing.

(323) 454. *beholde:* 1545 ed., "be bolde." ¶ 455. *be:* 1569 ed., "lie." ¶ 456. *ye:* the pardoner. ¶ 458. *you:* the poticary.

(324) 480. *manner:* i. e., manner of. ¶ 497. *All-Halowes*="all saints"; the ignorant pardoner takes the words to be the name of some particular saint.

(325) 526. *Seven Slepers:* the Seven Sleepers, according to legend, lived at Ephesus in the third century; on account of persecution for their Christian faith they fled to a cave, where they slept for some two or three centuries; upon awaking, they told of the miracle and died. ¶ 557. *Whiche on:* i. e., in which.

(326) 564. *mary:* a mild oath, from the name of the Virgin Mary; the same as the oath or exclamation "marry." ¶ 589. *on*=in. ¶ 590. *in*=to. *I passe you an ace:* i. e., I overplay you, my medicine having higher value than your pardons. ¶ 594. *hollydam:* the Virgin Mary. The correct form is "halidam," meaning "holiness," "sacred relic," etc., but popular etymology explained the word as "holy dame."

(327) 637. The early editions have "one" after "in"; the emendation is Professor Manly's.

(328) 656. The early editions give this line to the pedler, but ll. 670–74 show it is spoken by the palmer. Professor Manly made the correction. ¶ 679. *God:* i. e., Christ. ¶ 680. *you twayne:* the pardoner and the palmer.

(329) 682. *us twayne:* the pardoner and the poticary. ¶ 684. *ye:* inserted by Professor Manly. ¶ 703. In the following omitted passage the poticary tells a coarse tale of a wonderful cure which he wrought.

(330) 793. *out of hande:* at once. ¶ 799. *geare:* his pardons and relics. ¶ 813, 814. It was a popular superstition that to sneeze was a bad omen, which could be averted in the way illustrated in the text.

(331) 831, 832. The allusion is to the cycle of miracle plays given at Coventry every year, on Corpus Christi Day, the Thursday after Trinity Sunday. ¶ 835. *me*=my.

(332) 892. *in presens:* i. e., into the presence of the Devil; "in presence" is the regular court phrase for an audience with a monarch.

(334) 999. A line has evidently dropped out, as the rhyme shows; it is missing in all the editions. ¶ 1000. *taried:* the reading of the 1569 ed.; 1545 and Copland eds., "maried."

(335) 1014. *Poules Churche Yard:* an inclosure near St. Paul's Cathedral, London, a center for the book trade. ¶ 1032. *ten bones:* fingers. ¶ 1041. *prevy tythe:* an insinuation that the pedler has been bribed by the palmer. ¶ 1044. *Thy wyves x commandementes:* " 'Ten commandments' seem to have been cant terms for the nails of the hands."—Dodsley.

(338) 1144. *ye:* the palmer. ¶ 1149. *ye:* the pardoner. ¶ 1165. *say the sarvyes apoynted:* 1545 ed., "praye for soule departed.

(339) 1185. *hym*=himself.

GLOSSARY

GLOSSARY

NOTE.—Words spelled with either "i" or "y" are not always given in both forms. Words having the following peculiarities of form are usually not explained:

(1) Plurals in "is" or "ys," instead of "s" or "es."
(2) Present participles in "and" or "ande," instead of "ing.'
(3) Preterites and past participles in "it," instead of "ed.'
(4) Past participles indicated by the prefix "i" or "y"—as "ido," "idon," for "done"; "i-beo," "y-be," for "been"; "y-bore," for "borne.

A

A, have.
A, in, on, of
A', all.
Abaisit, abashed.
Abate, overthrow, surprise.
Abhomynable, abominable.
Abilgheit, appareled.
Abiten, bite.
Able, suitable, seemly; adapt, make ready, empower.
Abod, abode, waited
A-bof, abuf, abuven, above.
Abon, abone, aboone, above.
Abrayde, abreyde, awake, awoke.
Abrode, abroad.
Abusyoun, misuse, deceit, wrong.
Abute, abuten, about.
Abyde, tarry
Ac, but.
Accomber, encumber, overwhelm.
Achate, buying; *achatour*, caterer, buyer
Achieve, succeed
Acolen, embrace.
Acord, agreement; *acorde*, agree, beseem; *acordaunt*, in accordance with.
Acorse, curse.
Acquerne, squirrel (fur).
Acqueynce, acquaintance.
Acquite, pay.
Adai, aday, by day.
Adaunt, daunt.
Added, a-dead, dead.
Adihte, order.
Adoun, a-downe, down, adown.
Adrad, afraid; *adrede*, dread, fear
Adubmente, adubbement, adornment
Adunest, dinnest.
Advysement, consideration, deliberation.

Adyte, prepare, ordain, dispose.
Ae, one.
Aengles, angels.
Aferd, afraid.
Aff, off.
Affeir, conduct, demeanor.
Affile, file, polish.
Affray, fear, fright; affright.
Affyaunce, trust.
After, afterward; behind, along, according to.
Aganis, against, in preparation for
Agaste, make aghast, frighten.
Agayne, ageyn, agens, against.
Agen, ageyn, again.
Aghlegh, fearless.
Aghlich, fearful, dreadful.
Aglyghte, slipped from.
Ago, agon, gone.
Agu, ague.
Agult, been guilty, sinned.
Ain, own.
Aither, either.
Al, all; wholly.
Al, although.
Al, awl.
Alace, allace, alas.
Alane, alone.
A-lawe, below, down.
Al be, albeit, although.
Alderbest, best of all.
Algate, always, in any case, assuredly.
Alichtyn, light.
Alkin, allkin, of all kinds, every sort of.
All, altogether, wholly.
Alle, all.
Almaist, almost.
Almous, almoyse, alms, pittance.
Alre, of all; *alre-worste*, worst of all

Als, al so, also.
Als, alse, also, al-so, as like, so.
Alterait, altered.
Altherfirst, first of all, at first.
Althyng, all things.
Al-to, all too.
Alyght, alighted.
Amaille, enamel.
Amblere, ambler, easy-paced horse.
Amene, ameyn, mild, pleasant.
Among, amonge, at intervals; all the while.
Amorettis, love-knots.
A-morwe, on the morrow.
Amoure, love.
Amys, amiss.
An, a, an, one.
An, in, on, at; *an nyght*, by night.
An, and.
Anamalit, anamayld, enameled; *anamalyng*, enameling.
Ance, once.
Ancres, anchorites.
And, an.
And, if.
Ane, a, one.
Aneuch, enough
Anhanged, hanged.
Aniht, anight, by night.
Anis, once.
Anker, anchor.
Anlas, dagger.
Anone, anoon, anon, at once; *anon-right. anoon-ryght*, straightway, immediately
Anoynt, anointed.
Ant and.
Anunder, under.
Anwolde, power.
Apayede, satisfied, pleased.
Apert, openly, manifestly.
Apiked, trimmed.
Apon, upon.
Aport, deportment.
Appayreth, grows worse.
Appose, question (oppose with a question).
Appreve, approve.
Aqwhyte, acquit, pay.
Ar, ere.
Aras, arras, tapestries.
Archar, archer *archares, archearis, archeris* archers
Archery, archers in a body.
Are, ere, before.
Areir, behind, in the past.

Areste, areest, arrest, stop.
Arghe, timid, afraid; become timid.
Aright, exactly, just, wholly.
Arme, poor.
Armonye, harmony.
Armypotent, powerful in arms
Arn, are.
Aros, arose
Aros, arros, arrows; *arow*, arrow.
A-roume, at a distance.
Arrerage, arrears.
Arsounz, saddle-bows
Artilye, artillery.
Artow, art thou.
Arwes, arrows.
As, as if; according to; in order to.
Asay, essay, try.
Ase, as.
Asent, assent, concord.
Aspille, spill, ruin.
Aspyit, espied.
Assay, trial, experiment; *assayit*, essayed, tried, attacked.
Assente, agree to.
Assined, assigned.
Assoilen, absolve; *assoillyng*, absolution.
Ast, hast.
Astert, escape, start, start aside.
Astonied, astonished.
Astored, stored.
Asure, azure.
A-sweved, dazed (as if asleep).
Asyse, form, fashion.
Ate, at the.
At-flith, flieth away.
Athel, noble.
At-holde, retain.
Atled, aimed, designed.
Atones, at once.
Atount, astonished
Atour, over.
At-schet, shot away.
Attempre, temperate.
Attournay, attorney, deputy.
Auctoritee, authority.
Auctour, author.
Auful, awful, inspiring awe.
Auhte, ought.
Auld, old.
Aumayl, enamel.
Auncian, ancient, old.
Aureat, golden
Austeir, austere, cruel.

Auther, either.

Avance, avaunce, advance.

Avaunt, boast; *avauntynge,* boasting; *avauntour,* boaster.

Avayle, sink.

Aventure, adventure, happening, luck.

Avisioun, vision.

Avowe, vow.

Avoy, fie!

Avys, avyse, advice, consideration.

Aw, all.

Awa, away.

Await, ambush.

Awe, ewe.

Awei, a-wey, away.

Awen, own.

A-whaped, amazed, stupefied with fear.

A-wharf, whirled round.

Awoik, awoke.

A-wreke, avenged.

Awyn, own.

Axe, ask; *axt,* asked; *axinge,* asking.

Axis, accession of sickness, pain

Ayein, again.

Ayen, ayenst, against.

Ayerishe, aerial.

B

Ba, ball.

Babewynnes, grotesque architectural ornamentations.

Bable, bauble.

Bacheler, a novice in arms, a young knight.

Bagit horss, stallion.

Baid, abode.

Baill, bale, woe.

Bair, bare.

Bait, feed.

Baith, boith, both.

Bakbyttaris, backbiters.

Bake, prepare, make ready; baked.

Balas, a kind of ruby.

Baldly, boldly.

Bale, sorrow; *balfull,* baleful, destructive.

Balgh, round, smooth.

Balke, ridge of ground.

Balled, bald.

Ballet, ballad; *ballattis, ballettis,* ballads, songs.

Balys, troubles, evils.

Bandis, bindings, ties.

Bane, bone.

Bane, death.

Baneist, banyst, banished.

Baner, banner.

Banis, murderers.

Bar, bare.

Barbe, axe-edge.

Bare, thoroughly, completely.

Baren, bore, conducted.

Baret, strife.

Barganeris, wranglers.

Barlay, by Our Lady.

Barm, bosom.

Barmkyn, rampart.

Barne, bairn, child.

Barnth, burneth.

Barres, bars, stripes.

Basnetes, basnites, basinets, helmets.

Basse, lower.

Bataille, battle; *batailled,* having indentations like a battlement.

Bathe, both.

Baundoun, dominion, control.

Bawdrik, baldric, belt.

Bawe, bow.

Baxsteres, bakers (female).

Bayly, baily, district.

Bayne, prompt.

Baysment, abasement.

Bayst, is abashed.

Baythen, grant.

Be, by; *be, be that,* by the time that.

Be, been.

Bearneth, burn.

Beau, beautiful, fair.

Beche, valley.

Be-com, went.

Bede, bid, offer; offered.

Bedis, prayers.

Bedone, worked.

Beer, bore.

Beere, clamor, noise.

Beestly, like a beast.

Befalle, befits.

Befe, beef.

Beft, struck.

Beggestere, female beggar.

Begouth, begowth, began.

Behalding, beholding.

Behet, behite, promise

Be-hoves, behoove

Beighe, collar

Beir, bear.

Beir, boar.

Bekes, beaks.

Bele, boil, burn.
Belive, *belyve*, quickly.
Belle, beautiful.
Belly-huddroun, sluggard.
Bely, belly.
Bem, beam; *bemes, bemez, bemys*, beams.
Bemeneth, means, signifies.
Bemes, horns, trumpets.
Ben, be, are, been.
Bende, bent.
Bene, fair, well, gracious.
Benedicite, bless you.
Bent, coarse grass; grassy field.
Beo, be, are; *beoth*, be, are, there are.
Ber, beore, bore.
Berand, neighing.
Berd, beard; *berdlez*, beardless.
Bere, bier.
Bere, beren, bear, bore; *berez*, bears; *bere the face*, turned the face.
Bergen, shelter, preserve.
Bergh, hill.
Beriall, beryl-like.
Beris, barley's, of barley.
Berkyng, barking.
Bern, bairn, child.
Berye, berry.
Besene, furnished, arrayed.
Beste, best; *atte beste*, in the best way.
Beste, beast; *bestys*, beasts.
Besy, busy.
Bet, betere, better, rather.
Bet, bete, beat.
Betake, commit.
Bete, amend, cure.
Beteiche, bequeath.
Beth, be, are.
Betydde, happened, befallen
Beugh, bough; *bewis, bewys*, boughs.
Bewsprytt, bowsprit.
Beyn, pleasant, fair.
Bi, by, during, in, about, in regard to.
Bicoom, became.
Bidder, beggar.
Bifalle, befallen, happened; *bifel, bi-ful*, (it) befell.
Biforen, biforne, before.
Bighes, collars.
Bigon, begun.
Bigredet, cry out at.
Bi-growe, overgrown.
Bi-grypte, gripped.
Bigyle beguile.

Bihat, promises; *bihoten*, promised.
Bi-heold, beheld.
Bihove, behoove, be needful.
Bikennen, commend.
Bikkir, attack; *bikkerit*, attacked.
Biknowen, acknowledge, confess; *biknewe*, confessed.
Bilden, build.
Bile, bill.
Bi-ledet, pursue, chase.
Bi-lefeth, believe; *bilefves, bi-leve*, beliefs.
Bilefve, bileve, abide, remain; remain silent.
Billie, comrade, mate.
Binne, within, into the inner room.
Birk, beech.
Birnyng, burning.
Bi-schricheth, shriek at.
Bi-seo, see.
Bisette, used.
Bisily, busily.
Bismotered, besmutted.
Bi-stolen, stolen.
Bi-swiketh, betrays, deceives.
Bit, cutting blade or edge.
Bit, bids.
Bi-talt, shaken.
Bitaucte, gave to.
Bi-telle, justify.
Bithenche, bethink; *bi-thouht*, bethought.
Bitwixe, betwixt, between.
Biwreyest, betrayest.
Bi-wyled, beguiled, tricked.
Blac, blake, black.
Blaght, white.
Blaiknit, made bleak, deprived.
Blane, stopped.
Blanke, nugatory, of no effect.
Blate, exposed, bare.
Blaunner, a kind of (white ?) fur.
Blayke, white.
Ble, color.
Bleaunt, linen robe.
Blende, blent, mingled.
Blenk, shine, glisten.
Blenk, blink, glance; *blenking*, look.
Blente, blinds.
Bleo, complexion.
Blered, bleared, blurred.
Blesand, blazing.
Blewe, blue.
Blo, blue, pale.
Blome, bloom, blossom; *blomez, blomys* blossoms; *blomyt*, covered with blossoms.

Blonk, horse.

Blosme, blosmen, blossoms.

Blou, blow.

Bloweth, bloometh.

Blubred, foamed.

Bluid, blood.

Blunk, horse.

Blunt, faint.

Blutheliche, blithely.

Blwe, blue.

Blycande, glittering; *blykked*, shone.

Blyithnes, blitheness.

Blynne, cease.

Blysnande, shining.

Blysse, bless; *blyssyd, blyssit, blyste*, blest, blessed.

Blythe, joy.

Blyve, quickly, soon.

Bobbe, bough.

Bocher, butcher; *bocheres*, butchers.

Bocht, bought.

Bod, abode.

Bode, body.

Boden, prayed, asked.

Bode-words, tidings.

Bodin, prepared, arrayed.

Bogh, boghe, bend one's steps, go, walk.

Bogh, behooves, is necessary.

Bohe, bough.

Bokeler, buckler, shield.

Boles, bulls.

Bolles, boles, tree-trunks.

Bolne, swell.

Bomen, bowmen, archers.

Bon, good.

Bon, bone.

Bonc, bank.

Bonched, banged, struck.

Bond, bound; *bonde*, band.

Bone, boon, prayer.

Bonet, bonnet; *bonnettis*, bonnets.

Bonk, bank, height; *bonkkez*, banks.

Boold, bold.

Boon, bone.

Boote, remedy.

Boras, borax.

Bord, board.

Bordes, borders; *bordour*, border.

Bore, born.

Borelych, burly, huge.

Boris, boar's.

Born, borne.

Borne, burn. brones, *bornes*, brook's.

Bornyst, burnished.

Borrow, ransom, set free; lay in pledge forego.

Boste, boast; *bostaris*, boasters.

Bot, bit.

Bot, bote, but, unless; *bot and*, and also.

Bote, remedy.

Boterflye, butterfly.

Botes, bootes, boots

Botiler, butler.

Botme, bottom.

Botouns, buttons.

Bought, requited, atoned for.

Boult, bolt.

Boun, bowne, ready, prepared.

Bounden, boundin, bound.

Bounte, goodness, kindness.

Bour, boure, bowr, bower, bedroom, inner private apartment in a castle or mansion.

Bout, without.

Box, boxwood.

Boxomnesse, submission.

Boys, bows.

Brae, brow; hillside, river-bank.

Braggaris, braggers.

Braid, broad, open.

Brak, broke.

Brande, sword.

Brandeist, swaggered.

Branschis, branches.

Brast, burst; *brastyng*, bursting.

Brathe, brathes, fierceness, eagerness, violence.

Braule, brawl.

Braundysch, brandish.

Braw, brave, fine, handsome.

Brawden, woven.

Brayde, awoke, started; threw; *braydes*, draws.

Brayden, embroidered.

Braye, slope, river-bank.

Brayn, mad.

Bred, breed, bread.

Brede, breed; have whims.

Breek, would break.

Breem, bream, a kind of fish

Bref, brief.

Breid, breadth; *on breid*, abroad out.

Breif, write; letter, writ.

Breird, blade; *on breird*, on the increase.

Breist, breast.

Breke, break, open.

Breme, clear, distinct, loud.

Breme, fierce; *bremly*, fiercely, boldly.

Bren, bran.
Brende, *brenden*, burned; *brennes*, burns; *brennynge*, burning; *brent*, burnt.
Brent, high, steep.
Brerd, surface.
Bresed, rough.
Brest, voice.
Bret-ful, brimful.
Breved, told, related.
Brewesteres, brewers (female).
Brict, *brighte*, *briht*, bright; brightness.
Briddes, *bridis*, birds.
Brist, burst.
Broche, *brotch*, brooch.
Brod, *brode*, *brood*, broad.
Brode, brood.
Bronde, brand; *brondes*, hearth-fires.
Brook, *brouke*, *brouken*, use, enjoy.
Brothe, angry, fierce; *brothely*, angrily.
Brouct, brought.
Broun, *broune*, brown.
Browd, broad; *browd arrow*, arrow with a broad head.
Bruke, brook.
Brukkil, brittle.
Brunt, blow.
Brycht, *brygt*, *bryht*, bright.
Bryddez, birds.
Brydill, bridle.
Brymme, river, stream; bank.
Bryttlynge, breaking up, cutting up.
Buen, be, been; *bueth*, be, are.
Bugge, buy.
Buit, help.
Bukis, books.
Bukkes, bucks.
Bulluc, bullock.
Bulte, bolt.
Bumbard, lazy, stupid.
Bur, *burre*, blow, assault; force, hitting power.
Burd, board; *hard on burd*, close alongside.
Burde, ought, it behooved.
Burdoun, burden, musical accompaniment.
Burgeis, *burgeys*, burgess, citizen.
Burne, man, knight; *burnez*, men.
Burned, *burnyst*, burnished.
Bus, *buss*, *busk*, bush.
Busk, make ready.
Buskez, goes.
Busyez, busies, troubles.
But, *bute*, *buten*, but, unless, except, without; *but if*, unless.

Butiller, butler.
Buxom, *buxoum*, yielding, obedient.
By, be.
By, to; *as by*, as to, as regards.
By, *bye*, buy.
By and by, at once, immediately.
By-calt, recalled.
Byckarte, skirmished.
Byddᵹs, *bydez*, *bydis*, abides, remains; bide.
By-dene, *bydeen*, quickly, at once.
Byears, biers.
Byers, buyers.
Bygate, begot.
By-gonne, begun.
Byl, bill.
Bylis, boils.
Bylle, bill, halberd, sword.
Byn, been, be.
Bynethe, beneath.
Bynne, bin.
By-qwethe, bequeath.
Byre, cow-house, barn.
Byseme, beseem, become.
Byside, aside.
Byte, take hold of, touch.
Bytte, see *bit*.
Byttour, bitterns.
Byynge, buying.

C

Caas, cases.
Cace, case; *in cace*, perchance.
Cach, catch, take, acquire; *caches*, takes; *caght*, caught.
Cair, care; *cairful*, full of care; *cairen*, care.
Cald, cold; *calder*, colder.
Calling, behavior.
Calste, callest.
Calve, calf.
Cam, came.
Can, know, knows.
Can, gan, began, did.
Capados, hood, cap.
Caple, horse.
Capoun, capon, fowl.
Carefull, causing care.
Carf, carved.
Carioun, *caroyne*, *carren*, carrion, flesh.
Carkes, carcase, body.
Carp, speech; *carpe*, talk, chatter, say.
Cas, chance.

Cast, throw; speak; plan, intend, conjecture, contrive; *caste*, purpose; *casten*, planned; *casten hem*, purposed.

Casuelly, by chance.

Catapuce, lesser spurge.

Cative, caitiff, wretched; *caytyfe*, caitiff; *catyvis*, cowards.

Cattes, cattis, cat's.

Caught of, received.

Cauld, cold.

Cawmyt, calmed.

Ceint, cincture, girdle.

Celestyne, celestial.

Celicall, heavenly.

Cemmed, folded, twisted.

Cerges, wax tapers.

Ceruce, white lead.

Cever, reach, attain.

Chaffare, trading.

Chaist, chaste.

Chapman, merchant, huckster.

Char, chariot, car.

Chays, chase.

Cheere, cheir, cheer.

Cheffe, cheften, chief, chieftain.

Cheke, cheek.

Chekke, evil turn or trick.

Chele, chill, cold.

Chenzie, chain; *chenyeit*, covered with chain-armor.

Cher, chere, face, countenance, mien, appearance, behavior.

Cherising, cherishing.

Cherle, churl, peasant.

Chese, choose; *chees*, chose.

Cheselys, pebbles.

Chevallere, chevalier, man-at-arms, knight.

Cheven, thrive.

Chevisaunce, borrowings.

Cheyne, chain.

Chife, chiftane, chief, chieftain.

Chiknes, chickens.

Chilce, childishness.

Chist, chest, ark.

Chivachye, campaign.

Chop, stroke.

Chos, chose.

Chose, go.

Choys, choice.

Chydand, chiding.

Chylder, chylderyn, children.

Chyssell, chisel-like, thin and sharp.

Cidre, cedar

Cipres, cypress.

Cite, city.

Clam, climbed.

Clanly, cleanly, purely, wholly.

Clarke, clerk, cleric, priest.

Cleading, clothing.

Cleif, cleave, split.

Cleir, clear.

Clene, clean, fair; *clennesse*, cleanness.

Clent, clinched, shut.

Clepe, clepen, call.

Cler, clere, clear, fair, bright, shining; clearly.

Clerk, learned man; *clergealy*, in the manner of a clerk.

Clethit, clothed.

Cleve, cottage.

Cleve, cleave, adhere.

Cleven, cleave, part, separate; *clewis*, clefts.

Clivre, claws

Cloches, clutches.

Clomben, climbed.

Clos, close, cloos, enclose, enclosed, closed; *clos, closs*, close, enclosure, yard

Clot, clod, soil, earth.

Cloude, clod.

Clout, patch; *clutes*, clouts, rags.

Clowes, claws.

Clynge, cling.

Cniht, knight.

Cnokez, knockest.

Coarted, coarcted, confined.

Cofer, coffer, cofre, coffer, chest, small trunk for clothes.

Cogge, cog.

Coghed, coughed.

Col-blake, coal-black.

Cold, colde, could.

Colde, disastrous.

Cole, cowl.

Colerik, coleryk, choleric.

Colers, collars.

Colfox, coal-fox, fox with black markings.

Collep, drinking-cup.

Colliar, collier.

Colling, blacking.

Color, cholera.

Colpons, shreds.

Com, come, comen, came; *come*, coming.

Comaundes, commend.

Combre-world, encumberer or troubler of the world.

Comly, comlych, comely.

Commune, common; *comunly*, *in commune*, commonly, in common.

Compace, plan.

Compassinges, contrivances.

Complecciouns, complexions, temperaments.

Composicioun, composition, agreement, contract.

Compouned, compounded.

Compted, accounted.

Comunes, commons.

Con, *cone*, can.

Con, did; see *can*.

Conable, famous.

Condicion, *condicioun*, nature, disposition.

Condicionel, conditional.

Confort, comfort.

Conne, *conneth*, know, know how.

Connyng, cunning, knowledge, skill, discretion; cunning, skilful.

Conscience, tenderness of feeling.

Conseil, *conseille*, counsel, council.

Contek, contest, strife.

Contenaunce, show, display.

Contening, containing.

Contre, *contree*, country, earth.

Contreved, contrived.

Conversation, life.

Conynges, conies, rabbits.

Coode, could.

Coolde, cold; *on coolde*, on the cold ground.

Coom, *coomen*, come, came.

Cop, *coppe*, cup; *coppis*, cups.

Cop, top.

Cope, cape, cloak; *copis*, cloaks.

Copen, cheapen, bargain for.

Copill, couplet, stanza.

Corage, heart.

Cornys, corn's, of corn.

Coroune, crown.

Corp, *corps*, *corpes*, *corpis*, body.

Correnoch, coronach, war-cry, death-song.

Cors, curse; *corsedest*, cursedest.

Corsiare, courser.

Corss, body.

Corss, coin having a cross on it.

Cort, court.

Cortays, courteous.

Cortel, kirtle.

Corven, carved, cut.

Cosses, kisses.

Costes, manners, virtues.

Cosyn, cousin.

Couchit, adorned.

Coud, *coude*, did, could, knew; *coude no good*, was untrained; *coudna*, could not.

Countit, accounted; *countour*, accountant, auditor, mathematician; counting-board, abacus.

Countrefete, counterfeit, imitate

Counzie, motion.

Courtepy, coarse coat.

Courtyns, curtains.

Couthe, known, well-known.

Coveite, coveted; *coveitise*, *covetyse*, covetousness, avarice.

Covyne, deceit.

Cowde, could.

Cowle, caul, cabbage.

Cowthe, knew.

Crabbed, *craibit*, perverse.

Cracche, *cracchy*, scratch.

Craftes, trades, arts, abilities; *crafty*, skilful; *craftely*, skilfully.

Craig, crag.

Crap, crept.

Creische, grease, fat

Cresped, crisped.

Cresse, cress, mite.

Crie, cry; *cride*, *cryden*, cried.

Crips, crisp, curly.

Croked, *croken*, crooked.

Crokez, sickles.

Crokettis, small curls.

Crokke, crock, earthenware vessel.

Crome, crumb.

Crop, top, summit; *croppes*, *croppis*, tops, shoots.

Cropure, crupper.

Croun, crown; *crounyng*, crowning tonsure.

Croupe, crept.

Crowse, lively.

Croys, cross.

Crulle, curly.

Cryke, creek.

Cu, cow.

Cuccu, *cucu*, cuckoo.

Culd, could.

Culled, killed.

Cullour, color.

Cume, *cumen*, *cumeth*, come; *cummyn*, come.

Cumly, comely.

Cunde, kind; *cunne*, kinds.

Cunne, can.

Cure, care; *do no cure*, (I) care not; *curious*, careful, wrought with care; *curiosite*, careful workmanship.

Curnels, seeds.

Curs, curse, excommunication.

Curteys, courteous; *curteisye*, courtesy.

Custe, character, habits.

Cuthe, make known; *could*, knew how to; *cuthest*, knowest.

Cuvatyce, covetousness.

Cwemde, pleased.

D

Dai, day; *dai-rim*, day-rim, early dawn.

Dalt, dealt.

Dam, stream.

Dameselis, damsels.

Dampnable, damnable; *dampnacion*, damnation.

Dans, dance.

Dare, tremble.

Dasewed, dazed.

Daueth, dawneth.

Daun, lord, sir.

Daungere, danger, harm, injury; *in daunger*, under his jurisdiction; *daungerous*, hard, severe.

Daunte, tame, subdue.

Daw, jackdaw, simpleton; untidy person.

Dawenynge, dawning.

Dayerye, dairy.

Dayesye, daisy; *dasyis, dayes-eyes*, daisies.

Day-sterre, day-star.

De, dee, die; *dede*, deaden; *deed*, dead; *deeth*, death.

Dece, dees, daïs.

Dee, do; *dede*, did; *dedyst*, didst; *dede, deid*, deed.

Deel, deal, whit; *deelen*, deal.

Defendit, defended, warded off.

Defte, gentle, meek.

Defundand, pouring down.

Defye, digest.

Deghe, die.

Degouted, dropped down.

Degree, rank, station.

Deid, dead; death; *deidly*, deadly.

Deigned: him deigned not, it seemed to him not worthy, he disdained.

Deill, deal.

Deip, deep.

Deir, dear.

Deis, dies.

Del, dele, deal.

Del, dele, dole, sorrow.

Dele, dale.

Dele, devil.

Deliver, quick, nimble, active; *delyverly*, quickly, nimbly.

Delyt, delyte, delight.

Dem, deme, demen, judge.

Demme, grow dim.

Demure, decorous, modest.

Denely, loud.

Denes, Danish.

Denned, dinned, resounded.

Denned, dennede, hid (as in a den).

Deor, wild animal.

Deore, dear; *deores*, dear ones, lovers.

Deoveles, devils'; *deovlen*, devils.

Deowes, dews.

Departe, departen, make to depart, part, divide, separate.

Depaynt, depeynted, painted, covered with paintings.

Depured, depurit, purified.

Dere, harm, injure, hurt; *dereth*, harms; *deres*, harms.

Derke, dark; *derknesse*, darkness.

Derlyng, darling.

Derne, secret, crafty.

Derrere, dearer; *derrest*, dearest, most worthy; *derthe*, dearness, worth.

Dervely, stoutly.

Derworth, precious.

Descrive, describe.

Desdeyne, disdain.

Despitous, cruel, pitiless.

Dest, doest, makest, causest.

Destruye, destroy.

Dette, debt; *dettelees*, debtless.

Deu, dew.

Develes, devils; *develes*, devils'.

Devit, deafened.

Devoyde, destroy, remove, put away.

Devys, devyse, direction, opinion; describe, recount.

Dewty, duty.

Dewyne, dwine, pine.

Dey, deye, die.

Deye, dairymaid.

Deyntee, deynty, dainty, rare; *deyntees*, dainties.

Deys, daïs, raised platform.

Did, made; *dide*, did.

Digele, secret, secluded.

Diggs, ducks.
Dight, dighte, make ready, pronounce.
Digne, worthy; proud, disdainful.
Dine, dinner.
Dinna, do not.
Dischevele, with hair in disorder.
Diseis, misery.
Disjone, breakfast.
Dispence, expense, expenditure.
Dispite, dispyte, despite, contempt, scorn; *in his dispite,* in scorn of him.
Displesaunte, displeasing.
Disporte, cheer, amuse; sport, pleasantry.
Dissagysit, disguised.
Dissymilance, dissimulation; *dissimilour,* dissembler; *dissymlit,* dissembling, false.
Disstryez, destroys; *distruyeth,* destroy.
Ditee, ditty.
Diurnal, of the day.
Do, make, cause.
Doc, duke.
Doctrine, teaching, instruction.
Doddy, fool.
Doel, dole.
Doen, betaken.
Doge, dog.
Doghter, daughter; *doghtren,* daughters.
Dois, does.
Dok, tail.
Dokes, ducks.
Dokked, docked, cut short.
Dol, dole, grief.
Dolven, buried.
Dom, dome, doom, mind, judgment.
Don, done, done, caused, put, brought.
Done, down.
Donge, dung, manure.
Donk, dank, moist; *donketh,* dampen, moisten.
Donne, do.
Donne, dun.
Doolie, doleful, mournful.
Doomes, judgments, decisions.
Doon, do; *dooth,* doth.
Doris, doors.
Dorste, durst, dared.
Dosyn, dozen.
Doth, do; *dotz,* does, dost.
Doubilnes, doubleness, deceit.
Doubtaunce, doubt; *double,* fear.
Douchter, doughtre, daughter.
Dougheti, doughte, doughty.
Dought, could.

Doun, down; *dounes,* downs, hills.
Doute, doubt, fear; *doutelees,* doubtless.
Douthe, people.
Dowbyll, double; *dowbillis,* doubles; *dowblit,* doubled.
Dowene, down; *downes,* downs, hills.
Dowte, doubt, hesitation; *but dowt,* without doubt.
Dowyne, dwine, pine.
Doys, does.
Dozeyn, dozen.
Drad, afraid.
Drap, drop.
Drawne, draw near.
Dre, endure.
Drecched, troubled.
Dred, dreaded; *drede, dreid,* fear, dread, doubt, make to fear; *dredful,* full of dread, timid.
Dregh, fiercely
Dreghe, endure.
Dreinchen, drinchen, drench, drown; *dreynt,* drowned.
Drem, music.
Dremit, dreamed.
Dresse, make ready, prepare, direct, made ready, prepared.
Dreve, drive, pass.
Dreye, drie, endure.
Drigten, Lord.
Drivande, driving, advancing; *driveth,* drives, rushes; *drof,* drove.
Drogges, drugs.
Drogh, drew.
Drowrie, dowry.
Drunckart, drunkard; *drunken,* drunkenness.
Drwry, dreary, sad.
Dryghe, endure; impassive, unmoved.
Dryghly, heavily, slowly
Dryghtyn, dryhten, lord.
Dryve, drive, strike; *dryven forth,* pass; *dryvars,* drivers
Dubbed, dubbet, decked.
Duches, duchess'.
Dud, dude, duden, did, caused.
Duddroun, sloven.
Duelle, dwell.
Dulce, sweet.
Dule, sorrow, mourning.
Dun, down.
Dunne, dun.
Dunt, dint, blow.

Durande, during.
Duresse, harshness.
Durres, doors.
Dut, dutte, doubted, feared.
Dwell, tarry, linger.
Dyches, ditches.
Dye, die; *dyed*, died.
Dyght, prepare, set in order; prepared, done; *dyght me*, prepared; *dyghtande*, being made ready.
Dyke, dig dikes or ditches.
Dyne, dynne, din, noise.
Dynt, dynte, blow; *dynttez*, blows.
Dyryge, dirge.
Dyscreven, descry, be seen.
Dytees, ditties.

E

Ear, ere, before.
Earding-stowe, dwelling-place.
Earen, ears.
Ech, eche, echon, each, each one.
Edefie, edefy, build up, replenish.
Edye, blessed, rich.
Ee, eye.
Eeris, ears.
Eet, ate.
Effect, reality, fact, practice.
Eft, efte, again, afterwards; *efter, eftir*, after.
Egal, equal.
Egge, edge.
Eghe, eye; *egen*, eyes.
Egle, eagle.
Eigh, eye.
Eik, eke, also.
Eiled, ailed.
Eir, ere.
Eir, heir.
Eird, earth; *eirdly*, earthly.
Ek, eke, also.
Elacyon, elation.
Eld, old; *ealde, elde*, old age; *eldre*, elder.
Elevait, elevated, elated.
Ellebor, hellebore.
Ellen, ell.
Elles, ellis, els, else, elsewhere, otherwise; *ellez*, if that.
Elnyerde, ell-yard.
Elyng, ailing.
Em, uncle.
Embassades, embassies.
Embosed, plunged into the wood.

Emerad, emeraut, emerald.
Emispery, emyspery, hemisphere.
Empeireth, is impaired, grows worse.
Emperice, empress.
Enamilit, enameled.
Enbrauded, enbroud, embroidered.
Encensyng, expelling by perfume
Enchace, pursue, seize.
Enclynande, inclining, bowing.
Encres, increase.
Ende: set tale on ende, began his story.
Endite, compose; *endytyng*, inditing, composing.
Endlang, along.
Endynge, ending.
Ene, eyes.
Enesed, clipped(?).
Eneuch, enough.
Enfourme, inform.
Engendren, are produced.
Englene, angels'.
Engyned, racked.
Enker, bright.
Enlumynyng, illumining, enlightening
Enmy, enemy; *enmyes*, enemy's.
Ensample, example.
Ensew, ensue, follow.
Entendement, understanding, perception.
Entente, heed; *ententyf*, attentive; *ententyfly*, attentively.
Entere, entire.
Enterit, entirt, entered.
Entist, enticed.
Entyse, acquire.
Entunes, tunes.
Envye, vie, strive.
Envyned, stored with wine.
Er, ere, before, first.
Erbe, herb; *erbez*, herbs, herbage; *erbe yve*, herbive, ground pine.
Erbere, arbor.
Erchedeknes, archdeacon's.
Erd, earth; *erde*, land, abode.
Ere, ear.
Erewe, slow.
Ern, eagle.
Erneth, run.
Ernde, eronde, errand, business.
Erys, ears.
Eschaunge, exchange.
Eschue, eschew, shun.
Ese, ease; *esed*, entertained.
Est, east.

Estat, state, condition, high station or rank, *estatlich*, *estatly*, stately, dignified.
Este, delicacy, dainty.
Esy, easy, moderate.
Etayn, giant.
Ete, eat; *et*, ate.
Ethe, ask.
Ethe, easily.
Eure, fate, luck.
Evele, evil, ill.
Even, *evene*, smooth, moderate; exactly, aright.
Evereche, *everyche*, *evrich*, *everichone*, every, everyone.
Evin, *evyn*, evening, eve.
Evy, heavy.
Evyll, ill.
Ewiry, every.
Expone, *expoun*, expound, describe, explain, interpret.
Ey, egg.
Eye, awe.
Eyen, eyes.
Eyleth, *eylyt*, aileth.
Eyre, air.
Eyther, either.

F

Fa, fall.
Fache, fetch.
Facture, fashioning, shape, feature, aspect.
Facultee, occupation, profession.
Fade, hostile.
Fader, father; *faderis*, father's.
Fadge, short, fat person.
Faght, fought.
Faille, doubt.
Fair, fare.
Faire, fairly, well, gracefully; *fairnesse*, fair and gentle means.
Fairlies, wonders.
Falce, false.
Falcounn, falcon.
Faldying, a kind of coarse cloth.
Falle, befall; *falleth*, fall, befits; *falle*, *fallen*, happened; *faire falle*, be prospered.
Fals, false; *falshed*, *falssyng*, falsehood.
Falt, falters.
Famulier, familiar.
Fand, found.
Fanes, vanes.
Fange, take.
Fannand, waving, flowing.

Fantoum, phantom.
Fare, far.
Fare, *faren*, go, go away; *faren*, gone.
Fare, conduct, manner, business, proceeding, experience, condition.
Farsed, stuffed.
Faste, near.
Faught, fought.
Fauldit, folded.
Fauned, fawned on.
Faunt, child, maiden.
Faut, fault; *fautlest*, faultless; *fawty*, faulty.
Fax, hair.
Fay, *faye*, faith, loyalty.
Fayly, fail; *faylyd*, missed.
Fayn, *fayne*, fain, glad.
Fayn, vane; *fanys*, vanes, banners.
Faynt, faint, weak; *fayntyse*, faintness, weakness.
Faynynge, feigning.
Fayteden, begged falsely.
Fe, fee, pay, wages.
Feale, fail.
Feare: in feare, together.
Fech, *feche*, fetch.
Fede, faded, decayed.
Fedme, fathoms.
Feere, see *feare*.
Feere, fear.
Feersly, fiercely.
Feghtyng, fighting.
Feid, enmity, ill-will.
Feirer, fairer, more beautiful.
Feildis, fields.
Feill, experience, knowledge.
Feir, fear.
Feir, array, equipment.
Feire, fair; *feirer*, fairer.
Feist, feast.
Feit, feet.
Feitch, fetch.
Feith, faith.
Fela, *felawe*, *felawh*, fellow; *felaschipe*, *felawshyp*, fellowship.
Feld, *felde*, field.
Fele, much, many.
Fell, fierce, bold, cruel; *felly*, fiercely, boldly.
Fendes, fiends.
Fenyeit, feigned.
Fenyl, fennel.
Feole, many.

Feorthe, fourth.

Fer, far.

Ferde, fared, went, proceeded, acted.

Ferde, fere, fear; *fered, ferde*, afraid, frightened.

Fere, companions; *in fere*, in company.

Feres, carries.

Ferked, ran; *ferkkes*, rides.

Ferleis, marvel; *ferly*, marvel, wonder; *ferlis* marvels; *ferly*, wondrously.

Ferne, far off, distant.

Fernie, covered with fern.

Ferre, far, farther; *ferreste*, farthest.

Ferst, first.

Ferthyng, small or smallest portion (farthing, fourth part).

Fest, fast, made fast, confirmed; *festne*, fasten.

Festys, feasts.

Fet, fett, fetch; fetched, brought.

Fet, fete, feet.

Fet, feedeth; *fete*, feed.

Feth, faith.

Fetisly, exactly, elegantly; *fetys*, elegant.

Fetures, features, members; *feutred*, featured.

Fewir, fever.

Feye, fated to die.

Feyn, fain, glad.

Feynd, fiend.

Feyne, feynen, feign.

Feyrest, fairest.

Feyth, faith.

Fflee, fly.

Ffrawart, froward.

Fiere, companion.

Fiftene, fifteen.

Figurait, figured.

Fihte, fight.

Fil, fell.

Fild, filled.

Filde, field.

Fildore, gold thread.

Fille, chervil, a kind of herb.

Filstnede, helped.

Finden, find.

Fir, for.

Fir, fire.

Firret, ferrets.

Fistela, fistula.

Fit, section of a poem.

Fithele, fiddle.

Flaghe, flew.

Flaghte, plot of ground, flat.

Flagraunte, fragrant.

Flambe, flame.

Flang, flung.

Flastynge, flashing.

Flatour, flatterer; *flattereris*, flatterers.

Flaugh, flawe, flew.

Flaumbande, flaming.

Flaunes, custards.

Flayn, arrow.

Fle, flee, flee, fly; *fleo*, fly; *fles*, fleest; *fleigh*, flew.

Fleetinge, flowing; *flete, fleten*, flow, float.

Fleme, exile; banish.

Flet, floor.

Flex, flax.

Fley, flew; *fleynge*, fleeing.

Fleyce, fleece, covering.

Flihst, flyest.

Flo, flay.

Flode, flood, sea.

Floghe, fled.

Flonc, flung.

Flor, flour, flower; *flour-de-lys*, fleur-de-lis, lily; *floure-jonettis*, flowers of the great St. John's wort.

Flot, flowed, floated; *flow*, overflow, flood.

Flowen, flew.

Floytyng, fluting, playing on a flute.

Flude, flood.

Flurted, flowered, figured.

Flyghes, flies.

Flyte, quarrel, strive.

Flytte, float.

Fnast, breath; *fnaste*, breathe.

Fo, foe.

Foch, fetch.

Fode, food.

Fol, foul.

Folde, folded.

Folde, earth.

Folden, grant.

Fole, fool.

Fole, foal, young horse.

Folgande, following, in proportion, suitable; *folged, folowit, folwed*, followed.

Folye, folly.

Femon, foeman; *fomen*, foemen.

Fonde, find, found; *fond*, found.

Fonde, try.

Fone, foe.

Fonge, take.

Fonte, surveyed, scanned.

Foo, roughly.
Foond, found, provided for.
For, because, because of, against, before.
Forby, by, past.
For-dolked, mortally wounded.
Fordward, forward.
Forgaf, forgave.
Forgane, over against.
For-garte, lost.
Forgeten, forgotten.
Forgh, ford.
Forgit, forged, fashioned.
For-go, for-gon, forego.
For-lete, lost.
For-lete, stop, leave off.
Forloren, lost, ruined.
Forloyn, note of recall.
Forme, first, foremost.
Forme: in forme, with formality.
Forn-cast, premeditated.
Forne, before, formerly.
Fornes, forneys, furnace, fire.
For-payned, severely troubled.
Forpyned, wasted away by torment.
For-quhy, because.
Fors, force, matter, consequence; *do no fors*, make no account.
For-se, foresee.
Forser, fortress, stronghold, place of refuge.
Forslewthen, waste by sloth.
Forst, first.
Forster, forester.
Fort, until.
Forte, for to.
For-the, for-thi, for that reason, therefore.
Forthren, further, help.
Forth-rihtes, straightway.
Fortill, for to, in order to.
For-tirit, tired.
Fortune, fortune.
Forvayit, went astray.
Forwandred, tired with wandering.
Forward, foreward, agreement.
Forwaryed, cursed.
Forwery, very weary.
For-why, because.
Forwityng, foreknowing; *forwot*, foreknows.
Forwreyen, accuse.
For-yelde, requite.
For-yet, forgets; *for-yete, foryeten*, forgotten.
Foryeve, forgive.
Fostere, forester.

Fot, fote, foot; *to fotte*, on foot; *fote-hoot*, hot-foot, in haste.
Fother, cart-load.
Fou, variegated or spotted (fur)
Foudre, thunderbolt.
Foul, foule, fowl, bird.
Foule, foul; *foulest*, ugliest.
Founce, bottom.
Founded, come; *foundez*, goes.
Founes, fawns.
Fowel, fowl, bird; *fowlez*, birds; *foweler*, fowler, bird-hunter.
Fowll, foul.
Foyned, pushed at.
Fra, frae, fram, from.
Frak, moved fast.
Frame, benefit, advantage.
Fraward, froward, perverse.
Frayne, ask; *frayst*, ask, asked; *frayste*, sought.
Fre, free, generous, bountiful, noble, admirable.
Freake, freik, man; *freckys*, men.
Frech, fresh.
Freend, frende, friend.
Frely, beautiful.
Fremyt, strange.
Frere, friar.
Fret, adorned; *fret-wise*, in the manner of fret-work.
Freyke, man.
Frinde, friend.
Fro, from, from the time that, since.
Frounses, contracts.
Frount, front, forehead.
Froward, perverse, adverse, unfavorable.
Fructuus, fertile, abundant.
Fryte, fruit.
Fryth, wood.
Fudder, great amount.
Fude, food.
Fugele, fowls, birds; *fugeles*, bird's; *fugel-kunne*, fowl-kind, bird-kind.
Fu', full.
Ful, fully.
Ful, fell.
Ful, fule, foul.
Fule, fool.
Fulfilled, filled full.
Fume, perfume, odor.
Fumelere, fumatory, a bitter medicinal plant.
Fundament, foundation.
Funden, found.

Fur, fire.
Fure, fared, went.
Furth, forth, out, from.
Furtherynges, furtherings, help.
Fust, fist, hand.
Fyall, turret, pinnacle
Fyiftene, fifteenth.
Fyked, shrank.
Fynde, provide for.
Fyne, cease, end, die.
Fynnys, fins.
Fyr, fire; *fyre-flawcht*, lightning.
Fyrre, farther.
Fyrte, fearful, trembling.
Fyrth, frith, bay.

G

Ga, gae, go; *gaed*, went.
Gabbe, talk idly, lie.
Gables, cables.
Gadderaris, gatherers; *gadderit, gadrede*, gathered.
Gaif, gave.
Gaip, gape.
Gaitrys, dogwood.
Galegale, noisy fellow, singsong.
Gallandis, gallants.
Galle, gall, bitterness.
Game, gamen, merriment, sport, pleasure; *gamed*, it pleased.
Gamountis, capers.
Gan, began, did.
Gan, gane, gone.
Gang, gange, go, walk.
Ganyde, gained.
Gar, make, cause; *garez*, make; *gard, garde, gart, garten*, made, caused.
Gargat, throat.
Garleek, garlic.
Garnisoun, garrison.
Gast, aghast.
Gat, got.
Gate, way, course, road, ford.
Gat-tothed, having teeth wide apart
Gaudi, gaud, ornament.
Gay, finely dressed.
Gayn, useful, meet; *gaynez*, gains, avails.
Geates, goats.
Gederes, gederez, gathers, takes, lifts.
Geere, gear, tools, instruments, apparel.
Gees, geese.
Gefve, give; *gef*, gave; *geftes*, gifts.
Gekkis, mocking gestures.

Gemme, gemmez, gems.
Gente, gentil, gentyll, gentle, noble, gracious, well-born; *gentilesse, gentilnes*, gentleness, nobility.
Gere, gear, affair; *gered*, geared, accoutered.
Gerner, garner.
Gert, made.
Geserne, axe.
Gesse, guess, suppose.
Gest, goest.
Gest, story, tale; *gestiours*, story-tellers.
Gete, get; *gete, geten*, got, begotten.
Geve, give.
Geynest, most gracious one.
Ghostly, spiritual.
Gide, guide.
Gilofre, gilly flower
Gilt, sinned; guilt.
Gin, if.
Gipoun, doublet.
Gipser, pouch, purse.
Girles, young people.
Gise, guise, way, fashion.
Giserne, axe.
Glace, glance.
Gladande, gladding; *glade*, glad; *gladur*, gladder; *glaid*, gladden; *glaidsum*, gladsome.
Glans, glance.
Gle, glee.
Glede, live coal; *gledy*, glowing, burning, ardent.
Glem, gleam; *glemys*, gleams
Glemen, gleemen, musicians.
Glemered, glimmered.
Glent, glente, glanced, glinted, gleamed, shone; glided; shrank, flinched.
Glenyng, gleaming.
Gletering, glittering.
Glode, glade.
Glopnyng, fright.
Glore, glory
Glose, gloss; explain.
Glotones, gluttons; *glotonye*, gluttony; *glotoun*, glutton.
Glydande, gliding; *glydez*, glides.
Glyfte, looked.
Glyght, shone, glistened.
Glysnande, glistening.
Glytrand, glittering.
Gobet, gobbet, piece.
God, gode, good; *godes*, good's, of good; *godly*, graciously, courteously; *godhede*, goodness.

Godes, gods; *Godes, Godez*, of God, God's; *goddys*, gods'; *Goddot*, God knows.

Gog, God.

Gogelinge, guggling.

Goliardeys, buffoon.

Gome, man.

Gomen, games, sports.

Gomme, gum.

Gon, gone, go, walk; *gonde*, gone.

Gong, gait.

Gonne, began, did.

Good, goods, property; *goodely*, kindly.

Goon, go.

Goost, ghost, spirit.

Goot, goat.

Gordel, girdle.

Gossips, gossops, cronies.

Gost, ghost, spirit; *gostely*, spiritual.

Gost, goest; *goth*, go, goeth; *gotz*, goes.

Goud, good.

Goud, gowd, gold; *gouden*, golden.

Goune, gown.

Graith, make ready.

Grame, anger, harm, vexation.

Gramercy, great thanks.

Granis, groans.

Grattest, greatest.

Graunt, grant, permission.

Graunt mercy, great thanks.

Gravayl, gravel, pebbles.

Grave, bury; *graven, gravin*, buried.

Graynez, grains.

Graythe, ready; *graythed*, made ready, arrayed; *graythely*, quickly.

Gre: in gre, in good part.

Greahondes, greyhounds.

Grece, gristle of the neck.

Gree, degree, high rank, victory.

Greet, weep, cry out; *greeting*, weeping.

Greffe, grief.

Greit, great; *greetnes*, greatness.

Greit, grit, gravel.

Grem, greme, anger, grief, harm.

Grenne, grinned.

Gresse, grass.

Gret, grete, great; *gretter*, greater.

Grete, weep; *gret*, wept.

Grette, greeted.

Greved, grieved; *grevis*, grieves.

Greves, grevez, grevis, groves.

Grey, gray (fur).

Greyn, grain.

Greyn, green.

Grill, grumble.

Grip, vulture.

Gris, young pigs.

Grislich, grisly, horrible.

Grit, great.

Gromylyoun, gromwell, grey millet.

Grope, probe, test.

Grouf, groveling posture.

Ground, ground-work, texture.

Gruch, grucche, grudge, grumble, complain; *grudge*, begrudge.

Grund, grunde, ground.

Grundlike, ravenously.

Grundyn, ground, sharpened.

Grunzie, snout.

Grwe, good-will.

Gryed, trembled.

Gryndel, angry, fierce; *gryndelly*, wrathfully; *gryndel-layk*, fierceness, anger.

Gryndelston, grindstone.

Grys, a kind of gray fur.

Gryte, great.

Gud, gude, guid, good; *gudely*, goodly; *gudeliare*, goodlier.

Guerdoun, guerdon, reward.

Gulteth, sins.

Gunne, did.

Gyiss, disguising, mask, masquerade.

Gylt, gild.

Gyng, assembly.

Gynglen, jingle.

Gyngure, ginger.

Gynnen, gynneth, begin; *gynnis*, beginnest.

Gyrdez, spurs.

Gyrle, girl.

Gyrnd, grinned.

Gyternere, gittern, guitar.

H

Ha, hall.

Ha, habbe, habbeth, have; *habbes*, hast.

Habergeoun, short coat of mail.

Habitacles, niches.

Habite, dress.

Hable, enable to be or do.

Habundant, abundant.

Hace, hoarse.

Hackstock, timber.

Hadde, hade, had; *hadez*, hadst; *hadna*, had not.

Hae, haf, have; *haes*, has.

Hagher, fit.

Haif, have.

Hailsum, wholesome.
Hait, hot.
Halce, neck.
Halched, looped, fastened.
Halde, hold; *haldin*, held, kept.
Hale, recess, corner.
Hale, wholly; *halesum*, wholesome.
Haled, trimmed.
Hales, rushes.
Halfe, half, side; *a Goddes halfe*, for God's sake; *halfendel*, the half part; *halflyng*, half, partly.
Halke, corner, covert.
Halle, large room.
Halled, rushed.
Halm, handle.
Hals, neck.
Halt, holds.
Halte, halt, maimed.
Halve, halves, sides; behalf.
Halwes, hallowed persons, saints; shrines.
Halyde, hauled, pulled.
Ham, am.
Hame, home; *hamelynes*, familiarity.
Han, have.
Han, hand; *out of hand*, at once.
Hange, hang; *hang*, hung.
Happe, good fortune, joy.
Happit, wrapped.
Harbery, lodging.
Hard, closely.
Hard, *harde*, heard.
Hardily, certainly; *hardyly*, *hardi'y*, boldly; *hardyar*, hardier.
Haris, hairs.
Harlot, ribald; *harlottis*, vile fellows.
Harm, misfortune.
Harneised, harnessed, accoutered, mounted; *harnys*, harness.
Harre, hinge.
Harrow, help!
Has, behest, command.
Hase, has.
Hasell, hazel.
Hasped, enclosed.
Hast, haste; *hastely*, quickly, promptly; *hastyf*, hasty.
Hastou, hast thou.
Hat, *hatte*, am called, is called; *hattes*, *hattest*, art called.
Hathel, nobleman, knight.
Hatrent, hatred.
Hatture, hotter.

Hatz, has, hast.
Hauberghe, hauberk, cuirass.
Haunt, skill.
Haunten, practice, use.
Havekes, hawks.
Haven, have; *havest*, hast; *havet*, *haveth*, hath; *havede*, had.
Having, behavior.
Haw, livid.
Hawbergh, hauberk, cuirass.
Hawtane, haughty; *hawtesse*, haughtiness.
Haylsed, hailed, saluted.
He, he, she it, they.
He, high.
Heade, heed; *headfull*, heedful.
Heal, hail.
Heale, health; *evil heale*, disaster.
Hearnes, herons.
Heaste, hest, promise.
Heawyng, hewing.
Hed, *hede*, *heed*, head; *hedlez*, headless.
Hedyr, hither.
Heeld, held.
Heep, heap, crowd.
Heer, *heere*, hair.
Heeth, heath.
Heft, haft, handle.
Heg, *heghe*, high.
Hegge, hedge; *hegis*, hedges.
Heh, high; *hehest*, highest.
Heid, heed.
Heigh, high.
Heill, heel; *heild*, heeled.
Heillie, haughty, disdainful.
Heir, here.
Heird, hear it.
Heit, heat, heating.
Heke, eke, also.
Helder, the more.
Heldet, moved, went back; *heldez*, rides.
Hele, healing, health, welfare, pleasure.
Hele, heel.
Heled, hidden.
Helpyn, help.
Hem, them.
Heme, hem, skirt.
Hemmed, embroidered.
Hende, district.
Hende, still.
Hend, *hende*, *hendi*, *hendy*, handy, dexterous, kind, gracious, gentle; *hendest*, handiest, most courteous; *hendeliche*, *hendely*, courteously, kindly.

Heng, hung.
Hens, hence.
Hente, get; *hent*, seized, caught.
Heo, she, it, they; *heom*, them; *heore*, their.
Heolde, held.
Heonne, thence.
Heorte, heart.
Heovene, heaven.
Her, here.
Her, here, hair.
Her, here, their.
Herbere, garden for herbs and flowers.
Herbergage, harborage, lodging.
Herberwe, harbor, inn.
Herde, herdsman.
Here, heren, hear.
Here, host, army.
Here-biforne, before now.
Hered-men, retainers, courtiers.
Heremyte, hermit.
Herestow, hearest thou.
Herke, herkne, herkneth, hearken.
Herle, twist, fillet.
Hermyne, ermine.
Hernes, brains.
Her-of, hereof.
Her-on, here-on.
Herre, higher.
Hert, hart.
Herte, heart; *hertelees*, heartless; *hertyth*, heartens, encourages.
Heryed, praised.
Herys, hairs.
Hes, has, have.
Het, was promised· *hette*, promised; *hettez*, didst promise.
Hete, heat; *helt*, hot.
Heterly, quickly, suddenly.
Hethene, heathen.
Heu, hue.
Heve, heavy.
Heve, heven, heave, raise, exalt.
Heved, head.
Hevede, had.
Hevene-riche, of heaven's kingdom; *hevenliche, hevenysh*, heavenly; *hevynnys*, heavens.
Hew, hewe, hue.
Hewen, hewn, forged, shaped.
Hey, heych, heye, high.
Hi, her, they.
Hichest, highest.
Hiddouss, hideous.

Hider, hither.
Hiegh, high; *hier*, higher, nearer; *highlich*, noble, admirable.
Hight, promise.
Hight, highte, is called, was called, called.
Hii, they.
Hin, hinne, inn, dwelling.
Hinde, gentle, courteous.
Hine, him.
Hipes, hips.
Hippit, hopped.
Hir, hire, her, herself, their.
Hirde, herdsman, shepherd.
Hire, hear.
His, is.
Hit, it.
Hitte, hit.
Ho, she, they.
Hode, hood, helmet.
Hoge, huge.
Hoilsum, wholesome.
Hoir, old, feeble.
Hoked, hooked.
Holden, hold, keep.
Hole, holle, whole; *holly*, wholly.
Holgh, holwe, hollow.
Holland, linen.
Holt, wood; *holte-wodez*, holt-woods.
Holyn, holly.
Hom, home.
Homered, hammered, struck.
Hond, hand.
Hondele, handle.
Hondreth, hondrith, hundred.
Honest, honorable, creditable; *honestli*, honorably; *honestye*, honor.
Hony, honey.
Hoo, stop!
Hoold, hold.
Hoole, whole; *hoolly*, wholly.
Hooly, slowly.
Hoomly, homely.
Hoot, hoote, hot.
Hope, think, suppose.
Hor, their.
Hord, horde, hoard.
Hordom, whoredom; *horsen*, whoreson, bastard.
Hors, hoarse.
Hors, horse, horses.
Hosen, leggings, gaiters.
Ho-so, whoso.
Hostell, hostelry, inn; *hostiler*, innkeeper.

Hote, hot.

Hoten, be called.

Hounger, hunger.

Hounte, hunt.

Houris, morning prayers.

Houves, hoods, coifs.

Hoved, hovered, waited.

Hoves, hoofs.

Howp, hope.

Howped, whooped.

Hu, how.

Hude, hood.

Hud-pykis, misers.

Huere, their.

Huke, frock, dress.

Hulles, hills.

Humblesse, humbleness, meekness.

Humblynge, rumbling.

Hundreth, hundred.

Hunte, hunter.

Hurdaris, hoarders.

Hure and hure, especially.

Hurne, corner, nook.

Huyle, while.

Hwan, when.

Hwat, what.

Hwe, hue; *hwes*, hues.

Hwenne, when.

Hwere, where.

Hwil, hwile, while.

Hwo, who.

Hy: in hy, in haste.

Hy, high; *on hy*, upright; *hyer*, higher, upper.

Hydous, hideous.

Hye, hyghe, hie, hasten; *in hyghe*, in haste.

Hyght, height.

Hyght, promised.

Hyme, him.

Hyndreste, hindmost.

Hyne, hence.

Hyne, hind, peasant, servant; hinds, servants.

Hyng, hang.

Hypped, hopped, limped.

I

I, in.

I wis, indeed, forsooth, surely.

Ibet, bettered, amended.

Ich, I; *ichabbe*, I have; *icham*, I am; *ichot*, I know; *ichulle*, I shall

I-cundur, more akin.

Idel, idle.

Idole, image.

I-fallyng, fallen.

I-fere, companions.

I-herde, ihord, heard.

I-hote, called.

Ikindled, whelped, born.

Ile, I will.

I-leste, last.

Ileved, lived.

I-leyd, laid.

I-lich, like.

Ilka, ilke, every; same

Illumynat, illumined.

Ilome, often.

I-meind, mixed.

Imprentit, imprinted.

In, inn.

In, into, upon; *in till, in to* in.

Incontynent, instantly.

Incress, increase.

Inestimable, beyond estimate, too precious.

Infect, of no effect, invalid.

In-fere, together.

Influent, having influence.

Infortune, misfortune.

Innogh, in-noghe, i-nohe, inoughe, enough.

Impugnen, impugn.

Inquyrit, inquired.

Inspired, breathed upon.

Intelligible, intelligent.

Into, in.

Invention, fiction.

Invy, envy.

In-with, within.

I-peint, painted.

Iqueme, please.

Iren, iron.

Is, his.

Ischit, issued.

I-scrud, clothed.

Ise, I will.

I-seh, iseyen, saw; *iseo*, seen.

I-shote, shot, poured.

I-somned, assembled.

Ispeke, spoken.

Ithohten, they thought.

I-thrunge, pressed near.

Ived, fed.

Ivere, companions.

Iworthe, happen.

I-wysse, indeed, forsooth, surely.

J

Jaggit, cut into jags, pinked.
Jakkis, leathern jackets.
Jangle, jangill, chatter, prate; *jangeler janglere*, babbler, idle talker.
Japers, jesters; *japes*, tricks.
Jaw, wave.
Jeet, jet.
Jenepere, juniper.
Jeopardie, chance.
Jet, mode, fashion.
Jet, go, strut; *jetter*, boaster.
Jimp, slim.
Jolif, joly, joyful, jolly, pleasant; *olyte*, jollity.
Jornay, journey.
Jowall, juel, jewel; *juelere*, jeweler.
Juge, iugge, judge; *iugged*, judged.
Juste, joust, tilt in tournament.

K

Kachez, reins up; *kaght*, caught, took.
Kalle, call.
Kanel, collar, neck.
Kast, cast.
Kavelacion, strife.
Kay, left.
Kechone, kitchen.
Keep, care, heed; *keip*, keep; *keipt*, kept.
Kell, cap, head-dress.
Kempes, warriors.
Kems, combs; *kempte*, combed.
Ken, kin, mankind.
Ken, know; *kend*, known, recognized; *kenned*, taught.
Kendlit, kindled.
Kene, bold.
Kepe, keep, protect, take care.
Kerchere, kerchief, head-cover.
Kerved, carved.
Kest, knot; trick.
Kest, keste, cast, threw.
Kethat, cassock, long robe.
Keve, turn.
Kevel, gag.
Kever, recover.
Keverez, descends, obtains.
Kin, kindred; *kinde*, nature, character; *kindeschipe*, kinship, acquaintance.
Kilted, tucked up.
Kirtillis, kirtles.
Kitoun, kitten.
Klyfez, klyffez, cliffs.

Knarre, knotted, thickset fellow.
Knarrez, cliffs.
Knave, boy; *knaves*, servants.
Knaw, know; *knawen*, known.
Knelyng, kneeling.
Knet, knit, twined.
Knicht, knight; *knichtlie*, knightly.
Knokled, having projections, craggy.
Knorned, knobbed, rough.
Knyff, knife; *knyvis*, knives.
Knyled, kneeled.
Konyng, cony or rabbit (fur).
Kort, court.
Koyntly, cunningly; *koyntyse*, cunning.
Kunnes, kind's, of kind.
Kvre, cover.
Kyd, showed, manifested; *kydde*, declared; well-known, renowned.
Kye, kyne, kine, cows.
Kylde, killed.
Kynde, kind, nature, kinship; *kynde wytte*, natural intelligence; *kyndely*, properly.
Kyne, royal; *kyngriche*, kingdom.
Kynnellis, battlements.
Kyrf, cut, blow.
Kyrkis, kirks, churches.
Kyst, cast.
Kyste, chest.
Kyth, land, country.
Kythe, make known, show; *kythit*, shown.

L

Laas, lace, cord, string.
Lach, take.
Lad, ladden, led, taken.
Ladyis, ladies.
Laft, lafte, laften, left, ceased, delivered.
Lage, law, custom.
Laghes, laughs.
Laght, took, caught, received.
Laike, play.
Laip, lap.
Lait, late.
Laith, loath.
Lak, lack, want; *lakit, lakkyt*, lacks; *lakkede*, lacked.
Lake, shroud.
Lan, land; *landis*, lands.
Lansing, running.
Lant, lent, gave.
Lap, leaped.
Lappe, fold, cloth; *lapped*, wrapped, folded.
Lappez, borders, laps.

Large, freely, broadly, coarsely; *larges*, liberality.
Lascht, lashed.
Lasse, less.
Lat, let; *latting*, letting.
Lathed, invited.
Lathly, loathsome.
Latoun, *latten*, a compound of copper and zinc.
Lauched, laughed.
Laughte, caught.
Launde, clear space in a wood.
Lauriol, spurge laurel.
Law, low; *lawfully*, in a low voice.
Lawe, mount.
Lawhing, laughing.
Lawsez, looses.
Lawtie, loyalty.
Lay, law.
Lay, lodged.
Lay, lay down, wager.
Laykez, sports.
Layned, hidden, kept secret.
Layser, leisure.
Layt, lightning.
Layt, *layte*, look, seek.
Lazar, *lazarous*, leper.
Leafdi, lady.
Lease, lose.
Least, last.
Least, lest.
Ledden, speech.
Lede, people, retinue.
Lede, lead; *ledyt*, led; *ledyth*, leadeth; *ledes-man*, leader, guide.
Leed, cauldron.
Leef, dear, agreeable.
Leef, leaf.
Leene, lean.
Leere, learn.
Lees, lost.
Leet, let.
Lef, dear.
Lef, leaf.
Lefve, leave, farewell.
Legge, liege.
Legges, *leggis*, legs.
Leghe, lay.
Leid, lead.
Leid, persons, folk.
Leide: bi leide, lain down.
Leide, laid, leaned; *leidest*, laidst.
Leif, leave. permission.

Leif, live.
Leip, leap.
Leir, learn.
Leive, leave.
Lekes, leeks.
Lelly, loyally, faithfully.
Leman, lover, mistress.
Leme, glide away.
Lemed, gleamed, shone; *lemand*, *lemyng*, shining, gleaming, glittering; *lemes*, *lemis*, beams, gleams.
Lende, dwell.
Lene, lend; *lende*, lent.
Leng, longer; *lenghe*, *lenkthe*, *lenthe*, length; *on lenghe*, *on lenthe*, a long time; *upon lenghe*, at length.
Lenge, linger, stay, dwell; *lent*, tarried, remained.
Lent, leaned, departed; *lenynge*, leaning.
Lenten, Lent, spring.
Leof, *leofve*, dear, pleasing.
Leosen, lose.
Leoun, lion.
Lere, countenance.
Lere, learn, be learned; *lered*, learned; *lerne*, learn.
Les, less; *lest*, least.
Lese, lose.
Lesing, lying; *lesingis*, lies.
Lest, pleasure, delight; (it) pleased.
Leste, *lestez*, lost.
Lesteth, lasteth.
Let, *lett*, hinder, prevent, refrain, refrain from; *lette*, hindered; *let*, hindrance, obstacle; *lette*, delay.
Lete, looks, behavior; *lette*, acted.
Leten, considered.
Letez, let.
Lethe, moderate.
Letterure, learning.
Letuaries, electuaries, medical pastes.
Leude, man.
Leudly, lewdly, ignorantly, wickedly.
Leun, lion.
Leute, loyalty.
Leve, permit, grant.
Leve, cease, leave; *levis*, leaves.
Leve, believe; *levez*, believes.
Leve, dearly; *lever*, dearer, more pleasant, rather.
Levedi, lady.
Levit, lived; *levyth*, liveth.
Lewche, laughed.

Lewed, lewde, unlearned, ignorant.
Lewte, lewtye, loyalty.
Ley, lie, lay; *leyd,* laid.
Leyff-tenante, lieutenant.
Lhouth, loweth.
Lhude, loud.
Libardes, leopards.
Libbe, live; *libbyng,* **living.**
Liche: i liche, alike.
Lichery, lechery.
Licht, alight.
Licour, liquor.
Lict, light.
Lides, lids.
Lief, love.
Lifdaye, life's day, lifetime; *lif-lode,* liveli
hood; *lifve,* life.
Liggen, lie, lodge.
Ligten, alight, descend.
Likede, (it) pleased; *liki,* like, please.
Likerous, delicate, dainty.
Likned, likened.
Lim, limb.
Ling, long grass, heather.
Lipne, trust.
Lipper, leper.
List, is pleased, are pleased, **pleasest.**
List, liest; *lith,* lieth.
Litarge, litharge, white lead.
Lith, limb.
Litherlurden, disease of laziness.
Lobyes, lubbers.
Lock, look.
Lodlich, loathsome, hateful.
Lof, loaf.
Logge, lodging; *logged,* lodged.
Loghe, water.
Loh, laughed.
Lok, loke, look; *lokyde,* looked, saw.
Loke, loki, lock, guard, preserve; *loke,*
loken locked. shut.
Lomb, lamb.
Lome, often.
Lome, tool, axe.
Lond, londe, land; *in londe,* away.
Longes, lungs.
Longeth, longes, belongs.
Looth, loath, disagreeable.
Lopen, leaped.
Lordynge, lordling.
Lore, learning, knowledge, teaching.
Lorn, lorne, lost.
Los, fame.

Lose, loose.
Losel, worthless fellow.
Losengeour, flatterer, deceiver.
Lossum, lovesome, lovable, lovely.
Lote, bow, inclination of the head.
Lote, lot.
Lote, sound; *lotez,* words.
Loth, lothe, loathsome, hateful; *lother,*
more displeasing; *lothlich,* loathly; *lotheth,*
becomes loathsome to.
Loughe, laughed.
Louked, looped, fastened.
Louse, loose; *lousit.* loosened, let fly.
Loute, bow down, bow down to.
Loverd, lord.
Lovery, portion, allowance.
Lovies, loves; *lovieth,* love.
Lowande, shining.
Lowd, loud; *lowd and still,* under all cir-
cumstances.
Lowed, stooped.
Lowerd, lord.
Lowghe, lowh, laughed.
Lowne, still, quiet.
Luce, pike, a kind of fish
Luche, laughed.
Lud, loud.
Lud, voice, language.
Lud, lude, man, knight.
Luf, lufe, love; *lufis,* love's, of love; *luffaris,*
lovers; *lufiare,* lovelier; *luflych, luflyly,*
lovingly, graciously, courteously.
Luf-daungere, love-dominion.
Luik, luke, look.
Luken, lock, shut.
Lunzie, loins.
Lur, loss; *lurez,* losses.
Lust, pleasure, delight; *luste,* (it) would
please; *lustie,* lusty, pleasant, fair; *lustiar,*
more pleasant; *lustily,* pleasantly.
Lust, list, hear; *luste,* listened.
Lut, lutte, bowed, stooped.
Lutel, little.
Luveden, luved, loved.
Lycam, body.
Lycht, light.
Lyckely, likely.
Lyf, life, person; *lyfly,* in a lifelike way.
Lyff-tenant, lieutenant.
Lyghe, lie.
Lyght, lyht, alight, descend; *lyghte,* alighted.
Lyhte, light; *lyghtly, lyghtlich,* lightly,
easily, quickly.

Lynge, line, lineal descent.

Lyis, lies.

Lyk, lyke, like, as if, alike.

Lykyng, pleasure.

Lylye, lily.

Lymeres, hounds in leash

Lymes, limbs.

Lynde, lyne, linden, tree.

Lyndes, loins.

Lyne, lain.

Lyre, complexion.

Lyst, listen.

Lyst, (it) pleases; *lyste*, desire, longing.

Lyte, little; *on lyte*, a little; *girt a lyte*, girded loosely.

Lyth, lieth.

Lythe, assuage.

Lyvar, liver.

Lyve, life; *on lyve*, alive; *be lyve*, quickly; *lyvis*, life's; *lyveden*, lived.

Lyveree, livery.

M

Ma, man.

Maad, made.

Mach, match.

Mack, make; *madde*, made.

Mad, made, weary, sad.

Madde, made.

Madde, go mad; *maddyng*, folly; *made*, mad.

Magger, maugre, in spite of; *in the magger*, in spite of.

Maghtyly, mightily.

Maid, made.

Maille, mail, armor.

Mair, more; *maist*, most.

Maister, master; *maistres*, masters; *maistresse*, mistress; *maistried*, mastered; *maistrye*, mastery, superiority; *a fair for the maistrye*, a fair one to have authority.

Maistow, mayest thou.

Makand, makkand, making; *make*, compose, write; *makynge*, composing poetry.

Make, mate.

Malancolye, malencolie, melancholy.

Male, mail, armor.

Male, mail, bag; *male-hors*, pack-horses.

Malice, malys, malice, misery.

Malte, melted, dissolved.

Malte, speak.

Manace, menace.

Mandeth, mends, increases.

Mane, man; *manes*, man's.

Maneir, maner, manner, manner of, kind of.

Manian, many an.

Mansed, menaced.

March, border; *march-parti*, borderside.

Mare, more.

Margarys, marjorys, pearls.

Marres, marrest, destroyest.

Marvayle, marvel.

Mary-bones, marrow-bones.

Mase, maze, confusion, trick, deception.

Maship, mastership.

Mate, confound, disable; *mat, mate*, dead, dull in appearance; overcome, dejected.

Mateere, mater, matter.

Matutyne, matutinal, of the morning.

Maugree, maugre, in spite of.

Maun, must.

May, maiden.

Mayct, mayest.

Mayit, sported.

Mayk, make.

Mayn, great, powerful; *mayne*, main, strength.

Maystres, mistress.

Me, my.

Me, men, one.

Meal-pock, meal-poke, meal-bag.

Meany, meanye, company, retinue, household.

Med, mead, meadow.

Mede, meede, meed, reward.

Medlee, medley, of a mixed color.

Meet, close-fitting.

Meit, meat.

Mele, discourse, talk; *meles*, talks; *meled*, spoke.

Melly, mêlée, combat.

Memorial, memory.

Mendez, amends.

Mene, mean, common, poor; middle course, golden mean.

Meneth, moaneth.

Menis, men's.

Menske, graciousness; *menskes*, honors; *mensked*, adorned.

Menstrale, minstrel.

Ment, mixed, mingled.

Meny, household.

Merbell, marble.

Mercy, thanks.

Mere, mare.

Mere, lake, stream, water: *meres*, waters.

Merely, merrily.

Merk, mark, bound.

Merse, topcastle, a protected place at a masthead.

Mervaille, mervele, merwell, marvel; *mervaylez*, marvels; *mervaylous*, marvelous.

Mery, merye, merry, pleasant.

Meschaunce, mischance.

Meschef, meschief, harm, trouble, mishap.

Meshe, mash, beat into a mass.

Messe, mass.

Mest, most, almost.

Mesure, measure, moderation; *mesurable*, moderate.

Met, dreamed.

Mete, measure; meet, suitable, fit.

Mete, meat; *mete-nythinges*, meat-niggards.

Meten, dream; *mette*, dreamed; *hym mette*, dreamed; *meteles*, dream.

Meven, move; *meved*, moved.

Meyne, meynee, crew, company, retinue.

Mich, much; *mickle*, much, great.

Micte, might.

Mid, with; *mid hwan*, with what.

Middel, middle, waist; *middlis*, middles.

Midding, dung-heap.

Migte, might; *mihti*, mighty.

Mikel, great.

Miles, animals.

Min, mine, my.

Ming, mingle, mix.

Ministres, ministers, officers.

Misliketh, displeases.

Mister, master, achieve.

Mit, with.

Mithe, conceal.

Mo, more.

Moche, mochel, mochil, much, great.

Mod, mode, mood, mind; *mody*, moody.

Moder, mother.

Moe, more.

Moght, might.

Moich, moist, misty.

Moir, more.

Molde, mold, earth; *moldez*, earth.

Molte, melted; *moltin*, molten.

Momme, mum, least sound.

Mon, man.

Mon, moan.

Mon, must.

Mone, moon; *monethes*, months.

Monie, many.

Monische, admonish.

Monne, men's; *monnes*, man's.

Monnyn-day, Monday.

Mony, money.

Moon, moan.

Moot, notes on a horn.

Moote, may.

Mor, more.

Moralitee, moral lesson.

Mordre, murder; *mordred*, murdered; *mordrour*, murderer.

Mormal, sore.

Morne, mourn; *mornyng*, mourning, sorrow.

Morne, morow, morowing, morrow, morning.

Mort, death-note, blast on the horn to announce the death of game.

Mortel: bed mortel, death-bed.

Morwe, morning; *by the morwe*, in the morning.

Mose, titmouse.

Most, very great.

Most, moste, mosten, must.

Mot, mote, may, must.

Mote, argument, speech.

Mottelee, motley.

Moucte, might.

Moul, mold, earth.

Mountez, amounts, avails.

Mowe, may.

Mowse, mouse.

Molaynes, bits.

Muchel, muchele, much, great; *muckel* greatness, great size.

Mufe, move.

Muhe, may.

Mulne, mill.

Munt, blow, aim, purpose.

Munt, feigned.

Murehthe, murhthe, mirth, joy; *murgeth*, make merry, gladden; *murie*, merry; *muryly*, merrily.

Murning, mourning; *murnit*, mourned.

Mus, mice.

Musit, mused.

Muthe, mouth.

Muwen, may.

Mychel, much

Mycht, might; *mychti, mychty*, mighty.

Myddlez, midst, middle of.

Myd-iwisse, with certainty, surely.

Myhte, might.

Mykel, much.

Myllan, Milan steel.

Myn, mind, attend.

Myn one, myself; *myne allone*, by myself.

Myneyeple, long gauntlet.

Mynn, think.

Mynours, miners.

Mynstrales, minstrels.

Mynt, aim, blow; *myntest*, struckest; *myntez*, strikes.

Myry, merry, pleasing; *myryeste*, merriest, pleasantest.

Mys, mice.

Mys, tunic.

Mys, sin; *mysses*, sins, faults.

Mys-boden, wronged.

Myschief, damage, harm.

Mysduden, did amiss.

Myse-tente, misunderstood.

Mysse, lack, want; lose, get rid of.

Mysse-yeme, misuse

Myster, trade.

Mythe, escape.

Myttanis, mittens.

N

Na, no, not.

Nabbe, nabbeth, have not; *nadde*, had not.

Nafre, never.

Naght, not, naught.

Nam, name.

Nam, am not.

Nam, took.

Namo, namore, no more.

Nane, none.

Nanis, nonce.

Napoplexie, nor apoplexy.

Nar, nare, nor.

Narette, impute to.

Narewe, narwe, narrow, narrowly, closely.

Nas, was not, (it) was not.

Nat, not.

Natheles, nevertheless.

Naunt, aunt.

Nauther, nawther, neither.

Naver, never.

Ne, not, nor.

Nece, niece.

Nedder, adder, serpent.

Nedels, needles.

Nedely, necessarily; *nedez*, needs, of necessity.

Nee, nor.

Neet, cattle.

Negge, neghe, draw near; *neghe, neh*, nigh.

Neid, need.

Neir, ne'er.

Nel, nelle, will not.

Nempne, name.

Neod, need, needs.

Ner, near; *nerre*, nearer.

Nere, never.

Nere, were not.

Nese, nose.

Nethar, neither.

Nevene, name.

Nevew, nephew.

New-fangelnesse, love of novelty.

Nextin, next.

Ney, nigh; *neygheboris*, neighbors.

Nict, nicht, nihte, night; *the nicht*, to-night: *nihtes-when*, in the night-time.

Nikked, denied.

Nis, is not.

Nither, nether, down, below.

Nixt, next.

No, nor.

Nobley, nobility.

Nobot, nothing but(?).

Nocht, noght, noht, naught, not.

Nodye, noddy, simpleton.

Nolde, would not.

Nombre, number.

Nome, name.

Nomen, took.

Nomon, no man.

Non, none.

Non, none, noon.

Nones, no.

Nones, nonys, nonce, the once.

Noon, none.

Noot, know not.

Norice, nurse; *norising, norissyng*, nourishing.

Norland, northland.

Norne, call.

Nose-thirles, nosethrels, nostrils.

Nostow, thou knowest not; *not*, know not

Notabilitee, notable thing.

Note, business, profit.

Note, throat-knot (?).

Noth, not.

Not-heed, crop-head, head with hair cut short.

Nother, neither.

Nou, now.

Nouct, nout, nouth, not.

Nouthe, just now.

Nouther, neither

Nowight, nowiht, not, nothing.
Nowor, nowhere.
Nowt, nowth, not, nothing.
Nowthe, now.
Noyouse, troublesome.
Noyss-thyrlys, nostrils.
Nu, now.
Nuke, nook.
Nul, nulle, will not.
Nusten, knew not.
Nuthe, now.
Nutshales, nutshells.
Ny, nye, nigh, close.
Nyce, foolish.
Nye, vex, trouble.
Nygard, niggard.
Nyghtertale, night-time.
Nyhtegales, nightingales.
Nys, foolish, stupid.
Nys, is not.
Nyste, knew not.

O

O, of.
O, one.
Obeysaunces, acts of obedience.
Observance, conduct; mode of playing and singing.
Obstract, abstract.
Obumbrat, overshaded.
Occiane, ocean.
Ochane, a cry of woe.
Ociositie, idleness.
Of, off, from, out of; for, on account of, in respect of.
Of-dradde, in dread, afraid.
Off, of.
Of-slaghe, slain; *of-sloghen*, slew.
Of-teoned, vexed.
Of-thincheth, repents, makes sorry; repent.
Of-thowed, thawed away.
Oge, oghne, own.
Oght, aught, something.
Oght, ohte, bold, brave.
Oille, oil.
Okkeraris, usurers.
On, a, an, one.
On, in, of.
One, own.
One, alone; *onely*, only; *ones, onis*, once.
Onslydez, unfolds, opens.
Onsware, answer.
Oo, aye, continually.

Oo, oon, oone, one; *in oone*, in the same condition; *after oon*, according to one standard, of uniform excellence.
Operacyon, workmanship.
Opinioun, reputation.
Opne, open.
Or, ore, ere, before.
Ore, one.
Orfeverye, goldsmith's work.
Orient, eastern; the East.
Orisoun, prayer; *oritore*, oratory, place of prayer.
Orlogge, horologe, clock.
Ornat, ornate, beautiful.
Orpedly, boldly.
Ost, host; *ostel*, hostel, dwelling.
Oter, otter (fur).
Oth, of the.
Other, either, or; the other, the second; *otherweies*, otherwise.
Ou, you.
Ouersylit, covered over.
Ouirquhelmit, overwhelmed.
Ouirthorte, athwart, across.
Ounces, small portions.
Oundy, wavy.
Oune, own.
Oures, hours; prayers appointed for certain hours of the day.
Ourheldand, covering over; *our-helit*, covered over.
Ourthwort, athwart, across.
Outrely, utterly, entirely.
Out-sterte, started out.
Over, over to, up to the point of; besides.
Overal, all over; everywhere; more than all.
Over-dede, excess.
Overest, uppermost.
Over-go, go by.
Over-seh, looked down on, despised.
Overshette, overshot.
Overspradde, overspread.
Over-take, overcome.
Overture, opening.
Over-walt, overcome.
Ovyth, oweth, ought.
Owar, oware, hour.
Owel, awl.
Owen, owin, owyn, own.
Owher, anywhere.
Owtbrastyng, bursting out.
Oynons, onions.

P

Pace, go on, surpass.

Padzane, pageant.

Palays, paleys, palace.

Pane, piece of cloth inserted in a garment for ornament.

Panis, pains.

Pansing, thinking.

Panter, fowler's net, snare.

Pappe, pap, breast.

Paraunter, peradventure.

Pardé, pardee, par Dieu (a mild oath).

Parell, peril; *parellous*, perilous.

Parfit, perfect.

Parishens, paroschienes, parishioners.

Part, divide, deal, give.

Parti, side; *partye*, sides; *uppone a parti*, aside.

Partit, parti-colored, variegated.

Partlez, partless, portionless.

Partye, partner.

Pas, pace, footpace; *pase*, paces.

Passe, extent.

Passen, surpass, conquer; passed, surpassed.

Passis, pass.

Pastance, pastime.

Pastees, pasties.

Pay, paye, pleasure; *payed*, pleased.

Payred, impaired.

Payttrure, breast-armor for a horse.

Peces, pieces.

Pees, peace.

Peire, pair, set.

Pekke, peck.

Pelure, costly fur.

Pendaundes, pendauntes, pendants.

Pensiwe, pensyf, pensive, sad.

Pented, pertained.

Penuritie, penury.

Peple, people.

Pepyns, seeds, apple-seeds.

Perdurably, permanently

Pere, peer, equal.

Perell, peril.

Peren, appear.

Perez, pears.

Perfet, perfect; *perfitly*, perfectly.

Perilouslych, perilously.

Perrie, jewelry.

Pers, cloth of sky-blue color

Persavit, perceived.

Perse, pierce.

Persewit, pursued, followed; *persute*, pursuit.

Person, parson.

Pes, peace.

Pese, peas; *pescodes*, peas-cods, pea-pods.

Pete, pity.

Peyce, piece (of ground), field.

Peyned, took pains; *peyned him*, put him to the trouble; *peynest thee*, puttest thee to the trouble.

Philomene, philomel, nightingale.

Piche, pitch.

Pieteous, piteous.

Pigges, pigs'.

Piled, having little hair.

Pilwe-beer, pillow-case.

Pin, door-pin, inside latch.

Pinched, pleated.

Pinkynge, blinking.

Pitee, pity; *pitous*, piteous, compassionate.

Plaiding, disputing; *plait*, dispute, debate.

Plane, playne, level, smooth.

Playned, mourned, lamented.

Plededen, pleaded.

Pleigntes, complaints.

Plenie, plenty, abundance, fullness (of time).

Plesand, pleasant; *plesaunce, plesere*, pleasure.

Pleyen, pleyne, play, disport; *pleyed*, played.

Pleyn, full; entirely; *pleynly*, completely.

Pleyne, complain, lament; *pleyned hem*, complained.

Plicht-anker, sheet-anchor.

Plonttez, plants.

Plye, plight.

Plyght, fault; harm, danger.

Plyte, plight, condition.

Pobbel, pebble.

Poke, bag.

Pole, pool, stream.

Poleist, polysed, polished, cleaned.

Pomely, dappled.

Poraille, poor; *porre*, poor; *porful*, very poor.

Porfyl, hem.

Portes, gates.

Portrature, form; *porturat*, portrayed, outlined.

Possed, pushed.

Possede, possess.

Potshordes, potsherds.

Poure, power.

Poure, pouren, pore, look.

Povre, poor.
Poweer, power.
Powped, tooted, blew.
Poynaunt, poignant, pungent.
Poyned, trimmed, ornamented.
Poynt, case, condition.
Practisour, practitioner.
Prangled, pressed.
Praty. pretty.
Precios, precious.
Prees, press, throng.
Preest, priest; *preistis*, priests.
Pref, proof; *preif*, prove, test.
Prelat, prelate.
Prent, imprint, stamp.
Pres, prese, press, throng.
Presently, at once.
Presse, mold.
Prest, preste, ready.
Pretely, prettily.
Preve, prove; proof, of proved strength.
Prevy, privy, secret; *prewelie*, privily.
Prey, pray; *preyden*, prayed; *preyeres*, prayers.
Preyse. praise; *preysynges*, praisings.
Pricasour, pricker, hard rider; *prikyng*, spurring, riding.
Pricliss, pricks, annoys.
Prime, about nine A.M.
Primordyall, first beginning.
Pris, price; prize.
Probacioun, proof.
Proceede, go to law.
Promys, promise.
Prophytabylle, fruitful.
Propre, peculiar, own; *proprely*, appropriately; *propretee*, property, peculiar characteristic.
Proved, was proved.
Prow, prowe, profit.
Prowes, prowess.
Proyne, preen, trim feathers with the beak.
Prudence, wisdom.
Pruyde, pride.
Prys, pryse, price, value, esteem; *bear the pryse*, have the pre-eminence.
Pucell, virgin, maid.
Pu'd, pulled, plucked.
Pulder, powder.
Pulled, plucked.
Pultrye, poultry.
Purchas, things acquired, proceeds of begging.

Purchasour, conveyancer; *purchasyng*, conveyancing.
Pured, furred.
Pured, purified.
Purfiled, trimmed.
Purpour, purple.
Purs, purse.
Purtreye, portray, draw.
Pyece, piece, thing.
Pyght, placed,
Pyll, strip, spoil.
Pynakled, having pinnacles or peaks.
Pynche, find fault.
Pyne, punishment, torment; *pyned*, tormented; *Goddes pyne*, the Passion of Christ.
Pyonys, peonies.
Pysan, gorget, neck-armor.
Pyte, pity.

Q

Quat, quhat, what, lo; *quat-so*, whatsoever.
Quath, quoth.
Quelle, kill.
Quen, quhen, when.
Quene, queen.
Quere, quhere, where; *queresoever*, wheresoever.
Queth, bequest (?).
Quethen, whence.
Quettyng, whetting.
Quha, who; *quhais*, whose; *quham*, whom.
Quhair, quhar, quhare, where; *quhareby*, whereby.
Quheill, wheel.
Quhi, quhy, why.
Quhich, quhilk, quhilkis, which.
Quhile, quhill, while, till.
Quhyp, whip.
Quhyrlys, whirls along, drives.
Quhyte, dissembling.
Quic, quick, alive.
Quiere, choir.
Quight, quit, clear, free.
Quite, quhite, white.
Quite, requite.
Quo, quho, who; *quhois*, whose; *quhom*, whom; *quo-so*, whosoever.
Quod, quoth.
Quycke, quick, alive.
Quyle, quhyle. while.
Quyrry, quarry, dead game.
Quyt, quhyte, white.

Quyte, requite, reward; quit, avenged.
Qwelp, whelp.

R

Raas, onset, course.
Racis, races, kinds.
Rad, afraid.
Rad, read.
Rade, rode.
Radly, readily, promptly.
Rage, rave, be mad, behave wantonly.
Raght, reached; *raghtez*, gavest.
Ragman, papal bull.
Raid, rode.
Raine, reign.
Rais, raise, rose.
Rak, noise.
Rake, course, way.
Randez, paths, borders.
Rapely, quickly.
Rasores, razors.
Ratheled, rooted.
Rather, sooner.
Ratones, rats.
Raughte, reached, got, grown.
Rawez, rows.
Rawthe, terrible.
Raxled, roused, awoke.
Raye, a kind of striped cloth.
Raykande, going, flowing; loud.
Rayled, bordered.
Rayleth, puts on.
Raynez, reins.
Raysoun, reason.
Reade, take heed, take counsel.
Reane, rain.
Reas, rouse.
Reboytit, driven back; *rebute*, rebuttal, repulse.
Recche, rech, reck, care; *recchelees, recheles*, careless, indifferent, regardless.
Receit, receipt.
Rechased, driven back.
Reches, extends; *rechez*, reachest, offerest.
Recorde, remind.
Recure, remedy.
Red, rede, advice, counsel; *rede*, advise, counsel; *redde*, said; *redden*, advised.
Rede, read.
Rede, red.
Redely, redly, readily, soon.
Redempte, redeemed.
Redez, managest.

Redis, reeds.
Reed, advice, counsel; counselor.
Reed, red.
Refete, feed, refresh.
Reflayr, odor.
Reflex, reflection.
Refourme, renew.
Refute, defense.
Regale, regal; *regne*, reign; *regnes*, realms.
Regrait, regret, complaint.
Reherce, rehercen, rehearse.
Reid, advise.
Reid, red.
Reiffis, bereaves, robs.
Reight, reached.
Reird, uproar.
Reiseth, raiseth.
Rejosit, rejoiced.
Reke, smoke.
Reken, beautiful; *rekenly*, nobly, courteously.
Rekene, reckon; *reknyd*, reckoned.
Rele, encounter.
Relece, release.
Reled, rolled.
Releved, raised up, revived.
Relusant, resplendent.
Rem, roar, cry.
Remeid, remedy, cure; find remedy.
Remenaunt, remnant, rest.
Remes, realms.
Remeves, removes.
Remorde, blame.
Renable, fluent, loquacious.
Renke, man.
Renne, rennen, run.
Renon, renoun, renown.
Rent, revenue, income.
Rente, split.
Renzie, rein.
Reowe, rue, grieve.
Repen, reap.
Replecciouns, repletions.
Reportour, reporter, umpire.
Rere, proceed.
Rescowe, rescue.
Resedew, residue.
Resette, place of reception.
Reson, resoun, ressoun, reason, right; statement, speech, talk; *resouns, resouns*, opinions, words.
Resownyt, resounded.
Ressave, receive.
Restayed, restrained.

Reste, arrest.

Retchlesse, reckless.

Rethor, rhetorician, writer; *rethorik*, rhetoric, art of expression.

Retrete, relate.

Reule, reulen, rule.

Reve, rive, rob, drive away; *reving*, robbery.

Reverence, respect, respectful manner; *at the reverence*, in honor of, for the sake of; *reverenced*, greeted.

Reverez, streams.

Revers, reverse.

Revest, reclothed; *revestyng*, reclothing.

Revin, raven.

Revis, tears.

Rew, rewe, rue, pity, take pity; *reweth me*, makes me sorry.

Rewme, realm.

Reyne, rain.

Reysed, gone on military expeditions.

Ribaudye, ribaldry.

Riche, realm, kingdom.

Riche, noble (steed); *richesse*, riches, nobility.

Richt, rict, right, riht, rihte, right, just, justly, exactly.

Rimed, stretched.

Rise, branch, bough.

Rispis, marsh grass.

Ritt, runs.

Riving, tearing.

Roches, rochis, rocks.

Rod, rode.

Rode, rood, cross.

Rode, redness, complexion.

Rof, cut, blow.

Rofe. roof.

Roghe, rough.

Roghte, recked, cared.

Roial, royal; *roialliche*, royally.

Rokkes, rocks, cliffs.

Role, roll.

Ronge, rang, resounded, rung.

Ronk, rank, large; bold, strong.

Ronne, run; *bludy ronne*, run over with blood.

Rood, rod.

Rood, rode.

Roos, rose.

Roost, roste, roast.

Roote, rote, root.

Ropen, reaped.

Ros, rose; *rosere*. rose-garden.

Rote, a kind of fiddle.

Rotten, rat.

Roun, whisper; *roun, roune, rune*, song, *rounes*, whispers, murmurs.

Rounce, rouncy, horse, nag.

Rourde, sound.

Rous, fame.

Rout, company.

Rout, route, noise, roar.

Routhe, ruth, pity.

Rove, cleft, cut.

Rowd, rolled, wound.

Rowme, room, space.

Rownande, whispering, murmuring; *rownaris*, whisperers.

Rowp, croak.

Rubarde, rhubarb.

Ruchched, ruched, settled, ordered, fixed.

Rudeliche, rudely.

Rueth, ruth.

Ruged, rugged, shaggy.

Rughe, rough.

Ruke, rook.

Ruled, well-mannered.

Rumpillis, rumples, folds.

Runisch, violent, sudden; *runischly*, roughly fiercely.

Rurd, noise, clamor.

Ruse, praise.

Rused, roused.

Rute, root.

Ryal, ryalle, royal; *ryalmes*, realms.

Rych, ryche, noble, resplendent; nobles; *rychesse*, riches.

Ryched, prepared, arranged; *ryght*, prepares.

Rycht, right; *ryghtwysnes*, righteousness.

Ryd, rid, release, set aside.

Ryshes, rushes.

Rysyt, arise.

Ryveris, river's; *rywir*, river.

Ryvez, rives, cleaves.

S

Sa, sae, so.

Sabill, sabyll, sablyne, sable.

Sad, sade, serious, grave, constant, stedfast; *saddest*, most serious; *sadly*, gravely, steadily.

Saf, safe, save, except.

Saffer, sapphire.

Safforne, saffron.

Saghe, word.

Saghte, peace, reconciliation.

Saif, save.

Sair, sore.

Sait, seat.

Sal, sall, shall.

Sale, hall.

Salt. assault.

Saluse, salute; *salust*, saluted.

Same, shame.

Samin, samyn, same.

Sanct, saint.

Sangwyn, sanguine, blood-color, ruddy; cloth of blood color, red cloth.

Sank, blood.

Sar, sore; *sarar*, sorer.

Sarvi, serve; *sarvyes*, service.

Saufly, safely.

Saugh, saw.

Sautrye, psaltery, harp.

Save, safe; *save-condyt*, safe-conduct.

Saverly, savory, sweet; *savour*, like, relish; savor, taste.

Sawcefleem, red and pimpled.

Sawez, words.

Sawgh, say, saw.

Saye, essay, try.

Sayn, say; *say, sayede*, said; *saytz*, sayest.

Saynt, samite, rich silk.

Scade, cleft.

Scalled, scalyt, scaled, scabby.

Scathe, harm, misfortune, injury.

Schaddow, image.

Schafte, spear.

Schaghe, grove, wood.

Schalk, man, knight.

Schane, shone.

Schapin, shaped.

Scharp, sharp (axe).

Scheild, shield.

Scheir, shear, cut.

Schende, schent, destroy.

Schene, shining, bright, beautiful, clear; bright (axe).

Schere, purify, refine.

Scherez, shears, divides.

Scherp, sharp.

Schevin, shaven.

Schew, show, appear.

Schilde, shield.

Schill, shrill.

Schir, sir.

Scho, she.

Scholes, hangs down (?).

Schome, shame.

Schone, schoone, shoes.

Schop, shaped, provided.

Schore, shore, earth, ground.

Schorne, purified, refined.

Schorte shorten (the time), amuse.

Schoure, shower.

Schowvez, shoves, pushes.

Schrank, sunk, pierced.

Schrevin, shriven, absolved.

Schrewis, sinners.

Schrowdith, enshrouds, clothes, invests.

Schrylle, shrill, clear.

Schuik, shook.

Schulde, should; *schule, schulle*, shall.

Schunt, flinching.

Schwne, shun, protect.

Schyire, schyr, schyre, bright, clear, pure; *schyre*, bright (neck).

Schylderes, shoulders.

Schymeryng, shimmering.

Schyn, shall.

Schynand, shining; *schynez*, shines.

Schyndered, severed.

Science, knowledge, learning.

Sclayne, slain; *scle, scloo*, slay.

Sclendre, slender.

Scole, school; *scoleye*, go to school

Scowtes, caves.

Scrippull, scruple.

Scroggs, underwood.

Scryppis, scrips knapsacks

Se, saw.

Seaven, seven.

Seche, seek.

Secree, secret.

Sed, sede, seed.

See, sea.

See, seat.

See, protect.

Seege, siege.

Seeke, sick.

Seel, seal.

Seen, see.

Sege, seat.

Segg, man; *segges*, men

Segge, sedge.

Segge, seggen, say, may say.

Segh, seh, seigh, saw; *seis*, seest.

Seide, said; *of seide*, spoke of; *for seide*. aforesaid; *sein*, say; *seist*, sayest; *seith*, saith

Seiknes, sickness; *seke*, sick.
Seker, sure.
Selcouth, seldom known, rare.
Selde, seldom.
Sele, prosperity.
Seles, seals.
Self, selfsame, same.
Selhthe, happiness.
Selk, silk.
Selles, cells.
Selliche, *selly*, wonderful, strange; *sellyez*,
    wonders.
Sely, simple, helpless.
Semblaunt, semblance, countenance.
Semblyde, assembled.
Seme, *semly*, seemly; *semely*, becomingly;
    semlokest, seemliest, most lovely; *semyt*,
    seemed.
Sen, since.
Sendal, thin silk.
Send, *sende*, sends, sent.
Sene, seen.
Sene, truthful.
Sengeley, alone.
Sens, incense.
Sent I me, I assent.
Sentement, sentiment, feeling, passion.
Sentence, sense, meaning, subject, theme,
    opinion.
Seo, see.
Seolve, self.
Seorewe, sorrow.
Seoththe, sith, since afterwards.
Seowe, sowed.
Sep, sheep.
Ser, *sere*, sire, sir.
Sere, several, diverse.
Sereyn, serene.
Serjauntz, sergeants-at-law, lawyers.
Serk, sark, shirt.
Sertayne, certainly.
Servez, serves; *serwit*, served; *servisable*,
    willing to serve.
Sesed, ceased.
Sesed, seized.
Seson, *sesoun*, *sesson*, season.
Sete, seat; *seten*, sat.
Sete, *setten*, set, bind.
Sew, sue.
Sewed, pursued, followed; *seweth*, follows.
Sey, sea; *seyis*, seas.
Sey, saw.
Seye, *seyne*, *seyt*, say.

Seyl, sail.
Seynd, singed, broiled.
Seysoun, season.
Shadwe, shadow.
Shake, shaken.
Shale, shall; *shaltow*, shalt thou.
Sham, shame.
Shap, *shapen*, shape, form, plan; *shape me*,
    prepare me; *shaped*, made; *shaply*, fit.
Sharpe, steep.
Shathmont, hand-span.
Shawe, show, report.
Shear, several.
Shedes, sheds; *sheede*, shed.
Shee, shoe; *sheene*, shoes.
Sheeldes, French coins stamped with shields.
Sheld, shield.
Shenden, shame, harm; *shent*, *shente*,
    destroyed, hurt; *shenshipp*, shame, dis-
    grace.
Shene, bright.
Shepe, shepherd.
Sheres, shears.
Sherte, shirt.
Shete, shoot.
Shette, shut.
Shewith, showeth.
Shilde, shield.
Shir, bright, clear.
Shirreve, sheriff.
Sho, she.
Sho, shoe.
Shold, should; *shole*, *sholen*, shall.
Shome, shame.
Shonye, shun.
Shoon, shone.
Shoope, *shope*, shaped, prepared, made,
    ordained, dressed; *shopen*, dressed as.
Shorte, shorten; *shortly*, in short, to be brief.
Shot, money, coin.
Shot-anker, sheet-anchor; a main reliance.
Shote, shoot, shot.
Shoud, should.
Shoures, showers.
Shrewe, beshrew, curse; sinner, tyrant.
Shrighte, *shriked*, shrieked.
Shroudes, clothes.
Shul, shall; *shulde*, should.
Shuldres, shoulders.
Shyars, shires.
Sic, such.
Siching, sighing.
Sigh, *sih*, saw; *sihte*, sight.

Sike, sick.

Sike, sigh.

Siker, assure, confirm; *sikerer*, surer, more reliable; *sikerlike*, *sikerly*, surely, truly, assuredly.

Silden, shield.

Sile, betray.

Siller, silver.

Sin, *sins*, since.

Sindrie, *sindry*, sundry, several.

Sined, shined, shone.

Singuleer, single, private, individual.

Sipe, ship.

Sipers, cypress, thin stuff for veils.

Sit, sits.

Sith, *sithe*, *sithen*, since, afterward.

Sithe, time; *sithes*, times.

Skaldand, scalding.

Skayved, wild, desolate.

Skil, reason.

Skinkled, sparkled.

Skowland, scowling, overhanging.

Skwez, shades.

Skyis, sky's; *skyiss*, skies.

Skylful, reasonable; *skylle*, reason; *skyllez*, reasons.

Sla, slay; *slaghte*, stroke; *slaghtere*, slaughter.

Slade, valley, dell.

Slak, hollows, dales.

Slake, stop, cease, desist, neglect.

Slan, *slawe*, slain.

Slaw, slow.

Sle, *slee*, *sleath*, slay; *slean*, slain.

Sleepe, slept; *sleper*, sleeper.

Sleighte, *sleyht*, sleight, skill, trick, trickery, devices.

Sleit, sleet.

Sleuthe, sloth.

Slich, *sliche*, slime, plaster.

Slode, slid.

Slokes, cease.

Sloo, slay; *sloghen*, *sloughe*, *slow*, slew; *slone*, slain.

Slouthe, sloth; *slute*, slattern.

Sma, small.

Smake, scents.

Smarte, smartly; *smartly*, quickly.

Smert, *smerte*, smart, give pain; *smertith*, smarteth.

Smoot, smote.

Smorit, smothered.

Smothe, smooth; *smothely*, smoothly.

Smuke, smoke.

Smyte, smites.

Snese, sneeze.

Snybben, reprove, chide.

Snyrt, cut.

So, as, as if; *so . . . . so*, so . . . . as.

Sobir, quiet; *sobirly*, quietly.

Soche, such.

Sodaym, sudden; *sodeynly*, *sodenely*, suddenly.

Soght, sought.

Solas, solace, mirth.

Solde, should.

Solempne, festive, cheerful; *solempnely*, pompously.

Solle, soul.

Solle, shall.

Som-del, somewhat.

Somer, summer.

Somers, sumpter-horses, pack-horses.

Somnour, summoner; *somonynge*, summoning.

Sonde, sending, messenger.

Sone, son.

Sone, soon, forthwith; *soner*, sooner; *eft sonez*, again, likewise.

Song, *songe*, sung; *songe*, songs

Soote, sweet.

Sooth, true, truth; *soothly*, truly; *soothfastnesse*, truth.

Soper, supper.

Soppis, juices, moisture.

Sor, pain; *sore*, *soore*, sorely.

Sore, soar.

Sorghe, sorrow; *sori*. sorry, wretched.

Sorquydryghe, surquedry, pride.

Sort, company.

Sort, destiny.

Sorwe, sorrow; *sorweful*, sorrowful.

Sot, fool.

Soth, *sothe*, truth. true.

Sothery, soft and smooth(?).

Sould, should.

Soun, *sounn*, *soune*, sound.

Sounzie, care; *with sounzie*, with care, unwillingly.

Souple, supple.

Sourquydrye, pride.

Sours, springing up, ascent.

Soverayn, *sovereyn*, sovereign, supreme; *sovereynly*, supremely, most of all.

Sovethe, seventh.

Sowne, sound; *sownynge*, sounding; *sownynge in*, tending to, promoting.

Sowres, bucks in their third year.

Soyr, sorrel.

Soyte, suit.

Space, course.

Spale, splinter, cleft stick.

Spangis, spangles.

Sparlyr, calf of the leg.

Sparred, rushed.

Sparthe, battle-axe.

Sparwe, sparrow.

Spece, species, kind, creature.

Speche, speech; *speik*, speak.

Speid, speed; *gude speid*, fast, quickly.

Spelle, speech, story, long tale.

Spendyd, extended, placed in rest; *spenet*, fastened; *spenned*, clasped, enclosed; *spenne*, span, space, interval.

Spere, sphere.

Speten, spit.

Spetos, sharp.

Spety, speedy.

Spire, tall grass.

Spittaill, hospital.

Splendent, resplendent, shining.

Splene, spleen.

Sponne, spun, grew.

Spores, spurs; *sporne*, spurn, kick.

Sprad, *spredis*, *spreid*, spread.

Sprangis, rays.

Spreit, sprite, spirit.

Sprent, *sprente*, sprang, spurted.

Sprit, started.

Sprynge, spring.

Sprynkland, moving swiftly with undulatory motion.

Spures, spurs; *spurnis*, spurnest, kickest.

Spysez, aromatic plants.

Spyt, spite.

Squelonde, squealing, crying.

Squyar, *squyer*, squire, attendant on a knight.

Staat, estate, condition.

Stablit, made stable, quieted.

Stad, bestead, beset.

Stage, story.

Stale, stole; stealing.

Stalle, bring, place.

Stalworthe, stalwart.

Stane, stone; *stannyris*, small stones.

Stant, stands, consists.

Starc, stark.

Staren, shine.

Stean, stone.

Stedde, *stede*, stead, place.

Stede, *steid*, steed.

Stefne, voice.

Steill, steel.

Steir, stir up.

Stek, stuck, fitted tight.

Stel-bawe, steel-bow, saddle.

Stele, steel, handle.

Stele, steal.

Stel-gere, steel gear, armor.

Stellefye, make into a star.

Stem, ray of light; *stemed*, shone.

Stemd, *stemmed*, stopped.

Stent, stinted, stopped.

Stent, stretched.

Stepe, bright.

Stere, stir; prevent.

Stere, *sterre*, *stern*, star; *sternez*, stars.

Sterne, stern (men).

Steropes, stirrups.

Stert, tail.

Stert, *sterte*, started, darted.

Steven, *stevin*, sound, voice, conference; *at steven*, within reach of the voice.

Stewe, fish-pond.

Stich, stitch.

Stickit, stuck.

Stif, strong, brave; strongly, bravely.

Stightlez, sits, dwells.

Stirte, *stirten*, started.

Stoc, *stok*, stock, tree-trunk.

Stod, stood.

Stodie, study.

Stoken, secured, fixed.

Stonge, stung.

Stoon, stone; *stonyt*, stone; *ston-stil*, stonestill.

Stoor, store.

Stope, advanced.

Stot, stallion, horse, cob.

Stound, *stounde*, time, hour.

Stound, sudden pain; *stoundes*, pains.

Stour, *stoure*, combat, battle, conflict.

Stovys, vapors.

Stower, hour.

Stowned, astounded.

Stowrand, stirring, darting.

Strabery, strawberry.

Stran, strand, shore.

Strang, strong.

Straught, straight.

Straunge, strange, foreign.

Stray, astray.

Strayght, straightway; strait, narrow.

Strayne, restrain, curb.

Strecche, stretch; *streight*, stretched.

Streght, straight, straightway.

Streit, *streite*, strait, narrow, scanty, strict drawn; closely, tightly.

Strekene, stricken.

Strem, stream, river.

Stremande, shining; *stremowris*, streamers.

Streyneth, constraineth.

Streyte, straitly, strictly.

Streyves, strays.

Strike, hank.

Striketh, runs.

Strocke, struck.

Stroke, strode.

Strondes, strands, shores.

Strot, contest.

Strothe, hidden (?), secure (?).

Strydez, strides, mounts.

Strye, destroy.

Strythe, firm position with feet wide apart.

Stude, stood.

Stude, stead, place.

Sturez, brandishes.

Sturne, stern, severe, bold; *sturnely*, boldly.

Sturt, trouble.

Sturtes, stirrups.

Styghtel, set, dispose.

Stynt, *stynte*, stint, stop, cease; *stynst*, stint; *stynt*, *stynttyde*, stopped.

Stythly, strongly.

Suar, *suer*, sure, trusty; *suerly*, surely, safely.

Sudaynly, suddenly.

Suereth, sweareth.

Suete, sweet.

Sueving, dreaming.

Suffisant, sufficient; *suffisaunce*, sufficiency.

Suffre, *suffren*, suffer, allow.

Suich, *suilk*, such.

Suld, should.

Sulghart, shining.

Sulghe, soil, earth.

Sulle, shall.

Sulve, self.

Sum, some; *sumdeill*, somewhat.

Sumere, summer.

Suppois, suppose.

Supportacyon, support.

Surfet, fault.

Surmounteth, surpasses.

Surquidre, pride.

Sustene, sustain.

Suster, sister; *sustren*, *sustres*, sisters.

Sute, suit, fashion.

Suth, sooth, truth.

Swak, throw.

Swal, swelled.

Swalte, died.

Swane, swan.

Swange, loins.

Swangeande, flowing, rushing.

Swappe, swoop.

Swapte, smote.

Swardit, swarded, grass-grown.

Sware, answer.

Sware, square.

Swat, sweated.

Swathbondes, swaddling-bands; *swatheling* swaddling.

Sweete, sweat.

Swefte, swift.

Sweines, servants.

Sweir, slothful; *sweirness*, sloth.

Sweit, sweat.

Sweit, sweet; *sweitnes*, sweetness.

Swelt, fainted, died.

Swenche, molest.

Sweore, neck.

Swerd, sword.

Swere, swear.

Swete, sweat.

Swete, sweet, good.

Sweven, dream.

Sweyved, sounded.

Swich, *swiche*, such.

Swike, traitor; *swikelmen*, treacherous men.

Swike, cease.

Swithe, very; quickly.

Swo, so, as if.

Swogh, sough, murmur.

Swoghe, deathlike.

Swon, swan.

Swonken, *swunken*, toiled, labored.

Swote, sweet.

Swoun, swoon.

Swyn, swine.

Swynk, *swynke*, *swynken*, toil, work; *swynkere*, toiler.

Swyre, neck, throat.

Swyth, *swythe*, quickly.

Sybb, related by blood, akin.

Sych, such.

Sycht, sight.

Syde, side; *sydes*, sides; *on syde*, aside askance.

Syen, seen; *syghe*, see; *syghe, syhe*, saw; *syghte, syhte*, sight, insight.

Syis, times.

Sykyng, sighing.

Symple, simple, foolish.

Syn, syne, since, afterward, then.

Syne, sin.

Synge, sing.

Synglure, uniqueness.

Syngne, sign.

Synneles, sinless.

Synopar, cinnabar, a brown pigment.

Sypres, cypress.

Syre, man.

Syse, times.

Syt, set.

Sythe, scythe.

Sytole, citole, a musical instrument.

T

Ta, tookest.

Tabard, coarse mantle.

Tabide, to abide.

Tacched, attached; *taches*, attaches, ties.

Taffata, taffeta, a kind of silk.

Taght, taught.

Taidis, toads.

Takel, takyll, tackle, arrow.

Takning, takyn, token.

Tale, story, talk; *talen*, tell tales.

Tale, reckoning, account; *litel tale hath he told*, little account he made.

Talenttyf, desirous.

Tancrit, transcribed.

Tane, the one.

Tane, taken.

Tape, tappe, tap, blow.

Tappestere, female tapster, barmaid.

Tapycer, upholsterer.

Targe, charter, document.

Tarie, tarry, delay.

Tarmegantis, termagants, quarrelsome persons.

Tartre, tartar.

Tas, takes.

Tassay, to essay, to try.

Tasselez, tassels.

Tat, that.

Taxeth, appoints, assigns.

Tayk, take.

Te, the.

Teche, teach.

Teches, manners, qualities.

Tell, till.

Telle no store, reckon no account, set no store; *telth*, tells, reckons, esteems.

Tempest, agitate.

Tempred, tempered, tuned.

Tendit, held its course.

Tene, vexation, anger; *tenez*, sorrows.

Tent, tente, tend, guard, attend.

Teon, teone, vexation, grief, injury.

Teris, tears.

Tespye, to spy out.

Tett, lock.

Thair, there; *thairout*, thereof.

Thair, their; *thame*, them, themselves.

Than, thane, the; that.

Than, then.

Thane, than.

Thapocalips, the Apocalypse.

Thar, their.

Thar, thare, there, where; *tharvore*, therefore; *thar-mid*, therewith, besides.

Tharraye, the array.

Thas, of the.

That, so that; *that ne come*, before came.

Thalempre, temperate.

The, thee; they; who; he who.

The, thee, prosper.

Thear, those; their.

Thef, thief.

Theh, thei, though.

Thei, theo, they.

Thenche, think.

Thencrees, the increase.

Thengendrynge, the engendering.

Thenges, things.

Thenke, think.

Thenne, when.

Thennes, thens, thence.

Theos, this, these.

Ther, there, there, where; *ther as*, where; *thereas*, whereas; *therfore*, for that; *therto*, in addition, besides; *ther-while* while that, so long as.

Ther, their.

Thes, this, these; *thet*, that.

Thi, thie, thee.

Thider, thither.

Thik, thike, thick.

Thilke, that same.

Thimber, heavy.

Thin, thine, thy.

Thinche, seem; *thincthe*, (it) seems.

Thir, these, those; *this*, these, thus; *thisse, this; thise*, these.

Tho, the, those; then, when; *tho . . . tho*, when . . . . then.

Thocht, thought.

Thogh, though.

Thoght, thoghte, (it) seemed.

Thole, tholien, tholieth, endure; *tholis*, suffers, allows.

Thon, then.

Thonk, thanked.

Thonkes, thoughts'.

Thoo, then.

Thore, there.

Thorgh, thorowe, thorrow, thoru, through.

Thou, though.

Thow, thou.

Thrae, through.

Thrange, throng, pierce.

Thrawe, time, while.

Thrawen, wound.

Thredis, threads.

Threo, three.

Threteth, threatens.

Threpe, reproof.

Threw, intertwined.

Thrid, thridde, thride, third; *thries*, thrice.

Thriftily, carefully.

Thrinne, therein.

Thriste, bold.

Thriste, thrust.

Thritty, thirty.

Thro, bold, eager, angry.

Throge, course.

Throtis, throttis, throats.

Throu, throuch, throw, thrych, through.

Throwe, time, while.

Throwout, throughout.

Thrynges, throngest. pressest.

Thu, thou.

Thuhte, seemed, thought.

Thurgh, through; *thurghout*, quite through.

Thurste, thirst.

Thwarle, tight, hard.

Thwong, thong.

Thycke, fast.

Thynk, thing.

Thynketh, (it) seems.

Thynne, thin.

Tide, time.

Til, till, to.

Tilie, till.

Tipet, tippet, hood, cowl.

Tiptoon, tiptoes.

Tirled, rattled.

Tirneden, turned.

Tissew, thin undergarment.

Tite, quickly.

To, as to, for.

To, too.

To, two.

Tocke, took.

Toforowe, heretofore.

Toft, high place.

To-gadere, togideres, togidre, together.

Tok, toke, took.

Tole, toll; *tollen*, take toll; *tolleres*, toll-collectors.

Tole, tool.

Tomit, emptied.

Tomorwe, tomorrow.

Ton, the one.

Tone, good condition.

Tonge, tongue.

Tonne, tun, cask.

Tool, weapon.

Toom, empty.

Toon, toes.

Topace, topaz.

Toppyng, mane(?).

Tor tedious.

Tornes, turns.

To-schuke, shook.

Tothar, the other.

To-tose, tear to pieces.

Toun, town; enclosure, farm.

Toune: to toune, in its turn.

Toure, tower.

Tourne, turn.

Toward, in respect to, regarding.

Towe, two.

Towen, pulled, drawn.

Trace, track, course.

Traisoun, treason.

Traist, trust.

Tramort, corpses.

Tratour, traitor.

Trauthe, trawthe, traweth, troth, faith.

Travayle, travel; work.

Traysoun, treason.

Tre, tree, tree, shaft, wood; *treis*, trees.

Trendeled, rolled.

Tresor, treasure; *tresorere*, treasury.

Tressit, tied in tresses; *tressour*, headdress.

Tretys, long and well-proportioned.

Tried, proved.

Trieliche, choicely.

Trompe, trumpet.

Trone, throne.
Trouth, troth; *trouthe*, truth; *trowe*, trust.
Trumpour, deceiver.
Trwe, true; *trwly*, truly.
Tryed, proved; choice.
Tryghe, trust.
Trylle, twirl.
Trymlit, trembled.
Tryst, trust; *trystell-tree*, trysting-tree; *tryst-yly*, faithfully.
Tueyne, twain.
Tuik, tuke, took, occupied.
Tukest, pluckest, teasest.
Tukked, tucked up, girded about.
Tul, till.
Tunge, tongue.
Tuo, two.
Turkeys, turquoises.
Turmentowres, tormentors.
Twaw, tweye, two; *twyes*, twice; *twynne*, twain.
Twayned, twind, parted, separated; *twyned*, deprived; *twynne*, depart, go.
Twistis, twigs.
Twynnen, twined.
Tyde, tied.
Tyde, time.
Tydif, small bird, titmouse, wren.
Tykelnesse, instability.
Tynde, bough, branch.
Tyne, lose; *tynt*, lost.
Tynst, tinged, colored.
Tyse, entice.

U

Uch, uche, ulche, each.
Udir, other, each other.
Ule, owl.
Umbe-foldes, folds around.
Umbe-gon, fallen around.
Umbe-pyght, set around.
Umbe-torne, around.
Umbrage, shadow.
Umquhile, whilome, formerly.
Unabaisitly, unabashed, fearlessly.
Unblomit, unblossomed.
Un-cortoyse, discourteous.
Uncouth, unknown, strange.
Under, during; *under than*, during these things, meanwhile.
Underfoe, undertake.
Undergrowe, undergrown, undersized.
Undermynde, undermine.

Understondeth, understand, learn.
Undertake, affirm, guarantee.
Unethe, scarcely, hardly.
Unfere, infirm.
Unhelthe, unhelhthe, sickness, disease.
Unkeveleden, ungagged.
Unknawin, unknown.
Unkynde, unnatural.
Unlapped, unbound.
Un-mete, immense; *unmethe*, immoderateness.
Unneth, useless.
Unneth, unnethes, hardly, scarcely, with difficulty.
Unorne, old, worn-out.
Unrightes, unryht, unrighteousness.
Unsasiable, insatiable.
Unselthe, unhappiness.
Unstrayned, untroubled.
Unswerde, answered.
Un-til, untyll, unto.
Un-trawthe, unfaithfulness; *untrewe*, untruly.
Unwelde, weak.
Unwiht, monster; monstrous, uncanny
Un-wille, unpleasing.
Un-wraste, bad, dirty.
Un-wreste, weakly, badly.
Unyliche, unlike.
Up, upon; *upper*, higher.
Uphie, uphold.
Ure, our.
Ut, out.
Uther, other; *uthiris*, others.
Uus, us.
Uvele, evil; evilly.
Uych, uyche, each.

V

Vache, cow, beast.
Vaire, fair.
Vaistie, waste, ruined.
Valay, valley.
Vareth, fare, go.
Variant, varying.
Vavasour, sub-vassal, squire.
Vayned, brought.
Vele, many.
Venerye, hunting.
Venesoun, venison.
Vengeable, vengeful.
Venter, venture.
Veole, many.

Veorre, afar.
Verament, truly.
Verdit, verdict, judgment.
Vered, raised. lifted; *verez*, raises.
Verey, *verray*, very, true; *verrayly*, truly.
Vers, verses.
Verteth, turneth, boundeth (?).
Vertu, power.
Vesage, visage, face.
Vesytacion, visitation.
Veyl, veil.
Veyne, vain.
Veyne, vein.
Viage, voyage, journey.
Vice, error, fault.
Vileinye, unbecoming speech, ill-breeding.
Vitaille, victuals.
Volde, folds, ways.
Vor, for; *vor-thi*, therefore.
Vote, foot.
Vouch it safe, vouchsafe it, bestow it; *vouche-sauf*, vouchsafe.
Voyde, leave.
Vule, foul.
Vylanye, unbecoming conduct, discourtesy, fault.
Vyse, visage, face.

W

Wa, wall.
Wa, woeful.
Wace, was.
Wad, would; *wadna*, would not.
Wae, woe.
Wag, waddle.
Waist, waste, unpeopled.
Wait, knows, know.
Wak, damp, moist.
Waken, watch over.
Wa'king, walking.
Wakkest, weakest.
Wald, would.
Wale. choose, seek.
Walet, wallet.
Walking, awake.
Wallis, waves.
Wallydrag, big-bellied person.
Walt, *walte*, wielded, possessed, held.
Walter, welter, roll, turn over.
Wame, womb, belly; *wamiss*, bellies.
Wan, colorless.
Wan, whom.
Wan, won, arrived at.

Wandez, wand's, handle's.
Wane, multitude (?).
Wane, weening, knowing; *will of wane*, at a loss what to do.
Wanene, whence; *wanne*, when.
Wanis, dwellings.
Wantoun, wanton, wild, frolicsome; *wantonnes*, *wantonness*, mirth, playfulness.
Wap, blow.
War, ware, **were**.
War, aware, wary, prudent; *ware*, beware; *war him*, beware.
Wardmotes, ward-meetings.
Ware, use; *waret*, acted, dealt.
Wareine, warren, place for keeping animals.
Warke, work.
Warldes, *warldis*, world's.
Warlo, warlock, wizard, imp.
Warly, warily.
Warni, *warny*, warn.
Warp, threw, cast, uttered.
Warry, curse; *waryit*, cursed.
Wars, worse.
Wast, waist.
Waste, solitary, solitary places; *wastours*, wasters.
Wastel-breed, cake-bread.
Wat, what.
Wat, quoth.
Wat, *wate*, knows, know.
Waterlees, waterless, out of water.
Wathe, injury.
Watz, wast, was.
Wayke, weak.
Wayned, sent, brought.
Wayted, watched; *wayted after*, awaited, expected; *waytez*, looks.
We, ah.
Weal, raise welts by clenching (?).
Weare, were.
Webbe, weaver; *webbez*, webs, **cloths**.
Weddeen, wedding.
Wedder, weather.
Wede, weed, garment.
Wedous, widows.
Weel, well.
Weet, *weete*, wet, **rain**.
Weid, weed, dress.
Weie, way.
Weil, *weill*, well.
Weiping, weeping.
Weir, war.
Weird, fate, destiny.

Wel, well, much, many.

Welde, wield, rule, have power, possess.

Wele, weal, wealth, prosperity, happiness.

Welewed: for welewed, withered.

Welke, walked.

Welkyn, welkin, sky.

Wellis, springs, streams.

Well-wight, very strong.

Welt, disposed of.

Wely, joyous.

Wemen, women.

Wemme, spot, blemish.

Wende, went, wenden wend, go, turn; *wend, wende*, went.

Wene, doubt.

Wenen, ween, think; *wenes, wenst*, thinkest; *wende*, thought.

Went, footpath.

Weode, plant.

Weole, weal.

Weope, weep.

Weppen, weapon.

Wer, wore.

Werblis, warbles.

Wercheth, work.

Werdlys, world's.

Were, doubt.

Were, war.

Were, where.

Wered, wereden, wore.

Weren, wern, were.

Werke, werken, work, **do.**

Werle, garland (?).

Wernyng, refusal.

Werpeth, cast, throw.

Werre, war.

Wers, worse.

Werte, wart.

Werthe, entertainment, host.

Wery, weary.

Wes, was.

Weste, go westward.

Westernays, perversely.

Wete, know.

Wete, weten, wet.

Weve, pass.

Weven, weave; *weved*, wove; *weveres*, weavers.

Wex, wexen, wax, grow, become; *wex*, became.

Weyeden, weighed; *weyhte*, weight.

Weyes, ways.

Weyl, weylle, well.

Weylaway, wel-a-way, alas.

Weyte, wait, attend.

Weyves, waifs.

Whair, where; *whaireir*, where'er.

Whallez, whale's.

Wharred, whirred.

What, lo; *what so*, whatever; *whatten*, what.

Wheder, whether; whither.

Whelkes, blotches.

Wher, where; *wher so*, wheresoever.

Wher, where, whether.

Whete, wheat.

Whether, whither; nevertheless, yet.

Whette, whetted.

Whiche, who.

Whider, whither.

Whipper, whopper, something that beats everything else.

Whit, white.

Whoys, whose.

Whyle, the while, once, for a while; *whyllys*, whilst.

Whyrlande, whirling.

Wi, with.

Wiche, which.

Wickit, wicked.

Widdercock, weathercock.

Wide, wide apart.

Wifves, wives, women.

Wihte, wights, creatures.

Wikke, wicked.

Wilc . . . . so, whichsoever.

Wile, while; *sum wile*, sometimes.

Wile, will.

Will, wille, wild, astray.

Wille, will, pleasure; *with wille*, quickly.

Wimpel, covering for the head and neck.

Win, winne, joy, pleasure, delight.

Winna, will not.

Wirdis, words.

Wis, surely.

Wis, wise.

Wise, guide.

Wise, way, ways.

Wiste, knew, thought.

Wit, with, against.

Wit, mind, intelligence; *wit, wite, witen*, know; *wityng*, knowing.

Wite, keep, guard.

With that, on condition that.

Withere, hostile.

With-holden, retained, confined.

Withouten, besides.

Withseye, gainsay.

With-ute, without, besides.

Witlis, witless.

Wlatsom, loathsome.

Wlonk, fair, beautiful.

Wlyteth, whistle, pipe.

Wnto, unto.

Wo, woeful, sad.

Woche, which, of what sort.

Wod, wode, wood.

Wod, wode, mad; *wodenes*, madness, fury.

Wode, woad, blue pigment.

Woderove, woodruff, asphodel.

Woe, woeful, sorry.

Woik, woke.

Wol, wole, wolle, wolleth, will, wish; *wolt*, wilt; *wold, wolde*, wished, would; *woltestow*, wouldst thou.

Wolde, plain, earth.

Wolle-websteres, wool-weavers (female).

Wolteryng, weltering, rolling.

Wolwarde, with wool next the skin.

Womanheid, womanhood.

Wombe, belly.

Won, wan.

Won, win, come to.

Won, when.

Won, wone, dwelling, retreat; *wone*, dwell.

Wonder, wonderful; *wonderly, wonderlych, wonderliche*, wonderfully; *wonders*, very, extremely.

Wone, one.

Wone, want, lack, misery.

Wone, wont, custom; *wone, woned*, wont, accustomed.

Wonen, wonnen, won, come, come to.

Wonges, cheeks.

Wonne, when.

Wont, wonte, want, lack; *wonted*, wanted lacked.

Wonyng, wailing.

Wonynge, dwelling, mansion; *wonys*, dwells; *wonyes*, dwellest.

Wood, mad.

Wook, woke.

Woone, waning, growing less.

Woot, wot, know.

Wop, weeping.

Worch, work, do; *worchis*, works; *worchyng*, working.

Wore, weir, dam.

Wore, were.

Worschip, worsipe, worship, honor.

Wortes, wortez, herbs.

Worth, worthe, be.

Worthe, worthilych, worthy; *worthy*, distinguished, honorable.

Wost, wottest, knowest; *wostow*, knowest thou, thinkest thou.

Wote, wot, know, knows.

Wothe, wouche, harm, injury.

Wounder, wonderfully, very.

Wount, wont, used.

Wowes, wooes; *wowyng*, wooing.

Wox, grown, become.

Wrabbed, rabid(?).

Wracheit, wretched.

Wraghte, wrought.

Wraik, vengeance, retribution; *wraikfull*, vengeful.

Wrait, wrote.

Wrange, wrong.

Wrathed, made angry; *him wrattheth*, he becomes angry.

Wraw, headstrong, perverse.

Wrecche, wretched; *wrechis*, wretches, niggards.

Wreke, wreken, wreak, avenge.

Wrenche, twists, deceits.

Wring, wring (the hands), wail.

Write, written.

Writelinge, trilling.

Wro, cave, corner.

Wroken, wreaked, avenged.

Wrooth, wroth, angry; *wrothe*, angrily; *wrotheloker*, more angrily.

Wroughte: for wroughte, worn out.

Wrth, shall be.

Wruxled, folded, wrapped, clad.

Wryte, writing.

Wrythe, writhe, turn.

Wu, how.

Wude, wood.

Wul, wulleth, will.

Wulvine, she-wolf.

Wunest, dwellest; *wuneth, wunye*, dwell.

Wunne, bliss, joy.

Wurchep, wurchyp, worship; *wurchepyd*, worshiped.

Wurth, shall be.

Wuste, knew.

Wy, why.

Wy, woe!

Wyd, wide.

Wydwe, widow.

Wygh, wyghe, wyht, wight; *wyghez,* wights.
Wyght, strong and active.
Wyiss, wise, way.
Wyld, combed.
Wyld, wild creatures. deer.
Wyle, wile, trick.
Wylfull, voluntary; *wyll,* wish; *wylnez,* wilt, wishest.
Wylyde, wild, amorous.
Wyn, wine; *wynes,* of wine.
Wyn, wynne, bliss.
Wynde, enclose, shut up.
Wynne, goodly.
Wynne, win.
Wynt, turns, directs.
Wypped, struck.
Wyppit, bound.
Wyrde, fate.
Wys, wyse, wise, prudent; wise men; *as wys,* as surely (as).
Wyschande, wishing.
Wyse, way.
Wystly, attentively.
Wysty, waste, desert.
Wyt, know, learn, see; *wyter,* wise.
Wyther, opposite.
Wyve, wife; *wyves,* wife's.

X

Xal, xul, shall; *xalt,* shalt; *xulde,* should.

Y

Y, I.
Y, one.
Yae, every.
Yaf, gave.
Yare, quickly.
Yare, years.
Yarkkez, dispenses, makes ready, disposes.
Ychabbe, I have; *ycham,* I am.
Yche, each.
Y-crased, cracked.
Ye, yea.
Ye, eye; *yen,* eyes.
Yebent, bent.
Yeddynges, songs.
Yede, went.
Yederly, promptly.
Yeerd, yard.
Yef, if.
Yeid, went.
Yeir, year.
Yeidhall, guild-hall.
Yeldyde, yielded; *yeldynge,* yielding.

Yelleden, yelled.
Yeman, yeoman; *yemanly,* yeomanly.
Yemen, care for.
Yenoughe, enough.
Yeo, ye.
Yep, active; *yeply,* actively, promptly.
Yerde, stick; *yerdes,* wands, shoots.
Yer, yere, year.
Yerle, earl.
Yerly, early.
Yes, ye shall.
Yest, yeast.
Yestreen, yester even, last night.
Yet, gate.
Yeve, yeven, give.
Y-fere, together.
Ye-feth, in faith.
Yghe, yhe, eye; *yhen,* eyes.
Y-halowed, hallooed to.
Yif, if.
Yifte, gift.
Ying, young.
Yis, yes.
Yit, yet.
Yive, give.
Y-lad, led, carted.
Yle, isle.
Y-lent, arrived, come.
Y-liche, y-lyke, alike, equally; *y-lyk,* like.
Ympnis, hymns.
Ynde, bright-blue color.
Ynogh, y-noh, ynou, y-nough, ynowh, enough.
Yode, went.
Yol, Yole, Yule, Christmas.
Yoldyn, yielded, given up.
Yone, yon.
Yonge, young; *yonge, yonghede,* youth.
Yore, fore.
Yore, long time.
Yot, went.
Yow, yowe, you.
Yrn, yrne, iron.
Yse, ice.
Y-seye, seen.
Y-stalled, installed.
Y-teyed, tied.
Yth, in the.
Yut, yet.
Yve, ivy.
Yvore, ivory.
Ywar, wary.
Y-wympled, having a wimple; see *wimpel.*
Y-yirned, yearned, been anxious.

BIBLIOGRAPHY

BIBLIOGRAPHY

GENERAL WORKS

HISTORY AND SOCIAL CONDITIONS. A Short History of the English People, by J. R. Green (London, 1874; Harper). Epochs of English History, ed. by M. Creighton (Longmans, 1874–87): England a Continental Power (1066–1216), by L. Creighton; The Early Plantagenets, by William Stubbs; The Houses of Lancaster and York, by James Gairdner; The Early Tudors, by C. E. Moberly; The Tudors and the Reformation, by M. Creighton. The Making of England, The Conquest of England, 2 vols., by J. R. Green (Macmillan, 1881, 1883). Old English History, by E. A. Freeman (Macmillan, 1869). Early Britain, by A. J. Church (Unwin, 1889; Story of the Nations series). Anglo-Saxon Britain, by Grant Allen (Society for Promoting Christian Knowledge, 1882; Early Britain series). History of the Norman Conquest, 6 vols., by E. A. Freeman (Oxford University Press, 1867–79). Short History of the Norman Conquest, by E. A. Freeman (Oxford University Press, 1880). Norman Britain, by W. Hunt (Society for Promoting Christian Knowledge, 1884; Early Britain series). Post-Norman Britain, by H. G. Hewlett (Society for Promoting Christian Knowledge, 1886; Early Britain series). Social England, ed. by H. D. Traill, Vols. 1–3 (Cassell, 1894–95; Putnam). Mediaeval England, English Feudal Society from the Norman Conquest to the Middle of the Fourteenth Century, by Mary Bateson (Putnam, 1904; Unwin). Chaucer and His England, by G. G. Coulton (Methuen, 1908; illustrated). In the Days of Chaucer, by T. Jenks (New York, London, 1904). Court Life under the Plantagenets, by H. Hall, F. S. A. (Sonnenschein, 1890). England in the Time of Wycliffe, by G. M. Trevelyan (Longmans, 1899). English Wayfaring Life in the Middle Ages (fourteenth century), by J. J. Jusserand, translated from the French by L. T. Smith (Unwin, 1888; the French version, 1884). England in the Fifteenth Century, by W. Denton (Bell, 1888; Macmillan). Town Life in the Fifteenth Century, 2 vols., by Mrs. J. R. Green (Macmillan, 1894). English Villages, by P. H. Ditchfield (Methuen, 1901; Pott). Mediaeval London, 2 vols., by Sir Walter Besant (Black, 1906). London in the Time of the Tudors, by Sir Walter Besant (Black, 1904).

HISTORY OF LITERATURE. The Cambridge History of English Literature, ed. by A. W. Ward and A. R. Waller, Vols. 1, 2 (Cambridge University Press, 1908; Putnam). Histoire de la littérature anglaise, by H. A. Taine, Vol. 1 (Paris, 1863); English translation by H. van Laun, 1871 (Holt, 1896). Histoire littéraire du peuple anglais, by J J. Jusserand, Vol. 1 (Paris, 1894); English translation, A Literary History of the English People, Vol. 1 (Unwin, 1895; Putnam). English Literature, an Illustrated Record, by Richard Garnett and Edmund Gosse, Vol. 1 (Macmillan, 1903). A Short History of English Literature, by George Saintsbury (Macmillan, 1898). Periods of European Literature, ed. by George Saintsbury (W. Blackwood, 1897–1904; Scribner): The Dark Ages, by W. P. Ker; The Flourishing of Romance and the Rise of Allegory, by George Saintsbury; The Fourteenth Century, by F. J. Snell; The Transition Period, by G. G. Smith. History of English Poetry, 4 vols. (1774–81), by Thomas Warton, ed. by W. C. Hazlitt (Reeves, 1871). A History of English Poetry, by W. J. Courthope, Vol. 1 (Macmillan, 1895). Characteristics of English Poets from Chaucer to Shirley, by William Minto (W. Blackwood, 1874). Chambers' Cyclopaedia of English Literature (Lippincott, 1902–4; new ed.). Dictionary of National Biography (Smith, 1885–1901; Macmillan). Encyclopaedia Britannica (Black, 1875—; ninth ed.). Geschichte der englischen Litteratur, 2 vols. (from the beginning to 1557), by B. ten Brink (Berlin, 1877, 1889); English translation: Early English Literature (to Wiclif), translated by H. M. Kennedy (Holt, 1883; Bell, Bohn ed.); History of English Literature (Wyclif, Chaucer, Earliest Drama Renaissance), translated by W. C. Robinson (Holt, 1893; Bell,

Bohn ed.). Sketch of the History of Anglo-Saxon Literature, by Henry Sweet (in Hazlitt's ed. of Warton's History of English Poetry; see above). History of Early English Literature, from Its Beginnings to the Accession of Alfred, by S. A. Brooke (Macmillan, 1892). English Literature from the Beginning to the Norman Conquest, by S. A. Brooke (Macmillan. 1898; many translations into modern 'English). English Literature from the Norman Conquest to Chaucer, by W. H. Schofield (Macmillan, 1906). The Age of Chaucer, by F. J. Snell (Bell, 1901; Macmillan). The Age of Transition (1400–1580), 2 vols., by F. J. Snell (Bell, 1905; Macmillan). A History of English Dramatic Literature, by A. W Ward, Vol. 1 (Macmillan, 1875; rev. ed., 1899). The Mediaeval Stage, 2 vols., by E. K. Chambers (Oxford University Press, 1903). Shakspere's Predecessors in the English Drama, by J. A. Symonds (Smith, Elder, & Co., 1884). The English Religious Drama, by K. L. Bates (Macmillan, 1893). English Mysteries, by A. Ebert (Jahrbuch für romanische und englische Litteratur, Vol. 1; Berlin, Leipzig, 1859). A Literary History of Scotland, by J. H. Millar (Scribner, 1903). Three Centuries of Scottish Literature, by Hugh Walker, Vol. 1 (Maclehose, 1893; Macmillan). The History and Poetry of the Scottish Border, by John Veitch (Maclehose, 1877). The Feeling for Nature in Scottish Poetry, 2 vols., by John Veitch (W. Blackwood, 1887). Englische Metrik, 2 vols., by J. Schipper (Bonn, 1881–89). A History of English Prosody, from the Twelfth Century to the Present Day, by George Saintsbury, Vol. 1 (Macmillan. 1906).

COLLECTIONS OF POEMS. Bibliothek der angelsächsischen Poesie, 4 vols., ed. by C. W. M. Grein (Göttingen, 1857–64; new ed., 5 vols., ed. by R. P. Wülcker (Cassel and Leipzig, 1883–98). The Exeter Book, Part I, ed. by I. Gollancz (Early English Text Society Publications, original series, No. 104; Paul, 1895; texts, with rendering into modern English, of Christ, St. Guthlac, Azariah, Phoenix, St. Juliana, Wanderer, Endowments of Men, A Father's Instruction). Select Translations from Old English Poetry, ed. by A. S. Cook and C. B. Tinker (Ginn, 1902; renderings, mostly in verse, of Banished Wife's Complaint, Battle of Brunanburh, Battle of Maldon, Deor's Lament, Dream of the Rood, Husband's Message, Judith, Phoenix, Ruined City, Seafarer, Wanderer, Widsith, of extracts from Andreas, Beowulf, Charms, Christ, Elene, Exodus, Genesis, Gnomic Verses, Riddles, and of a few other poems). An Old English Miscellany, ed. by R. Morris (Early English Text Society Publications, original series, No. 49; Trübner, 1872; A Bestiary, Proverbs of Alfred, Moral Ode, religious poems of the thirteenth century). A Middle English Reader, ed. by O. F. Emerson (Oxford University Press, 1905). Specimens of Early English (1150–1393), 2 vols., ed. by R. Morris and W. W. Skeat (Oxford University Press, 1872–1879; notes and glossary: new ed., 1894). Specimens of English Literature (1394–1579), ed. by W. W. Skeat (Oxford University Press, 1871; notes and glossary). The Works of the English Poets from Chaucer to Cowper, 21 vols., ed. by A. Chalmers (London, 1810). Specimens of Lyric Poetry (in the time of Edward I), Specimens of Old Christmas Carols, ed. by T. Wright (Percy Society Publications, Vol. 4; London, 1841). Songs and Carols, Now First Printed from a Manuscript of the Fifteenth Century, ed. by T. Wright (Percy Society Publications, Vol. 23; London, 1847). Political, Religious, and Love Poems, ed. by F. J. Furnivall (Early English Text Society Publications, original series, No. 15; Trübner, 1866; Paul, 1903, new ed.). Ancient Poetical Tracts of the Sixteenth Century, ed. by E. F. Rimbault (Percy Society Publications, Vol. 6; London, 1842). Abbotsford Series of the Scottish Poets, 4 vols., ed. by G. Eyre-Todd (Hodge, 1891–93; Vol. 1, Thomas the Rhymer, Barbour, Andrew of Wyntoun, Henry the Minstrel; Vol. 2, James I, Henryson, Dunbar, Douglas; Vol. 3, Lindsay, Pellenden, James V, Maitland, Alexander Scott, Alexander Montgomerie; Vol. 4, ballads). Selections from the Early Scottish Poets, ed. by W. H. Browne (Johns Hopkins Press, 1896; notes and glossary). Scottish Minor Poets, ed. by Sir G. Douglas (Scott, 1891; Canterbury Poets ed.). Dunbar Anthology (1401–1508), ed. by Edward Arber (Oxford University Press, 1901; British Anthologies series; much from Dunbar and Henryson). Specimens of the Pre-Shaksperean Drama, 2 vols., ed. by J. M. Manly (Ginn, 1897; Athenaeum Press ed.). A Select Collection of Old English Plays, originally published by Robert Dodsley in 1744, re-ed. by W. C. Hazlitt (Reeves, 1874; Vol. 1 includes Interlude of the Four Elements, Every-man, Hickscorner, The Pardoner and the Friar, The World and the Child, The Four PP; Vol. 2 includes Interlude of Youth, Lusty Juventus, Disobedient Child, Marriage of Wit and Science). English Miracle Plays, Moralities, and Interludes, ed. by A. W. Pollard (Oxford University Press, 1890; most of the works are abridged; notes and glossary).

DICTIONARIES. An Anglo-Saxon Dictionary, 4 vols. and a supplement, by J. Bosworth and T. N. Toller (Oxford University Press, 1882–98, 1908). The Student's Dictionary of Anglo-Saxon, by Henry Sweet (Oxford University Press, 1897). Middle-English Dictionary, by F. H. Stratmann, rev. by Henry Bradley (Oxford University Press, 1890; Macmillan). A Concise Dictionary of Middle English, by A. L. Mayhew and W. W. Skeat (Oxford University Press, 1888).

BALLADS

EDITIONS. The English and Scottish Popular Ballads, 5 vols., ed. by F. J. Child (Hough-ton, 1882–98; Stevens). English and Scottish Popular Ballads, ed. by H. C. Sargent and G. L. Kittredge (Houghton, 1904; Cambridge ed.). Old English Ballads, ed. by F. B. Gummere (Ginn, 1894; Athenaeum Press ed.). Percy's Folio Manuscript, 3 vols., ed. by J. W. Hales, F. J. Furnivall, and F. J. Child (Trübner, 1867–68). Percy's Reliques of Ancient English Poetry (1765), 3 vols., ed. by H. B. Wheatley (Sonnenschein, 1890); 2 vols., ed. by J. V. Prichard (Bell, 1876; Macmillan; Bohn ed.). Ritson's Ancient Ballads and Songs (1790–91), ed. by W. C. Hazlitt (Reeves, 1877).

CRITICISM. F. B. Gummere: Primitive Poetry and the Ballad (Modern Philology, Vol. 1; The University of Chicago Press, 1903–4); The Beginnings of Poetry (Macmillan, 1901); The Popular Ballad (Houghton, 1907; Types of English Literature series). J. W. Hales: Folia Litteraria (Seeley, 1893; Macmillan). W. M. Hart: Ballad and Epic, a Study in the Development of the Narrative Art (Studies and Notes in Philology and Literature, Vol. 11; Ginn, 1907). W. P. Ker: Epic and Romance (Macmillan, 1897). F. Liebrecht: Zur englischen Balladen-poesie (Englische Studien, Vol. 3; Heilbronn, Paris, London, New York, 1880). W. E. Mead: Color in the English and Scottish Ballads (in An English Mis-cellany; Oxford University Press, 1901).

GEOFFREY CHAUCER

EDITIONS. Works, 6 vols., ed. by W. W. Skeat (Oxford University Press, 1904). Stu-dent's Chaucer, ed. by W. W. Skeat (Oxford University Press, 1895; complete works). Works, ed. by A. W. Pollard, H. F. Heath, M. H. Liddell, W. S. McCormick (Macmillan, 1898; Globe ed.). Minor Poems, ed. by W. W. Skeat (Oxford University Press, 1889; notes and glossary). A Parallel-Text Edition of Chaucer's Minor Poems, ed. by F. J. Furnivall (Chaucer Society Publications, 1st series, Nos. 21, 57, 58; Trübner, 1871). A Parallel-Text Print of Chaucer's Troilus and Criseyde, and Three More Parallel Texts, put forth by F. J. Furnivall (Chaucer Society Publications, 1st series, Nos. 63, 64, 87, 88; Trübner, 1881–82, 1894–95; nine texts). Chaucer's Troylus and Cryseyde Compared with Boccaccio's Filostrato Trans-lated by W. M. Rossetti (Chaucer Society Publications, 1st series, Nos. 44, 65; Trübner, 1873, 1883). Legend of Good Women, ed. by W. W. Skeat (Oxford University Press, 1888; notes and glossary). A Six-Text Print of Chaucer's Canterbury Tales, ed. by F. J. Furnivall (Chaucer Society Publications, 1st series, Nos. 1, 14, 15, 25, 30, 31, 37, 49, 72; Trübner, 1868–84). Canterbury Tales, 3 vols., ed. by R. Morris and W. W. Skeat (Oxford University Press, 1874–89; Prologue, Knightes Tale, Nonne Preestes Tale; Prioresses Tale, Sir Thopas, Monkes Tale, Clerkes Tale, Squieres Tale, etc.; Tale of the Man of Lawe, Pardoneres Tale, Second Nonnes Tale, Chanouns Yemannes Tale; notes and glossaries). Prologue, Knightes Tale, Nonne Prestes Tale, ed. by M. H. Liddell (Macmillan, 1901). Prologue, Knight's Tale, Nun Priest's Tale, ed. by A. Ingraham (Macmillan, 1902; Pocket Classics ed.). Can-terbury Tales, Modern Rendering into Prose of the Prologue and Ten Tales by Percy Mackaye (Fox, 1904). Prologue, Knight's Tale, Man of Law's Tale, Nun's Tale, Prioress's Tale, Squire's Tale, Legend of Good Women, Minor Poems, Romaunt of the Rose, done into Modern English by W. W. Skeat, 5 vols. (Chatto, 1904–7). Chaucer's Canterbury Tales for the Modern Reader, prepared and ed. by A. Burrell (Dent, 1908; Everyman's Library ed.). Canterbury Tales, ed. by John Saunders (Dent, 1889; paraphrases and extracts).

BIOGRAPHY AND CRITICISM. Essays on Chaucer (Chaucer Society Publications, 2d series, Nos. 2, 9, 16, 18, 19, 29; Trübner, 1868–92). A. C. Garrett: Studies on Chaucer's House of Fame (Studies and Notes in Philology and Literature, Vol. 5; Ginn, 1896). W. M. Hart: The Reeve's Tale, a Comparative Study of Chaucer's Narrative Art (Publications of the Modern Language Association, Vol. 23; Baltimore, 1908). William Hazlitt: Lectures on the English Poets (1818) (Dent, 1902–4; Macmillan, Bohn ed.). Life Records of Chaucer (Chaucer Society Publications, 2d series, Nos. 12, 14, 21, 32; Trübner, 1875, 1886). T. R. Lounsbury: Studies in Chaucer, 3 vols. (Harper, 1891; Osgood). J. R. Lowell: Literary Essays, Vol. 3 (Houghton; this essay, 1870). E. E. Morris: The Physician in Chaucer (in An English Miscellany; Oxford University Press, 1901; Putnam). Originals and Analogues of Chaucer's Canterbury Tales (Chaucer Society Publications, 2d series, Nos. 7, 8, 10, 15, 16, 20, 22; Trübner, 1872–88). K. O. Petersen: On the Sources of the Nonne-Prestes Tale (Radcliffe College Monographs; Boston, 1898). A. W. Pollard: Chaucer (Macmillan, 1893; Literature Primers series). T. R. Price: Troilus and Criseyde, a Study of Chaucer's Method of Narrative Construction (Publications of the Modern Language Association, Vol. 11; Baltimore, 1896). A. Rambeau: Chaucer's House of Fame in seinem Verhältniss zu Dante's Divina Commedia (Englische Studien, Vol. 3; Heilbronn, Paris, London, New York, 1880). R. K. Root: The Poetry of Chaucer (Houghton, 1906). W. H. Schofield: Chaucer (Macmillan; in preparation). J. C. Shairp: On Poetic Interpretation of Nature (Edinburgh, 1877: Houghton). M. H. Spielmann: The Portraits of Geoffrey Chaucer (Chaucer Society Publications, 2d series, No. 31; Paul, 1900). A. C. Swinburne: Miscellanies (Short Notes on English Poets) (Chatto, 1886; Scribner). J. S. P. Tatlock: The Development and Chronology of Chaucer's Works (Chaucer Society Publications, 2d series, No. 37; Paul, 1907). B. ten Brink: Chaucers Sprache und Verskunst (Leipzig, 1884); English translation, The Language and Metre of Chaucer (Macmillan, 1902). A. W. Ward: Chaucer (Macmillan, 1879; English Men of Letters series).

GAWAIN DOUGLAS

EDITIONS. Poetical Works, 4 vols., ed. by J. Small (Edinburgh, 1874).
CRITICISM. P. Lange: Chaucers Einfluss auf Douglas (Anglia, Vol. 6; Halle, 1883).

WILLIAM DUNBAR

EDITIONS. Poems, ed. by J Schipper (Vienna, 1891–94). Poems, ed. by J. Small (Scottish Text Society Publications, Nos. 2, 4, 16, 21, 29; W. Blackwood, 1884–93). Poems, ed. by Edward Arber (Birmingham, 1886; in English Scholar's Library).
BIOGRAPHY AND CRITICISM. J. Schipper: William Dunbar (Berlin, 1884). O. Smeaton: William Dunbar (Oliphant, 1898; Famous Scots series; Scribner).

EARLY MIDDLE ENGLISH POEMS

Bestiary (in An Old English Miscellany; see above, "General Works, Collections of Poems").

Bruce (by John Barbour), ed. by W. W. Skeat (Scottish Text Society Publications, Nos. 31–33; Blackwood, 1894); ed. by the same (Early English Text Society Publications, extra series, Nos. 11, 21, 29, 55; Trübner, Paul, 1870–89; reprinted, 1896). G. Neilson: John Barbour, Poet and Translator (Paul, 1900).

Brut, ed. by Sir F. Madden (London, 1847; published by the Society of Antiquaries).

Cleanness, ed. by R. Morris in English Alliterative Poems (Early English Text Society Publications, original series, No. 1; Trübner, 1864; rev. ed., 1869).

Cursor Mundi, ed. by R. Morris (Early English Text Society Publications, original series, No. 57, 59, 62, 63, 68, 99, 101; Trübner, Paul, 1875–92; four texts).

Genesis and Exodus, ed. by R. Morris (Early English Text Society Publications, origina series, No. 7; Trübner, 1865; rev. ed., 1873).

Ormulum, 2 vols., ed. by R. Holt (Oxford University Press, 1878).

Owl and the Nightingale, ed. by J. E. Wells (Heath, 1907; Belles Lettres ed.); ed. by T. Wright (Percy Society Publications, Vol. 11; London, 1843).

Patience, ed. by R. Morris in English Alliterative Poems (see above, "Cleanness").

Pearl, ed. by Israel Gollancz, with a modern rendering (Dent, 1891; Temple Classics ed.); ed. by C. G. Osgood, Jr. (Heath, 1906; Belles Lettres ed.); ed. by R. Morris in Early English Alliterative Poems (see above, "Cleanness"); Rendered into Modern English Verse by S. Weir Mitchell (Century Co., 1906); Rendered into Modern English by G. G. Coulton (London, 1906; in the metre of the original); Rendered in Prose by C. G. Osgood, Jr. Princeton, 1907). C. F. Brown: The Author of The Pearl, Considered in the Light of His Theological Opinions (Publications of the Modern Language Associa tion, Vol. 19; Baltimore, 1904). C. S. Northup: A Study of the Metrical Structure of the Middle English Poem Pearl (Publications of the Modern Language Association, Vol. 12; Baltimore, 1897). W. H. Schofield: The Nature and Fabric of the Pearl, and Symbolism. Allegory, and Autobiography in the Pearl (Publications of the Modern Language Association, Vols. 19, 24; Baltimore, 1904, 1909).

Poema Morale [or Moral Ode], ed. by R. Morris in An Old English Miscellany (see above, "General Works, Collections of Poems"), and in Old English Homilies, 1st and 2d series (Early English Text Society Publications, original series, Nos. 29, 34, 53; Trübner, 1868, 1873; Jesus College, Lambeth, and Trinity College MSS, respectively); translation into modern English, in Old English Homilies, 1st series; ed. by J. Zupitza (Anglia, Vol. 1; Halle, 1878); ed. by A. C. Paues from a newly discovered MS (Anglia, Vol. 30; Halle, 1907); in Specimens of Early English (see above, "General Works, Collections of Poems").

JOHN GOWER

EDITIONS. Complete Works, 4 vols., ed. by G. C. Macaulay (Oxford University Press, 1899–1901; English Works, in Vols. 2 and 3, 1901); English Works, same ed. (Early English Text Society Publications, extra series, Nos. 81, 82; Paul, 1900–1). Tales of the Seven Deadly Sins, being the Confessio Amantis, ed. by Henry Morley (Routledge, 1899; Carisbrooke Library ed.). Confessio Amantis, ed. by G. C. Macaulay (Oxford University Press, 1903; selections, with notes, etc.).

STEPHEN HAWES

EDITIONS. Poems, ed. by Edward Arber (Birmingham, 1884; in English Scholar's Library). The Pastime of Pleasure, ed. by T. Wright (Percy Society Publications, Vol. 18; London, 1845; reprint of 1555 ed.). Complete Poetical Works, ed. by A. K. Potter from 1509 ed. (in preparation).

ROBERT HENRYSON

EDITIONS. Poems, ed. by G. G. Smith (Scottish Text Society Publications, Nos. 55, 58; W. Blackwood, 1906, 1908). Testament of Cresseid (in Chaucerian and Other Pieces, ed. by W. W. Skeat; Oxford University Press, 1897; a supplement to the Complete Works of Geoffrey Chaucer); in Chalmers (see above. "General Works, Collections of Poems"). Poems and Fables, ed. by D. Laing (Edinburgh, 1865).

JOHN HEYWOOD

The Foure PP, ed. by J. M. Manly in Specimens of the Pre-Shaksperean Drama, Vol. 2 (see above, "General Works, Collections of Poems"). The Pardoner and the Friar (in A Select Collection of Old English Plays; see above, "General Works, Collections of Poems").

THOMAS HOCCLEVE

EDITIONS. Minor Poems, ed. by F. J. Furnivall (Early English Text Society Publications, extra series, No. 61; Paul, 1892). Regement of Princes, and Fourteen Minor Poems, ed. by F. J. Furnivall (Early English Text Society Publications, extra series, No. 72, Paul, 1897). In Chalmers (see above, "General Works, Collections of Poems").

JAMES I OF SCOTLAND

EDITIONS. The Kingis Quair, together with A Ballad of Good Counsel, ed. by W. W. Skeat (Scottish Text Society Publications, No. 1; W. Blackwood, 1884). In Chalmers (see above, "General Works, Collections of Poems").

CRITICISM. H. Wood: Chaucer's Influence upon James I (Anglia, Vol. 3; Halle, 1880).

WILLIAM LANGLAND

EDITIONS. Piers Plowman, ed. by W. W. Skeat (Early English Text Society Publications, original series, Nos. 28, 38, 54, 67, 81; Trübner, 1867–83; the three texts). Piers the Plowman, ed. by W. W. Skeat (Oxford University Press, 1869; 5th ed., rev., 1888; the "B" text). Vision of Piers the Plowman, Done into Modern Prose by K. M. Warren (Unwin, 1895; Macmillan); Done into Modern English by W. W. Skeat (Chatto, 1905).

CRITICISM. E. D. Hanscom: The Argument of the Vision of Piers Plowman (Publications of the Modern Language Association, Vol. 9; Baltimore, 1894). J. J. Jusserand: Les Anglais au moyen âge, l'épopée mystique de William Langland (Paris, 1893); English translation, Piers Plowman, a Contribution to the History of English Mysticism (Unwin, 1894; Putnam); Piers Plowman, the Work of One or of Five (Modern Philology, January, 1909, January, 1910; The University of Chicago Press). J. M. Manly: The Lost Leaf of Piers the Plowman; The Authorship of Piers Plowman (Modern Philology, January, 1906, July, 1909; The University of Chicago Press).

JOHN LYDGATE

EDITIONS. Troy Book, ed. by H. Bergen (Early English Text Society Publications, extra series, Nos. 97, 103; Paul, 1906, 1908; Books I–III). Temple of Glass, ed. by J. Schick (Early English Text Society Publications, extra series, No. 60; Paul, 1891). Pilgrimage of the Life of Man, ed. by F. J. Furnivall (Early English Text Society Publications, extra series, Nos. 77, 83; Paul, 1899, 1901). London Lickpenny, ed. by E. P. Hammond (Anglia, Vol. 20; Halle, 1898; two texts, from the MSS, and an argument against Lydgate's authorship). A Selection from the Minor Poems, ed. by J. O. Halliwell (Percy Society Publications, Vol. 2; London, 1840).

SIR DAVID LYNDSAY

EDITIONS. Poetical Works, 3 vols., ed. by D. Laing (Edinburgh, 1879). Works, ed. by J. Small and F. Hall (Early English Text Society Publications, original series, Nos. 11, 19, 35, 37, 47; Trübner, 1865, 1868; rev. ed., 1883).

MIDDLE ENGLISH METRICAL ROMANCES

King Horn, ed. by J. Hall (Oxford University Press, 1901); ed. by G. H. McKnight (Early English Text Society Publications, original series, No. 14; Paul, new ed., 1901).

Lay of Havelock the Dane, ed. by W. W. Skeat (Early English Text Society Publications, extra series, No. 4; Trübner, 1868; Oxford University Press, 1902). Havelock the Dane, a Close Translation by A. J. Wyatt (Clive, 1906): Rendered into Later English by Emily Hickey (Leamington Press, London, 1902).

Morte Arthure, ed. by E. Brock (Early English Text Society Publications, original series, No. 8; Trübner, 1865; new ed., 1871).

Romance of Guy of Warwick, ed. by J. Zupitza (Early English Text Society Publications, extra series, Nos. 25, 26, 42, 49, 59; Trübner, 1875–76, 1883).

Romance of Sir Beues of Hamptoun, ed. by E. Kölbing (Early English Text Society Publications, extra series, Nos. 46, 48, 65; Paul, 1885–86, 1894).

Sir Gawayne and the Green Knight, ed. by R. Morris (Early English Text Society Publications, original series, No. 4; Trübner, 1864; rev. ed., 1869). Sir Gawain and the Green Knight, Retold in Modern Prose by J. L. Weston (Nutt, 1898). Gawayne and the Green Knight, a Poem, by C. M. Lewis (Houghton, 1903; a free reworking of the old romance). J. L. Weston: The Legend of Sir Gawain, Studies upon Its Original Scope and Significance (Nutt, 1897).

Specimens of Early English Metrical Romances, 3 vols., by G. Ellis (London, 1805; Bell; Macmillan; Bohn ed.).

MIRACLE PLAYS

Brome Play of Abraham and Isaac, ed. by L. T. Smith (Anglia, Vol. 7; Halle, 1884).

Chester Plays, 2 vols., ed. by T. Wright (Shakespeare Society Publications; London, 1843, 1847); ed. by H. Deimling (Early English Text Society Publications, extra series, No. 62; Paul, 1893; Part I, containing the first thirteen plays).

Digby Mysteries, ed. by F. J. Furnivall (New Shakspere Society Publications; Trübner, 1882); reissue, as Digby Plays, with an incomplete "morality" of Wisdom, Who Is Christ (Early English Text Society Publications, extra series, No. 70; Paul, 1896; Killing of the Children, Conversion of St. Paul, Mary Magdalene, Christ's Burial and Resurrection).

Ludus Coventriae, a Collection of Mysteries, ed. by J. O. Halliwell (Shakespeare Society Publications; London, 1841). Two Coventry Corpus Christi Plays, ed. by H. Craig (Early English Text Society Publications, extra series, No. 87; Paul, 1902; the plays represent the annunciation, nativity, adoration of the shepherds and magi, flight into Egypt, slaughter of the innocents, presentation in the temple, and Jesus among the doctors).

Non-Cycle Mystery Plays, together with the Croxton Play of the Sacrament and The Pride of Life, ed. by O. Waterhouse (Early English Text Society Publications, extra series, No. 104: Paul, 1909).

Towneley Plays, ed. by G. England, intro. by A. W. Pollard (Early English Text Society Publications, extra series, No. 71; Paul, 1897).

York Plays, ed. by L. T. Smith (Oxford University Press, 1885).

MORALITY PLAYS

Everyman, ed. by W. W. Greg in Materialen zur Kunde des älteren englischen Dramas, Vol. 4 (Louvain; Leipzig; London; Nutt, 1904); ed. with intro. and notes (Bullen, 1902); ed. by J. S. Farmer (Gibbings, 1906); ed. by A. T. Quiller-Couch (Oxford University Press, 1908; Select English Classics ed.)

Kynge Johan (by John Bale), ed. by J. P. Collier (London, 1838; Camden Society Publications)

Lusty Juventus (in A Select Collection of Old English Plays; see above, "General Works, Collections of Poems").

Macro Plays, ed. by F. J. Furnivall and A. W. Pollard (Early English Text Society Publications, extra series, No. 91; Paul, 1904; Mankind, Wisdom, The Castle of Perseverance).

Magnyfycence (see below "John Skelton").

Marriage of Wyt and Syence (in A Select Collection of Old Plays; see above, "General Works, Collections of Poems").

Marriage of Wit and Wisdom, ed. by J. O. Halliwell (Shakespeare Society Publications; London, 1846).

Play of Wyt and Science, ed. by J. O. Halliwell (Shakespeare Society Publications; London, 1848); in Specimens of the Pre-Shaksperean Drama (see above, "General Works Collections of Poems").

OLD ENGLISH POEMS

1. *Beowulf*

EDITIONS AND TRANSLATIONS. Beowulf, ed. by M. Heyne, rev. ed. by A. Socin (Paderborn, 1898); ed. by A. J. Wyatt (Cambridge University Press, 1894; Putnam). Beowulf, Autotypes of the Unique Cotton Manuscript, with a Transliteration and Notes by J. Zupitza (Early English Text Society Publications, original series, No. 77; Trübner, 1882). The Tale of Beowulf, Done out of the Old English Tongue by William Morris and A. J. Wyatt (Longmans, 1895). Beowulf, Translated by C. G. Child (Houghton, 1904; Riverside Literature series; prose). Beowulf and the Fight at Finnsburg, Translation in Modern English Prose by J. R. C. Hall (Sonnenschein, 1901; Macmillan). The Deeds of Beowulf, translated by J. Earle (Oxford University Press, 1892; prose). Beowulf, Translated into Modern English Verse by J. L. Hall (Heath, 1892).

CRITICISM. F. A. Blackburn: The Christian Coloring in the Beowulf (Publications of the Modern Language Association, Vol. 12; Baltimore, 1897). J. Harrison: Old Teutonic Life in Beowulf (Overland Monthly, July, 1884). W. P. Ker: Epic and Romance (Macmillan, 1897). F. A. March: The World of Beowulf (Proceedings of the American Philological Association, 1882).

2. *Other Poems*

EDITIONS AND TRANSLATIONS. Battle of Brunanburh: translated into verse by Alfred Tennyson and into prose by Hallam Tennyson, in Select Translations (see below). Battle of Maldon, and Short Poems from the Saxon Chronicle, ed. by W. J. Sedgefield (Heath, 1904; Belles Lettres ed.); verse translation of Battle of Maldon by H. W. Lumsden, in Macmillan's Magazine, March, 1887, and in Select Translations (see below); translation, mostly in prose, by K. M. Warren, in English Literature from the Beginning to the Norman Conquest (see below). Christ, ed. by I. Gollancz (Nutt, 1892; with translation in blank verse); ed. and translated by the same in The Exeter Book (see below). Deor's Lament: verse translation in Select Translations and in English Literature from the Beginning to the Norman Conquest (see below). Dream of the Rood: blank-verse translation in Select Translations (see below). Elene, translated into English prose by L. H. Holt (Yale Studies in English, No. 21; Holt, 1904); translated by J. M. Garnett (Ginn, 1889; blank verse). Exodus and Daniel, ed. by F. A. Blackburn (Heath, 1907; Belles Lettres ed.). Judith, ed. by A. S. Cook (Heath, 1907; Belles Lettres ed.); translation by Henry Morley in his English Writers, Vol. 2 (Cassell, 1888) and in Select Translations (see below). Juliana, ed. by W. Strunk (Heath, 1907; Belles Lettres ed.); translation in The Exeter Book (see below). Phoenix: text and translation in The Exeter Book (see below); prose translation by A. S. Cook in Select Translations (see below). Seafarer: blank verse translation in Select Translations (see below). and in English Literature from the Beginning to the Norman Conquest (see below). Widsith: translation by Henry Morley in his English Writers, Vol. 2, and in Select Translations (see below).

For other poems see The Exeter Book, and Select Translations from Old English Poetry, under "General Works, Collections of Poems"; and English Literature from the Beginning to the Norman Conquest, by S. A. Brooke, under "General Works, History of Literature."

CRITICISM. W. E. Mead: Color in Old English Poetry (Publications of the Modern Language Association. Vol. 14; Baltimore, 1899). A. R. Skemp: The Transformation of

Scriptural Story, Motive, and Conception in Anglo-Saxon Poetry (Modern Philology, January 1907; The University of Chicago Press).

JOHN SKELTON

EDITIONS. Poetical Works, 2 vols., ed. by Alexander Dyce (London, 1843; Macmillan; Bohn ed.). Works, ed. by Edward Arber (Birmingham, 1887; in English Scholar's Library). Magnyfycence, a Moral Play, ed. by R. L. Ramsay (Early English Text Society Publications, extra series, No. 98; Paul, 1906). Selection from Poetical Works, ed. by W. H. Williams (Isbister, 1902). In Chalmers, Vol. 2 (see above, "General Works, Collections of Poetry"). Poetical Works (Boston, 1856; Houghton; British Poets ed.).

CRITICISM. F. Brie: Skelton-Studien (Englische Studien, Vol. 37; Leipzig, 1906).

INDICES

INDICES

INDEX OF AUTHORS

Cædmon (fl. 670), 34

Chaucer, Geoffrey (1340?-1400), 108

Cynewulf (fl. 750), 34

Douglas, Gawin (1474?-1522), 193

Dunbar, William (1465?-1530?), 184

Gower, John (1325?-1408), 100

Guildford, Nicholas de (fl. 1250), 57

Hawes, Stephen (1476?-1523?), 197

Henryson, Robert (1430?-1506?), 177

Heywood, John (1497?-1580?), 312

Hoccleve, Thomas (1370?-1450?), 165

James I of Scotland (1394-1437), 170

Langland, William (1330?-1400?), 102

Layamon (fl. 1200), 51

Lydgate, John (1370?-1451?), 166

Lyndsay, Sir David (1490-1555), 194

Skelton, John (1460?-1529), 201

INDEX OF TITLES

A Bestiary, 56

A Gest of Robyn Hode, 204

Abraham's Sacrifice, 265

Alysoun, 76

Babylon, or The Bonnie Banks o Fordie, 240

Ballads, 203

Beowulf, 1

Bonnie George Campbell, 254

Cædmon's Hymn, 34

Charms, 30

Confessio Amantis, 100

Cuckoo Song, 75

Cursor Mundi, 61

Early Middle English Poems, 49

Edward, 235

Everyman, 272

Genesis, 36

How Graunde Amoure Was Receyved of La Belle Pucell (from The Pastime of Pleasure), 197

Howe Remembraunce Made His Epytaphy on His Grave (from The Pastime of Pleasure), 200

Jock o the Side, 226

Johnie Cock, 224

Judith, 38

Kemp Owyne, 247

London Lyckpeny, 166

Lord Thomas and Fair Annet, 243

Mary Hamilton, 252

Mi Maister Chaucer, 165

Middle English Metrical Romances, 79

Miracle Plays, 254

Morality Plays, 272

Natura Leonis (from A Bestiary), 56

Old English Poems, 1

Piers the Plowman, 102

Poema Morale, 49

Riddle, 31

Sanct Salvatour, Send Silver Sorrow, 184

Satan's Speech (from Genesis), 36

Sir Gawayn at the Green Chapel (from Syr Gawayn and the Grene Knyght), 91

Sir Hugh, or The Jew's Daughter, 232

Sir Patrick Spens, 231

Springtime, 77

St. Stephen and Herod, 203

Sweet William's Ghost, 242

Syr Gawayn and the Grene Knyght, 83

The Banished Wife's Lament, 33

The Battle of Maldon, 44

The Book of the Duchesse, 108

The Brut, 51

The Canterbury Tales, 127
The Cleansing of Heorot (from Beowulf), 1
The Complaynt of Chaucer to His Purse, 164
The Cruel Brother, 239
The Dance of the Sevin Deidly Synnis, 189
The Deluge, 254,
The Dreme, 194
The Fight with the Dragon (from Beowulf), 19
The Foure PP, 312
The Frisian Wife, 31
The Goldyn Targe, 185
The Happy Land (from The Phœnix), 34
The Hous of Fame, 112
The Hunting of the Cheviot, 216
The Kingis Quair, 170
The Lay of Havelok the Dane, 79
The Legend of Good Women, 122
The Mariage of Witt and Wisdome, 296
The Moon and the Sun (Riddle), 31
The Nonne Preestes Tale (from The Canterbury Tales), 148
The Owl and the Nightingale, 57
The Pastime of Pleasure, 197
The Pearl, 66

The Phœnix, 34
The Prolog (from The Dreme), 194
The Prologue (from The Canterbury Tales), 127
The Prologue (from The Legend of Good Women), 122
The Prologue (from The Vision of William concerning Piers the Plowman), 102
The Proloug of the XII Buk of Eneados, 193
The Proverbs of Hendyng, 74
The Stranger at King Arthur's Court (from Syr Gawayn and the Grene Knyght), 83
The Testament of Cresseid, 177
The Three Ravens, 234
The Twa Sisters, 237
The Virgin's Song to Her Baby Christ, 79
The Vision of William concerning Piers the Plowman, 102
The Wanderer, 31
The Wee Wee Man, 251
Thomas Rymer, 249
Truth, 163

Ubi Sunt Qui ante Nos Fuerunt, 78

Why Come Ye Nat to Court, 201

INDEX TO FIRST LINES

	PAGE
A gentleman cam oure the sea	239
A povre wydwe, somdel stope in age	148
A, sirra, my masters	300
A thousand tymes have I herd men telle	122
Adam past nyne hundride yere	61
Against a sudden stitch	30
Against a swarm of bees	30
As I was wa'king all alone	251
Bewailing in my chamber thus allone	170
By myself, full sad, I utter this song	33
Bytuene Mershe ant Averil	76
Dear to the Frisian wife	31
Fle fro the prees, and dwelle with sothfastnesse	163
Four and twenty bonny boys	232
Grim tok the child, and bond him faste	79
"Haste thou ony grene cloth," sayd our kynge	211
Her mother died when she was young	247
High upon Highlands	254
I, God, that all the world have wrought	254
I have heard that far hence	34

I pray you all gyve your audyence 272
I saw a wight wondrously bearing booty 31
Ich am eldre than ich wes, a winter and ek on lore 49
Ich was in one sumere dale 57
In a somer seson, whan soft was the sonne 102
In to the Calendis of Januarie 194

Jesu, swete sone dere 79
Johny he has risen up i the morn 224

Lenten ys come with love to toune 77
Like as the rowling stone, we se 306
Lord Thomas and Fair Annet 243

Me thoghte thus: that hyt was May 108
Most myghty Makere of sunne and of mone 265
My sonne, drawe neare; give eare to me 296

Now God be here, Who kepeth this place 312
Now should we praise the Keeper of heaven's kingdom 34
Now wyl I of hor servise say yow no more 83

O maister deere and fadir reverent 165
Of Jupiter this finde I write 100
Off Februar the fyiftene nycht 189
Oft a lonely man looks for favor 31
Ones yet agayne 201

Peeter a Whifeild he hath slaine 226
Perle plesaunte to prynces paye 66

Ryght as the stern of day begouth to schyne 185

Sanct Salvatour, send silver sorrow 184
Seynt Stevene was a clerk in Kyng Herowdes halle 203
She doubted not the Glorious Creator's gifts 38
So then Healfdene's son seethed always 1
Sumer is icumen in 75

That came to pass afterwards 19
The good dame Mercy, with dame Charyte 200
The king sits in Dumferling toune 231
The kynge came to Notynghame 204
The leun stant on hille 56
The Persè owt off Northombarlonde 216
The twynklyng stremowris of the orient 193
Then he bade each of the youths 44
Then spoke the proud king 36
Thenne gyrdez he to Gryngolet, and gederez the rake 91
There came a ghost to Margret's door 242
There was twa sisters in a bowr 237
There were three ladies lived in a bower 240
There were three ravens sat on a tree 234
This duleful sentence Saturne tuik on hand 177
This egle, of whiche I have yow tolde 112
To London once my steppes I bent 166
To them whose shoulders doe supporte 308

To yow, my purse, and to non other wight 164
True Thomas lay oer yond grassy bank 249

Under than com tydinge 51

Well now, son Witt, the proofe is plaine 310
Were beth they that biforen us weren 78
Whan she it knewe, than ryght incontynent 197
Whan that Aprille with his shoures soote 127
"Why dois your brand sae drap wi bluid" 235
Wis mon halt is wordes ynne 74
Word 's gane to the kitchen 252